Behavior Therapy with Hyperactive and Learning Disabled Children

Behavior therapy with hyperactive and learning disabled children

BENJAMIN B. LAHEY
UNIVERSITY OF GEORGIA

New York • Oxford
OXFORD UNIVERSITY PRESS
1979

Copyright © 1979 by Oxford University Press, Inc.

Library of Congress Cataloging in Publication Data
Main entry under title:

Behavior therapy with hyperactive and learning disabled children.

   Bibliography: p.
   Includes index.
   1. Hyperactive children—Addresses, essays, lectures.
2. Learning disabilities—Addresses, essays, lectures.
3. Behavior therapy—Addresses, essays, lectures.
I. Lahey, Benjamin B. [DNLM:
1. Behavior therapy—In infancy and childhood.
2. Hyperkinesis—In infancy and childhood.
3. Hyperkinesis—Therapy.   4. Learning disorders—Therapy.
WS350.6.B419]   RJ506.H9B44   618.9′28′58   78-16344
ISBN 0-19-502478-8   ISBN 0-19-502479-6 pbk.

Printed in the United States of America

Preface

Although they have probably always been with us, the problems known as hyperactivity and learning disabilities have been the subject of extensive research and service only in the past twenty years. To say that children with these patterns of difficulties were misunderstood and underserved before this time would be a great understatement. Much changed, however, in the early 1960s when learning disabilities and hyperactivity became a major focus of public, professional, and scientific attention. Research expanded exponentially, and federal and state programs developed so rapidly that today virtually every public school system in the United States has a special program for at least some of its learning disabled and hyperactive children. It is fair to ask, however, if these changes have improved the lot of such children. Do we now possess a technology for effectively dealing with learning and behavior problems?

The chapters in this volume attempt to provide an answer to that question. They are organized in both an historical and conceptual framework. The historical perspective begins in the introductory chapter and extends throughout the volume. From this perspective, the past twenty years are divided into three brief "eras" based on the paradigm used to understand hyperactivity and learning disabilities. The first paradigm viewed them as medical-model disease entities, while the second paradigm shifted attention to overt behavior problems. In the latter model, intervention was not aimed at the vague mental "diseases" that were believed to underly the disorder, but rather at specific behaviors that were believed to be incompatible with effective classroom learning. It was felt that learning would proceed at normal rates if the incompatible behaviors were eliminated.

When this was shown to be untrue, the shift to the third paradigm occurred. In this model, attention has shifted to the direct modification of academic, cognitive, and physiological deficits, with resulting indirect improvements in other behavior problems.

Section I reviews the evidence for first paradigm models of assessment and treatment, and outlines new directions in the definition and assessment of hyperactivity and learning disabilities. Section II reviews evidence supporting second and third paradigm methods of behavior therapy. A variety of emerging viewpoints are portrayed which give definition to the continuing development of the third paradigm. Although the shortcomings in our knowledge are clearly visible, effective treatment outcomes can be seen for the first time for these populations of children. The third and final section of the volume contrasts behavior therapy techniques with psychopharmacological methods, highlighting the strong and weak points of each method.

I want to express my deep appreciation for the support of the University of Georgia during the preparation of this manuscript. As always, these efforts are dedicated to Susan, Megan, Edward, and Erin.

Athens, Georgia   B. B. L.
June 1978

Contents

Behavior intervention strategies

Behavior therapy and pharmacological treatments

Introduction

1. Current perspectives on hyperactivity and learning disabilities

BENJAMIN B. LAHEY   STEVEN A. HOBBS
DAVID L. KUPFER   ALAN DELAMATER

Philosopher of science T. S. Kuhn (1962) has described a phenomenon referred to as the "paradigm shift." On a few rare occasions in the history of a science, a genuinely new conceptualization or methodology attracts the attention of scientists and significantly changes the nature of theory and research in that field. Such paradigm shifts are generally followed by long periods in which most scientific activity is devoted to working out the details of the new paradigm. Scientific progress occurs during these periods in a quantitative sense, but qualitative developments do not occur until the next paradigm shift.

A similar analysis can be made of historical changes in the applied sciences. In the fields of psychology and education, particularly, major paradigm shifts can periodically be seen in the ways in which children and their problems are conceptualized. A rapid succession of these important shifts have occurred during the past twenty years surrounding the terms "learning disabilities" and "hyperactivity." In the late 1950s, a large population of children with serious learning and behavior problems "came into existence" with the invention of these terms. Although upwards of 10 percent of all children will be currently given one or both of the diagnostic labels of learning disabilities or hyperactivity during their childhood, the paradigms of psychology and education did not admit to the existence of such disorders prior to the 1950s. Clearly children had such problems prior to then, but they received little psychological and educational help because they did not fit into existing conceptualizations.

FIRST-PARADIGM THEORIES

The first paradigm shift occurring in the 1950s resulted in the *definition* of learning disabilities and hyperactivity as medical-model "disease" entities. Although different investigators defined learning disabilities in different ways (Lahey, 1976), all definitions included essentially the same basic elements:

Children are considered to be learning disabled if there are: (1) significant deficits in some area or areas of educational achievement, (2) normal overall scores on standardized intelligence tests, (3) no major behavior disorders, (4) no uncorrected sensory handicaps, and (5) no history of environmental deprivation. Following the first paradigm shift, all major theorists went on to posit explanations for such learning deficits in terms of various abnormalities in mental and/or neurological functioning as if learning disabilities were a type of disease.

The definition of hyperactivity is both simpler and more complex. Most theorists defined hyperactivity as an excessive level of motor activity, distractability, and impulsivity that brings the child into conflict with his or her environment (D. M. Ross & S. A. Ross, 1976). While this definition focuses on a cluster of overt behaviors, it is sufficiently vague to render assessment extremely difficult. As with the term "learning disabilities," all major theorists of the 1950s hypothesized neurophyschological deficits to account for the behavioral deviance. The identification of these children by any definition, however, must be considered a positive first step as it resulted in psychological and educational assistance for the first time in history.

NEUROPSYCHOLOGICAL THEORIES

The specific first-paradigm theories were of uneven quality and generated much controversy, but they dominated theory and practice for nearly twenty years. The first widely accepted theory of hyperactivity and learning disabilities treated them as brain damage syndromes because of similarities between some children and wartime neuropsychiatric patients who had suffered physical trauma. Because short attention span, distractibility, and high activity levels are typical in these populations, it was assumed that learning disabled and hyperactive children also suffer from brain damage, but of a "minimal" sort (Strauss & Lehtinen, 1947). These theorists reasoned that brain damage in hyperactive and/or learning disabled children was not extensive enough to produce full mental retardation, but had selective effects resulting in specific and variable patterns of academic deficits and overactivity.

Teaching methods similar to those developed for World War II brain-trauma victims were advocated. These centered around the elimination of environmental complexity, including blacking-out windows, painting rooms a uniform gray, separating students into cubicles, and requiring teachers to wear drab uniforms with no jewelry or makeup. Fortunately, a sensible, structured approach to academic instruction was also emphasized (Gillingham & Stillman, 1965).

When it became clear that hard evidence of brain damage was uncommon in the learning disabled and hyperactive populations, the term "minimal brain *dysfunction*" was substituted for "minimal brain *damage*" (Cruickshanck, 1967; Johnson & Myklebust, 1967). This reconceptualized the putative disorders of the brain in functional rather than anatomical terms, to the extent that the hypothesized disorders resembled "mental" disorders more than neurological ones. One influential brain dysfunction theory, for example, spoke in terms of disorders of "in-tersensory integration" (Johnson & Myklebust, 1967).

The concept of minimal brain dysfunction is still prevalent in the fields of medicine, education, and psychology, but brain damage theories are generally no longer considered valid in their original form. Many of the teaching methods derived from the early brain damage theories still linger on, however. As is too often the case, it is the more esoteric and less valid methods (reduction of environmental complexity) that have survived rather than the better methods (the systematic academic instruction of Gillingham & Stillman, 1965).

Recently, a major new direction for neuropsychological theories has arisen. Sophisticated research methods have been used to attempt to relate individual differences in neurological and biochemical variables to learning and behavior problems. Unlike previous organic theories, these recent hypotheses have been proposed in operational, testable form. It should be possible, therefore to determine if covariations between behavioral and physiological variables of this type might exist within the reasonably near future. While there is much empirical support for some of the newer neuropsychological theories (Feuerstein, Ward, & LeBaron, 1978), particularly those that posit chronic differences in autonomic arousal, the evidence is far from consistent and conclusive at this point (Barkley, 1977). One team of investigators (Lubar & Shouse, 1977) has generated considerable interest by suggesting through their preliminary clinical findings that arousal theory may be directly translatable into treatment methods for hyperactivity through the technology of biofeedback.

PERCEPTUAL AND PERCEPTUAL-MOTOR THEORIES

Shortly after the brain damage theories called attention to learning disabled and hyperactive children, a variety of theories were proposed that explained their difficulties in terms of "perceptual disorders." This family of theories variously implicated every sensory modality and defined perception in such broad Gestalt-like terms that virtually every intellectual process was included. But, while the spectrum of perceptual theories was broad, each theory was quite specific in postulating "causes" of learning and activity problems and in recommending methods to remediate the causative perceptual disorders.

Kephart (1971) and Delacatto (1966) suggested that perceptual-intellectual dysfunction arose when early motor-learning experiences were abnormal or inadequate. In theories that paralleled, but apparently did not stem from Piaget, Kephart and Delacatto believed that normal intellectual development could not proceed until the sensory-motor deficits had been remediated. Accordingly, they prescribed elaborate programs of physical exercises (walking balance beams, "angels-in-the-snow" calisthenics, forced changes in sleep positions, forced crawling as a means of locomotion). Kephart's rationale was that children needed to learn their body's orientation in space before they could perceive the spatial organiztion of letters and numbers. Delacatto, on the other hand, put forward an even more speculative theory involving highly controversial treatment methods that he felt would "reorganize" neural structures.

Gerald Getman (Getman and Kane, 1964) has proposed a perceptual-motor theory that emphasizes the role of ocular muscle movements and visual-motor integration. Based on this theory, he has developed a battery of visual-motor training exercises that form the basis of modern "developmental optometry." Such methods are widely used today by optometrists and others in an effort to treat children with learning and behavior problems.

Frostig and Horne (1964) and Fernald (1943) have suggested perceptual theories that place less emphasis on motor learning. Although they have given less attention to the question of etiology, they too have developed extensive programs to treat perceptual dysfunction. The widely used "Frostig Kits" attempt to remediate the visual perception of children through exercises such as copying abstract geometric figures. Fernald's program emphasizes the integration of the visual, auditory, kinesthetic, and tactile modalities through such techniques as using cut-out letters covered with sand paper. One method even attempts to remediate the "overemphasis" on the visual modality by teaching chldren to read raised letters or words that are "traced" on their backs while blindfolded (Blau & Blau, 1969).

PSYCHOLINGUISTIC THEORIES

Another theoretical approach views learning and behavior problems as the result of disorders of "psycholinguistic processes" (Kirk, McCarthy, & Kirk, 1968). Like the term "perception," however, the term "psycholinguistic" is used by these theorists in such broad terms as to be syn-onymous with the term "intelligence." Based on Osgood's (1957) model of psycholinguistic functioning, an instrument has been developed to "diagnose" specific areas of dysfunction (the Illinois Test of Psycholinguistic Abilities or ITPA), and a program for remediating such deficits has been proposed.

EFFECTIVENESS OF FIRST-PARADIGM REMEDIAL PROGRAMS

As noted above each of the variety of first-paradigm theories has given rise to a specific set of remedial procedures, often commercially published in the form of educational "kits." These have been widely used by educations, psychologists, and other professionals for many years and have been frequently evaluated through research. The empirical support for such methods is quite weak, however.

The environmental restriction methods arising from the brain damage and brain dysfunction theories have received less empirical scrutiny than most other methods. A review of the available research by Hallahan and Kauffman (1975), however, concludes that there is no reason to believe that environmental restriction improves academic achievement.

A much larger body of evidence focuses on perceptual training programs. These studies have been received by several investigators who have reached essentially the same conclusions: (1) few published studies are methodologically adequate even when judged by minimal standards, and (2) the few methodologically sound studies show no significant effects of any form of perceptual or perceptual-motor training on academic achievement when compared to untreated control groups (Goodman & Hammill, 1973; Hallahan & Kauffman, 1976; Lahey, 1976; A. D. Ross, 1976). Hammill and Larsen (1974) have reviewed the published studies on psycholinguistic training with similar results. The few adequate studies suggest no beneficial effects of psycholinguistic training.

In spite of the lack of data-based support, however, environmental restriction, perceptual training, and psycholinguistic methods are still widely used. This is apparently so because: (1) many methodologically inadequate studies have given the appearance of supporting such methods, (2) no viable alternatives to the unsupported methods have been made widely available especially through commercial sources, and (3) the choice of treatment methods is usually not based on experimental evidence in the applied "sciences."

THE SECOND-PARADIGM SHIFT: BEHAVIORAL APPROACHES

In the early 1970s, the beginnings of what now appears to be a full paradigm shift became evident. Numerous writers began discussing hyperactivity and learning disabilities not as labels for medical-model disease entities, but as labels that loosely refer to broad maladaptive patterns of behavior. That is, academic and activity problems were no longer viewed as *symptoms* of underlying neurological or psychological disorders, but rather as behavior problems that can be modified in the same manner as any other behavior disorder. Treatment was no longer directed at abstract, unseen mental/neurological processes, but was directed at the maladaptive and deficient behaviors themselves (Ayllon, Layman, & Kandel, 1975; Haring & Bateman, 1977; Lahey, 1976; K. D. O'Leary, Pelham, Rosenbaum, & Price, 1977; Ross, 1976). In a broader sense, this shift can be seen as one of the late ripples of the applied behaviorism paradigm shift of the 1960s, but to children who have been given the labels of hyperactivity and/or learning disabilities, it was a change of no small importance.

The first behavioral studies were devoted to the necessary demonstration that key behaviors of hyperactive and learning disabled children, such as overall gross motor activity and visual attending, could be changed using positive reinforcement (Novy, Burnett, Powers, & Sulzer-Azaroff, 1973; Patterson, Jones, Whittier, & Wright, 1965). Unfortunately the first result of these successful demonstrations was the launching of "advocates" who proclaimed the virtues of the behavioral approach in advance of substantial evidence and technological know-how. Since then, however, a considerable amount of substantiating and elaborating evidence was followed, with the years 1975–78 producing bumper crops. This research focused not only on larger-scale validations conducted in natural settings (K. D. O'Leary, Pelham, Rosenbaum, & Price, 1977; Lahey, 1976), but also began evaluating *alternative* behavioral strategies.

The topic of this book is the development of the behavioral approaches to learning disabilities and hyperactivity, skipping quickly from its inception to its elaboration between 1975 and the present. It is a hallmark of applied behaviorism that researchers and practitioners must constantly evaluate and refine their own methods. The critical attitude taken towards both traditional and behavioral methods by the authors of the selections contained in this volume is a sure sign of continued adherence to that dictum. The rapid development of methods and support for behavioral approaches in general is the encouraging outcome of that critical attitude. Still, it is essential that the evidence contained in this volume be taken as only *tentative* information, as much obviously remains to be learned, particularly about the long-term effects of behavioral and other methods of treatment.

In general, the behavioral approach to teaching and therapy is defined by three primary characteristics (Lahey & Johnson, 1978):

1. Individualization and mastery learning.

The educative process begins with the particular strengths and weaknesses of each individual child and advances only at the rate at which that child can progress. The child is allowed to learn each task to mastery before progressing to the next.

2. Direct teaching.

Behavioral methods are based on principles of learning and social influence that are aimed *directly* at the behaviors that need to be modified, rather than at inferred mental or physiological disorders that are believed to underly the maladaptive behavior.

3. Emphasis on measurement.

As can be clearly seen in the accompanying chapters, frequent or continual measurement of the behaviors to be changed is an essential part of teaching or therapy. The process of measurement provides continual feedback on the effectiveness, or ineffectiveness, of the behavior-change methods and allows modification of the procedures when necessary.

INAPPROPRIATE OR QUESTIONABLE TARGETS FOR BEHAVIORAL INTERVENTION

If a behavioral approach assumes that the deviant or deficient behavior is the problem itself, then the key step in any applied behavior analysis is obviously the selection of the "right" behavior(s) to modify. In the case of learning disabilities and hyperactivity, this is no easy task, as the behavior problems of such children are "complex," especially at first glance. The following discussion reviews current thinking and evidence on a number of potential targets for behavioral intervention.

1. Attention deficits:

A variety of theorists, of behavioral and other orientations, have suggested that deficits in "attention" are the core problems of both learning disabled and hyperactive children (Barkley, 1976; Douglas, 1972; A. Ross, 1976; D. Ross & S. Ross, 1976). Such children are referred to as "inattentive," "underselective," "distractible," and as having "short attention spans." Although these theorists have not made it clear if they are referring to deficits in peripheral attending behaviors (e.g., looking at the academic task) or deficits in an inferred central process of attention, these theories have in common the vague belief that stimuli are not being "received" in a normal fashion.

It would be tempting, therefore, to design behavioral treatment strategies to teach children to "attend" properly to relevant stimuli. A number of early behavioral investigations of learning disabled children did, in fact, take this strategy. Wolf, Giles, and Hall (1968), for example, gave token reinforcers to learning disabled children for attending or being "on-task" for brief periods of time. These tokens were later exchanged for small toys and were successful in markedly increasing the amount of on-task behavior. Novy, Burnett, Powers, and Sulzer-Azaroff (1973) similarly demonstrated the effectiveness of positive reinforcement in increasing the amount of attending behavior.

These and a number of other similar studies established the ease with which an apparently maladaptive characteristic of learning disabled and hyperactive children could be remediated. In theory, these improvements in attending behavior would lead naturally to improvements in learning, but unfortunately, these studies did not test their implicit assumption by collecting data on academic performance. When evidence was finally gathered, it was evident that teaching children to attend more to their academic tasks through positive reinforcement generally *does not* lead to improvements in academic learning (Ferritor, Buckholdt, Hamblin, & Smith, 1972; Kirby & Shields, 1972; Marholin, Steinman, McInnis, & Heads, 1975; Marholin & Steinman, 1977). This apparently promising approach to therapy has proved to be a false lead, at least at the present time.

2. Impulsivity

Another term used to describe the behavior of learning disabled and hyperactive children is "impulsive." The term has been popularized by Kagan (1966) who has defined impulsivity as the tendency to respond hastily to stimuli before "thinking through" alternative responses. Kagan has suggested that impulsive responding is a major cause of academic underachievement, but the concept of impulsivity has a number of methodological difficulties connected with it. Impulsivity is operationally defined in terms of performance on choice tasks, such as Kagan's Matching Familiar Figures Test (Kagan, 1966). Only children whose latencies are short and whose number of errors are high are considered to be impulsive. Defined in this manner, measures of impulsivity are correlated with a variety of academic measures. It is not clear, however, whether the correlational relationship is due to the high level of errors, the short latencies, or both, of the "impulsive" children.

Williams and Lahey (1977) explored this question by separately modifying accuracy and latency in children who had been defined as impulsive according to Kagan's criteria. They found that when the children were reinforced for accurate responding, their accuracy increased, but their brief latencies did not change. When other children were reinforced for long latencies, their latencies became longer, but their number of errors did not decrease. Moreover, reinforcing children for both long latencies and accurate responding was no more effective in reducing errors than reinforcement for accurate responding. In other words, "impulsive" or short-latency responding does not appear to be *functionally* related to accurate performance. The correlational relationship between "impulsivity" and academic deficits may reflect no more than a correlation between making errors on the Matching Familiar Figures Test and making errors on academic tasks. In any case, it does not seem necessary to modify impulsivity, in the sense of brief latencies, to increase the accuracy of responding in underachieving children. It seems sufficient to focus on the reduction of inaccurate responding.

3. Activity level

The key defining feature of hyperactivity is a perceived high level of motor activity. Most writers have been careful, however, to distinguish between just high activity levels and high activity levels that "bring children into conflict with their environments." While it is difficult to know what is meant by this vague phrase, the most reasonable interpretation is that high rates of *appropriate* behavior do not lead to a diagnosis of hyperactivity, while high rates of *inappropriate* behavior do lead to such labels. Indeed many of the rating scales that are used to assess hyperactivity contain a predominance of items relating to behavior problems rather than activity level, and there are some data which suggest that diagnosed hyperactive children do *not* differ from normal controls in gross motor activity at all (Saxon, Magee, & Siegel, 1977).

In terms of the selection of appropriate targets for behavioral intervention, this interpretation suggests that the behaviors that must be changed in hyperactive children are the same behaviors that must be changed in any child with behavior problems: *the inappropriate behaviors themselves.*

This interpretation raises the question of whether the inappropriate behaviors of diagnosed hyperactive children *can* be modified using the same behavior therapy methods used with other children with behavior problems. The chapters by K. D. O'Leary, Pelham, Rosenbaum, & Price (1977) and S. G. O'Leary & Pelham (1978) provide tentative evidence that the label of hyperactivity is irrelevant to the choice of treatment methods and the effectiveness of treatment. In addition, Dubey and Kaufman (Note 1) used the O'Learys' method in a large scale clinical and experimental study that further suggested that hyperactive children respond to behavior therapy in the same way as other children. The parents of seventy-three children defined as hyperactive according to strict criteria were given training in the use of behavior modification techniques. The training was conducted in small groups based on Becker's (1971) book, *Parents are Teachers*. As compared to before treatment, the children were rated by their parents as engaging in fewer inappropriate behaviors after the training program and in six-to-nine-month follow-up ratings. In one phase of the study, children in the experimental group were found to have improved more than did children in a delayed-treatment control group.

The results of this study are remarkably similar to, if not more successful than, a similar treatment outcome study using similar methods conducted with nonhyperactive "conduct problem" children by Kent and K. D. O'Leary (1977). The limitation of this entire series of studies, however, is that they used behavior rat-ings made by parents that were not independently substantiated by unbiased observers as the only dependent variables. While there are some data that partially validate such scales (Bolstad & Johnson, 1977), the results would have been much stronger had the studies employed measures that are less subject to extraneous bias.

4. Perceptual and cognitive disorders

A large number of studies attest to the fact that learning disabled and/or hyperactive children consistently differ from normal control children on a large number of perceptual and cognitive measures. These include matching visual stimuli (Cohen, Weiss, & Minde, 1972; Lahey & Lefton, 1976), vigilance tasks (Sykes, Douglas, Weiss, & Minde, 1971), and short-term memory (Swanson, 1977) to name only few.

For a number of reasons, it is not yet clear what meaning these findings may or may not have for the selection of targets for behavior intervention. First, it cannot yet be determined on the basis of available evidence whether this long list of deficits reflects genuine "disorders," or whether they reflect more general problems in the area of "attention" or "motivation." Second, the number of unsuccessful treatment programs that have been aimed at the remediation of perceptional and cognitive deficits (e.g., those by Frostig, Getman, Kirk) discourages further attempts in this area. This second point should not be given undue emphasis, however, since an evaluation of such remedial methods by the criteria of modern learning technology suggests that these early remedial methods were not firmly grounded in what is now known about human learning and transfer, to say the least. It may be that more sophisticated remedial approaches would be more successful.

Third, it does not appear to be *necessary,* in any case, to attempt to directly modify the disordered perceptual and/or cognitive processes. Several investigations have found that children diagnosed as having severe perceptual-cognitive disorders that are reflected in poor academic performance, showed marked improvement in their academic work when positive reinforcement was made contingent solely on accurate academic responding. Children diagnosed as having "perceptual disorders," for example, markedly improve in handwriting (Lahey, Busemeyer, O'Hara, & Beggs, 1977; Stromer, 1977) and the discrimination of letters (Lahey & McNees, 1975; Williams & Lahey, 1977) when reinforced for accurate responding. Similarly, short- and long-term memory for reading vocabulary improves when words are learned under conditions of reinforcement (Lahey & Drabman, 1974).

APPROPRIATE TARGETS FOR BEHAVIORAL INTERVENTION

While the dimensions of behavior mentioned above are apparently inappropriate targets for behavior-change methods, appropriate targets can be found. The criterion that must be applied to the choice of these targets is, which behaviors of children can adults *justifiably* modify? That is, which changes will actually benefit the children?

1. Conduct problems

The term "conduct problems" is being used in the sense defined by Peterson (1961). They are inappropriate behaviors such as noncompliance, aggression, disruption, being out-of-seat. Since these behaviors are generally considered to be maladaptive for both the individual and other individuals in the classroom or home, it would appear to be necessary to modify the frequency of these behaviors in *all* children for whom they are a problem.

The first question that must be answered, however, is are conduct problems prevalent among children who have been labelled hyperactive and/or learning disabled? This is clearly true for hyperactive children. When definitions refer to levels of activity that bring the child into conflict with his or her environment, the definitions are referring to *high rates of inappropriate behaviors*. High rates of appropriate behaviors (working math problems, washing cars, raking leaves) generally do not bring children into conflict with their environments, but high rates of inappropriate behaviors do.

Furthermore, as Kauffman and Hallahan (1978) have shown, the *behavioral* differences among children who have been labelled as emotionally disturbed, mentally retarded, and learning disabled are minimal, if not nonexistent. All three groups show high rates of both learning and conduct problems.

The next question that must be answered, then, is *can* the conduct problems of hyperactive and learning disabled children be modified with behavioral methods? Is it true that these children are "different" (e.g., organically impaired) and therefore cannot be helped except through medical intervention? A number of chapters in this volume provide encouraging evidence that high rates of conduct problems can be successfully reduced through behavioral procedures. These studies suggest, in fact, the very important possibility that children who have been labelled as hyperactive and/or learning disabled respond in essentially the same manner to behavioral interventions as any other children. Substantiating this point, the same investigators have found nearly identical results using their procedures on children who had been given the labels of "conduct problem" and "disruptive" as in the present chapters (Ayllon & Roberts, 1974; Kent & O'Leary, 1977). Thus, it seems both necessary and possible to modify the "conduct problems" of hyperactive and/or learning disabled children.

2. Academic learning

Another characteristic common to both learning disabled and hyperactive children is deficits in academic learning. Again, because of the social significance of academic achievement, it would seem necessary and justifiable to aim intervention procedures at this aspect of behavior. The question to ask again, however, is will such procedures be effective? The rationale upon which first-paradigm approaches to learning disorders were based is that academic intervention will not be successful until the underlying learning problems have been solved. Can, therefore, behavioral approaches to instruction result in more normal rates of learning in hyperactive and/or learning disabled children?

Several of the chapters in this volume provide evidence that such an approach can be successful. Clearly, reading, writing, and arithmetic can be taught more effectively to learning disabled and/or hyperactive children using behavioral methods of instruction (see the chapters by Lovitt, Lahey, and Stromer). What is critically needed, however, is well-controlled research on the long-term effectiveness of behavioral instruction with such children. Although a review of existing evidence is strongly supportive of behavioral teaching methods, the quality of the current research is lacking in a number of areas (Lahey, 1976, 1977).

THIRD-PARADIGM BEHAVIORAL APPROACH

If we accept the assumption that the two most justifiable and important targets for behavioral intervention in learning disabled and/or hyperactive children are academic learning and high rates of inappropriate behavior (aggression, being out of seat in school, noise making), the question becomes how should the modification of these two classes of behavior be *combined?* The original strategy of behavior therapists was to reduce the frequency of inappropriate behaviors that were believed to be incompatible with academic learning. The assumption was that learning would automatically improve to normal rates once the behavioral impediments to academic performance had been removed. Unfortunately, this assumption was not tested in the earlier studies, and when it was finally tested, it proved to be inaccurate. A number of studies have shown rather conclusively that when inappropriate classroom behaviors are reduced through behavioral methods, academic learning does not improve (Ferritor, Buckholdt, Hamblin, & Smith, 1972; Kirby & Shields, 1972; Marholin & Steinman, 1977; and Marholin, Steinman, McInnis, & Heads, 1975). Not only is this approach ineffective, but it may also be counterproductive in the long run. Winett and Winkler (1972) have suggested that in our emphasis on the control of behaviors *assumed* to be incompatible with learning, behaviorists may have encouraged some educators to create unnecessarily regimented and controlled classroom environments. Above all else, however, this episode should serve as a lesson to all empiricists to subject all important assumptions to experimental scrutiny as soon as possible.

An alternative approach to combining academic instruction and the control of inappropriate behavior can be seen in the recent work of Ayllon (Ayllon & Roberts, 1974; Ayllon, Layman, & Kandel, 1975), Broughton and Lahey (1978), and Marholin and Steinman (1977). In this approach, behaviors that are conducive to academic learning (the opposite of incompatible behaviors) are considered to be linked in a behavioral chain with accurate academic performance. If this assumption is valid, then the reinforcement of accurate responding (the terminal behavior in the chain) will result both in an increase in academic accuracy and in an increase in appropriate classroom behavior (and, by definition, a decrease in inappropriate classroom behavior).

Ayllon, Layman, and Kandel (1975) have provided an excellent demonstration of the usefulness of this approach with hyperactive and learning disabled children. Their subjects were three elementary-school children who had been diagnosed as both hyperactive and learning disabled,

took stimulant medication (Ritalin) prescribed to control their learning and behavioral problems, and showed low rates of accurate academic behavior. The procedure of reinforcing academic behavior was evaluated using a multiple baseline design across the two situations of mathematics and reading periods.

In the initial phase of the study, the three children were observed under normal or baseline conditions. Records were kept of the frequency of inappropriate behavior and the number of accurate responses in each mathematics and reading workbooks. After nine days, the children's medication was discontinued, resulting in sharp increases in the *rate* of inappropriate behavior for each child. Terminating the medication had little or no effect on academic behavior, but if anything, the rate of accurate academic responses increased slightly after Ritalin was discontinued. This finding illustrates the more general finding of Rie, Rie, Stewart, & Ambuel (1976) that, while stimulants do appear to reduce the rate of inappropriate behaviors in some children diagnosed as hyperactive, they clearly have no beneficial effects on academic learning in school settings.

After an additional baseline period without medication, the treatment program was initiated by giving each child one check (on an index card carried by the teacher) for each correct response in their mathematics workbooks. These checks could be exchanged later in the day for their choice of a variety of free-time or material backup reinforcers. The reinforcement contingency resulted in marked increases in both the accuracy of mathematics responses and sharp decreases in the rate of inappropriate ("hyperactive") behavior down to medication levels. At this time there were no changes in either class of behaviors during the reading period, but when reinforcement was made contingent upon correct reading responses, reading accuracy increased and the rate of inappropriate behaviors decreased. These findings have been consistently replicated by Ayllon, Layman, and Burke (1972); Ayllon and Roberts (1974); Broughton and Lahey (1978); Ferritor, Buckholdt, Hamblin, and Smith (1972); Marholin and Steinman (1977); and Marholin, Steinman, McInnis, and Heads (1975) on a broad range of children who had been given a variety of diagnostic labels indicating the potency and generality of this approach.

The implications of research on the reinforcement of terminal academic behaviors are extremely important. First, they strongly suggest that both the academic and high-rate inappropriate behaviors of hyperactive children can be successfully modified in actual school settings. Second, they suggest an efficient method by which the control of both classes of behavior can be effectively combined, because the reinforcement of academic behaviors is easier for teachers than the direct control of high-rate inappropriate behaviors.

Third, this procedure is advantageous to children in an important *humanistic* sense. It allows teachers to be both more objective and less restrictive in their behavior management procedures. Because teachers using this method generally provide response consequences only to academic behaviors, less subjective judgment is required in deciding what are the "appropriate" behaviors that should be reinforced. Even the problems involved in evaluating some types of academic work (creative writing, oral discussion) are minor compared to judgments of general classroom behavior. Removing a significant degree of subjectivity makes the control of behavior less subject to bias and, therefore, probably more "fair" overall.

Moreover, the reinforcement of terminal academic behaviors allows the *child* to determine, in a sense, what behaviors are *truly incompatible with academic learning*. If reinforcement increases the rate of academic progress to a satisfactory level, then any behaviors that were actually interfering with learning must have dropped out of the chain. If behaviors such as talking quietly to peers, sitting on the floor, and fidgeting in one's seat do not drop out of the chain, then by definition, they are not incompatible. The only rationale that a teacher could use to modify these behaviors would be to provide some evidence that the behaviors were disruptive to other children (lowered rates of academic progress, frequent complaints about the student's behavior or were harmful to the student in some other way (e.g., would make the child unpopular).

In actual practice, it appears that most of the behaviors that teachers generally *think* are incompatible with academic learning turn out to be so and drop out of the chain when academic behavior is reinforced. It may be necessary, however, for teachers to deal with a few serious infrequent misbehaviors, such as aggression, using other methods as well (Lahey & Johnson, 1978). In spite of this, the reinforcement of terminal academic behaviors does appear to provide the most effective and desirable method of simulta-

neously controlling classroom misbehavior and encouraging academic learning.

OTHER TREATMENT APPROACHES

In addition to the behavioral methods described above, two other approaches have been increasingly significant in the past decade, both in terms of the amount of research on the approaches and the extent to which they have been used in applied settings. These approaches are the use of "cognitive behavior therapy" and the use of stimulant medications.

COGNITIVE BEHAVIOR THERAPY

Investigations focusing on the role of self-generated verbalizations in controlling overt behavior (e.g., Bem, 1967; Meichenbaum & Goodman, 1969) have recently prompted a trend toward a treatment approach that can be classified as *cognitive* behavior therapy. Although this label has been applied to a large number of loosely related methods, the cognitive behavioral approach can be distinguished by two common elements in the area of hyperactivity and impulsivity (Kauffman & Hallahan, 1978). First, the child is exposed by means of direct instruction and/or modeling to a specific strategy which he/she is to implement. Second, the child is taught to covertly verbalize to him/herself certain instructions or commands which exemplify the strategy.

In an early study, Palkes, Stewart, and Kahanna (1968) trained ten hyperactive boys to instruct themselves aloud to "Look and think before I answer," prior to responding to stimuli from the Matching Familiar Figures (MFF), Embedded Figures (EFT), and Trail Making tests. Each of two pre- and posttraining measures of performance on the Porteus Maze Extension Series (PM) indicated that the self-instruction training group improved significantly over time and made significantly fewer errors at posttesting as compared to a no-treatment control group. In a subsequent study, Palkes, Stewart, and Freedman (1972) employed a third condition in which hyperactive boys were provided with a script of instructions to read silently prior to responding on the MFF and the EFT. Posttreatment comparisons among an overt self-instruction condition, the covert self-instruction (silent reading) condition, and a no-treatment control on a PM qualitative score yielded significantly greater improvement for only the overt self-instruction procedure. No significant differences among conditions were found on the PM measure of general intelligence. Further, no differences were observed among treatment conditions on either measure at 2 week follow-up.

Meichenbaum and Goodman (1971) used a cognitive procedure which incorporates modeling and training in self-instruction in treating five children placed in a special education class for "behavioral problems such as hyperactivity and poor self-control." Children initially observed an adult model performing various sensorimotor and problem-solving tasks while instructing himself aloud (e.g., "Draw the line down, down, good; then to the right; that's it . . . ."). Subsequently the children were asked to perform the modeled task themselves and to verbalize the same instructions to themselves first aloud, then while whispering to themselves, and finally covertly. Comparisons from pre- to posttreatment and at 4 week follow-up on a total of seven performance tasks (including the PM) yielded a significantly greater improvement for the cognitive training group (as opposed to subjects who were merely exposed to the task materials) on three of the measures: MFF latency, the WISC Picture Arrangement score, and a prorated WISC IQ score. Additional measures of actual classroom behavior and teacher ratings of the children's activity level, self-control, etc., revealed no treatment effects.

In similar investigations, Bender (1976) and Douglas, Parry, Marton, and Garson (1976) employed the procedures of Meichenbaum and Goodman (1971) in treating children diagnosed as hyperactive. In the Douglas et al. (1976) study, pre-post comparisons of 18 treated children with a no-treatment control yielded significant differences on 6 of 16 measures of performance. Similar pretreatment to follow-up comparisons indicated significant treatment effects on only MFF latency and error measures and on withdrawal and realistic responses on a story completion test. Significant treatment effects were not observed on teacher ratings of the children using the Connors Teacher Rating Scale (1969), on the PM, or on other memory, ability, achievement, and perception measures. Bender (1976) was even less successful in achieving lasting treatment effects. While cognitive training resulted in significant improvement in latencies of MFF-like tasks, it did not significantly reduce errors on those tasks nor did it lead to significant improvement on measures of MFF performance one day after termination of training.

Only one study of cognitive behavior modification procedures has demonstrated generalization of behavior change to the natural environment. Bornstein and Quevillon (1976) used methods similar to those of Meichenbaum and Goodman (1971) in the treatment of three preschool boys described as highly distractible, unable to follow directions, and overactive with short attention spans. However, early in training, tangible reinforcement was also included in order to motivate the children to attend to the model and to imitate the sensorimotor and problem-solving tasks. Rewards were then quickly faded as correct performance on the tasks increased. In addition, the instructional statements differed from those of Meichenbaum and Goodman (1971) as the child's self-instruction included imagining himself performing the activities in the classroom situation. Results indicated that relative to baseline measures the three children dramatically increased on-task behavior in the classroom during treatment and at 3 month follow-up.

Thus, studies of cognitive behavior modification methods have produced inconsistent results. Several investigations have demonstrated improvement on a variety of psychological tests (such as the MFF or PM) which seem to be related to the dimensions of hyperactivity and impulsivity, but not on behavioral measures in the natural environment. Moreover, these studies have generally employed weak no-treatment control groups and differed widely as to *which* psychological tests showed treatment effects. Conclusive evaluation of the efficacy of the cognitive behavior modification approach to hyperactivity and impulsivity awaits further investigations which attempt to measure and extend treatment effects beyond artificial measures used in the laboratory or clinic setting to hyperactive or impulsive behaviors occurring in the home or classroom.

STIMULANT MEDICATIONS

Although stimulants such as dextroamphetamine (Dexedrine) and methylphenidate (Ritalin) have been used with hyperactive and/or learning disabled children for many years, the use of these medications has significantly increased in recent times. Fortunately, there has been a corresponding increase in the availability of reasonably useful research on these medications, even if the upswing in research *followed* the increase in usage instead of preceding it, and medical practice has often failed to take heed of these research findings.

Although most investigations of the use of stimulants are characterized by a number of serious methodological flaws (Bosco & Robin, 1976; D. M. Ross & S. A. Ross, 1976; Sroufe, 1975), there seems to be enough interpretible evidence to justify at least four tentative conclusions (Barkley, 1976, 1977; D. M. Ross & S. A. Ross, 1976; Sprague & Baxley, in press):

1. Stimulants generally result in mean changes in a variety of laboratory measures of activity and cognitive performance when groups taking the medication are compared to placebo-control groups.
2. Stimulants generally produce ratings of "improved" by parents and teachers using rating scales containing items relating to what is referred to as hyperactivity and conduct problems, when treatment groups are compared to placebo-control groups.
3. Stimulants apparently do not produce any statistically significant mean changes in classroom academic performance compared to placebo-control groups.
4. Stimulants commonly produce a number of medical side-effects, including changes in cardiovascular functioning, depression of appetite and physical growth, and insomnia. Occasionally, they also produce side-effects such as nausea and discomfort, and may even worsen activity problems according to reports of parents and teachers. The long-term medical significance of these side effects is currently unknown, but they certainly appear to be significant enough to warrant serious concern and caution in the use of these medications.

A few recent studies have addressed themselves to the important question of the *relative* effectiveness of stimulant medications and behavior therapy. Although these studies suffer from a number of methodological shortcomings, they do suggest some very tentative conclusions. The most extensive study compared the effects of *behavior therapy plus methylphenidate*, to *behavior therapy plus placebo pills*, and to *methylphenidate alone* in thirty-four elementary-school-aged hyperactive children (Gittelman-Klein, Klein, Abikoff, Katz, Gloisten, & Kates, 1976). The children were evaluated on teacher and parent rating scales, global ratings by a psychiatrist, and direct behavioral observations in the school. The results were the same for every measure: The children who received stimulant medication plus behavior therapy improved more, but not statistically more, than children who received medication alone. Both groups, however, were statistically superior to the group that received behavior therapy and placebos, even though all three treatments resulted in significant improvement.

These results suggest that stimulant drug treatment alone is more effective than behavior therapy alone, and that the combination of the two treatments is no more effective than drug treatment alone. The only shortcomings of this study are the lack of a behavior therapy group without placebos, and the lack of detailed data presented on the direct behavioral observations.

Other studies that compared drugs and behavior therapy, however, do not confirm these findings. S. G. O'Leary and Pelham (1978) conducted a comparative study of seven hyperactive boys who were taking stimulant medications (Dexedrine, Ritalin, and Cylert). After baseline measures were taken on parent rating scales, the chidren were taken off the medications. This resulted in a rapid and marked rise in ratings of hyperactivity for the children. Following a brief training program in which the parents learned to modify the behavior of their children using behavior therapy techniques, however, the ratings of the children dropped to a level equal to that when the children were taking stimulant medications alone.

These findings suggest that behavior therapy may be as effective as stimulants in reducing hyperactive behavior. Although this study used only the weak measure of parent rating scales, its findings closely replicate the previously cited study by Ayllon, Layman, and Kandel (1975) which used direct observations of classroom behavior. They found that three children who had been taken off stimulant medication returned to the low drug levels of hyperactive behavior when reinforced for correct academic responding. Both studies, however, suffer from potential order effects since all of the children had been on medication prior to the behavior therapy. It may have been that behavior therapy would have been less effective if it had preceded rather than followed the stimulant medications.

A number of other studies which employed extensive observations of single subjects also suggest the conclusion that behavior therapy is approximately equal to stimulant medications in controlling high rates of inappropriate (hyperactive) behaviors (Pelham, 1977; Shafto & Sulzbacher, 1977; Strong, Sulzbacher, & Kirkpatrick, 1974; Stableford, Butz, Hasazi, Leitenberg, & Peyser, 1976; Wulburt & Dries, 1977). These studies generally found behavior therapy to be as effective and more consistent than drugs.

Taken together, these results tentatively suggest that both stimulant medications and behavior therapy are effective in reducing high rates of inappropriate behavior in children diagnosed as hyperactive. It cannot yet be determined whether one treatment is consistently more effective than the other, but the differences are probably not large if they do exist. However, two consistent findings do give the practitioner clear guidelines in the choice of treatments: (1) Stimulant medications have not been found to increase *academic* learning, whereas behavior therapy has been found to do so in many studies (cf. Lahey, 1976), and (2) stimulant medications have more known negative side effects of a potentially serious nature than does behavior therapy. For these reasons, it would seem most appropriate to begin interventions with a reinforcement program for correct academic responding (Ayllon, Layman, & Kandel, 1975) and training for parents in the direct control of high rates of inappropriate behavior (Kent & K. D. O'Leary, 1976; S. G. O'Leary & Pelham, 1978). Under normal circumstances, stimulant medications should be added to or substituted for behavior therapy *only* if behavior therapy has proved to be ineffective and stimulant medications are deemed to be medically safe (i.e., an acceptable risk) for the child. Hopefully, such instances will be infrequent.

CONCLUSIONS

Taken at face value, the preceding discussion suggests that behavioral approaches provide useful methods for correcting the behavioral and academic problems of children who have been labeled hyperactive and/or learning disabled. The extensive research of the past few years is sure to be interpreted in that manner by many and lead to renewed advocacy for behavioral approaches in applied settings. For some purposes, however, it would be more prudent to view the existing body of research summarized in this volume as hypothesis-generating rather than hypothesis-confirming. To summarize previous comments, the present evidence on behavioral approaches is insufficient in a number of respects:

1. The few studies that are both well designed and have used the most sophisticated dependent variables of direct observations by blind observers of specific behaviors or academic performance (e.g., Ayllon, Layman, & Kandel, 1975; Wulbert & Dries, 1977) generally used the smallest number of subjects. Studies which employed large numbers of well-selected subjects (e.g., K. D. O'Leary, Pelham, Rosenbaum, & Price, 1977; Rosenbaum, K. D. O'Leary, & Jacob, 1975) have generally used weak subjective ratings of behavior by adults who knew which children had received treatment and which had not. Only the large and well-designed study by Gittelman-Klein, Klein, Abikoff, Katz, Gloisten, & Kates (1976) used both types of measures, and it suffered from inadequate reporting of data.

2. Even if the most positive interpretation of the literature on behavioral approaches is accepted, the implications of these studies for clinical applications are limited by the short-term nature of the studies. None of the studies extend through even a single academic year, and most cover far shorter time periods. The extensive study of Gittleman-Klein and her associates, for example, covers only an eight-week period. It is simply not possible to conclude on the basis of existing evidence that applied programs that must extend over a full school year, or more likely over several school years, will be successful. Long-term, rigorous evaluations of treatment outcome are sorely needed. A few long-term studies of behavioral treatment for academic deficits are in the literature and show apparently positive results (Haring & Hauck, 1969; Nolen, Kunzelmann, & Haring, 1976). Long-term evaluation of stimulant treatment, on the other hand, has not been encouraging (Weiss, Minde, Werry, Douglas, & Nemeth, 1971), but none of these follow-up studies of either treatment approach has utilized any method of experimental control whatsoever.

Where does that leave us? As scientists we must follow up the suggestive evidence of existing studies and conduct large-scale, long-term, rigorous evaluations of the several behavioral approaches to hyperactivity and learning disabilities. Until this is done, further research on the scale of existing experiments will probably add little or nothing to our knowledge.

As practitioners, however, we obviously cannot wait until these improved experiments are conducted. We must implement those treatment procedures that appear to offer the best hope of helping children who currently have problems.

1. No other psychological treatment approach

has received as much research support as the behavioral approach. Given the methodological deficiencies that characterize research on all of the treatment approaches, the behavioral methods seem to be the most effective. Few comparisons of different approaches have been conducted, but the evidence supporting behavioral approaches has been consistently positive, while the data on other approaches has been decidedly inconsistent.

2. The use of stimulants, within the limits of existing data, appears to be as effective if not more so than behavioral methods in controlling high rates of inappropriate behavior, but given the medical side effects, the lack of effect on academic behavior, and the early findings of poor long-term effectiveness, stimulants should generally be the treatment of last resort. Clearly there is no reason to use stimulants with children with learning deficits who are not hyperactive as they are currently prescribed.

3. Many of the methodological deficiencies that are significant for scientific purposes are less serious considerations for the practitioner. For example, the long-term evaluations of behavioral treatment show academic gains of more than one grade-level of achievement per academic year in groups of children. Because neither control group nor within-group control methods were used, we cannot conclude which aspect of the treatment package produced the academic gains. Simple time-related confounds can be reasonably ruled out because consistent gains of this magnitude have rarely if ever been reported for this population. But placebo, teacher expectancy, or other unintentional effects could be responsible for the academic gains rather than the supposedly active parts of the behavioral treatment package. Knowing this information may be of no importance, however, to practitioners who simply want to find a treatment program that will result in large academic gains over long periods of time, regardless of which elements of the program are responsible for the effectiveness.

A similar conclusion may be reached concerning the use of scales for parent and teacher ratings of hyperactive children. Because of the way in which these scales have been used, it cannot be concluded that the behavior of children who were rated as being improved *actually changed.* Some validating evidence exists to suggest that this is the case (Bolstad & Johnson, 1977; Gittleman-Klein et al., 1976), but it may not be necessary for these scales to reflect actual behavior changes to be useful. One major goal of treatment is to modify the behavior of hyperactive children so that they "come into conflict with their environments" less frequently and less seriously. If a treatment program leads parents and teachers to *perceive* the child as improved, then a major goal of treatment may have been achieved.

In summary, therefore, the now extensive behavioral research on hyperactive and/or learning disabled children has serious shortcomings in terms of experimental design, adequacy of dependent measures, and the paucity of long-term evaluations. These inadequacies strongly suggest the need for additional and improved research. The consistently positive nature of current findings, and the fact that some of the scientific shortcomings may not be serious concerns to the practitioner, strongly recommends behavioral methods in comparison to other available treatment methods. The remaining chapters of this volume will add considerable meat to this barebones overall view and, more importantly, allow readers to reach their own conclusions.

REFERENCE NOTE

1. Dubey, D. R., & Kaufman, K. F. *Home management of hyperkinetic children.* Unpublished manuscript, Melville, New York, Sagamore Children's Psychiatric Center, 1978.

REFERENCES

Ayllon, T., Layman, D. & Burke, S. Disruptive behavior and reinforcement of academic performance. *Psychological Record,* 1972, *22,* 315–323.

Ayllon, T., Layman, D., & Kandel, H. J. A behavioral-educational alternative to drug control of hyperactive children. *Journal of Applied Behavior Analysis,* 1975, *8,* 137–146.

Ayllon, T., & Roberts, M. Eliminating discipline problems by strengthening academic performance. *Journal of Applied Behavior Analysis,* 1974, *7,* 71–76.

Barkley, R. A. Predicting the response of hyperkinetic children to stimulant drugs: A review. *Journal of Abnormal Child Psychology,* 1976, *4,* 327–348.

Barkely, R. A. A review of stimulant drug research with hyperactive children. *Journal of Child Psychology and Psychiatry,* 1977, *18,* 137–165.

Becker, W. S. *Parents are teachers.* Champaign: Research Press, 1971.

Bem, S. L. Verbal self-control: The establishment of effective self-instruction. *Journal of Experimental Psychology,* 1967, *74,* 485–491.

Bender, N. N. Self-verbalization versus tutor verbalization in modifying impulsivity. *Journal of Educational Psychology*, 1976, *68*, 347–354.

Blau, H., & Blau, H. *A theory of learning to read by modality blocking*. San Raphael, California: Academic Therapy Publications, 1969.

Bolstad, O. D., & Johnson, S. M. The relationship between teachers' assessment of students and the students' actual behavior in the classroom. *Child Development*, 1977, *48*, 570–578.

Bornstein, P. H., & Quevillon, R. P. The effects of a self-instructional package on overactive preschool boys. *Journal of Applied Behavior Analysis*, 1976, *9*, 179–188.

Bosco, J. J., & Robin, S. S. (Eds.). The hyperactive child and stimulant drugs: Definition, diagnosis, and direction. *School Review*, 1976, *85*, 1–175.

Broughton, S. F., & Lahey, B. B. Direct and collateral effects of positive reinforcement, response cost, and mixed contingencies for academic performance. *Journal of School Psychology*, in press.

Cohen, N. J., Weiss, G., & Minde, K. Cognitive styles in adolescents previously diagnosed as hyperactive. *Journal of Child Psychology and Psychiatry*, 1972, *13*, 203–209.

Cruickshank, W. *The brain-injured child in the home, school, and community*. Syracuse, N.Y.: Syracuse University Press, 1967.

Delacatto, C. *Neurological organization and reading*. Springfield, Ill.: Charles C. Thomas, 1966.

Douglas, V. I. Stop, look and listen: The problem of sustained attention and impulse control in hyperactive and normal children. *Canadian Journal of Behavioral Science*, 1972, *4*, 259–282.

Douglas, V. S., Parry, P., Marton, P., & Garson, C. Assessment of a cognitive training program for hyperactive children. *Journal of Abnormal Child Psychology*, 1976, *4*, 389–410.

Fernald, G. *Remedial techniques in basic school subjects*. New York: McGraw-Hill, 1943.

Ferritor, D. E., Buckholdt, D., Hamblin, R. L., & Smith, L. The noneffects of contingent reinforcement for attending behavior on work accomplished. *Journal of Applied Behavior Analysis*, 1972, *5*, 7–18.

Feuerstein, M., Ward, M., & LeBaron, S. Critical issues in the neuropsychological and neurophysiological assessment of children with learning and behavior problems. In B. B. Lahey & A. E. Kazdin (Eds.), *Advances in clinical psychology* (Vol. 2). New York: Plenum, 1978.

Frostig, M., & Horne, D. *The Frostig program for the development of visual perception:* Chicago: Follett Educational Corporation, 1964.

Getman, G. N., & Kane, E. R. *The physiology of readiness: An action program for the development of perception for children*. Minneapolis, Minn.: Programs to Accelerate School Success, 1964.

Gillingham, A., & Stillman, B. *Remedial training for children with specific disability in reading, spelling and penmanship* (7th ed.). Cambridge, Mass.: Educators Publishing Service, 1965.

Gittleman-Klein, R., Klein, D. F., Abikoff, H., Katz, S., Gloisten, A. C. & Kates, W. Relative efficacy of methylphenidate and behavior modification in hyperkinetic children: An interim report. *Journal of Abnormal Child Psychology*, 1976, *4*, 361.

Goodman, L., & Hammill, D. The effectiveness of Kephart-Getman activities in developing perceptual-motor and cognitive skills. *Focus on Exceptional Children*, 1973, *4*, 1–9.

Hallahan, D. P., & Kauffman, J. M. Research on the education of distractible and hyperactive children. In W. M. Cruickshank & D. P. Hallahan (Eds.), *Perceptual and learning disabilities in children*. Vol. 2, *Research and theory*. Syracuse, N.Y.: Syracuse University Press, 1975.

Hallahan, D. P., & Kauffman, J. M. *Introduction to learning disabilities: A psycho-behavioral approach*. Englewood Cliffs, N.J.: Prentice-Hall, 1976.

Hammill, D. D., & Larsen, S. The effectiveness of psycholinguistic training. *Exceptional Children*, 1974, *41*, 5–15.

Haring, N. G., & Bateman, B. *Teaching the learning disabled child*. Englewood Cliffs, N.J.: Prentice-Hall, 1977.

Haring, N. G., & Hauck, M. A. Improved learning conditions in the establishment of reading skills with disabled readers. *Exceptional Children*, 1969, *35*, 341–352.

Johnson, D., & Myklebust, H. *Learning disabilities: Educational principles and practices*. New York: Grune & Stratton, 1967.

Kagan, J. Developmental studies in reflection and analysis. In A. H. Kidd & J. H. Rivoire (Eds.), *Perceptual development in children*. New York: International Universities Press, 1966.

Kauffman, J. M., & Hallahan, D. P. Learning disability and hyperactivity. In B. B. Lahey & A. E. Kazdin (Eds.), *Advances in clinical child psychology* (Vol. 2). New York, Plenum, 1978.

Kent, R. N., & O'Leary, K. D. A controlled evaluation of behavior modification with conduct problem children. *Journal of Consulting and Clinical Psychology*, 1976, *44*, 586–596.

Kephart, N. *The slow learner in the classroom*. Columbus, Ohio: Merrill, 1971.

Kirby, F. D., & Shields, F. Modification of arithmetic response rate and attending behavior in a seventh-grade student. *Journal of Applied Behavior Analysis*, 1972, *5*, 79–84.

Kirk, S. A., McCarthy, J. J., & Kirk, W. D. *Illinois test of psycholinguistic abilities*. Urbana: University of Illinois Press, 1968.

Kuhn, T. S. *The structure of scientific revolutions*. Chicago: University of Chicago Press, 1962.

Lahey, B. B. Behavior modification with learning

disabilities and related problems. In M. Hersen, R. Eisler, P. Miller (Eds.), *Progress in behavior modification* (Vol. 3). New York: Academic Press, 1976.

Lahey, B. B. Research on the role of reinforcement in reading instruction: Some measurement and methodological deficiencies. *Corrective and Social Psychiatry*, 1977, *23*, 27–32.

Lahey, B. B., Busemeyer, M. K., O'Hara, C., & Beggs, V. Treatment of severe perceptual-motor disorders in children diagnosed as learning disabled. *Behavior Modification*, 1977, *1*, 123–240.

Lahey, B. B. & Drabman, R. Facilitation of the acquisition and retention of sightword vocabulary through token reinforcement. *Journal of Applied Behavior Analysis*, 1974, *7*, 307–312.

Lahey, B. B., & Johnson, M. S. *Psychology and instruction*. Glenview: Scott, Foresman, 1978.

Lahey, B. B. & Lefton, L. A. Discrimination of letter combinations by good and poor readers. *Journal of Special Education*, 1976, *10*, 205–210.

Lahey, B. B. & McNees, M. P. Letter discrimination errors in kindergarten through third grade: Assessment and operant training. *Journal of Special Education*, 1975, *9*, 191–199.

Lahey, B. B., McNees, M. P., & Brown, C. C. Modification of deficits in reading for comprehension. *Journal of Applied Behavior Analysis*, 1973, *6*, 475–480.

Marholin, D., & Steinman, W. M. Stimulus control in the classroom as a function of the behavior reinforced. *Journal of Applied Behavior Analysis*, 1977, *10*, 465–478.

Marholin, D., Steinman, W. M., McInnis, E. T., & Heads, T. B. The effect of a teacher's presence on the classroom behavior of conduct-problem children. *Journal of Applied Behavior Analysis*, 1975, *3*, 11–25.

Meichenbaum, D., & Goodman, J. Reflection-impulsivity and verbal control of motor behavior. *Child Development*, 1969, *40*, 785–797.

Meichenbaum, D., & Goodman, J. Training impulsive children to talk to themselves: A means of developing self-control. *Journal of Abnormal Psychology*, 1971, *77*, 115–126.

Nolen, P. A., Kunzelmann, H. P., & Haring, N. G. Behavioral modification in a junior high training disabilities classroom. *Exceptional Children*, 1967, *34*, 163–168.

Novy, P., Burnett, J., Powers, M., & Sulzer-Azaroff, B. Modifying attending-to-work behavior of a learning disabled child. *Journal of Learning Disabilities*, 1973, *6*, 217–221.

O'Leary, K. D., Pelham, W. E., Rosenbaum, A., & Price, G. H. Behavioral treatment of hyperactive children: An experimental evaluation of its usefulness. *Clinical Pediatrics*, 1977, *15*, 274–279.

O'Leary, S. G., & Pelham, W. E. Behavior therapy and withdrawal of stimulant medication with hyperactive children, *Pediatrics*, in press.

Osgood, C. A behavioristic analysis. In *Contemporary approaches to cognition*. Cambridge: Harvard University Press, 1957.

Palkes, H., Stewart, M., & Freedman, J. Improvement in maze performance of hyperactive boys as a function of verbal-training procedures. *Journal of Special Education*, 1972, *5*, 337–342.

Palkes, H., Stewart, M., & Kahana, B. Porteus Maze performance of hyperactive boys after training in self-directed verbal commands. *Child Development*, 1968, *39*, 817–826.

Patterson, G. R., Jones, R. W., Whittier, J. E., & Wright, M. A. A behavior modification technique for the hyperactive child. *Behaviour Research and Therapy*, 1965, *2*, 217–226.

Pelham, W. E. Withdrawal of a stimulant drug and concurrent behavioral intervention in the treatment of a hyperactive child. *Behavior Therapy*, 1977, *8*, 473–479.

Peterson, D. R. Behavior problems of middle childhood. *Journal of Consulting Psychology*, 1961, *25*, 205–209.

Rie, H. E., Rie, E. D., Stewart, S., & Ambuel, J. P. Effects of Ritalin on underachieving children. *Journal of Consulting and Clinical Psychology*, 1976, *44*, 250–260.

Rosenbaum, A., O'Leary, K. D., & Jacob, R. G. Behavioral intervention with hyperactive children: Group consequences as a supplement to individual contingencies. *Behavior Therapy*, 1975, *6*, 315–323.

Ross, A. D. *Psychological aspects of learning disabilities and reading disorders*. New York: McGraw-Hill, 1976.

Ross, D. M., & Ross, S. A. *Hyperactivity: Research, theory, and action*. New York: Wiley, 1976.

Saxon, S. A., Magee, J. T., & Siegel, D. S. Activity level patterns in the hyperactive Ritalin responder and nonresponder. *Journal of Clinical Child Psychology*, 1977, *6*, 27–29.

Shafto, F., & Sulzbacher, S. I. Comparing treatment tactics with a hyperactive preschool child: Stimulant medication and programmed teacher intervention. *Journal of Applied Behavior Analysis*, 1977, *10*, 13–20.

Sprague, R. L., & Baxley, G. B. Drugs used for the management of behavior in mental retardation. In N. R. Ellis (Ed.), *Handbook of mental deficiency* (2nd ed.). Hillsdale, N.J.: Erlbaum Associates, in press.

Sroufe, L. A. Drug treatment of children with behavior problems. In F. D. Horowitz (Ed.), *Review of child development research* (Vol. 4). Chicago: University of Chicago Press, 1975.

Stableford, W., Butz, R., Hasazi, J., Leitenberg, H., & Peyser, J. Sequential withdrawal of stimulant drugs and use of behavior therapy with two hyperactive boys. *American Journal of Ortho-psychiatry*, 1976, *46*, 302–312.

Strauss, A., & Lehtinen, L. *Psychopathology and education of the brain-injured child*. New York: Grune Stratton, 1947.

Stromer, R. Remediating academic deficiencies in learning disabled children. *Exceptional Children*, 1977, *43*, 432–440.

Strong, C., Sulzbacher, S. I., & Kirkpatrick, M. A. Use of medication versus reinforcement to modify a classroom behavior disorder. *Journal of Learning Disabilities*, 1974, *7*, 214–218.

Swanson, H. L. Nonverbal visual short-term memory as a function of age and dimensionality in learning-disabled children, *Child Development*, 1977, *48*, 52–55.

Sykes, D. H., Douglas, V. I., Weiss, G., & Minde, K. K. Attention in hyperactive children and the effects of methlphenidate. *Journal of Child Psychology and Psychiatry*, 1971, *12*, 129–139.

Weiss, G., Minde, K., Werry, J. S., Douglas, V.,

& Nemeth, E. Studies on the hyperactive child: VIII. Five-year follow-up. *Archives of General Psychiatry*, 1971, *24*, 409–414.

Williams, M., & Lahey, B. B. The functional independence of response latency and accuracy: Implications for the concept of conceptual tempo. *Journal of Abnormal Child Psychology*, 1977, *5*, 371–378.

Winnet, R. A., & Winkler, R. C. Current behavior modification in the classroom: Be still, be quiet, be docile. *Journal of Applied Behavior Analysis*, 1972, *5*, 499–504.

Wolf, M. M., Giles, D. K., & Hall, R. V. Experiments with token reinforcement in a remedial classroom. *Behaviour Research and Therapy*, 1968, *6*, 51–64.

Wulbert, M., & Dries, R. The relative efficacy of methylphenidate (Ritalin) and behavior-modification techniques in the treatment of a hyperactive child. *Journal of Applied Behavior Analysis*, 1977, *10*, 21–32.

II

Basic concepts and critical issues

The chapters in this section discuss a number of fundamental issues surrounding the assessment and treatment of hyperactivity and learning disabilities. A variety of competing viewpoints and practices are compared and critically evaluated. The disappointing performance of the most widely practiced approaches revealed in these chapters sets the stage for the discussion of behavioral procedures that follows.

The chapters by Hammill, Goodman, and Wiederholt (Chap. 2), Hammill and Larsen (Chap. 3), and Brundage-Aguar, Forehand, and Ciminero (Chap. 17) review the experimental evidence on treatment approaches derived from traditional (perceptual, perceptual-motor, and psycholinguistic) theories and find that the data do not support their use. Similarly, Dubey (Chap. 4) critically examines and rejects theories that relate learning disabilities and hyperactivity to minimal disorders of the nervous system.

The chapters by Sulzbacher (Chap. 6); Rie, Rie, Stewart, and Ambuel (Chap. 7); and Barkley (Chap. 8) are concerned with the effects of stimulant medication on hyperactive behavior. They demonstrate that in spite of many methodological difficulties with the research literature, stimulants can be shown to exert powerful influences on the behavior of children, particularly a narrowly defined subset of children described as having attention-span/distractibility problems. It is equally clear, however, that stimulants do not improve the academic performance of such children. More discussion of these topics is included in Section IV, in which the relationship between stimulant medications and behavior therapy is examined.

Critical issues relating to the assessment process are addressed in this section by Paternite, Loney, and Langhorne (Chap. 10), Magliocca, Rinaldi, Crew, and Kunzelmann (Chap. 11), and Bremer and Stern (Chap. 12). In view of the frequently reported difficulties in finding useful psychometric measures of hyperactivity and learning disabilities (Feuerstein, Ward, & LeBaron, 1978; Sandoval, 1977), alternate strategies involving direct observations of behavior in the classroom (Magliocca et al.) and in laboratory settings (Bremer & Stern are described. Paternite, Loney, and Langhorne discuss the controversial relationship between socioeconomic status (SES) and hyperactivity and find that activity problems per se are no more frequent in lower SES groups than upper ones, but that other behavior problems which might lead to a diagnosis of hyperactivity appear to be more common in the lower SES groups. Sandoval, Lambert, and Yandell (Chap. 13) examine the current diagnostic procedures used by physicians in assessing hyperactivity and find them seriously insufficient. The same conclusions could probably be reached about the assessment procedures used by most members of all professional groups, however.

A number of significant issues were considered to be beyond the scope of this volume. For example, K. D. O'Leary, Rosenbaum, and Hughes (1978) have recently concluded that fluorescent lighting is not a cause of hyperactivity as has been frequently asserted by others. Similarly, Spring and Sandoval (1976) have concluded that food additives are apparently a causative factor in very few, if any, cases of hyperactivity.

REFERENCES

Feuerstein, M., Ward, M. M., & LeBaron, S.W.M. Neuropsychological and neurophysiological assessment of minimal brain dysfunction. In B. B. Lahey & A. E. Kazdin (Eds.), *Advances in clinical child psychology* (Vol. 2). New York, Plenum, 1978.

O'Leary, K. D., Rosenbaum, A., & Hughes, P. C. Fluorescent lighting: A purported source of hyperactive behavior. *Journal of Abnormal Child Psychology*, in press.

Sandoval, J. The measurement of the hyperactive syndrome in children. *Review of Educational Research*, 1977, 47, 293–318.

Spring, C., & Sandoval, J. Food additives and hyperkinesis: A critical evaluation of the evidence. *Journal of Learning Disabilities*, 1976, 9, 28–37.

2. Visual-motor processes: can we train them?

DONALD HAMMILL   LIBBY GOODMAN
J. LEE WIEDERHOLT

The preoccupation of some educators, psychologists, physicians, optometrists, and parents with sensorimotor training is one of the more remarkable phenomena in special education of the last fifteen years. This interest has stimulated the development of many perceptual-motor training programs, varying from sequenced instructional packages to loosely structured collections of activities. Of these, the contributions of Frostig and Horne (1964), Kephart (1971), Getman (1962), Getman and Kane (1964), Getman and others (1968) have been particularly prominent.

While these professionals may differ slightly among themselves regarding particular theoretical points or remedial techniques, they seem to agree on two fundamental assumptions—1) that visual-motor adequacy is important, if not essential, to cognitive development and subsequent academic success, and 2) that these visual-motor processes are in fact trainable in most children by their methodology. The validity of these assumptions has been widely, and often uncritically, accepted by members of the educational and lay community. As a result, visual and motor training programs have been widely implemented in the schools, countless instructional hours have been devoted to such training—often at the expense of academic activities—and large sums of money have been spent on these projects. After a decade and a half of intensive vi-sual-motor training in our schools, it is time to ask if the allocation of time, the expenditure of funds, and the untold efforts of teachers and children have been worthwhile.

Discussions relating to visual perception are made difficult by the variety of definitions of the term "perception" which are currently being used by professionals in the field. Hammill (1972) located thirty-three definitions of perception in the current literature and summarized them as follows:

To some theorists, the entire receptive process is called "perception." To others a distinction is made between "sensation"—that is, the passive reaction of the receptor cells, a reaction not involving memory—and "perception"—that is, the remainder of the receptive process. Others write only of "sensation" and "cognition" where "perception" is subsumed under "cognition." Still others distinguish among "sensation," "perception" and "cognition." In this case, the processes which involve thinking, meaningful language, problem solving and so on are assigned to "cognition" while those dealing with non-symbolic, non-abstract properties of the stimuli—for example, size, color, shape, texture, sequence—are relegated to "perception." (p. 553)

The last definition will be used operationally for the purposes of this paper. To summarize that definition, visual perceptual processes are those brain operations which involve interpreting and

From *The Reading Teacher*, February 1974, 469–478. Reprinted by permission of the authors and the International Reading Association.

organizing the physical elements of the stimulus rather than the symbolic aspects of the stimulus, and are usually referred to as visual discrimination and spatial relationships. Visual perceptual tasks can, therefore, be differentiated readily from lower and higher order visual processing tasks—for example, visual acuity and reading comprehension respectively. We believe that this is essentially the same distinction Getman makes when he differentiates between "sight" and "vision." In practice, almost all assessment devices adhere to this definition—Frostig's Developmental Test of Visual Perception, Bender's Visual-Motor Gestalt Test, Graham-Kendall's Memory for Designs Test, Colarusso-Hammill's Motor-Free Test of Visual Perception, the Benton, the Beery-Buktenica, the Haworth, the Winter Haven, and selected subtests from the Wechsler and Illinois Test of Psycholinguistic Abilities batteries, among many other examples. All of these tests include tasks which require matching of geometric or nonsense forms, fine visual-motor coordination activities, and the distinction of embedded figures (figure-ground).

Actually it is precisely these kinds of skills which most of the visual perception training programs, such as those of Frostig-Horne, Kephart, and Getman, attempt to develop. To date, a large body of research literature has accumulated which relates to the effects of these particular training programs on the visual-motor, cognitive, and academic growth of children. This paper attempts to review the efficacy research which pertains to these approaches. Each section will be concluded with a brief overview of school-based research which was designed by us to evaluate these programs.

FROSTIG-HORNE PROGRAM

This section is devoted to a description of the Frostig-Horne program and to a discussion of the effects of such training on the perceptual, school readiness, and academic achievement of children. A more detailed discussion of both the Frostig test and training program is available elsewhere (Hammill & Wiederholt, 1972).

The Frostig-Horne perceptual development program is comprised of 359 worksheets divided into sets roughly analogous to the subtests of the DTVP, Eye-Hand Coordination, Figure Ground, Form Constancy, Position in Space, and Spatial Relations. Within each set the worksheets are arranged in easy-to-difficult order. In addition, exercises are recommended for children who might require more basic training in body image, gross and fine muscular coordination, and eye movement control. Frostig suggests that language, auditory and visual perception, basic concepts, and social skill training be integrated into the use of the worksheets. These worksheets are not exclusively for use with children who fail the DTVP, but are offered as a supplement to regular preschool, kindergarten, and first grade programs.

If one supplements an educational program with heavy doses of Frostig-Horne, will the children evidence a commensurate improvement in reading skill? To our knowledge, Frostig has never said that they would, though this is implied in their work, yet, many teachers have used the materials for the expressed purpose of enhancing reading proficiency. Arciszewski (1968), Bennett (1968). Forgone (1966), Fortenberry (1968), Jacobs (1968), Jacobs, Wirthlin and Miller (1968), Lewis (1968), Linn (1967, 1968), Mould (1965), O'Connor (1968), Rosen (1966), Sherk (1968), Widerholt and Hammill (1971) and Buckland and Balow (1973) have studied the effects of the Frostig-Horne program on reading. These investigations varied widely with regard to statistical expertise, types and numbers of subjects, number of different trainers, tests used, and overall quality. Surprisingly, in thirteen of these fourteen studies, the authors concluded that concomitant improvement in reading *cannot* be expected as a result of systematic use of the Frostig-Horne program.

The single exception was Lewis, whose study contained serious methodological shortcomings because he included only five subjects, used no control groups, and trained only three hours a week for ten weeks. The results of this study are perplexing; the subjects made significant improvement in reading while failing to improve significantly in visual perception, the latter presumably being the skill trained! Though Linn concluded that perceptual training in kindergarten gave pupils a better start in mastering first grade activities, this investigation is listed as a negative one because the differences on the Metropolitan Achievement Tests between trained and nontrained children at the end of the first grade were not statistically significant.

Since most readiness tests include various perceptive tasks as subtests, one might expect to obtain significant improvement on readiness scores as a result of training children with the Frostig-Horne materials. Seven studies which dealt with this proposition were located. Of these, four investigators reported that perceptual training did not measurably influence readiness performance (McBeath, 1966; Simpkins, 1970; Wiederholt & Hammill; Buckland and Balow, 1973). Support for such training was provided by Alley and others (1968), Cowles (1968), and Frostig (1970). The conflicting nature of these research findings does not permit definitive statements, pro or con, regarding the efficacy of the Frostig-Horne materials when used as a supplement to school readiness programs.

The fundamental question remains: What kind of success have researchers had in stimulating visual-motor growth by using the Frostig-Horne program? Of the eight studies which used the Frostig-Horne materials and which provided control groups, employed at least twenty experimental subjects, and conducted training for fifteen or more weeks, six studies (Alley, 1968; Alley and others, 1968; Arciszewski; Cawley and others, 1968; Jacobs, 1968; Jacobs and others, 1968; Wiederholt and Hammill, 1971) reported no statistical difference between trained and nontrained subjects. Only Mould found such training beneficial in developing perceptual processes.

Other studies that used small samples, had no control groups, and/or trained for only short periods of time tended to find the program instructionally beneficial in improving visual perception. However, because of the weaknesses in their designs, these investigations must be interpreted with unusual caution (Bennett, 1968; Forgone, 1966; Maslow and others, 1964; Rosen, 1966; Talkington, 1968; Tyson, 1963). Another study (Allen and others, 1966) reported that the program led to improvement in several areas of visual perception in mentally retarded children. However, this conclusion must be discounted owing to an error in the analysis of variance table which, if corrected, would indicate insignificant results. Lewis's findings, mentioned previously with regard to reading, were also not significant.

MORE EVIDENCE

This trend is further demonstrated in the research we designed and executed in the Philadelphia public schools (Wiederholt and Hammill, 1971). One hundred and seventy subjects from among 520 pupils in eighteen kindergarten and first grade classes in three schools were randomly assigned to experimental or control subgroups. The U.S. census tract data indicates that the school

neighborhoods are below the city average on median family income and above the city average for male unemployment, receipt of public assistance, and juvenile crime.

In addition to Frostig's DTVP, the Slosson Intelligence Test, the Metropolitan Readiness Tests, and the Metropolitan Achievement Tests were administered to the subjects at the beginning of the study. In addition to the DTVP, the Philadelphia Readiness Test and the Philadelphia Reading and Arithmetic Tests served as posttest measures, as the Metropolitan tests proved to be unsuitable for this purpose. At the time of the pretest, differences between treatment groups were not statistically significant on chronological age, intelligence, perception, or achievement variables.

At the conclusion of the training period, all of the Frostig-Horne worksheets were collected from the teachers and completed sheets were counted. Only subjects who had completed 100 or more sheets were included in the study. Fourteen youngsters from the experimental groups were disqualified because they had not been trained sufficiently. In addition fourteen of the experimental subjects and twelve of the control subjects had moved from the school, were ill throughout the posttesting period or were otherwise unavailable. In all, 130 pupils remained in the study. From among these, twenty-one experimental subjects and twenty-four of the control subjects were found to have pretest PQs of below ninety, and they comprised perceptually handicapped subgroups. Pretest differences between the experimental and control subjects for the remaining sample and perceptually handicapped subsample were not significant on any of the variables.

Training sessions covered sixteen weeks. On the average each child completed 186 worksheets. Because subjects were selected by a random procedure, the number of students in each teacher's class varied from three to seven children per teacher. The median number of children being trained per teacher was five. Some teachers had access to fulltime aides, while others were provided with part-time aides. In some schools, lead teachers and reading teachers cooperated with classroom teachers in administering the worksheets. Because of this, some teachers were able to provide daily sessions for each child while others trained their pupils on an alternate day basis.

The classroom teachers and their aides, as well as lead teachers and reading teachers, were enrolled in ten one-hour staff development meetings which were dispersed throughout the training period. The purpose of these meetings was to instruct the teachers to administer the DTVP and the Frostig-Horne program properly and to provide an opportunity to deal with problems which might arise during the training period. We made periodic visits to the classrooms to give additional support to the teachers.

Teachers received a complete package of worksheets for each of their pupils in the experimental group and were instructed to train the experimental pupils using all five sets of worksheets. In order not to waste time or bore the children, the teachers began each set with worksheet number 1 and skipped by fives until they reached the point where the subject experienced noticeable difficulty. They then dropped back five worksheets and proceeded from that point, one worksheet at a time. Some subjects moved rapidly through the program, while others progressed one sheet per session and only after supplemental activities were introduced.

None of the t ratios associated with posttest differences between the experimental and control groups were significant at the 0.5 level of confidence. Analyses relating to the performance of the perceptually handicapped subsamples yielded similar results.

Additional analyses indicated that subjects who completed the most exercises earned higher perceptual scores than those who did the fewest exercises. This finding suggested that perceptual growth was related to the number of worksheets accomplished and that our negative findings might have been the result of insufficient training. Therefore, the performance of twenty-three pupils who had completed 200 or more worksheets was analyzed. Differences between this group and its control group on the pretest measures were not significant. The posttest analyses yielded no significant t ratios associated with readiness or achievement measures, but did yield a significant t on the total score of the DTVP. Of the twenty-three subjects, nine were classified as perceptually handicapped. Even though they had completed 200 exercises, their performance on the DTVP did not differ significantly from their control group. However, the responses of the fourteen non-perceptually handicapped subjects to training was responsible for the highly significant t.

In this study the pupils who were trained in visual perception scored no higher than their controls on the academic or readiness tests. There-fore, the use of this program as a supplement to traditional readiness activities or as a method for facilitating the mastery of reading and arithmetic does not appear to be warranted. Students who completed over 200 sheets improved significantly in visual perception. Unfortunately, the improvement was made by perceptually adequate students rather than by the perceptually handicapped students, the group most in need of training. Therefore, the use of this program as a remedial method is not supported. Since these last conclusions are based on analysis using a small number of students, those who were trained in excess of 200 sheets, interpretation of results must be made cautiously. However, the reader should recall that analyses based on the original sample of sixty pupils who completed on the average 186 sheets failed to reveal any beneficial effects in visual perception when trained with the Frostig-Horne package.

KEPHART-GETMAN TECHNIQUES

A review of forty-two intervention studies in which the Kephart or Getman training techniques were utilized has been compiled by Goodman and Hammill (1973). Many of the studies employed a composite training program composed of activities drawn from more than one source. Unfortunately, many of them suffered from serious methodological inadequacies, such as use of too few subjects, short periods of training, and failure to use a control group; as a result, their findings could not be accepted with confidence. Criteria were established to identify the "better" research reports—that is, those studies which 1) had at least twenty experimental subjects, 2) provided at least twelve weeks or sixty sessions of training, and 3) utilized an experimental control group design.

Of the forty-two studies, sixteen satisfied all of the criteria. The studies meeting all the criteria included the works of Falik (1969), Faustman (1967), Garrison (1965), Getman and Kane (1964), Goodman (1973), Halliwell and Solan (1972), Hiers (1970), Keim (1970), Lipton (1969), McBeath (1966), McRaney (1970), O'Connor (1968), Okada (1969), Pryzwanski (1969), Turner and Fisher (1969), and Wimsatt (1967).

Of these "better" designed reports, eleven studies were concerned with the effects of visual-motor training on visual-motor performance. In all, twenty-five measures of visual-motor ability were included in the posttest batteries of these studies. The results were, for the most part, insignificant. The experimental subjects performed significantly better than the control subjects in only four instances. But in O'Connor's study the significant result is suspect due to a difference in the teacher-pupil ratio between the experimental and control groups (1:10 versus 1:30 respectively).

The effects of visual-motor training on school readiness were investigated in eight studies in which nine posttest criteria of readiness were used. Significantly better readiness scores favored the trained subjects on three of the nine posttests (Hiers; Lipton; Turner and Fisher). The results of two of the "positive" studies are puzzling, however. Hiers noted improvement on the cognitive and auditory subtests but not on the visual-motor subtests of the Metropolitan Readiness Test, and Turner and Fisher found improved readiness without a concomitant improvement in visual-motor skills, a most curious finding. In the latter instance, the authors themselves suggest that the positive treatment effect may have been due to the confounding variables and not the treatment.

The effects of visual-motor training on intelligence, school achievement, and language functioning were investigated in ten studies which included fifteen different posttest analyses. Experimental subjects performed significantly better in only six of these. Wimsatt, using kindergarten, first, and second grade students, found that the experimental kindergarten children made significant gains in reading aptitude but not in intelligence, while the first and second graders apparently did not benefit at all from the training program.

In light of the limited treatment effect, he concluded that there is little evidence that visual-motor training benefits general learning abilities. In contrast, significantly better performance on tests of reading comprehension for first graders who received supplemental perceptual-motor training in addition to their regular reading program were found by Getman and Kane and by Halliwell and Solan. Faustman reported significantly greater gains in word recognition ability for the experimental group. Okada found that treatment produced significant improvement in the psycholinguistic functioning of first grade experimental children.

While reviewing the literature related to the application of the Kephart and Getman training programs, only one study was found in which visual-motor training was used with orthopedically handicapped children (Hendry, 1970). In this study, a small group of multihandicapped children demonstrated improvements on selected visual-motor skills after participation in six-week training programs. However, interpretation and generalization of these findings are limited due to the inadequate research design of the study. The lack of studies using orthopedically handicapped subjects is unfortunate. Presumably, such children need remedial training.

These considerations led us to plan and implement an intervention study in which physically handicapped children would have an opportunity to participate (Goodman, 1973). Forty-four children enrolled in preschool classes for physically handicapped children in the greater Philadelphia area sponsored by the Easter Seal Society for Crippled Children and Adults were the subjects for the study. The children ranged in age from twenty-six to eighty-one months. Their global functioning as measured by Doll's Preschool Attainment Record ranged from 1.9 to 5.3 years.

The children were classified into two general etiological categories—those with muscular or neuromuscular disorders and those with skeletal deformities. Half of the sample were cerebral palsied, while nine suffered other less common conditions—spina bifida, hydrocephalus, birth defects, brain damage (unspecified), muscular atrophy, central nervous system disease (unspecified), amyotonia congenita, osteogenita imperfecta, and post cerebral trauma. The degree of motor impairment among the children varied from mild to severe.

After pretesting, the children were randomly assigned to either an experimental or control group. Analysis of the pretest established the pretreatment equivalence of the two groups. The training program itself was a composite program made up of activities from the Kephart and Getman-Kane programs with some additional activities from Getman's earlier work included. The experimental subjects participated in small groups of individual training sessions about three times a week for a period of approximately five months. Specific activities were selected and presented in accordance with the needs and abilities of the children. Control children participated in only the regular preschool program.

The effects of the training on the visual, motor, and integrated visual-motor functioning of the children were assessed. Criterion measures included the Ayres Space Test, the Position in Space subtest from the Frostig DTVP, the Seguin Form Boards, and Manikin Puzzle from the Merrill Palmer Scale of Mental Tests, the Imitation of Postures and Crossing the Mid-Line subtests from the Southern California Perceptual-Motor tests, and an informal Motor Development Checklist specially designed for use in this study. Contrary to expectations, the experimental subjects did not perform significantly better than the control subjects on any of these tests at the end of the training period. In fact, the group differences did not even consistently favor the experimental children. It would appear that participation in the supplemental visual-motor program was no more effective than participation in the regular preschool program regarding the enhancement of visual-motor functioning.

By itself, this study cannot be viewed as conclusive evidence of the nonefficacy of the Kephart and Getman-Kane training activities. It does, however, take on added significance when combined with other intervention studies.

To conclude, the results of attempts to implement the Frostig-Horne materials and Kephart-Getman techniques in the schools have for the most part been unrewarding. The readiness skills of children were improved in only a few instances. The effect of training on intelligence and academic achievement was not clearly demonstrated. Particularly disappointing were the findings which pertained to the effects of such training on perceptual-motor performance itself. For if the training is not successful in this area, can the positive benefits of such instruction reported by a few authors be anything other than spurious?

We have little doubt that any interested person who reads the efficacy literature will conclude that the value of perceptual training, especially those programs often used in schools, has not been clearly established. If he concludes that such training lacks solid support, he may begin to question the purchase of attractively packaged materials which some companies offer teachers along with unsubstantiated claims concerning their merits, the practice of providing perceptual-motor training to all school children in the name of readiness training, and the assumption that a lack of perceptual-motor adequacy causes a considerable amount of academic failure.

REFERENCES

Allen, R. M., I. Dickman and R. Haupt. "A Pilot Study of the Immediate Effectiveness of the Frostig-Horne Training Program with Educable Retardates." *Exceptional Children*, vol. 33 (1966), pp. 41–2.

Alley, G. "Perceptual-Motor Performance of Mentally Retarded Children after Systematic Visual-Perception Training." *American Journal of Mental Deficiency*, vol. 73 (1968), pp. 247–50.

Alley, G., W. Snider, J. Spencer and R. Angell. "Reading Readiness and the Frostig-Horne Training Program." *Exceptional Children*, vol. 35 (1968), p. 68.

Arciszewski, R. A. "Effects of Visual Perception Training on the Perceptual Ability and Reading Achievement of First Grade Students." *Dissertation Abstracts*, vol. 29 (1968), p. 4174-A.

Argenti, R. M. "The Effects of Systematic Motor Training on Selected Perceptual-Motor Attributes of Mentally Retarded Children." *Dissertation Abstracts*, vol. 29 (1968), p. 3853-A.

August, I. "A Study of the Effects of a Physical Education Program on Reading Readiness, Visual Perception and Perceptual-Motor Development in Kindergarten Children." *Dissertation Abstracts*, vol. 31 (1970), p. 2212-A.

Ayres, J. A. *Southern California Perceptual-Motor Tests*. Los Angeles, California: Western Psychological Services, 1968.

Ball, T. S. and C. L. Edgar. "The Effectiveness of Sensory-Motor Training in Promoting Generalized Body Image Development." *Journal of Special Education*, vol. 4 (1967), pp. 387–95.

Bennett, R. M. "A Study of the Effects of a Visual Perception Program upon School Achievement, IQ and Visual Perception." *Dissertation Abstracts*, vol. 29 (1968), p. 3684-A.

Benyon, S. D. *Intensive Programming for Slow Learners*. Columbus, Ohio: Charles E. Merrill, 1968.

Bosworth, M. H. "Pre-Reading Improvement of Visual-Motor Skills." *Dissertation Abstracts*, vol. 23 (1967), p. 3545-A.

Buckland, P. and B. Balow. "Effects of Visual Perceptual Training on Reading Achievement." *Exceptional Children*, vol. 39 (1973), pp. 299–304.

Cawley, J. F., W. H. Burrow and H. A. Goodstein. "An Appraisal of Head Start Participants and Non-Participants." Research Report OEO4177. Office of Economic Opportunity. Storrs, Connecticut: University of Connecticut, 1968.

Cowles, J. D. An Experimental Study of Visual-Perceptual Training and Readiness Scores with Certain First Grade Children. Unpublished doctoral dissertation, University of Alabama, 1968.

Early, G. H. and N. C. Kephart. "Perceptual-Motor Training and Academic Achievement." *Academic Therapy Quarterly*, vol. 4 (1969), pp. 201–06.

Edgar, C. L., T. S. Ball, R. B. McIntyre and A. M. Shotwell. "Effects of Sensory-Motor Training on Adaptive Behavior." *American Journal of Mental Deficiency*, vol. 73 (1969), pp. 713–20.

Emmons, C. A. "A Comparison of Selected Gross-Motor Activities of the Getman-Kane and the Kephart Perceptual-Motor Training Programs and Their Effect upon Certain Readiness Skills of First Grade Negro Children." *Dissertation Abstracts*, vol. 29 (1968), p. 3442-A.

Falik, L. H. "The Effects of Special Training in Kindergarten with Second Grade Reading." *Journal of Learning Disabilities*, vol. 2 (1969), pp. 325–9.

Faustman, M. N. Some Effects of Perception Training in Kindergarten on First Grade Success in Reading. International Reading Association Convention. Seattle (May 1967), ERIC ED 017-397.

Fisher, K. L. "Effects of Perceptual-Motor Training on the Educable Mentally Retarded." *Exceptional Children*, vol. 38 (1971), pp. 264–6.

Forgone, C. Effects of Visual Perception and Language Training upon Certain Abilities of Retarded Children. Unpublished doctoral dissertation, George Peabody College for Teachers, 1966.

Fortenberry, W. D. Effectiveness of a Special Program for Development of Word Recognition by Culturally Disadvantaged First Grade Pupils. ERIC ED 027 368, 1968.

Frostig, M. Pilot Program in Early Childhood Education, Compton City School District, 1970. Unpublished report. Project 75-E.I.A.

Frostig, M. and D. Horne. *The Frostig Program for Development of Visual Perception*. Chicago, Illinois: Follett, 1964.

Garrison, E. B. A Study in Visual-Motor Perception Training in First Grade. ERIC ED 031-292, 1965.

Getman, G. N. How to Develop your Child's Intelligence. Luverne, Minnesota: Getman, 1962.

Getman, G. N., E. R. Kane, M. R. Halgren, and G. W. McKee. *Developing Learning Readiness*. Manchester, Missouri: Webster Division, McGraw-Hill, 1968.

Getman, G. N. and E. R. Kane. *The Physiology of Readiness: An Action Program for the Development of Perception for Children*. Minneapolis, Minnesota: Programs to Accelerate School Success, 1964.

Goodman, L. The Efficacy of Visual Motor Training for Orthopedically Handicapped Children. *Rehabilitation Literature*, vol. 34 (1973), pp. 299–304.

Goodman, L. and D. Hammill. "The Effectiveness of Kephart-Getman Activities in Developing Perceptual-Motor and Cognitive Skills." *Focus on Exceptional Children*, vol. 4 (1973), pp. 1–9.

Hallahan, D. P. and W. Cruickshank. *Psychoeducational Foundations of Learning Disabilities*. Englewood Cliffs, New Jersey: Prentice-Hall, 1973.

Halliwell, J. W. and H. A. Solan. "The Effects of a Supplemental Perceptual Training Program on Reading Achievement." *Exceptional Children*, vol. 38 (1972), pp. 613–21.

Hammill, D. "Training Visual Perception Processes." *Journal of Learning Disabilities*, vol. 5 (1972), pp. 552–59.

Hammill, D. and J. L. Wiederholt. "Appropriateness of the Metropolitan Tests in an Urban Poor Neighborhood." *Psychology in the Schools*, vol. 3 (1971), pp. 49–50.

Hammill, D. and J. L. Wiederholt. "Review of the Frostig Visual Perception Test and the Related Training Program." *The First Review of Special Education*, L. Mann and D. Sabatino, Eds. Philadelphia: Journal of Special Education Press, 3515 Woodhaven, 1972.

Haring, N. W. and J. M. Stables. "The Effect of Gross Motor Development on Visual Perception and Eye-Hand Coordination." *Physical Therapy*, vol. 46 (1966), pp. 129–35.

Haworth, M. R., C. C. Auvinen and K. P. Scott. "Improving Perception: A Multisensory Approach." *Teaching Exceptional Children*, vol. 1 (1969), pp. 33–41.

Hendry, B. C. "The Effects of Gross-Motor Movements on the Perceptual-Motor Development of Primary Age Multiply Handicapped Children." *Dissertation Abstracts*, vol. 31 (1970), p. 5231-A.

Heriot, J. T. "A Perceptual Motor Program for Preschool Retardates: A Pilot Study." *Dissertation Abstracts*, vol. 28 (1967), p. 1197-B.

Hiers, M. H. "A Comparison of the Readiness Test Performance of a Group of Primary Level Educable Mentally Retarded Children Instructed on Visual-Motor Perception Tasks and a Comparable Group Receiving No Prescribed Instruction." *Dissertation Abstracts*, vol. 31 (1970), p. 6440-A.

Jacobs, J. N. "An Evaluation of the Frostig Visual-Perception Training Program." *Educational Leadership*, Vol. 25 (1968), pp. 332–40.

Jacobs, J. N., L. D. Wirthlin and C. B. Miller. "A Follow-Up Evaluation of the Frostig Visual Perceptual Training Program." *Educational Leadership Research Supplement*, vol. 4 (1968), 169–75.

Keim, R. P. "Visual-Motor Training, Readiness, and Intelligence of Kindergarten Children." *Journal of Learning Disabilities*, vol. 3 (1970), pp. 256–59.

Kephart, N. C. *The Slow Learner in the Classroom*. (2nd ed.) Columbus, Ohio: Charles E. Merrill, 1971.

Lazroe, J. J. "An Investigation of the Effects of Motor Training on the Reading Readiness of Kindergarten Children." *Dissertation Abstracts*, vol. 1 (1968), pp. 642–53.

Lewis, J. N. "The Improvement of Reading Ability through a Developmental Program in Visual Perception." *Journal of Learning Disabilities*, Vol. 1 (1968), pp. 652–53.

Linn, S. H. "A Follow-Up: Achievement Report of First Grade Students after Visual-Perception Training in Kindergarten." *Academic Therapy Quarterly*, vol. 3 (1968), pp. 179–80.

Linn, S. H. "From the Classroom: Visual Perceptual Training for Kindergarten Children." *Academic Therapy Quarterly*, vol. 4 (1967), pp. 255–58.

Lipton, E. D. "The Effects of Physical Education Programs to Develop Directionality of Movement of Perceptual-Motor Development, Visual Perception, and Reading Readiness of First Grade Children." *Dissertation Abstracts*, vol. 30 (1969), p. 2362-A.

Lyons, C. V. and E. B. Lyons. "The Power of Visual Training." *Journal of the American Optometric Association*, vol. 26 (1954), pp. 255–62.

Maloney, M. P., T. S. Ball and C. L. Edgar.

"Analysis of the Generalizability of Sensory-Motor Training." *American Journal of Mental Deficiency,* vol. 74 (1970), pp. 458–69.

Maslow, P., M. Frostig, D. W. Lefever and J. R. B. Whittlesey. "The Marianne Frostig Developmental Test of Visual Perception: 1963 Standardization." *Perceptual and Motor Skills,* vol. 19 (1964), pp. 463–99.

McBeath, P. M. "The Effectiveness of Three Reading Preparedness Programs for Perceptually Handicapped Kindergarteners." *Dissertation Abstracts,* vol. 27 (1966), p. 115-A.

McClanahan, L. J. "The Effectiveness of Perceptual Training for Slow Learners." *Dissertation Abstracts,* vol. 28 (1967), p. 2560-A.

McCormick, C. C., J. N. Schnobrich, S. W. Footlik and B. Poether. "Improvement in Reading Achievement through Perceptual-Motor Training." *The Research Quarterly,* vol. 39 (1968), pp. 627–33.

McRaney, K. A. "A Study of Perceptual Motor Exercises Utilized as an Early Grade Enrichment Program for the Improvement of Learning Activity and Motor Development." *Dissertation Abstracts,* vol. 31 (1970), p. 2935-A.

Meyerson, D. W. A Reading Readiness Training Program for Perceptually Handicapped Kindergarten Pupils of Normal Vision. Final Project Report No. 6-8724. Washington, D.C. Office of Education, Bureau of Research, May 1967.

Mould, R. E. An Evaluation of the Effectiveness of a Special Program for Retarded Readers Manifesting Disturbed Visual Perception Unpublished doctoral dissertation, Washington State University, 1965.

Murray, B. A. Suggested Method for the Preschool Identification of Reading Disability. ERIC ED 025-055.

O'Connor, C. "Effects of Selected Physical Activities upon Motor Performance, Perceptual Performance and Academic Achievement of First Graders." *Perceptual Motor Skills,* vol. 29 (1968), pp. 703–09.

Okada, D. M. "The Effects of Perceptual and Perceptual Motor Training on the Visual Perception, Auditory Perception and Language Performance of Institutionalized Educable Mental Retardates." *Dissertation Abstracts,* vol. 30 (1969), p. 2857-A.

Pryzwanski, W. E. "The Effects of Perceptual-Motor Training and Manuscript Writing on Reading Readiness Skills in Kindergarten." *Dissertation Abstracts,* vol. 31 (1969), p. 384-B.

Rosen, C. L. "An Experimental Study of Visual-Perceptual Training and Reading Achievement in First Grade." *Perceptual and Motor Skills,* vol. 22 (1966), pp. 979–1086.

Rutherford, W. L. "The Effects of a Perceptual-Motor Training Program on the Performance of Kindergarten Pupils on Metropolitan Reading Tests." *Dissertation Abstracts,* vol. 25 (1965), pp. 4583–84.

Sapir, S. G. A Pilot Approach to the Education of the First Grade Children with Problems in Body Schema, Perceptual-Motor or Language Development. ERIC ED 024-163.

Sherk, J. K. "A Study of the Effects of a Program of Visual Perception on the Progress of Retarded Readers." *Dissertation Abstracts,* (1968), p. 4392-A.

Shipe, D. and S. Miezitis. "A Pilot Study in the Diagnosis and Remediation of Special Learning Disabilities in Preschool Children. *Journal of Learning Disabilities,* vol. 2 (1969), pp. 579–92.

Simpkins, K. W. "Effect of the Frostig Program for the Development of Visual Perception on the Readiness of Kindergarten Children." *Dissertation Abstracts,* vol. 30 (1970), p. 4286-A.

Simpson, D. M. "Perceptual Readiness and Beginning Reading." *Dissertation Abstracts,* vol. 21 (1958), p. 1858.

Stutsman, R. *Guide for Administering the Merrill-Palmer Scale of Mental Tests.* New York: Harcourt, Brace & World, 1931.

Talkington, L. W. "Frostig Visual Perceptual Training with Low Ability Level Retarded." *Perceptual and Motor Skills,* vol. 27 (1968), pp. 505–06.

Turner, R. V. and M. D. Fisher. The Effects of a Perceptual Motor Training Program under the Readiness and Perceptual Development of Culturally Disadvantaged Kindergarten Children. ERIC ED 041-633.

Tyson, M. C. "Pilot Study of Remedial Visuo-Motor Training." *Special Education,* vol. 52 (1963), pp. 22–25.

Webb, R. C. "Sensory-Motor Training of the Profoundly Retarded." *American Journal of Mental Deficiency,* vol. 74 (1969), pp. 823–95.

Wimsatt, W. R. "The Effects of Sensory-Motor Training on the Learning Abilities of Grade School Children." *Dissertation Abstracts,* vol. 28 (1967), p. 347-B.

Wiederholt, J. L. and D. D. Hammill. "Use of the Frostig-Home Perception Program in the Urban School." *Psychology in the Schools,* vol. 8 (1971), pp. 268–74.

3. The effectiveness of psycholinguistic training

DONALD D. HAMMILL   STEPHEN C. LARSEN

Psycholinguistics is the study of language, as related to the general or individual characteristics of the users of language. It includes the processes by which a speaker or writer emits signals or symbols and the processes by which these signals are interpreted. In addition, attention is given to the way that the intentions of one individual are transmitted to another and, reciprocally, the way that the intentions of another person are received. In short, psycholinguistics deals with the psychological functions and interactions involved in communication.

While there are many theories of psycholinguistic functioning, the schemata presented by Osgood (1957) has had the greatest impact on education. The Osgood model encompasses two dimensions of language behavior, language processes and levels of organization. The process dimension includes decoding, association, and encoding. Decoding refers to the receiving and perceiving of stimuli, the recognition of what is seen or heard. Association implies the ability to manipulate linguistic symbols, the inference of relationships from what is seen or heard. Encoding is the expression of linguistic symbols, the use of skills necessary to express thoughts.

The processes just described are mediated at any one of three levels of neural organization. The most basic level is that of projection, which relates receptor and muscle events to the brain. The second organizational level is integration, which provides for the sequencing and organization of incoming and outgoing "messages." The most complex level of organization is the representational. At this level, the more sophisticated mediating operations necessary for meaningful symbolization are employed.

The educational applications of these particular psycholinguistic principles have generated both assessment techniques and remedial language programs. It was this model which Kirk, McCarthy, and Kirk (1968) adapted and used to construct the *Illinois Test of Psycholinguistic Abilities* (ITPA). This diagnostic instrument was designed to measure specific functions of psycholinguistic behavior and provides a framework for the amelioration of language disorders. The ITPA clinical model and the original Osgood schema have served as the basis for several remedial and developmental programs that are used extensively in schools (Karnes, 1968; Dunn & Smith, 1966; Bush & Giles, 1969; Minskoff, Wiseman, & Minskoff, 1972).

Psycholinguistic training is based upon the assumption that discrete elements of language behavior are identifiable and measurable, that they provide the underpinning for learning, and that if defective they can be remediated. When using

From *Exceptional Children*, 1974, *41*, 5–14. Reprinted by permission of The Council for Exceptional Children. Copyright 1974 by The Council for Exceptional Children, 1920 Association Drive, Reston, Virginia 22091.

this approach, an additional assumption is made that the cause of the child's learning failure is within himself and that strengthening weak areas will result in improved classroom learning. If this assumption is valid, then programs designed to alleviate psycholinguistic deficits would be appropriate and viable. However, if this assumption is not valid, much time, effort, and money is needlessly expended. Only through the accumulated results of carefully designed research may the efficacy of psycholinguistic training be proved to be of value. The purpose of this article is to report the results of studies that have attempted to develop psycholinguistic skills.

PROCEDURES

Only studies which used the ITPA or one or more of its subtests as the criterion for improvement of language behavior were reviewed. As the ITPA is based primarily upon the constructs of Osgood and as most of the training programs were generated either from the ITPA or from the original Osgood theory, it was felt that this stipulation would be the most efficient in determining the efficacy of psycholinguistic training. It was also assumed that the researchers who conducted these studies believed that there was some relationship between the ITPA and their intervention programs or they would not have selected this test to demonstrate the effects of their program.

The characteristics of the studies reviewed are presented in Table 3-1. The table includes (a) the names of the researchers; (b) the publication date of the research; (c) the number, (d) type, and (e) age of the experimental and control subjects; (f) the basic approach used with the experimental group, e.g., prescriptive (individualized) where a special program is designed for a child on the basis of diagnostic procedures or general (nonindividualized) where children are exposed to an overall language stimulation program; (g) the specific kind of experimental training, e.g., selected activities based on an ITPA psycholinguistic model (usually author designed but similar to the Kirk and Kirk, 1971, or Bush and Giles, 1969, activities), the *Peabody Language Development Kits* (PLDK), or other teaching systems; (h) the estimated duration of the treatment period; and (i) the number of hours devoted to training. The following example demonstrates how the table should be read. In 1967, Mueller and Dunn evaluated the effectiveness of the PLDK, a general, nonindividualized approach to teaching language. Their experimental and control subjects were elementary school aged educa-

ble mentally retarded children. More than 20 subjects were in each group. The experimental subjects received in excess of 50 hours of training over a more than 20 week period.

While some of the researchers compared the experimental subjects with a variety of contrast subjects, e.g., those who received remedial reading instruction or speech therapy, we were interested only in the experimental-control group analyses. In all instances, the results discussed in this review refer to comparisons between children trained in language and those who received no formal instruction of any kind or those who were enrolled in "traditional" programs.

RESULTS

The findings of these studies are summarized in Table 3-2. A "+" indicates that the author reported that the trained subjects did considerably better than nontrained subjects on a particular ITPA subtest. A "0" indicates that the control subjects were equal to or better than the experimental subjects on a subtest analysis. In most of the cases "+" and "0" are the same as statistical significance (.05 level) or nonstatistical significance respectively. Where this is not the case, the author's name is numbered and a description of the procedures used to designate the study's analyses as "+" or "0" are described in a footnote. The footnotes are also used to explain those occasions where our interpretations of a study's findings differed from its author's.

The reader will notice the many blank spaces in Table 3-2. This occurs because some authors used the 9 subtest 1961 ITPA and others used the 12 subtest 1968 version. Some researchers were concerned only with selected subtests while others were interested in the ITPA total score and not at all in the subtests. The effects of training on Auditory Closure and Sound Blending are almost nonexistent which was likely due to the fact that these subtests only became available with the publication of the revised ITPA and are only supplemental tests in that version. Visual Closure is also a new subtest, but it is included in the ITPA proper and has therefore been studied more frequently.

For these analyses, no distinction is made between the 1961 and 1968 versions of the ITPA. To avoid confusion, the terminology of the more recent version is used throughout this review. It was our opinion that differences between the two tests were of a technical nature, e.g., some subtests were lengthened, instructions were altered slightly, names of the subtests were changed; but

Table 3-1. Characteristics of psycholinguistic training studies

Authors	Date	Number E	Number C	Type	Age	Approach	Exp. method	EHT	DOT
Blessing	1964	2	2	1	UTE	2	1	3	2
Blue	1970	2	2	2	UTE	2	1	1	2
Bradley et al.	1966	2	2	2	2+3	1	1	3	3
Carter	1966	3	3	3	2	2	2	2	3
Clasen et al.	1969	2	2	3	1	2	2	3	1
Crutchfield	1964	1	1	1+2	2+3	2	1	1	2
Dickie	1968	3	3	3	1	2	3	2	3
Dunn & Mueller	1966	3	3	3	2	2	2	3	3
Dunn & Mueller	1967	3	3	3	2	2	2	3	3
Ensminger	1966	3	3	3	2	2	2	3	3
Forgnone	1967	3	3	1	2	2	2	2	2
Gazdic	1971	3	2	4	2	2	2	3	3
Gibson	1966	2	2	1	2	2	2	2	3
Gray & Klaus	1965	3	3	3	1	2	3	3	3
Guess et al.	1969	3	3	2	3	2	2	3	3
Hart	1963	1	1	4	2	1	1	1	1
Hartman	1967	3	3	3	1	1	1	3	3
Hodges & Spicker	1967	2	2	3	1	2	3	UTE	3
Jones	1970	3	3	3	1	2	2	2	2
Karnes et al.	1970	3	3	3	1	2	1	3	3
Lavin	1971	3	3	3	1	2	3	3	3
Leiss	1974	3	3	2	2+3	2	1	3	3
McConnell et al.	1969 (a,b,c)	3	3	3	1	2	3	3	3
Minskoff	1967	1	1	1	3	1	1	1	3
Mitchell	1967	3	3	3	1	2	2	UTE	1
Morgan	1972	3	3	3	1	2	3	3	3
Morris	1967	*	*	*	*	2	2	3	3
Mueller & Dunn	1967	3	3	1	2	2	2	3	3
Painter	1966	1	1	3	1	2	3	2	1
Runyon	1970	2	2	1	2	2	1	2	3
Saudargas et al.	1970	2	1	1	2	1	2	1	2
Sapir	1971	2	1	4	2	2	3	UTE	3
Schifani	1972	1	1	1	3	2	2	3	3
Siders	1970	3	3	3	2	2	3	3	3
Smith	1962	2	2	1	2	2	2	1	2
Spollen & Ballif	1971	3	3	4	1	1	1	3	3
Stearns	1967	2	1	3	1	1	3	2	2
Strickland	1967	3	3	3	1	2	1	UTE	2
Wiseman	1965	1	1	1	2	1	1	2	1

*Information not obtained

CODE

Subjects
Number
  E = Experimental
  C = Control
  1 = 5 to 10
  2 = 11 to 20
  3 = 20+
Type
  1 = EMR
  2 = TMR
  3 = Disadvantaged
  4 = Other
Age
  1 Preschool
  2 = 6 to 11 years
  3 = 11+ years
  UTE = unable to estimate

Approach
1 = prescriptive/individualized
2 = general/nonindividualized

Exp. method:
1 = Selected activities, based on
    ITPA model
2 = PDLK
3 = Other

EHT (*Estimated hours of training*):
1 = 30
2 = 30 to 50
3 = 50+
UTE = unable to estimate

DOT (*Duration of training*):
1 = 10 weeks
2 = 10 to 20 weeks
3 = 20+ weeks

Table 3-2. Results of studies which attempted to train psycholinguistic processes

Researcher	AR	VR	AA	VA	VE	ME	GC	VC	ASM	VSM	AC	SB	Total
Blessing					+								
Blue													0
Bradley et al.[1]	+	+	0	+	+	+	+		0	0			+
Carter	+	+	+	+	+	+	+		+	+			+
Clasen et al.	0	+	0	+	0	0	0		0	0			0
Crutchfield[2]	+	0	0	0	0	0	0		0	+			0
Dickie			0		0								
Dunn & Mueller[3]	0	0	+	+	+	0	0		0	0			+
Ensminger	0	0	+	0	+	0	0		0	0			0
Forgnone													0
Gazdic													0
Gibson	0	0	0	0	0	0	0		0	0			0
Gray & Klaus	+	+	+	+	+	0	+		+	+			+
Guess et al.[4]													0
Hart[5]	0	0	+	+	+	+	0		+	+			+
Hartman	0	0	0	0	0	0	0		0	0			0
Hodges & Spicker													0
Jones[6]	+	0	0	0	+	+	0	0	0	0			0
Karnes et al.	0	+	+	0	0	0	+		0	0			+
Lavin	0	0	0	0	0	0	0	0	0	0			0
Leiss	0	0	0	0	0	0	0	0	0	0			0
McConnell et al.	+	0	+	+	+	+	+		+	+			+
Minskoff[7]				+	0	+			0	0			0
Mitchell	0	0	0	0	0	0	0		+	0			0
Morgan	0	0	+	+	+	0	0	+	0	0			+
Morris			+		+		0						+
Mueller & Dunn	0		0				0			0			+
Painter	0	0	+	0	0	+	0		0	0			
Runyon													+
Saudargas et al.	0	0	0	0	0	0	0	0	0	0	0	0	+
Sapir		0	+	0	+	+			+	0			+
Schifani[8]	0	0	0	0	0	0	0	0	+	0			+
Siders	0		0		0		0						
Smith[9]	+	+	+	+	+	+	+		0	+			+
Spollen & Ballif													0
Stearns[10]	0	0	+	+	+	0	0		0	0			0
Strickland			+						+				0
Wiseman	0	0	0	0	+	+	0		+	0			+

CODE:

+ means experimental subjects did considerably better than control subjects
0 means control subjects were equal to or better than experimental subjects

ITPA Subtests: AR = Auditory Reception, VR = Visual Reception, AA = Auditory Association, VA = Visual Association, VE = Verbal Expression, ME = Manual Expression, GC = Grammatic Closure, VC = Visual Closure, ASM = Auditory Sequential Memory, VSM = Visual Sequential Memory, AC = Auditory Closure, SB = Sound Blending, Total = Total Language Age

FOOTNOTES:

1. Bradley et al. neglected to report the significance of difference in gain scores between experimental and control groups for the Auditory Sequential Memory subtest. Inspection of their Table 1 clearly indicates that the difference would be nonsignificant.

2. Crutchfield did no tests of significance but did provide pretest and posttest subtest means. It was therefore possible to calculate pre-post gains for experimental and control subjects. His experimental subjects were subdivided into a younger ($N = 9$) and older ($N = 8$) group, but no such division was made of the control subjects ($N = 15$). Because of the similarity in the N's of the two experimental groups, they were combined and their mean gains compared with those of the control group. Of the nine subtests, the gains of five favored the control subjects; in two instances, the differences were 2 months or less; and only two cases, where the differences exceeded seven months, could be taken as positive evidence of training.

3. Dunn and Mueller undertook two studies, one dealt with the effects of training on the total ITPA score (1966) while the other dealt with the subtests (1967). No tests of significance were reported for the latter. Instead pre- and posttest means for the experimental and control groups and gain scores are provided. On four of the nine subtests gains favored the control subjects and these are recorded as "0" in Table 2. In addition two subtests, Auditory Reception and Visual Sequential Memory, are also recorded as "0." In each of these cases the difference between experimental and control groups on both the pretest and the posttest was less than two months. The results for Auditory Association, Visual Association, and Verbal Expression clearly demonstrated the positive effects of training and are recorded "+."

4. The Guess et al. sample was posttested twice—once at the end of the 9 month training period and again 9 months later. Differences between experimental and control groups were not significant at the first testing but were significant at the last testing. The nonsignificant value is used in Table 2 because "followup" research was not dealt with in this review.

5. Hart does no tests of significance on his subtest data. He did provide the pre- and posttest means for his experimental and control groups. It was then possible to estimate gain scores. On one subtest, Auditory Reception, the gains favored the control group; on two others, Visual Reception and Grammatic Closure, the gains of the experimental group exceeded those of the control groups by four or fewer months. These subtests were arbitrarily recorded as "0." The other differences all favored the experimental group and ranged from 5 to 24 months.

6. Jones did no subtest analyses, though she did provide pre-post means for experimental and control groups (p. 119) which made it possible to compute gain scores for the groups. On an additional four subtests and the total scores, the differences favored the experimental group by less than 2 points. These eight analyses are recorded as "0" in Table 2. The remaining three analyses favored the experimental group by differences ranging from 2.4 to 5.6 points and are recorded "+."

7. Minskoff used the .10 level of confidence in his dissertation. As all other authors in this table employed the .05 level, we reinterpreted Minskoff's findings using the .05 level in order to be consistent.

8. In his dissertation, Schifani tests only the significance of the differences relating to the ITPA total score. As he provided means and standard deviations for the subtests, it was possible to compute the significance of subtest differences.

9. Smith reported no analyses regarding the significance of differences between experimental and control groups. It was possible, however, to compute the mean gain scores for the groups from data provided. The control subjects regressed or made no gain on five subtests and gains of less than 3 months on the four subtests, while the experimental subjects registered gains on all subtests ranging from 3 to 13 months. In Table 2 all the subtests with the exception of Auditory Sequential Memory are designated "+"; however, because of the small N, if analyses could have been run on these data, some of the results might have been nonsignificant.

10. Stearns only tested the significance of the differences between experimental and control groups on the total ITPA score. Subtest means were provided but not the associated standard deviations. He concluded, from inspection, that training appeared to positively affect three of nine subtests.

the basic constructs of the two remained essentially the same. This opinion is supported by the work of Waugh (1973) who compared the tests and concluded that for most purposes they could be used interchangeably.

Table 3-2 should be read as follows: Sapir reported that special psycholinguistic instruction was beneficial in developing the abilities measured by Auditory Association, Verbal Expression, Manual Expression, Auditory Sequential Memory, and the total ITPA Language Age. Such training was found to be no more beneficial than that in traditional classes regarding Visual Reception, Visual Association, or Visual Sequential Memory. No analyses were undertaken pertaining to the remaining ITPA subtests.

The authors of the 39 research studies reported (or provided the necessary information which allowed us to calculate and report) the results of 280 comparisons between the performance of experimental and control subjects on the subtest scores and the total scores of the ITPA. It was therefore possible to compute the percentage of

analyses which indicated that special psycholinguistic training was beneficial.

VARIABLES ON INSTRUCTION EFFECTIVENESS

When integrating the information provided in Tables 3-1 and 3-2, one can evalute the effectiveness of such instruction on differing types of children, e.g., retarded, disadvantaged, preschool, and elementary. The percentage of analyses, by subgroup, which found the intervention successful is found in Table 3-3. Where analyses were few, i.e., less than five, as was the case with Auditory Closure and Sound Blending, percentages were not computed.

Fifteen authors (103 analyses) studied the value of psycholinguistic training with retarded subjects with less than encouraging results. There was not a single subtest for which a majority of the researchers reported that training was beneficial. Therefore, the value of training retarded subjects in psycholinguistics has not been demonstrated to date.

The 18 authors (154 analyses) who used the instruction with disadvantaged children were apparently more successful, especially regarding improvement in associational and verbal expressive ability. However, as the positive percentages are only in the 50s and as most of the subtests of the ITPA did not respond to instruction, support for training disadvantaged children in psycholinguistic skills is at best limited.

The effects of age on training was probed at the preschool level by 15 authors (121 analyses) and at the elementary level by 19 authors (143 analyses). Apparently the training programs used to date emphasize the development of Auditory Association abilities at the preschool level and expressive language abilities at the elementary level. Once again, the positive findings are limited to the representational level subtests.

Eight of the researchers (70 analyses) used a prescriptive approach, i.e., they diagnosed their subjects, usually with the ITPA, and designed programs specifically for each child. This approach was apparently successful in stimulating visual associational and expressive language abilities. The nonindividualized approach to instruction, in which all children are exposed to a set program, was studied by 30 authors (208 analyses) and was evidently minimally effective in teaching auditory associational and verbal expressive abilities.

Two kinds of curricula were employed most often: the "selected activities" approach, used by 13 researchers (85 analyses), and the PLDK approach, used by 16 researchers (112 analyses). The selective activities approach was found to be useful in stimulating skills necessary to do well

on the Manual Expression subtest. With the exception of Verbal Expression, the PLDK does not seem to be an efficient method for developing language processes.

The figures at the bottom of Table 3-3 associated with "Total" are of particular interest in that they reflect the overall situation relative to psycholinguistic training accomplished to date. It is apparent that for the most part, researchers have been unsuccessful in developing those skills which would enable their subjects to do well on the ITPA. The Verbal Expression subtest seems to be the most responsive to intervention, while Visual Closure, Grammatic Closure, Visual Reception, and Auditory Reception are the most resistant.

Each ITPA subtest relates to a particular psycholinguistic construct in the Osgood-Kirk model, i.e., level, process, and channel (modality). By assigning each subtest to its appropriate construct and by computing the percentages of "+'s" it is possible to estimate the success which researchers have had in stimulating the theoretical psycholinguistic dimensions underlying the ITPA. These constructs, the subtests which comprise them, and the percentages of positive analyses are presented in Table 3-4.

COLLECTIVE RESULTS

The collective results of the studies reviewed suggest that the idea that psycholinguistic constructs, as measured by the ITPA, can be trained by existing techniques remains nonvalidated. Comparatively speaking, the most encouraging findings pertained to training at the representational level, especially the expressive process. The most discouraging results were associated

Table 3-3. The percentage of analyses, by subgroup, which found psycholinguistic training to be successful

	ITPA subtests [1]												
Subgroups	AR	VR	AA	VA	VE	ME	GC	VC	ASM	VSM	AC	SB	Total
Retarded subjects	33	25	13	33	40	44	22	—	22	20	—	—	50
Disadvantaged subjects	27	29	59	50	50	29	27	—	33	21	—	—	40
Preschool subjects	27	27	54	45	42	27	27	—	33	18	—	—	31
Elementary subjects	31	25	43	46	57	54	23	—	31	29	—	—	56
Prescriptive approach	17	17	33	57	57	57	17	—	29	14	—	—	50
Nonindividualized approach	32	28	52	39	50	33	25	20	37	26	—	—	46
Selected activities	29	29	38	29	44	50	29	—	33	25	—	—	42
PLDK activities	27	30	42	40	55	30	17	—	30	18	—	—	47
TOTAL	28	24	48	44	52	40	23	20	35	23	—	—	47

1. For ITPA subtest code, see Table 3-2.

Table 3-4. Psycholinguistic constructs, the ITPA subtests which comprise them, and the percentage of positive analyses

Language dimensions	Constructs	ITPA subtests [1]	Percentages of positive analyses
Levels	Representational	AR, VR, AA, VA, VE, ME	40
	Automatic	GC, VC, ASM, VSM, AC, SB	25
Processes	Reception	AR, VR	27
	Organization	AA, VA, GC, VC, ASM, VSM, AC, SB	33
	Expression	VE, ME	46
Modalities	Auditory-Vocal	AR, AA, VE, GC, ASM, AC, SB	37
	Visual-Motor	VR, VA, ME, VC, VSM	32

1. For subtest code, see Table 3-2.

with training at the automatic level, the receptive and organizing processes, and both the auditory-vocal and visual-motor modalities.

There is one additional observation worth noting, i.e., the recent findings are considerably less encouraging regarding the benefits of training than were those of the earlier research. In the studies located, 110 experimental-control comparisons were made between 1962 and 1966; 73 comparisons were made between 1967 and 1969; and 98 between 1970 and 1973. The percentages supporting training were 52, 31, and 21 respectively. As we can generate no satisfactory explanation for this finding, we choose merely to report the observation without comment.

Additional analyses were undertaken to investigate the effects of hours of training and length of the training period on subject improvement. As the results indicated these were not significant variables, they are not reported.

DISCUSSION

It seems as though we are confronted with at least three possible explanations which could account for the findings of this review: (a) the ITPA is an invalid measure of psycholinguistic functioning, (b) the intervention programs and/or techniques are inadequate, and (c) most psycholinguistic dimensions are either untrainable or highly resistant to stimulation.

VALIDITY OF THE ITPA

Some researchers have reported that the subtests of the ITPA lack independence, and as a consequence the test measures only one or two psycholinguistic factors. These findings are usually based on factor analyses which used only the

ITPA subtests or used the subtests with measures of achievement or intelligence. Such efforts may relate to the test's content validity but contribute little to estimating the test's construct validity, which is critical to this review. Sedlack and Weener (1973) have provided a particularly noteworthy review of the ITPA factor analytic research.

Only Hare, Hammill, and Bartel (1973) and Newcomer, Hare, Hammill, and McGettigan (1974) have factored the ITPA subtests with specifically designed psycholinguistic criterion tests. The findings suggest that only one subtest, Visual Sequential Memory, is clearly inadequate, and for the most part the subtests load independently and on factors which are easily recognizable in terms of the Osgood-Kirk constructs. Support was found for the concept of the levels, the processes, and the auditory-vocal modality. The visual-motor modality was not substantiated, however.

ADEQUACY OF THE TRAINING PROGRAMS

It seems likely that the instructional programs are uneven in that they seem to emphasize training associative and expressive abilities to the comparative exclusion of training receptive and automatic skills. This may be inherent in the programs, or teachers may avoid such activities and show preference for the associative and expressive activities. In any event, important variables are apparently not being taught using the presently available instructional systems.

It is suggested that teachers who attempt to train psycholinguistic processes pay particular attention to those skills which have been slighted up to now. It is particularly important to do so if the teacher accepts the still questionable hypothesis of Kass (1966), Sabatino (1973), Wepman (1960), Bartin (1971), and Golden and Steiner (1969), among many others, that automatic level skills can be used to differentiate between good and poor readers and that deficits in these abilities may contribute to or even cause appreciable reading failure.

TRAINABILITY OF PSYCHOLINGUISTIC PROCESSES

The positive findings regarding Verbal Expression suggest that at least one of the skills tapped by the ITPA may be responsive to training. This leads one to speculate that under different situations, using improved techniques, others might also respond to instruction. Still, the results to the review strongly indicate that neither the ITPA subtests nor their theoretical constructs are particularly ameliorative. Approximately 70 percent or better of the analyses were unsuccessful in training Grammatic Closure, Visual Sequential Memory, Visual Closure, Visual and Auditory Reception, automatic level skills, receptive processes, or visual-motor modality skills.

Therefore, whether some of the subtests are unresponsive to instructional efforts because they are basically impossible or extremely difficult to teach, because the training programs do not provide sufficient attention to them, or because the ITPA subtests are not appropriate measures of these constructs, we cannot say. This is a matter for future research to clarify.

IMPLICATIONS

One of the major implications to be drawn from this review of research is that the efficacy of training psycholinguistic functionings has not been conclusively demonstrated. These findings are of importance when considering the amount of time, effort, and money that is currently being devoted to providing exceptional children with training programs designed to increase psycholinguistic skills. A concerted effort should be made to determine conclusively that the constructs are trainable by available programs and/or to identify the characteristics of the children for whom such training is beneficial.

Efforts should also be directed to establishing the effectiveness of training on educationally relevant variables. If this type of research indicated that psycholinguistic skills can be stimulated and that as a consequence academic abilities do improve, then educators could proceed with some

assurance having evidence that training such skills is worthwhile. Until these results are available, however, programs designed to improve psycholinguistic functioning need to be viewed cautiously and monitored with care so that children experiencing difficulty in school will not be subjected to meaningless and irrelevant activities that will result only in a waste of valuable time.

REFERENCES

Bartin, N. The intellectual and psycholinguistic characteristics of three groups of differentiated third grade readers. Unpublished doctoral dissertation, State University of New York, Buffalo, 1971.

Blessing, K. R. An investigation of a psycholinguistic deficit in educable mentally retarded children: Detection, remediation and related variables. (Unpublished doctoral dissertation, University of Wisconsin, Madison) *International Dissertation Abstracts*, 1964, **25**, 2327.

Blue, C. The effectiveness of a group language program with trainable mentally retarded children. *Education and Training of the Mentally Retarded*, 1970, **5**, 109–112.

Bradley, B. H., Maurer, R., & Hundzial, M. A study of the effectiveness of milieu therapy and language training for the mentally retarded. *Exceptional Children*, 1966, **33**, 143–149.

Bush, W. J., & Giles, M. T. *Aids to psycholinguistic teaching*. Columbus, Ohio: Charles E. Merrill, 1969.

Carter, J. L. The effect of a language stimulation program upon first grade educationally disadvantaged children. *Education and Training of the Mentally Retarded*, 1966, **1**, 169–174.

Clasen, R. E., Spear, J. E., & Tomaro, M. P. A comparison of the relative effectiveness of two types of preschool compensatory programming. *The Journal of Educational Research*, 1969, **62**, 401–405.

Crutchfield, V. M. E. The effects of language training on the language development of mentally retarded children in Abilene State School. (Unpublished doctoral dissertation, University of Denver) *International Dissertation Abstracts*, 1964, **25**, 4572.

Dickie, J. P. Effectiveness of structured and unstructured (traditional) methods of language training. In M. A. Brottman (Ed.), Language remediation for the disadvantaged pre-school child. *Monograph of the Society for Research in Child Development*, 1968, 33 (124), 62–79.

Dunn, L. M., & Mueller, M. W. The efficacy of the Initial Teaching Alphabet and the *Peabody Language Development Kit* with grade one disadvantaged children: After one year. IMRID papers and reports. Institute on Mental Retardation and Intellectual Development, George Peabody College, 1966.

Dunn, L. M., & Mueller, M. W. Differential effects on the ITPA profile of the experimental version of level #1 of the *Peabody Language Development*

Kits with disadvantaged first grade children. IMRID papers and reports. Institute on Mental Retardation and Intellectual Development, George Peabody College, 1967.

Dunn, L. M., & Smith, J. O. *The Peabody Language Kits.* Circle Pines, Minn.: American Guidance Service, 1966.

Ensminger, E. E. The effects of a classroom language development program on psycholinguistic abilities and intellectual functioning of slow learning and borderline retarded children. Unpublished doctoral dissertation, University of Kansas, 1966.

Forgnone, C. Effects of visual perception and language training upon certain abilities of retarded children. (Unpublished master's thesis, George Peabody College) *International Dissertation Abstracts,* 1967, **27,** 1197-A.

Gazdic, J. M. An evaluation of a program for those children ascertained to be not ready for regular first grade placement. Unpublished master's thesis. Northeastern Illinois State College, Chicago, 1971.

Gibson, R. C. Effectiveness of a supplemental language development program with educable mentally retarded children. (Unpublished doctoral dissertation, University of Iowa) *International Dissertation Abstracts,* 1967, **27,** 2726-A.

Golden, N. E., & Steiner, S. R. Auditory and visual functions in good and poor readers. *Journal of Learning Disabilities,* 1969, **2,** 476–481.

Gray, S. W., & Klaus, R. A. An experimental preschool program for culturally deprived children. *Child Development,* 1965, **30,** 887–898.

Guess, D., Ensminger, E. E., & Smith, J. O. A language development program for mentally retarded children. Final report. Project No. 7-0815, Grant No. OEG-0-8-070815-0216 (032), Bureau of Education for the Handicapped, August 1969.

Hare, B., Hammill, D. D., & Bartel, N. Construct validity of selected ITPA subtests. *Exceptional Children,* 1973, **40,** 13–20.

Hart, N. W. M. The differential diagnosis of the psycholinguistic abilities of the cerebral palsied child and effective remedial procedures. *Special Schools Bulletin,* No. 2, Brisbane, Australia, 1963.

Hartman, A. S. A long-range attack to reduce the educational disadvantage of children from poverty backgrounds. 1965–66, Progress Report to the Ford Foundation. Department of Public Instruction, Harrisburg, Pennsylvania, 1967.

Hodges, W. L., & Spicker, H. H. The effects of preschool experiences on culturally disadvantaged children. In W. W. Hartub & N. L. Smothergill (Eds.), *The young child: Review of research.* Washington, D.C.: National Association for the Education of Young Children, 1967.

Jones, E. L. H. The effects of a language development program on the psycholinguistic abilities and IQ of a group of preschool disadvantaged children. (Unpublished doctoral dissertation, University of Arkansas, Fayetteville) *International Dissertation Abstracts,* 1970, **31,** 2761-A.

Karnes, M. B. *Helping young children develop language skills: A Book of activities.* Washington, D. C.: The Council for Exceptional Children, 1968.

Karnes, M. B., Teska, J. A., & Hodgins, A. S. The effects of four programs of classroom intervention on intellectual and language development of four-year-old disadvantaged children. *American Journal of Orthopsychiatry,* 1970,**40,** 58–76.

Kass, C. E. Psycholinguistic disabilities of children with reading problems. *Exceptional Children,* 1966, **32,** 533–539.

Kirk, S. A., & Kirk, W. D. *Psycholinguistic learning disabilities: Diagnosis and remediation.* Urbana: University of Illinois Press, 1971.

Kirk, S. A., McCarthy, J. J., & Kirk, W. D. *Illinois Test of Psycholinguistic Abilities.* Urbana: University of Illinois Press, 1968.

Lavin, C. M. The effects of a structured sensory-motor training program on selected cognitive and psycholinguistic abilities of preschool children. (Unpublished doctoral dissertation, Fordham University) *International Dissertation Abstracts,* 1971, **32,** 1984-A.

Leiss, R. H. The effect of intensity in a psycholinguistic stimulation program for trainable mentally retarded children. Unpublished doctoral dissertation, Temple University, 1974.

McConnell, F., Horton, K. B., & Smith, B. R. Effects of early language training for culturally disadvantaged preschool children. *The Journal of School Health* 1969, **39,** 661–665.(a)

McConnell, F., Horton, K. B., & Smith, B. R. Language development and culturally disadvantaged. *Exceptional Children,* 1969, **35,** 597–606. (b)

McConnell, F., Horton, D. B., & Smith, B. R. Sensory-perceptual and language training to prevent school learning disabilities in culturally deprived preschool children. Final report, Project No. 5-0682, Grant No. OEG-32-52-7900-5025,USOE Bureau of Research. The Bill Wilkerson Hearing and Speech Center, Nashville, Tennessee, August 1972. (c)

Minskoff, E., Wiseman, D. E., & Minskoff, J. G. *The MWM program for developing language abilities.* Ridgefield, N.J.: Educational Performance Associates, 1972.

Minskoff, J. G. A psycholinguistic approach to remediation with retarded-disturbed children. (Unpublished doctoral dissertation, Yeshiva University, New York City) *International Dissertation Abstracts,* 1967, **28,** 1625-A.

Mitchell, R. S. A study of the effects of specific training in psycholinguistic scores of Head Start children. (Unpublished doctoral dissertation) *International Dissertation Abstracts,* 1968, **28,** 1709-A.

Morgan, D. L. A comparison of growth in language development in a structured and traditional preschool compensatory education program. (Unpublished doctoral dissertation, United States International University, San Diego) *International Dissertation Abstracts,* 1972, **32,** 4388-A.

Morris, S. K. Results of a study using the *Peabody*

Language Development Kit: Level P. (Exper. ed.) Unpublished master's thesis, Vanderbilt University, 1967. Cited by L. M. Dunn & J. O. Smith, *The Peabody Language Kits.* Circle Pines, Minn.: American Guidance Service, 1966.

Mueller, M. W., & Dunn, L. M. Effects of level #1 of the *Peabody Language Development Kits* with educable mentally retarded children—An interim report after 4½ months. IMRID papers and reports. Institute on Mental Retardation and Intellectual Development, George Peabody College, 1967.

Newcomer, P., Hare, B., Hammill, D. D., & McGettigan, J. Construct validity of the ITPA subtests. *Exceptional Children,* 1974. **40,** 509–510.

Osgood, C. E. Motivational dynamics of language behavior. In M. R. Jones (Ed.), *Nebraska symposium on motivation.* Lincoln: University of Nebraska Press, 1957.

Painter, G. The effect of a rhythmic and sensory motor activity program on perceptual motor spatial abilities of kindergarten children. *Exceptional Children,* 1966, **33,** 113–116.

Runyon, M. J. L. The effects of a psycholinguistic development language program on language abilities of educable mentally retarded children. Unpublished master's thesis, Cardinal Stritch College, 1970.

Sabatino, D. Auditory perception: Development, assessment, and intervention. In L. Mann & D. A. Sabatino, *The first review of special education.* Philadelphia, Pa.: JSE Press, 1973.

Saudargas, R. A. Madsen, C. H., & Thompson, F. Prescriptive teaching in language arts rememdiation for Black rural elementary school children. *Journal of Learning Disabilities,* 1970, **3,** 364–370.

Sapir, S. G. Learning disability and deficit centered classroom training. In J. Hellmuth (Ed.), *Deficits in cognition.* Seattle: Special Child Publications, 1971.

Schifani, J. W. The relationship between the *Illinois Test of Psycholinguistic Abilities* and the *Peabody Language Development Kit* with a select group of intermediate educable mentally retarded children. (Un-

published doctoral dissertation, University of Alabama) *International Dissertation Abstracts,* 1972, **32,** 5076-A.

Sedlak, R. A., & Weener, P. Review of research on the *Illinois Test of Psycholinguistic Abilities.* In L. Mann & D. A. Sabatino, *The first review of special education.* Philadelphia, Pa.: JSE Press, 1973.

Siders, S. K. An analysis of the language growth of selected children in a first grade Title 1 project. (Unpublished doctoral dissertation, Kent State University) *International Dissertation Abstracts,* 1970, **30,** 4158-A.

Smith, J. O. Group language development for educable mental retardates. *Exceptional Children,* 1962, **29,** 95–101.

Spollen, J. C., & Balif, B. L. Effectiveness of individualized instruction for kindergarten children with a developmental lag. *Exceptional Children,* 1971, **38,** 205–209.

Stearns, K. E. Experimental group language development for psycho-socially deprived preschool children. (Unpublished doctoral dissertation, Indiana University, Bloomington) *International Dissertation Abstracts,* 1967, **27,** 2078-A.

Strickland, J. H. The effect of a parent education program on the language development of underprivileged kindergarten children. (Unpublished doctoral dissertation, George Peabody College) *International Dissertation Abstracts,* 1967, **28,** 1633-A.

Waugh, R. Comparison of revised and experimental editions of the ITPA. *Journal of Learning Disabilities,* 1973, **6,** 236–238.

Wepman, N. N. Auditory discrimination, speech, and reading. *Elementary School Journal,* 1960, **60,** 325–333.

Wiseman, D. E. The effects of an individualized remedial program on mentally retarded children with psycholinguistic disabilities. (Unpublished doctoral dissertation, University of Illinois, Urbana) *International Dissertation Abstracts,* 1965, **26,** 5143-A.

4. Organic factors in hyperkinesis: a critical evaluation

DENNIS R. DUBEY

Over the last decade, and particularly within the past several years, the diagnostic label "hyperkinetic" has been increasingly applied to a large number of school-aged children who are characterized by excessive motor movement, impulsivity, and difficulties in maintaining attention. At the same time, the term "minimal brain dysfunction" has achieved similar popularity in the diagnosis of many children with these characteristics; in fact, many hyperkinetic children are assumed to have minimal brain dysfunction to some degree—"minimal" because definite signs of brain damage are rarely manifest in these children.

Although many of the brain-injured children identified by Strauss and Lehtinen[40] were hyperkinetic, children who were not clearly brain-damaged were seen to manifest similar behavior. Many of these children possessed less unequivocal signs of nervous system abnormality, and thus the concept of the minimally brain-damaged child became recognized. It was noted, however, that many of these signs (e.g., abnormal electroencephalogram and poor motor coordination) were absent in significant numbers of hyperkinetic children; furthermore, the relationship of these signs to actual brain damage had not been well-delineated. This prompted use of the term "minimally brain-*dysfunctioned*" to describe the child who was hyperkinetic and who may or may not have had signs of neurological dysfunction. The behavior of these children was sufficient for some to infer the presence of a central nervous system deviation.

The notion that hyperkinesis has an organic basis has a number of implications for the hyperkinetic child. It suggests, first of all, that the treatment will be medically oriented; currently the treatment of choice for hyperkinesis is central stimulant medication (dextroamphetamine sulfate, methylphenidate hydrochloride, or mangesium pemoline). The assumption of an organic basis, and the frequently dramatic effects of medication, can lead to a diminished emphasis on preventative efforts.[10] Further, the assumption of organicity could lead both child and parents to absolve themselves of responsibility for the child's behavior. Finally, assumption of organicity could lead the persons involved to ignore important psychological and educational aspects of the therapy process.

Such limitations certainly can, and are, being dealt with by clinicians. In themselves, they are not a basis for discarding ideas of organic etiology. Given that these possible ramifications do exist, however, it becomes crucial to evaluate seriously the functional role of organic deviations in the development of hyperkinetic disor-

From *American Journal of Orthopsychiatry*, 1976, *46*, 353–366. Copyright © the American Orthopsychiatric Association, Inc. Reproduced by permission.

der. This review will critically examine the research concerning five major types of organic factors and their relationship to hyperkinesis— eletroencephalographic studies, studies of neurological soft signs, biochemical studies, studies of pregnancy and birth complications, and genetic studies. Within each area, the evidence for and against the presence of causative organic factors will be weighed, and particular attention will be paid to the evaluation of studies on a methodological as well as a conceptual basis.

ELECTROENCEPHALOGRAM STUDIES

The electroencephalogram is an indirect method of assessing brain activity. It reflects the summation of electrical potentials generated throughout the brain, particularly in the higher cortex. The clear association between EEG patterns and some types of behavioral dysfunction, notably epilepsy, has led researchers to use the EEG as a tool in the determination of neurological factors in a wide variety of behavior disorders.

A relatively high percentage of EEG abnormality (20%–80%) has been found in groups of hyperkinetic children. Several of the studies reporting such figures, however, fail to provide comparative data on normal controls,[16,18,35,36] which undermines conclusions that EEG abnormalities differentially affect hyperkinetic children. As the EEG interpretation itself is somewhat subjective and the criteria for abnormality may differ across investigators, it would be unwise to make comparisons with clinically-known norms of abnormality. Further, many of the higher percentages have been noted in groups of hyperkinetic children having known neurological disease,[1,18] which is not the case for most hyperkinetic children.

When comparisons with normal children have been made, results have been equivocal. Neither Werry and his colleagues[49] nor Satterfield et al.[34] found significant differences in the frequency of abnormality between hyperkinetics and normal controls, although Burks[2] did find such differences. Werry, Weiss and Douglas[50] found differences in the type of abnormality, but no differences in the incidence of abnormality. Findings by Caute, Niedermeyer and Richardson[5] were similar to those of Burks,[2] yet the hyperkinetic children in their group were selected for the presence of "soft" neurological signs, making their sample an atypical one.

Other comparisons have been made to nonhyperkinetic children who nonetheless manifest behavior disorders. If hyperkinetic children do possess an abnormally high prevalence of EEG abnormalities, and these abnormalities are related to the hyperkinesis itself, then the abnormalities in hyperkinetic children might be expected to differ in degree or in kind from the abnormalities present in other diagnostic groups. The only findings in such comparisons have been negative.[19,41,49,51] The EEG records of hyperkinetic children have proven indistinguishable from those of other diagnostic groups.

Absence of a relationship between EEG abnormality and hyperkinesis is further suggested by the failure to note differences between those hyperkinetic children who demonstrate the abnormality and those hyperkinetic children who show normal EEG tracings. The failure to find such differences in the areas of clinical symptomatology,[5] severity of disturbance,[36] and psychological test performance[19] suggests strongly that the presence of an EEG abnormality in some hyperkinetic children may be more of an irrelevant association than an etiological factor.

Finally, even in instances in which an EEG abnormality is present, the nature of that abnormality must be considered in attributing serious consequences to the dysfunction. In fact, there is general agreement that the most common "abnormality" is not of the marked paroxysmal variety but rather a general excess of slow-wave activity,[5,18,49,51] the significance of which is highly uncertain. In addition, the amount of slow-wave activity in the EEG appears not to change, even upon behavioral improvement as a result of the administration of stimulant medication.[49] Further, there has been no attempt to determine the level of slow-wave activity in the hyperkinetic child that is "excessive." It may well be that the differences among studies, in their comparisons of abnormality between diagnostic groups, are due to differences in the criteria for labeling a tracing abnormal. Lenient criteria could account for differences which are statistically, *but not clinically,* significant.

The studies described above have been concerned with EEG measurements under "standard" clinical conditions—that is, the EEG was assessed under conditions of wakeful resting, drowsiness, photic stimulation, or post-hyperventilation. Much attention has been paid, however, to one study in which the EEG was assessed under less typical conditions. Laufer, Denhoff and Solomons[20] determined the amount of Metrazol required to produce a neurophysiological and muscular response to photic stimulation in hyperkinetic and nonhyperkinetic children. Their finding that hyperkinetics had a lower photo-Matrazol threshold led them to conclude that hyperkinetic children have a lower threshold for neuronal disorganization as a result of a defect in the diencephalon. These results, however, must be viewed with caution. In the first place, patients in this study were obtained from a residential psychiatric hospital, indicating that their disturbance was much more severe than that exhibited by the hyperkinetic child who is able to remain a functioning member of his own home and school. Thus generalization to the majority of children diagnosed hyperkinetic are unwarranted. In addition, the nonhyperkinetic control groups also consisted of severely disturbed, institutionalized children, thereby allowing no judgments to be made concerning differences in threshold of neuronal disorganization between hyperkinetic and normal children. Finally, the hyperkinetic children had a high incidence of postnatal contributors to brain damage, once again making the sample atypical. As such, the results of the nonreplicated study by Laufer et al.[20] do little to establish a neurological difference between hyperkinetic and normal children.

In sum, despite common belief, there is only minimal evidence to support the notion that the EEG of hyperkinetic children differs from that of normal controls and other diagnostic groups. When abnormalities are present in particular children, the significance of the abnormalities is unclear. In general, abnormalities occur in approximately 20%–50% of a given sample, leaving 50%–80% of the sample unaccounted for. Further, there is no relationship between presence of abnormality and clinical severity or symptomatology.

STUDIES OF "SOFT" SIGNS

There exists a widespread notion that hyperkinetic children are characterized by "soft" neurological signs. Soft signs include such characteristics as immature reflexes and poor motor coordination. Neurological signs are considered "soft," as opposed to "hard," when their actual presence is uncertain or when the relationship between their presence and specific central nervous system damage is unclear. Their presence is also highly age-dependent. Because of these characteristics, soft signs have been considered either a reflection of minimal brain damage or of immature development of nervous system structures.

Although a high prevalence of soft signs in hyperkinetic children has been noted,[1,16,19,35,36] few published reports have included groups of comparison children. Both Wikler et al.[51] and Werry et al.[49] found that hyperkinetic children had significantly more soft signs than did normal children; however, Wikler et al.[51] found hyperkinetic children to have no more soft signs than behavior-disordered, nonhyperkinetic controls, while Werry et al.[49] did find such a difference. Hertzig, Bortner, and Birch[12] reported findings similar to those of Werry.[49] Unfortunately, children in the Hertzig[12] study were members of a class previously medically diagnosed as brain-injured, making it questionable to generalize from conclusions based on this group to the general population of hyperkinetic children whose disorder is not severe enough to render such placement.

Thus, it is unclear whether the presence of soft signs is related to hyperkinesis per se or is a characteristic of disordered children in general. If the latter is the case, then the presence of soft signs in hyperkinetic children provides little information about an organic basis for the behaviors associated with the hyperkinetic syndrome. It is also important to note that significant numbers of hyperkinetic children demonstrate no soft signs at all. Evaluations have shown that approximately 40%–50% of hyperkinetic children have completely normal neurological exams.[16,19,35,36] Further, the number of signs detected is usually minimal. Satterfield et al.[35] and Kenny et al.[16] found that 78% and 92%, respectively, of their hyperkinetic children had fewer than three neurological signs. In addition, Kennard[15] found that soft neurological signs have no relationship to a "harder" neurological sign, the electroencephalogram. Thus, for most hyperkinetic children, the neurological exam for soft signs does not appear to be an important indicator of organicity.

It should also be pointed out that, with one exception,[12] the studies mentioned above all suffer from a major methodological defect, the failure to evaluate the children on a "blind" basis. Blind rating refers to a condition whereby judges evaluate the child's neurological status without knowledge of his diagnostic status. As the neurological exam is characterized by the observation of data that are of uncertain presence and that require subjective judgment by the clinician, there is danger of unintentional bias resulting in higher severity scores for hyperkinetic children than for normals. Future research which does not insure blind evaluation will be of limited value.

STUDIES OF BIOCHEMISTRY

Wender[47,48] has posited that the primary etiological agent of hyperkinesis is a biochemical imbalance involving one or more of the central nervous system neurotransmitters, e.g., serotonin, dopamine, and norepinephrine. The thrust of the argument is based on the fact that drugs known to influence the clinical manifestations of hyperkinesis (e.g., dextroamphetamine and imipramine) are also known to influence the levels of brain monoamines. Yet the influence of the drugs on both the behavior and the amine levels does not necessarily reflect the functional relation between the two. Because they may be independent, it becomes important to measure directly the brain monoamine levels of hyperkinetic children and to make comparisons with nonhyperkinetic controls.

Since direct measurement of these biochemical levels is impossible without the aid of surgery, such measurements have had to be indirect. Monoamines and their metabolites have been measured through urinalysis by Wender et al.[48] and by Rapoport and coworkers.[28] Neither group found any differences between hyperkinetics and controls. Wender's study[48] pointed out that, as urinalysis reflects total body production of monoamines, differences in CNS levels may be obscured. As a possible alternative to this method, Coleman[6] examined the levels of blood platelet-serotonin in hyperkinetic children. Although platelet-serotonin is produced in the gastrointestinal system and not in the CNS, it has been postulated[26] that the platelet serves as a functional model for the serotonergic CNS neuron. Coleman[6] found that hyperkinetic children had depressed levels of platelet-serotonin; however, many of these levels were similar to those observed in nonhyperkinetic children undergoing stress. Further, in two of the children, serotonin levels were shown to be clearly related to environmental manipulation and to approach normal levels when the children were temporarily removed from their homes. In a partial replication, Rapoport et al.[31] found no differences in platelet-serotonin between hyperkinetics and normal controls. The hyperkinetic children were then placed on drug therapy, but clinical response was found to be unassociated with change in serotonin levels.

In sum, hyperkinetic children do not carry abnormal levels of peripheral monomamines. Brain monoamine levels in children are unexplored and will probably remain so. As such, there exists no evidence at this time to support the notion of a biochemical abnormality in the majority of hyperkinetic children.

One biochemical factor that may be causative with a small subsample of hyperkinetic children is increased lead levels. Particularly in poor urban areas, children commonly ingest toxic levels of lead from old housepaint. David[8] found that hyperkinetic children from impoverished city areas had higher blood- and bone-stored lead levels than control children. In addition, hyperkinetic children for whom other probable causes could be determined did not have elevated blood lead levels. These results indicate that the hyperkinesis in the other children was a result of the lead and not vice-versa. In a related and interesting finding, Silbergeld and Goldberg[37] demonstrated that mice in whom overactivity had been induced by lead-ingestion showed "paradoxical" responses to amphetamine, methylphenidate, and phenobarbital (similar to the responses of hyperkinetic children), while control mice showed the typical adult response. Taken together, these two studies suggest strongly that lead may be an important factor in hyperkinetic children who have a history of lead pica. This is not likely to be a widespread phenomenon, but one limited to children of low-income, impoverished areas. The vast majority of hyperkinetic children would not be expected to manifest any biochemical abnormality.

STUDIES OF BIRTH FACTORS

It has been widely recognized that a number of pregnancy and birth complications, such as severe prematurity or anoxia, may be etiological agents for both physical and behavioral difficulties in the later life of the child. Most often cited in this regard are Pasamanick and his coworkers,[25] who found more pregnancy and birth complications in a group of children with a wide variety of behavior disorders than in a group of control children. They suggested a "continuum of reproductive casualty" whereby the severity of deviance in development was a function of the severity of the complication. The authors also reported their results to be even more salient when those children described as hyperkinetic were considered separately.

The work of Pasamanick prompted specific research into pregnancy and birth factors in the etiology of hyperkinesis. Werry, Weiss, and Douglas[50] reported a strong trend for hyperkinetic children to have been involved in more pregnancy and birth complications than control children. These differences, in fact, were extremely small maternal bleeding: 4 hyperkinetic vs. 3 control; toxemia: 1 hyperkinetic vs. 1 control; prematurity: 3 hyperkinetic vs. 2 control; birth trauma: 2 hyperkinetic vs. 0 control; anoxia: 3 hyperkinetic vs. 1 control). Stewart et al.[39] reported no significant differences in such factors between hyperkinetic and control children. Both of these studies, however, employed data gained from interviews with the mothers of these children, leaving open the possibility that selective recall biased the results. To overcome this difficulty, Minde, Webb and Sykes[22] obtained data from the actual birth records of their subjects. Although there were differences in the duration of labor, no differences were found between hyperkinetic and control children in the amount or severity of pregnancy and birth complications. In fact, the researchers commented that

the most striking finding of this study is the great similarity between the two groups in the incidence of severe prenatal and paranatal difficulties[22] (p. 360).

It should be clear that hyperkinetic children do not, as a group, suffer from an unusual number or severity of recognizable birth complications. Some recent work by Waldrop and her associates,[42,43,44] however, suggests the influence of more subtle prenatal factors as etiological agents in the development of hyperkinesis. A summary of this work has been presented by Waldrop and Halverson.[43]

Waldrop's work is based on the observation that many children who are known to have major congenital defects, such as Down's syndrome, often have additional "minor physical anomalies" which are present from birth. The list of anomalies includes deviations such as abnormally large head circumference, malformed ears, and syndactylia of the toes, which are minor enough to go unnoticed by the casual observer. Some children with no obvious handicaps also have these anomalies, suggesting that some children may undergo subclinical deviations in embryological development which nonetheless may lead to observable behavior problems later on. Waldrop et al.[44] found that, in a group of normal

nursery school children, those who demonstrated behavior characteristic of hyperkinetic children had a greater number of minor physical anomalies than those who did not. This result was replicated with another group of young children and found to be stable over a five-year period.[43] In another study,[42] children selected by teachers as hyperkinetic were shown to have more anomalies than did nonhyperkinetic controls. Further, there was a significant correlation between number of anomalies and a subjective rank ordering of severity of condition. In sum, these studies suggest strongly that an etiological agent occurring early in pregnancy accounts in part for both minor physical anomalies and hyperkinetic behavior disorder.

None of Waldrop's studies included children who were clinically diagnosed as hyperkinetic. Rapoport[27,29,30] has partially replicated and extended Waldrop's work to a sample of hyperkinetic boys attending an outpatient clinic and receiving medication for their behavior. Within the sample of hyperkinetic children, Quinn and Rapoport[27] found low but significant positive associations between anomaly score and score on Conners's Teacher Rating Scale. Perhaps even more important, however, is the finding that, approximately half of those children with low anomaly scores demonstrated the disorder before the age of three, while 88% of those with high anomaly scores were reported to have demonstrated hyperkinesis before age three. This association between number of anomalies and age of onset of hyperkinesis suggests that those children who underwent a more severe prenatal deviation suffer from a greater contribution of organicity in their hyperkinesis.

It should be stressed that the associations found between anomaly score and severity of hyperkinesis, although statistically significant, have been low. The correlations reported have been .40[42] and .28[27] Thus, the highest correlation observed reveals that the variability in anomaly score accounts for only 16% of the variability in severity of hyperkinesis. This suggests that other factors may also contribute significantly to the development and maintenance of the hyperkinetic disorder.

It is also essential to recognize that the presence of physical anomalies is not a specific indicator for hyperkinesis. High anomaly scores have been found to be characteristic of hyperkinetic children,[42] overactive preschoolers,[44] children with congenital speech and hearing disorders,[43] and children prone to academic failure,[33] ans well as those with major defects such as Down's syndrome. Nonetheless, the presence of higher than normal anomaly scores in hyperkinetic children does strongly suggest that a subtle deviation in prenatal development can lead to both minor physical anomalies and behavioral deviance. The specific mechanism leading to hyperkinesis remains to be delineated.

GENETIC STUDIES

Although a number of researchers have sought to explain their findings of a higher incidence of organic factors in hyperkinetic children as a function of possible genetic mechanisms,[16,34,47] only a handful of reports have emerged concerning direct tests of the genetic hypothesis.

One way of investigating such an hypothesis is to look for aberrations in the chromosomal structure of hyperkinetic children. In the only study to do so, Warren et al.[45] found no evidence of sex chromosome aneuploidy (deviant number of sex chromosomes) or of deviations in structure or number in the complete karyotype.

An alternative to seeking abnormalities in the biological components of chromosome structure is to assume no biochemical abnormality but rather the transmission of a hyperkinetic disorder through normal genetic mechanisms. A popular method of exploring whether genetic transmission exists for many disorders has been twin studies, based on the premise that persons who share greater than the typical number of genes should have a higher than normal concordance for the disorder. Lopez[21] did find 100% concordance in four pairs of monozygotic twins and only 17% concordance in six pairs of dizygotic twins. His results are limited, however, by the extremely small sample size (ten) and the nonrandom selection of the sample. Even more importantly, as Lopez[21] pointed out, all of the monozygotic pairs were male, while two-thirds of the dizygotic pairs included females. This factor drastically compromises the conclusions, since hyperkinesis is known to occur much more frequently in males than in females. Thus, the observed differences in concordance between the two classes of twins may be wholly a function of the presence of females in the dizygotic sample. A more appropriate sample would include both male and female twin pairs in both categories of twins, but hyperkinetic females are rare and monozygotic female hyperkinetic twins are undoubtedly extremely rare. A reasonable alternative would be to include only males in both twin samples. At this point, however, twin data have not contributed to answering the question of genetic transmission.

Other studies that have sought to determine the familial relationship between hyperkinesis and various adult "personality disorders" have been cited as evidence for the genetic hypothesis. Morrison and Stewart[23] and Cantwell[3] both found that families of hyperkinetic probands had higher incidences of alcoholism, sociopathy, and hysteria than families of control subjects. (Investigation of disorders other than hyperkinesis is based on possible association between childhood hyperkinesis and adult disorders, since manifestations of hyperkinesis are considered to change following puberty.[46]) In addition, fathers of hyperkinetic children were more likely to report themselves as being hyperkinetic as children than were fathers of control children. These results, however, support either the genetic or the environmental hypothesis, as the authors were aware. Although genetic transmission is a possibility, parents who themselves have serious difficulties such as alcoholism are likely to have homes in which stress and inconsistent discipline are commonplace. Such an environment could produce a child with many manifestations of hyperkinesis. Further, fathers who have sons diagnosed as hyperkinetic may retrospectively consider themselves as having been hyperkinetic because 1) they identify with their sons and thereby associate their old behavior patterns with those of their children, who are now being diagnosed hyperkinetic, or 2) they now are exhibiting undesirable behavior patterns themselves and thus are more likely to consider themselves as having been problem children. In addition, the familial incidences of such disorders were far from uniform. Seventy-five percent of all fathers of hyperkinetic children were not considered hyperkinetic as children, and in 64% of families of hyperkinetics, neither parent was considered disordered. In short, such studies have provided no evidence that differentially supports the hypothesis of genetic transmission.

The most powerful research methodology for the determination of genetic factors is the adoption study, which has been used convincingly to demonstrate the genetic role in schizophrenia.[13,17]. In a variation of this design, Morrison and Stewart[24] compared the incidence of psychiatric illness in the families of hyperactives studied earlier[23,38] to the incidence of illness in families with hyperkinetic children adopted during infancy. In such a methodology, a lower incidence of parental disorder in the adoptive families would argue for the genetic hypothesis, since the hyperkinesis in the adopted children presumably could not be due to family disharmony and so must be the result of "bad genes." Morrison and Stewart[24] claimed that such is the case. They found significantly higher incidences of maternal hysteria and paternal alcoholism and sociopathy within the biological sample than within the adoptive sample, thus affirming the genetic hypothesis.

However, results of this study can be contested on methodological grounds. First, all diagnoses were made on a nonblind basis; that is, the interviewers were aware whether they were collecting data from a "biological" or an "adoptive" family. Thus unintentional rater bias is a strong possibility. In addition, whereas all families in the biologic group were solicited from a public outpatient clinic, half of the adoptive sample was recruited from private practitioners. This resulted in an adoptive sample with a higher socioeconomic status, and thus less likely to manifest psychiatric illness. Also, the adopted children lived with families with an average of 1.5 fewer children, another factor that tends to reduce family stress. There are, then, several factors which could explain the observation of reduced familial disorder in the adoptive sample aside from the variable of adoption itself. Adding to this reasoning the fact that there were no significant differences in the numbers of formerly hyperkinetic fathers and mothers between the two groups, there in fact appears to be little unassailable evidence of genetic transmission of hyperkinesis. (Very recently, Cantwell[4] reported a similar study with similar results; however, the problem of nonblind interviewing was present in this study also.)

Even if these methodological issues were resolved, it remains questionable whether an adoption study so designed would properly address the genetic question. No study of genetic factors in hyperkinesis has taken the most critical step, which is to evaluate the psychopathology in the natural parents of adopted hyperkinetic children. In order to demonstrate the role of genetics in hyperkinesis, it would be necessary to demonstrate not only that biological parents of nonadopted hyperkinetics exhibit more psychopathology than the adoptive parents of adopted hyperkinetics, but also that the biological parents of adopted hyperkinetics demonstrate more hyperkinesis than the adoptive parents. Such evidence would be strengthened further by the use of more objective indices of parental hyperkinesis, such as school records, which are based on more than a personal, retrospective, subjective evaluation by the parent himself. Only when these parents are studied will there be a sufficient basis for drawing valid conclusions about the role of genetics in hyperkinesis.

CONCLUSIONS

The evidence taken as a whole does not strongly support the notion that organic factors play a significant role in the behavior problems of most hyperkinetic children. The results from biochemical studies and studies of severe pregnancy and birth complications are clearly negative; results from electroencephalographic and neurological studies are conflicting; genetic studies are plagued by methodological difficulties. As such, the assumption that a hyperkinetic child suffers from minimal brain dysfunction or any other biological deviation is unwarranted in the absence of unequivocal data. For *most* hyperkinetic children, such data is unavailable.

Some may argue that, despite the failure to identify a particular organic etiological agent, the fact that a majority of hyperkinetic children do respond favorably to central stimulant medication suggests that the factors leading to hyperkinesis must be organic in nature. Such reasoning is unquestionably faulty. Certainly medication can have effects on persons who biologically are functioning normally, and these effects would not be due to a preexisting organic deviation. Further, medication is often beneficial to those who suffer disturbances clearly related to environmental circumstances, a prime example being the use of antidepressants to relieve symptoms of reactive depression. Thus the effect of medication on hyperkinetic behavior lends no support to the hypothesis of organic etiology.

It should be noted that, although there has been a failure to demonstrate the importance of biological factors in hyperkinesis, it has not been proven that such factors play no part. Certainly cases in which biological factors do play a role have been documented, such as with encephalitis,[9] lead,[8] and hypoglycemia. Such etiological factors appear to occur in only a small proportion of the hyperkinetic population, however, and among the majority of the 5%–10% of the school-aged population who are diagnosed hyperkinetic,[47] no such obvious factors appear.

One of the more likely explanations for the

failure to identify a single etiological agent is that hyperkinesis may be the result of different causative agents in different children. This would interfere with the identification of a single organic factor as being statistically more frequent in groups of hyperkinetic children than in normal children. This poses a dilemma for the researcher, but it is a dilemma which might be solvable through a more careful delineation of the physical and behavioral characteristics of the children. Typically hyperkinetic children are described no more specifically than as being restless, overactive, impulsive, and distractible. Common diagnostic measures, such as Conner's Rating Scale,[7] require no more than global ratings and thus do not provide specific information concerning the topography, frequency, and intensity of the child's behavior. As such, the present diagnostic procedures provide little basis for recognition of the particular behavioral characteristics of the individual child. If systematic and detailed descriptions of hyperkinetic children were to be made, however, it might be possible to classify subgroups of hyperkinetic children, and these subgroups might be found to relate to different causative agents.

Another factor that has severely limited the conclusions to be drawn from many of the studies discussed in this review is the deficiency in the methodological aspects of the research designs. Some of these have been specified above. Following are suggestions for strengthening future investigations of organicity in hyperkinesis:

Use of normal control groups

Every study investigating the incidence of a particular organic agent in a population of hyperkinetic children should employ a control group of normal children. Comparisons with normative data are unacceptable. Criteria for abnormality may differ among investigators when subjective judgments are involved and comparisons with clinically-known norms could provide spurious results. Groups should generally be matched on age, sex, socioeconomic status, and other factors that may be relevant to the particular investigation.

Use of deviant control groups

There may be many factors characteristic of disturbed children in general. Thus it is not only important to demonstrate that a characteristic is more common in hyperkinetic children than in normal children, but also to demonstrate that it is more common than in other disturbed children. It is otherwise difficult to argue that the characteristic is a relevant factor in the hyperkinetic aspects of the child's behavior. Further, the use of a deviant control helps to control for factors such as low motivation or high stress in a testing situation, which for the hyperkinetic child may contribute, for example, to poor performance on a motor coordination test in the neurological exam or to the presence of certain chemical levels in the blood.

Use of a generalizable population

Hyperkinetic children are not a homogeneous group, just as nonhyperkinetic children vary considerably. The most common hyperkinetic child, however, is not retarded, is not institutionalized, and does not attend classes for brain-injured children. Such children are important to study, but it would be unwise to extend one's conclusions based on these children to hyperkinetic children in general.

"Blind" examination

Whenever proper control groups are used, examiners should be unaware of each child's diagnostic status. The necessity for this increases as a function of the amount of subjective judgment required of the examiner and is relevant to EEG interpretation, the neurological examination, judgment of morphological deviations, and collection of interview data in genetic studies. Bias resulting from nonblind examination would be unintentional in most cases, yet knowledge of the child and particulary of the hypothesis under investigation could work in subtle ways to influence judgment in a particular direction.

Interjudge reliability

To insure that a particular judgment is not solely a function of the idiosyncratic evaluation of an examiner it is important to employ a second observer on at least some occasions. Agreement by the two would make it more likely that the judgment is valid, and again this is particularly important when a degree of subjectivity is involved. Measures of interjudge reliability in the studies reviewed here have been extremely scarce. Freeman[11] noted that he could find no study of the reliability of EEG interpretation of children's records.

Test-retest reliability of measures

Test-retest reliability refers to the stability of measures over time. If a child exhibits low blood serotonin levels on one occasion and not one week later, for example, the significance of the measure is thrown into question. Ritvo et al.[32] found that, of their group of children showing abnormal EEG tracings, nearly one-third showed normal tracings on one or more occasions. For these children, it was questionable whether or not their brains tended to function normally and whether their brain functioning was related to their deviant behavior.

Relationship between severity of organic and behavioral deviations

One might expect that the child who is more severely hyperkinetic might have a more severe organic deviation, if the organic factor is relevant to the hyperkinetic behavior. It is important to determine, then, whether these characteristics correlate to a significant degree within groups of hyperkinetic children. This has been done only infrequently in the research reviewed above. As mentioned earlier, EEG abnormality has been found to be unrelated to hyperkinesis,[36] while number of minor physical anomalies has been found to correlate low but significantly with severity.[42] Such measures are crucial in further studies of organic deviation.

Behavioral characteristics as determinants of biological indicators of organicity

Little has been made of the consideration that observed differences in organic indicators between hyperkinetic and normal subjects might be a *result*, rather than a cause, of the behavioral differences. Coleman[6] did find distinct variations in blood serotonin as a result of environmental manipulations, however, and Hughes[14] has reported that slow wave abnormalities in the EEG can be produced by stress and excessive movement. Thus, researchers must be extremely cognizant of behavioral factors which may influence their measures in addition to possible organic deviations. When possible, control groups may be matched with the hyperkinetic children on these measures, such as the use of a control group of delinquent children to match for low motivation.

In conclusion, hyperkinesis is a generic term which has been applied to large numbers of children demonstrating considerable variability in behavioral and biological functioning. No particular organic agent has emerged as a ubiquitous etiological factor, and although organic factors play a role in the hyperkinesis of some children, an assumption of organicity in the absence of clear indicators is unwarranted. The assessment of the hyperkinetic child should therefore be multimodal—including not only biological factors but educational and sociofamilial ones as well.

REFERENCES

1. Anderson, W. 1963. The hyperkinetic child: a neurological appraisal. Neurology 13:371–382.
2. Burks, H. 1960. The hyperkinetic child. Except. Chldrn 27:18–26.
3. Cantwell, D. 1972. Psychiatric illness in the families of hyperactive children. Arch. Gen. Psychiat. 27:414–417.
4. Cantwell, D. 1975. Genetic studies of hyperactive children: psychiatric illness in biologic and adopting parents. *In* Genetic Research in Psychiatry, R. Fieve, D. Rosenthal, and H. Brill, eds. Johns Hopkins University Press, Baltimore.
5. Capute, A., Niedermeyer, E. and Richardson, F. 1968. The electroencephalogram in children with minimal cerebral dysfunction. Pediatrics 41:1104–1114.
6. Coleman, M. 1971. Serotonin concentrations in whole blood of hyperactive children. J. Pediat. 78:985–990.
7. Conners, C. 1969. A teacher rating scale for use in drug studies with children. Amer. J. Psychiat. 126:884–888.
8. David, O. 1974. Association between lower lead level concentrations and hyperactivity in children. Environmental Hlth Perspectives May: 17–25.
9. Ebaugh, F. 1923. Neuropsychiatric sequelae of acute epidemic encephalitis in children. Amer. J. Dis. Chldrn 25:89–97.
10. Eisenberg, L. 1971. Principles of drug therapy in child psychiatry with special reference to stimulant drugs. Amer. J. Orthopsychiat. 41:371–379.
11. Freeman, R. 1967. Special education and the electroencephalogram: marriage of convenience. Spec. Ed. 2:61–73.
12. Hertzig, M., Bortner, M. and Birch, H. 1969. Neurologic findings in children educationally designated as ''brain-damaged.'' Amer. J. Orthopsychiat. 39:437–446.
13. Heston, L. 1966. Psychiatric disorders in foster home reared children of schizophrenic mothers. Brit. J. Psychiat. 112:819–825.
14. Hughes, R. 1961. An Introduction to Clinical Electroencephalography. J. Wright, Bristol.
15. Kennard, M. 1960. Value of equivocal signs in neurologic diagnosis. Neurology 10:753–764.
16. Kenny, T. et al. 1971. Characteristics of children

referred because of hyperactivity. J. Pediat. 79:618–622.

17. Kety, S. et al. 1968. The types and prevalence of mental illness in the biological and adoptive families of adopted schizophrenics. *In* The Transmission of Schizophrenia. D. Rosenthal and S. Kety, eds. Pergamon Press, London.

18. Klinkerfuss, G. et al. 1965. Electroencephalographic abnormalities of children with hyperkinetic behavior. Neurology 15:883–891.

19. Knobel, M., Wolman, M. and Mason, E. 1959. Hyperkinesis and organicity in children. Arch. Gen. Psychiat. 1:94–105.

20. Laufer, M., Denhoff, E. and Solomons, G. 1957. Hyperkinetic impulse disorder in children's behavior problems. Psychosomat. Med. 19:38–49.

21. Lopez, R. 1965. Hyperactivity in twins. Canad. Psychiat. Assoc. J. 10:421–426.

22. Minde, K., Webb, G. and Sykes, D. 1968. Studies on the hyperactive child—VI: prenatal and paranatal factors associated with hyperactivity. Devlpm. Med. Child Neurol. 10:355–363.

23. Morrison, J. and Stewart, M. 1971. A family study of the hyperactive child syndrome. Biol. Psychiat. 3:189–195.

24. Morrison, J. and Stewart, M. 1973. The psychiatric status of the legal families of adopted hyperactive children. Arch. Gen. Psychiat. 28:888–891.

25. Pasamanick, B., Rogers, M. and Lilienfeld, A. 1956. Pregnancy experience and the development of behavior disorder in children. Amer. J. Psychiat. 112:613–618.

26. Pletscher, A. 1968. Metabolism, transfer, and storage of 5-hydroxytryptamine in blood platelets, Brit. J. Pharmacol. Chemother. 32:1–16.

27. Quinn, P. and Rapoport, J. 1974. Minor physical anomalies and neurologic status in hyperactive boys. Pediatrics 53:742–747.

28. Rapoport, J. et al. 1970. Urinary noradrenaline and playroom behavior in hyperactive boys. Lancet (Nov):1141.

29. Rapoport, J. and Quinn, P. 1975. Minor physical anomalies (stigmata) and early developmental deviation: a major biologic subgroup of "hyperactive children." Inter. J. Ment. Hlth. (in press)

30. Rapoport, J., Quinn, P. and Lamprecht, F. 1974. Minor physical anomalies and plasma dopamine-beta-hydroxylase activity in hyperactive boys. Amer. J. Psychiat. 131:386–390.

31. Rapoport, J. et al. 1974. Platelet serotonin of hyperactive school age boys. Brit. J. Psychiat. 125:138–140.

32. Ritvo, E. et al. 1970. Correlation of psychiatric diagnoses and EEG findings: a double-blind study of 184 hospitalized children. Amer. J. Psychiat. 126:112–120.

33. Rosenberg, J. and Weller, G. 1973. Minor physical anomalies and academic performance in young school children. Devlpm. Med. Child Neurol. 15:131–135.

34. Satterfield, J. et al. 1972. Physiological studies of the hyperkinetic child: I. Amer. J. Psychiat. 128:1418–1424.

35. Satterfield, J. et al. 1973. Response to stimulant drug treatment in hyperactive children: prediction from EEG and neurological findings. J. Autism and Chldhd Schiz. 3:36–48.

36. Scatterfield, J. et al. 1974. Intelligence, academic achievement, and EEG abnormalities in hyperactive children. Amer. J. Psychiat. 131:391–395.

37. Silbergeld, E. and Goldberg, A. 1974. Hyperactivity: a lead-induced behavior disorder. Environmental Hlth Perspectives (May):227–232.

38. Stewart, M. and Morrison, J. 1973. Affective disorder among the relatives of hyperactive children. J. Child Psychol. Psychiat. 14:209–212.

39. Stewart, M. et al. 1966. The hyperactive child syndrome. Amer. J. Orthopsychiat. 36:861–867.

40. Strauss, A. and Lehtinen, L. 1947. Psychopathology and Education of the Brain-Injured Child. Grune and Stratton, New York.

41. Taterka, J. and Katz, J. 1955. Study of correlations between electorencephalographic and psychological patterns in emotionally disturbed children. Psychosomat. Med. 17:62–72.

42. Waldrop, M. and Goering, J. 1971. Hyperactivity and minor physical anomalies in elementary school children. Amer. J. Orthopsychiat. 41:602–607.

43. Waldrop, M. and Halverson, C. 1971. Minor physical anomalies and hyperactive behavior in young children. *In* Exceptional Infant: Studies in Abnormalities, vol. 2, J. Hellmuth, ed. Bruner/Mazel, New York.

44. Waldrop, M., Pedersen, F. and Bell, R. 1968. Minor physical anomalies and behavior in preschool children. Child Devlpm. 39:391–400.

45. Warren, R. et al. 1971. The hyperactive child syndrome: normal chromosome findings. Arch. Gen. Psychiat. 24:161–162.

46. Weiss, G. et al. 1971. Studies on the hyperactive child—VIII: 5-year follow-up. Arch. Gen. Psychiat. 24:409–414.

47. Wender, P. 1971. Minimal Brain Dysfunction in Children. John Wiley, New York.

48. Wender, P. et al. 1971. Urinary monoamine metabolites of children with minimal brain dysfunction. Amer. J. Psychiat. 127:1411–1415.

49. Werry, J. et al. 1972. Studies on the hyperactive child—VII: neurologic status compared with neurotic and normal children. Amer. J. Orthopsychiat. 42:441–450.

50. Werry, J., Weiss, G. and Douglas, V. 1964. Studies on the hyperactive child—I: some preliminary findings. Canad. Psychiat. Assoc. J. 9:120–130.

51. Wilker, A., Dixon, J. and Parker, J. 1970. Brain function in problem children and controls: psychometric, neurological, and electroencephalographic comparisons. Amer. J. Psychiat. 127:94–105.

5. A review of treatment approaches for hyperactive behavior

DIAN BRUNDAGE-AGUAR,   REX FOREHAND
ANTHONY R. CIMINERO

Treatment of hyperactivity has become a growing area of concern in recent years. The upsurge in interest is undoubtedly the result of the frequency with which the disorder occurs among children. Patterson (1964) surveyed the behavioral characteristics of children referred to a child guidance clinic and found that the most common problem behavior was hyperactivity. Recent estimates of the frequency of hyperactivity in school-age children in the United States range from 4% to 10% (Huessy, 1967; Stewart, Pitts, Craig, & Dierof, 1966). Studies of the prevalence of hyperactivity in children have noted that the disorder occurs more frequently among boys than girls (Disenhouse, 1972; Goggin, 1975; Miller, Palkes, & Stewart, 1973; Werry, 1969), decreases with age (Weiss, 1975), and occurs in all cultures (Weiss, 1975).

Hyperactivity itself refers to a cluster of behaviors that includes distractibility, short attention span, restlessness, frequent changes in activity, disruptiveness, aggression, and noncompliance (Burks, 1960; Patterson, Shaw, & Ebner, 1970). Failure to attend adequately to tasks is the most commonly cited problematic behavior of hyperactive children, especially by school personnel who constitute the most common referral source (Alabiso, 1972; Grinspoon & Singer, 1973). The common feature of each hyperactive behavior is the excessiveness of the behavior which is aversive to others. Patterson et al. (1970) have noted that the main difference between hyperactive and nonhyperactive children is not the behaviors emitted but the rate at which the behaviors occur.

The etiology of the disorder remains obscure; however, the following three etiological theories have dominated the development of therapeutic techniques in the area: (1) organic-physiological dysfunction, (2) deficits in the attentional mechanism, and (3) the learning theory approach (Bower & Mercer, 1975).

Since perceptual-motor problems were often observed in hyperactive children, an organic brain pathology was suggested as a physiological basis of hyperactivity (Stewart, Palkes, Miller, Young, & Welner, 1974). Treatment approaches based upon this theory are usually medical and emphasize treating the disorder by chemical means. Treatment approaches based on the attentional deficit theory have involved educational and classroom modifications (Strauss & Kephart, 1955). Suggested modifications in the classroom emphasize reducing excessive stimulation which is believed to exacerbate the distractibility of the child. Teaching methods focus on training the child to attend to tasks. Proponents of the learning theory approach view hyperactivity as learned behaviors which are maintained by environmental consequences. Treatment approaches

From the *Journal of Clinical Child Psychology*, 1976, 6, 3–10. Reprinted by permission of the Journal of Clinical Child Psychology.

based on this theory have involved teaching parents and teachers behavior modification principles and using direct conditioning procedures to modify hyperactive behavior.

A major problem in evaluating the effectiveness and desirability of any one of the major treatment approaches is that current research has not yet provided conclusive evidence for any etiological perspective (Lambert, Windmiller, Sandoval, & Moore, 1976). A second problem involves the identification of comparable samples of hyperactive children based on objective criteria. Prediction and diagnosis of hyperactivity based on physiological measures, such as EEGs, and on psychological tests have been unsuccessful (Alabiso, 1972; Grinspoon & Singer, 1973; Katz, Saraf, Gittleman-Klein, & Klein, 1975; Sroufe, 1975; Sroufe & Stewart, 1973). Another problem in evaluating the literature on the treatment of hyperactivity concerns the definition of what constitutes normal versus abnormal activity level. Since no norms are available, the identification of hyperactive children is largely a culturally relative and subjective judgment by the observer (Klein & Gittleman-Klein, 1975). Few studies (e.g., Minde, Levin, Weiss, Laviguerer, Douglas, & Sykes, 1971) have compared hyperactive children to "normal" children.

Despite the problems regarding the nature and identification of hyperactivity, the literature abounds with reports of clinical success in the management of hyperactivity. Therapeutic techniques for hyperactivity are reviewed in two major categories: medical and nonmedical management.

MEDICAL MANAGEMENT

Psychopharmacological management of hyperactivity is by far the most frequently used and established treatment method for hyperactivity (Grinspoon & Singer, 1973). A 1971 survey revealed that between 150,000 and 200,000 children of school age were receiving medication to reduce their hyperactive behaviors (Grinspoon & Singer, 1973). A 62% increase in the use of drug treatment for hyperactive children has been reported between 1971 and 1973 (Krager & Safer, 1974). Surveys indicate that from 5 % to 10% of elementary-school children are prescribed drugs to control their classroom behavior (Rogers, 1971).

Although there is widespread use of psychopharmacological agents to treat hyperactivity, the lack of well-controlled research studies concerning short- and long-term effects of drug agents in children confounds the reported effectiveness of chemotherapy. Sulzbacher (1973) reviewed 1,359 studies conducted between 1937 and 1971 on the effects of psychopharmacological agents on hyperactivity and other disorders with children and found only 27.5% used control measures. Furthermore, only 29 of the studies utilized any direct measures of behavior as a dependent variable. The most usual criteria in evaluating drug effects were parent and teacher verbal reports and rating scales which are generally unreliable and influenced by "halo" effects and rater biases (Gittleman-Klein & Klein, 1975; Schleifer, Weiss, Cohen, Elman, Cvejic, & Kruger, 1975).

INFREQUENTLY USED DRUGS

A number of chemical agents, including major and minor tranquilizers, antidepressants, and stimulants, have been used to treat hyperactivity. Except for the psychostimulants, most of the other pharmacological agents are used infrequently because of their negative side effects or the lack of support for their effectiveness with hyperactivity. For example, the major tranquilizers (e.g., phenothiazines) produce negative side effects in 60% of the children and impair their ability to learn and perform academic learning tasks adequately (Conners, 1971; Freibergs, Douglas, & Weiss, 1968; Greenberg, Deem, & McMahon, 1972; Sroufe, 1975; Weiss, Minde, Douglas, Werry, & Sykes, 1971; Werry, Weiss, Douglas, & Martin, 1966).

Other tranquilizers (e.g., hydroxyzine, diazepam, chlordiazepoxide) also have been prescribed for hyperactivity but have not been found effective (e.g., Greenberg et al., 1972; Wunderlich, 1973; Zrull, 1963). Antidepressants (viz., MAO inhibitors) produce hazardous side effects (e.g., toxic blood and liver damage) and are not usually recommended for children. In addition, no improvements in attentional processes or learning have been noted with their use (Forman, 1975).

Other pharmacological agents, including corticosteroids, lithium carbonate, caffeine, megavitamins, and specialized diets, have also been used for hyperactivity. Corticosteroids have been found to reduce distractibility in hyperactive children but also to produce serious side effects (Wunderlich, 1973). Lithium carbonate generally has been found to be no more effective than a placebo with hyperactive children (e.g., White-head & Clark, 1970).

In one uncontrolled study with caffeine, Schnackenberg (1973) reported clinical success in reducing hyperactive behaviors in eleven 9-year-old children by prescribing two cups of coffee per day. However, in a second study of caffeine effects on activity level and attention span in hyperactive children, no desirable behavioral effects were observed (Conners, 1975). Some data tentatively suggest that successful treatment of hyperactivity may result with the use of megavitamins (Cott, 1971; Wunderlich, 1973) and by removing from a child's diet certain foods that cause allergic reactions (Harvard, 1973; Wunderlich, 1973).

PSYCHOSTIMULANTS

By far, the most commonly used drugs in the treatment of hyperactivity are the psycho-stimulants: methylphenidate (Ritalin), dextroamphetamine (Dexedrine), amphetamine (Benzedrine), and magnesium pemoline (Cylert) (Sandoval, Lambert, & Yandell, 1976). Psychostimulant drugs have been found to result in less hyperactive behavior than any other chemical agent as children are observed to focus their attention better on tasks requiring sustained attention, exhibit less disruptive behavior, and behave more cooperatively with others (Bower & Mercer, 1975; Conley, 1973; Conners, 1971; Conners & Eisenberg, 1963; Conners, Eisenberg, & Barcai, 1967; Conners, Rothschild, Eisenberg, Stone, & Robinson, 1969; Douglas, 1975; Eisenberg & Conners, 1971; Solomans, 1971; Sprague, Barnes, & Werry, 1970; Sroufe & Stewart, 1973). Support for the use of psychostimulants in reducing hyperactivity is substantial, especially from school personnel (Conners, 1971; Grinspoon & Singer, 1973). However, there are various issues that need to be considered when evaluating the potential benefit of this form of chemotherapy. These issues include the effects of scholastic achievement, the negative side effects of stimulants, the need for regular monitoring and evaluation of drug effects by a physician, the nature of the drug effects, potential placebo effects of the medication, and the long-term effects of psychostimulants.

Relative to a placebo-control group, Conners (1972) reported improvements in spelling and reading for a drug treated group of children. In contrast, two studies by Rie, Rie, Stewart, and Ambuel (1976a, 1976b) have found that Ritalin does not enhance scholastic achievement (reading, spelling, math). Interestingly, teachers perceived the students as manifesting positive changes in achievement during the drug condition. Rie et al. (1976a) point out that when such misperception occurs, there may be no further effort to enhance the child's learning. Consequently, drugs may mask learning problems and lead to them being ignored.

A number of negative side effects have been found in 10%–20% of all children given psychostimulants. The most common effects are insomnia, irritability, stomach pains, loss of appetite, and crying. Rarer side effects, such as photosensitivity of the skin, increased heart rate, convulsions, and psychotic episodes, have also been reported (Cohen, Douglas, & Morganstern, 1971; Katz et al., 1975; Werry et al., 1966). Parents and teachers have been observed to often request that drug therapy be withdrawn because of undesired behavioral effects (Schleifer et al., 1975).

Although inconclusive, recent research into the long-term side effects of methylphenidate and dextroamphetamine treatment has revealed a 75%–83% suppression of expected yearly growth (Safer & Allen, 1975; Safer, Allen, & Barr, 1972). However, growth suppression has been reported to rebound following withdrawal of drugs (Safer et al., 1972).

Because of the frequency of side effects, adequate patient monitoring with chemotherapy is essential. Disenhouse (1972) found that hyperactive children who had the greatest contact with their physicians (i.e., weekly phone calls until desired response to drug dosage was obtained and monthly checkups) showed greater improvement on behavioral rating measures than children having minimal contact with their physicians (i.e., visited physician once or twice within six months). Investigators in the area have proposed that adequate monitoring requires the parent and child to visit the physician weekly until an adequate response to the drug has been maintained. Weekly school reports are also advised (Katz et al., 1975). Despite the precautions advised, 45% of the children receiving psychopharmacological treatment for hyperactivity are not being monitored adequately by their physicians (Sroufe, 1975): Most children are seen by their physicians only twice a month at most and many children begin medication without an office visit (Sroufe & Stewart, 1973).

The literature on placebo effects with hyperactivity reveals similar concerns regarding the effectiveness of the psychopharmacological management of hyperactivity. Although some studies (e.g., Conners, 1972; Conners & Eisenberg, 1963) indicate a greater change in hyperactive behavior for treated subjects than for placebo subjects, improvement has been reported in 35%–70% of the children given placebo, depending on the assessment measure used and the presence versus absence of blind evaluators (Sroufe, 1975; Sulzbacher, 1973). Parent, physician, and teacher expectations of a positive therapeutic change have been found to be sufficient in producing some behavioral change in an overwhelming number of children (Werry et al., 1966). In a study comparing the effects of a placebo and various types of stimulant agents on the psychometric and behavioral ratings of hyperactive children, it was found that there were no differences in the effects of drugs and placebo on behavior at either a 4 or 12 week assessment (Gittleman-Klein & Klein, 1975). Conrad, Dworken, Shai, and Tobiessen (1971) compared the effects of tutoring plus placebo, methylphenidate alone, and tutoring alone on achievement test measures and behavioral rating scales. Although children in the methylphenidate-alone condition improved in their behavioral ratings, only children in the tutoring plus placebo condition performed significantly better on achievement test measures. Christensen (1975) compared the effects of behavior modification plus methylphenidate and behavior modification plus placebo in treating 16 hyperactive institutionalized retardates. The two treatments were equally effective in modifying off-task and deviant behavior.

The findings from several follow-up studies of hyperactive children treated with psychostimulants provide data regarding the long term effects of such drugs. It should be noted that in most of these studies medication other than psychostimulants, such as tranquilizers, was used with some children at some point during treatment. Huessy, Metoyer, and Townsend (1974), in an 8 to 10 year follow-up of 84 teenagers who previously had been diagnosed as hyperactive, found that 18 of the teenagers had been placed in correctional institutions. The investigators concluded that hyperactive children are seriously at risk for later difficulties in life. Similarly, Minde, Weiss, and Mendelson (1972), in a five-year follow-up of 91 hyperactive children, found that although target symptomatic behaviors had decreased, the children still had problems relating to their responsibilities and environment.

Mendelson, Johnson, and Stewart (1971) found that although 92% of 83 teenagers studied had been treated with amphetamine or methylphenidate as children, only 50% were rated as improved behaviorally at follow-up. Seventy-five percent of the teenagers still manifested poor concentration, impulsivity, and defiance. Twenty-five percent were involved in antisocial acts, and most had school problems. Weiss, Minde, Werry, Douglas, and Nemeth (1971) also found a prevalence of academic difficulties in 64 teenagers who had been previously diagnosed as hyperactive. Attentional deficits were still manifested in 80% of the teenagers with concomitant underachievement in school.

Although psychopharmacological treatment is quite popular, the evidence shows that between 10% and 20% of children do not respond to chemotherapy (Katz et al., 1975; Novak, 1971). In addition, there are at present no valid predictors of responsiveness to drug therapy. Considering the research on the strength of placebo effects, of the possibility of adverse side effects with drug therapy, and the absence of long term effectiveness, application of this treatment approach requires strict and cautious prescription and monitoring (Cole, 1975). Some researchers in the area have concluded that because of the various problems and issues concerning drug treatment, it should remain a last alternative and should always be coupled with some type of training for parents and/or teachers in behavior management (Bendix, 1973; Bower & Mercer, 1975; Douglas, 1975; Grinspoon & Singer, 1973; Sroufe & Stewart, 1973).

NONMEDICAL MANAGEMENT OF HYPERACTIVITY

Although medication has been the most frequently used therapeutic intervention for hyperactive behavior of children, several nonmedical approaches have also been employed. These approaches have been used because of the problems associated with drugs (e.g., negative side effects) and parental concerns about use of chemical agents.

INFREQUENTLY USED APPROACHES

The effects of traditional psychotherapy techniques (i.e., play therapy, insight therapy) on hyperactivity have received little attention. However, at least one study suggests that such an approach is not successful in modifying hyperactive behaviors in children as assessed by parent verbal reports (Eisenberg, Gilbert, Cytryn, & Molling, 1961). Minimal success with psychotherapy also has been reported with children who simultaneously received psychopharmacological agents (O'Malley & Eisenberg, 1973).

A second nonmedical treatment approach has involved modifying the structure of the classroom. This procedure to reduce hyperactive behavior is based on the assumption that hyperactivity results from excessive environmental stimulation (Glennon & Nason, 1974; Strauss & Lehtinen, 1947). The use of cubicles to reduce classroom stimulation and thereby increase attending behavior has been implemented successfully (Bower & Mercer, 1975). Strauss and Kephart (1955) designed a special educational program for hyperactive children. The program involved minimizing classroom stimulation, simplifying academic materials, increasing classroom structure, and increasing tolerance for behavioral deviations. No data were presented on the effectiveness of their procedures.

A third approach, which is closely tied to the attentional deficit theory of hyperactivity, is cognitive self-instruction procedures for reducing hyperactive behaviors. These procedures attempt to help the child learn how to focus his/her attention on tasks and thereby gain some internal control over interfering hyperactive behaviors. Palkes, Stewart, and Kahana (1968) trained 20 boys to command themselves to "stop, look, and think before I do." Significant improvement on the Porteus Maze task, a measure of distractibility, was obtained after two one hour sessions in vocalized practice in self-commands. In a subsequent study with 30 boys under the same conditions, similar success was obtained (Paulkes, Stewart, & Freedman, 1972).

Meichenbaum (1971; Meichenbaum & Goodman, 1971) taught groups of hyperactive children through a modeling and practice with self-instruction procedure to improve their performance on the WISC and Porteus Maze. Children first observed a model demonstrate self-queries regarding the task, perform the task, and then correct or reinforce his performance of the task. Children were taught to verbalize, first overtly and then covertly. Assessment on the tasks one year following training revealed that their gains had been maintained. Using a procedure similar to the one employed by Meichenbaum (1971). Bornstein and Quevillon (1976) substantially increased the on-task classroom behavior of three 4-year-old hyperactive children enrolled in a Head Start Program. The gains were maintained at a follow-up 90 days after the beginning of the study.

Burns (1972) investigated the effects of self-verbalized commands on math performance and activity level in 45 hyperactive children. Achievement test results and direct behavioral observations of the children were obtained. Following twenty 30-minute training sessions, no significant treatment effects were found in any assessment measures.

With the exception of the Burns study, the cognitive self-instructional procedures show promise as an effective treatment for hyperactivity. Replications of the existing research, work with larger sample sizes, and examination of the effects of a multimodal approach (i.e., combining self-instructions with drug or behavior management) are now needed.

BEHAVIOR MODIFICATION

Behavioral management of hyperactivity is now the most frequently used nonmedical approach. Gaining impetus from the problems cited previously in research in the psychopharmacological treatment of hyperactivity, advocates of the behavioral approach emphasize that although drugs may make a child more manageable, they do not teach the child appropriate, nonhyperactive behaviors. Adequate treatment of hyperactivity involves treating the problem (i.e., the hyperactive behavior) rather than treating an inferred cause (Palkes et al., 1968).

The design and controls employed by researchers using behavior management procedures generally have been more rigorous than those used by researchers in other treatment areas. The majority of the studies have been conducted in classroom settings (e.g., Walker & Buckley, 1968). However, some studies have been completed in institutions (e.g., Christensen, 1975), laboratories (e.g., Seitz & Terdal, 1972), and homes (e.g., Risley, 1968). For review purposes, the studies will be examined by the principal treatment technique employed: presentation of positive reinforcement contingent upon either the nonoccurrence of hyperactive behavior or the occurrence of some alternate behavior; the withdrawal of positive reinforcement following the occurrence of hyperactive behavior; and the presentation of aversive stimulation contingent upon hyperactive behavior. In addition, several studies have reported training programs in which parents of hyperactive children are taught a variety of behavior management skills. These studies will be briefly reviewed.

REINFORCEMENT OF ALTERNATE BEHAVIOR

The treatment approach in most studies has been to reinforce the occurrence of an alternate behavior, typically a behavior that is incompatible with hyperactivity. Several studies (e.g., Twardosz & Sajwaj, 1972; Wolf, Hanley, King, Lachowicz, & Giles, 1970) conducted in classroom settings have successfully reinforced children with tokens plus subsequent back-up reinforcement for remaining in their seats. Typically, neither follow-up data nor increases in study behavior or academic performances have been reported.

In most classroom studies, the alternate reinforced behavior has been attending behavior. Typically the children are required to attend (looking in direction of the teacher or looking at assigned work) for a specified period of time in order to receive reinforcement. Tokens plus back-up reinforcers (Mitchell & Crowell, 1973; Walker & Buckley, 1968), primary reinforcement such as candy and trinkets (Kubany, Weiss, & Sloggett, 1971; McKensie, Clark, Wolf, Kothera, & Benson, 1968; Patterson, Jones, Whittier, & Wright, 1965), and social reinforcement (Allen, Henke, Harris, Baer, & Reynolds, 1967) have been used. In all studies, there was a reduction in hyperactive behaviors, including nonattending (e.g., McKensie et al., 1968; Walker & Buckley, 1968), movement (Patterson et al., 1965), disruptive or inappropriate off-task behavior (Mitchell & Crowell, 1973), and changes in activity (Allen et al., 1967) when treatment was implemented. At least in one study (Anderson, Note 1) primary reinforcement was faded out after hyperactive behaviors were reduced and praise was then sufficient to maintain such responses at a low level. In one study (Patterson et al., 1965) follow-up measures indicated that gains were maintained after treatment. Again, neither changes in academic performance nor follow-up, except in the Patterson et al. (1965) study, were measured.

In some classroom studies, the alternative behavior that has been reinforced is correct completion of academic work. Both Pigeon and Enger (1972) and Ayllon, Layman, and Kandel (1975) reduced hyperactive behaviors by reinforcing correct responses on academic tasks. The Ayllon et al. study is particularly noteworthy. Math and reading performance was assessed by workbook assignments, and targeted hyperactive behaviors were observed concurrently using a time-sampling procedure. A checkpoint system which enabled children to earn points for correct workbook assignments was employed. Academic performance and measures of hyperactivity were obtained in four phases: (1) on medication, (2) off medication, (3) reinforcement of math, and (4) reinforcement of reading. The results indicated that reinforcement was as effective as methylphenidate in decreasing hyperactive behaviors and was more effective in improving academic performance. This is the only study that has presented systematic data demonstrating concomitant decreases in hyperactive behavior and increases in academic performance.

Finally, some studies have reinforced more than one alternative behavior in attempting to decelerate hyperactivity. In the classroom, these alternate behaviors include completing assigned work, staying in seat, no fighting, and working on task. In laboratory settings, compliance, playing quietly, picking up toys, and positive interaction with adults are alternate responses which have been reinforced by an experimenter or by parents as part of parent-training programs. Varying types of tokens plus back-up reinforcers (Doubros & Daniels, 1966; O'Leary, Pelham, Rosenbaum, & Price, 1976; Rosenbaum, O'Leary, & Jacob, 1975; Wiltz & Gordon, 1974), primary reinforcement (Johnson & Brown, 1969), and social reinforcement (Daniels, 1973; Ebner, 1968; Kauffman & Hallahan, 1973; Seitz & Terdal, 1972; Vance, 1969) have been used as reinforcers. Again, in all studies positive outcomes resulting from treatment intervention were reported. However, neither systematic follow-up data nor, for the classroom studies, changes in scholastic achievement were reported in the studies.

WITHDRAWAL OF POSITIVE REINFORCEMENT

Two studies have been reported in which the primary intervention was the withdrawal of positive reinforcement. However, it should be noted that in several studies (e.g., Daniels, 1973; Vance; 1969) reported in the previous section the intervention agent (teacher, parent, or therapist) ignored hyperactive behavior in addition to reinforcing an alternate behavior. Sachs (1973) effectively reduced the hyperactive classroom behaviors of a child by placing him in a time-out room for 5 minutes contingent upon the hyperactive responses. Attending behavior in the classroom increased when hyperactivity was reduced by time-out.

In contrast to Sach's positive findings, Risley (1968) instructed a mother to implement a 10 minute time-out with her *autistic* child contingent on each instance of hyperactive climbing behavior in the home. No reduction in the target behavior occurred over 63 days of treatment.

PUNISHMENT

The presentation of an aversive stimulus contingent upon hyperactivity has occurred in two studies. In the study reported above in which time-out was ineffective in decelerating climbing behavior, Risley subsequently introduced shock contingent on climbing first in a laboratory setting and then in the home. In both instances, contingent shock produced an immediate decrease in climbing. In the laboratory, a concomitant increase in eye contact occurred. Gilandas and Ball (1975) reported a similar decrease in hyperactive behaviors of a profoundly retarded child when contingent shock was used.

PROGRAMS

Some reports have been published in which programs were described through which parents learned a variety of behavior management skills. Most of the work in this area has consisted of group counseling procedures (Katz et al., 1975). Eight- to ten-week parent groups are conducted for the purposes of teaching parents behavior management skills and enabling the parents to discuss common problems of their children. Parent verbal-report measures have been used to assess the effects of the group counseling procedures. Generally, parent groups have been reported to be successful in achieving their goals (Katz et al., 1975).

Schaefer, Palkes, and Stewart (1974) reported success in teaching nine sets of parents to modify the hyperactive behavior of their children. The training procedure employed involved two steps. Parents were first required to read *Child Management* (Smith & Smith, 1964) and *Parents Are Teachers* (Becker, 1971) and then to target specific problem behaviors of their children. Subsequently, a series of group sessions were held which focused on how to modify specified target behaviors. Role-playing, modeling, and program planning were used to teach reinforcement principles. Feighner and Feighner (1974) have reported similar successful results

using a group procedure to teach parents reinforcement and punishment skills to reduce hyperactivity. Furman and Feighner (1973) devised a videotaped training procedure to successfully teach parents of hyperactive children behavior modification skills. The changes were maintained at a 4 to 5 month follow-up.

Programs that teach parents and/or teachers a variety of behavior management skills certainly provide more help to the participants than instructing them in the use of only one skill (e.g., reinforcement of alternate behavior). Generalization of skills to new settings and behaviors should be enhanced by such programs. Furthermore, when the programs are conducted with groups of parents or teachers, the participants can benefit from each other's experiences and suggestions. Regardless of these benefits, systematic assessment of the effectiveness of such programs is necessary. Sufficient data are available to indicate that observations of changes in parent and child behaviors by independent observers, rather than parent reports, are necessary to realistically evaluate treatment effectiveness (see Forehand & Atkeson, 1976, for a review).

CONCLUSIONS

Existing literature on the effectiveness of various treatment approaches to modify hyperactivity is fraught with methodological problems and inconclusive findings. Considering the frequency of occurrence of hyperactivity in the general population, the problems associated with evaluating treatment alternatives are significant.

At present, chemotherapy with psychostimulant drugs remains the preferential choice; however, methodological problems in drug studies, the problem of idiosyncratic responses to drug therapy, and the possibility of adverse side effects suggest caution in the use of this treatment. Close monitoring must be exercised if a drug therapy approach is adopted. As evidenced by the drug follow-up data reported previously (e.g., Mendelson et al., 1971; Minde et al., 1972), even greater consideration in adopting a psychopharmacological treatment approach should be given to the fact that the drug agents do not cure hyperactivity. By reducing aversive hyperactive behaviors, drug treatment can serve to make parents and teachers less motivated to seek alternative solutions in dealing with children's hyperactive behaviors (Krippner, Silverman, Cavallo, & Healy, 1974; Sroufe & Stewart, 1973).

Parents and teachers support chemotherapy because children become more easily controlled, and changes in teaching and child-rearing practices can remain unmodified. Children support and depend on their medicine as they grow to believe that only chemical agents can control their disruptive behaviors. In sum, the indiscriminant use of the psychopharmacological approach may constitute an infringement on the child's rights, especially when it is selected in order to make the child submit to undesirable child rearing or teaching practices, and when it places an undue psychological burden on the children themselves by teaching them that they have no control over their own behaviors.

Behavior management training would appear to be a desirable approach to treating hyperactivity, primarily because it teaches the child how to behave appropriately and because it teaches parents and teachers how to maintain nonhyperactive behavior. In most studies in which behavioral intervention procedures were used, adequate experimental designs have been employed to allow a systematic evaluation of the effects of treatment. In addition, in those studies conducted in classroom settings, assessent of behavior change has been conducted by independent observers.

Unfortunately, three problems exist at present which prevent conclusive data regarding the effectiveness of behavior management procedures. First, in most studies, small sample sizes, often only a single subject, have been used. Second, other than the Ayllon et al. (1975) study, classroom studies have not examined the effects of treatment on academic performance but rather have been limited to the examination of treatment effects on decelerating hyperactive behavior. Third, follow-up data seldom have been collected.

Two treatment approaches would appear to merit further investigation. Each approach first involves a careful observational assessment of problematic behaviors in both the child's home and school to determine under what conditions hyperactive behaviors occur. In one approach, parents and teachers would be taught reinforcement principles in order to decrease inadvertant reinforcement for hyperactive behaviors and increase reinforcement for nonhyperactive behaviors. In addition, cognitive self-instructional procedures could be implemented with the child. If the child's behavior does not respond to these two approaches, chemical agents would then be administered and carefully monitored to aid in making the child's behavior accessible to reinforcement procedures.

Since there is evidence from well controlled studies (e.g., Conners et al., 1969; Sprague et al., 1970) that medication can have a rather immediate beneficial effect on hyperactivity, a second approach, a multimodal one, first using medication which is then followed by behavioral management techniques and cognitive self-instructional procedures might be most effective with children that do not respond initially to behavior management procedures. After the behavior is under environmental control, the medication could be faded out. This would take advantage of the immediacy of drug effects but would avoid the necessity of maintaining children on stimulants for long periods of time. A procedure similar to this was investigated by Christensen and Sprague (1973) who combined positive reinforcement for minimal seat movements with either methylphenidate or a placebo. The reinforcement procedure resulted in greater decreases in seat activity for the methylphenidate group. Although they only examined activity levels, the results suggest the need for further research on a multimodal approach to treating hyperactivity (Feighner, & Feighner, 1974; Stableford, Butz, Hasazi, Leitenberg, & Peyser, 1976).

REFERENCE NOTES

1. Anderson, D. B. *Application of behavior modification techniques to the control of a hyperactive child.* Unpublished Master's thesis. University of Oregon, 1964.

REFERENCES

Alabiso, F. Inhibitory functions of attention in reducing hyperactive behavior. *American Journal of Mental Deficiency, 1972, 77* 259–282.

Allen, K. E., Henke, L. B., Harris, F. R., Baer, D. M., & Reynolds, N. J. Control of hyperactivity by social reinforcement of attending behavior. *Journal of Educational Psychology,* 1967, 58, 231–237.

Ayllon, T., Layman, D., & Kandel, H. J. A behavioral-educational alternative to drug control of hyperactive children. *Journal of Applied Behavior Analysis,* 1975, **8,** 137–146.

Becker, W. C. *Parents are teachers: A child management program.* Champaign, Ill.: Research Press, 1971.

Bendix, S. Drug modification of behavior: A form

of chemical violence against children? *Journal of Clinical Child Psychology,* 1973, **2,** 17–19.

Bornstein, P. H., & Quevillon, R. P. The effects of a self-instructional package on overactive pre-school boys. *Journal of Applied Behavior Analysis,* 1976, **9,** 179–188.

Bower, K. B., & Mercer, C. D. Hyperactivity: Etiology and intervention techniques. *Journal of School Health,* 1975, **45,** 195–212.

Burks, H. F. The hyperkinetic child. *Exceptional Children,* 1960, **27,** 18–26.

Burns, B. The effect of self-directed verbal commands on arithmetic performance and activity level of urban hyperactive children (Doctoral dissertation, Boston College, 1972). *Dissertation Abstracts International,* 1972, **33,** 1782B. (Microfilms No. 72-22,884).

Christensen, D. E. Effects of combining methylphenidate and a classroom token system in modifying hyperactive behavior. *American Journal of Mental Deficiency,* 1975, **80,** 266–276.

Christensen, D. E., & Sprague, R. L. Reduction of hyperactive behavior by conditioning procedures alone and combined with methylphenidate. *Behaviour Research and Therapy,* 1973, **11,** 331–334.

Cohen, N., Douglas, V., & Morganstern, G. The effects of methylphenidate on attentive behavior and autonomic activity in hyperactive children. *Psychopharmacologia,* 1971, **22,** 282–294.

Cole, S. Hyperkinetic children: The use of stimulant drugs evaluation. *American Journal of Orthopsychiatry,* 1975, **45,** 28–37.

Conley, D. P. Effects of Ritalin on hyperactive children attending the Glendale Elementary Schools (Doctoral dissertation, Arizona State University, 1973). *Dissertation Abstracts International,* 1973, **34,** 1072A–1073A. (Microfilms No. 72-20,427).

Conners, C. K. Recent drug studies with hyperkinetic children. *Journal of Learning Disabilities,* 1971, **4,** 476–483.

Conners, C. K. Psychological effects of stimulant drugs in children with minimal brain dysfunction. *Pediatrics,* 1972, **49,** 702–708.

Conners, C. K. A placebo-crossover study of caffeine treatment of hyperactive children. *International Journal of Mental Health,* 1975, **4,** 132–143.

Conners, C. K., & Eisenberg, L. The effects of methylphenidate on symptomology and learning in disturbed children. *American Journal of Psychiatry,* 1963, **120,** 458–463.

Conners, C. K., Eisenberg, L., & Barcai, A. Effects of dextroamphetamine on children. *Archives of General Psychiatry,* 1967, **17,** 478–485.

Conners, C., Rothschild, G., Eisenberg, L., Stone, L., & Robinson, E. Dextroamphetamine sulfate in children with learning problems: Effects of perception, learning, and achievement. *Archives of General Psychiatry,* 1969, **21,** 182–192.

Conrad, W. G., Dworkin, E. S., Shai, A., and To-

biessen, J. E. Effects of amphetamine therapy and prescriptive tutoring on the behavior and achievement of lower-class hyperactive children. *Journal of Learning Disabilities,* 1971, **4,** 45–53.

Cott, A. Orthomolecular approach to the treatment of learning disabilities. *Schizophrenia,* 1971, **3,** 95.

Daniels, L. K. Parental treatment of hyperactivity in a child with ulcerative colitis. *Journal of Behavior Therapy and Experimental Psychiatry,* 1973, **4,** 183–185.

Disenhouse, H. A. An academic and social follow-up of children placed on dexedrine or ritalin for severe hyperactive or hyperkinetic disorders (Doctoral dissertation, University of Iowa, 1972). *Dissertation Abstracts International,* 1972, **4-A,** 1549A-1550A. (Microfilms No. 72-26,670).

Doubros, S. G., & Daniels, G. J. An experimental approach to the reduction of overactive behavior. *Behaviour Research and Therapy,* 1966, **4,** 251–258.

Douglas, V. I. Are drugs enough? To treat or to train the hyperactive child. *International Journal of Mental Health,* 1975, **4,** 199–212.

Ebner, M. J. An investigation of the role of the social environment in the generalization and persistence of the effect of a behavior modification program (Doctoral dissertation, University of Oregon, 1967). *Dissertation Abstracts International,* 1968, **28,** 3874B–3875B. (Microfilms No. 68-3979).

Eisenberg, L., & Conners, C. K. Psychopharmacology in childhood. In N. B. Talbot, J. Kagan, & L. Eisenberg (Eds.), *Behavioral science in pediatric medicine.* Philadelphia: Saunders, 1971.

Eisenberg, L., Gilbert, A., Cytryn, L., & Molling, P. A. The effectiveness of psychotherapy alone and in conjunction with perphenazine or placebo in the treatment of neurotic and hyperkinetic children. *American Journal of Psychiatry.al 1961,* **117,** 1088–1093.

Feighner, A., C., & Feighner, J. P. Multimodality treatment of the hyperactive child. *American Journal of Psychology,* 1974, **131,** 459–463.

Forehand, R., & Atkeson, B. M. Generality of treatment effects with parents as therapists: A review of assessment and implementation procedures. *Behavior Therapy,* in press.

Forman, P. Pharmacological intervention. In H. Myklebust (Ed.), *Progress in learning disabilities, Vol. III.* New York: Grune and Stratton, 1975.

Freibergs, V., Douglas, V. V., & Weiss, G. The effect of chlorpromazine on concept learning in hyperactive children under two conditions of reinforcement. *Psychophamacologia,* 1968, **13,** 299–310.

Furman, S., & Feighner, A. Video feedback in treating hyperkinetic children: A preliminary report. *American Journal of Psychiatry,* 1973, **130,** 790–796.

Gilandas, A. J., & Ball, T. Aversive conditioning

as a means of reducing aggressive behavior. *Australian Psychologist*, 1975, **10**, 45–49.

Gittleman-Klein, R., & Klein, D. Are behavioral and psychometric changes related in methylphenidate-treated, hyperactive children. *International Journal of Mental Health*, 1975, **4**, 182–198.

Glennon, C. A., & Nason, D. E. Managing the behavior of the hyperkinetic child: What research says. *Reading Teacher*, 1974, **27**, 815–824.

Goggin, J. E. Sex differences in activity level of preschool children as a possible precursor of hyperactivity. *Journal of Genetic Psychology*, 1975, **127**, 75–81.

Greenberg, L. Deem, M., and McMahon, S. Effects of dextroamphetamine, chlorpromazine and hydroxyzine on behavior and performance in hyperactive children. *American Journal of Psychiatry*, 1972, **129**, 299–310.

Grinspoon, L., & Singer, S. B. Amphetamines in the treatment of hyperactive children. *Harvard Educational Review*, 1973, **43**, 515–555.

Harvard, J. School problems and allergies. *Journal of Learning Disabilities*, 1973, **6**, 492–494.

Huessy, H. R. Study of prevalence and therapy of aborcatiform syndrome or hyperkinesis in rural Vermont. *Acta Paedopsychiatrica*, 1967, **34**, 130–135.

Huessy, H. R., Metoyer, M., & Townsend, M. Eight-ten year follow-up of 84 children treated for behavioral disorder in rural Vt. *Acta Paedopsychiatrica*, 1974, **40**, 230–235.

Johnson, S. M., & Brown, R. A. Producing behavior change in parents of disturbed children. *Journal of Child Psychology and Psychiatry*, 1969, **10**, 107–121.

Katz, S., Saraf, K., Gittleman-Klein, R., & Klein, D. Clinical pharmacological management of hyperkinetic children. *International Journal of Mental Health*, 1975, **4**, 175–181.

Kauffman, J. M., & Hallahan, D. P. Control of rough physical behavior using novel contingencies and directive teaching. *Perceptual and Motor Skills*, 1973, **36**, 1225–1226.

Klein, D. F., & Gittleman-Klein, R. Problems in the diagnosis of MBD and the hyperkinetic syndrome. *International Journal of Mental Health*, 1975, **4**, 46–60.

Krager, J. M., & Safer, D. J. Type and prevalence of medication used in the treatment of hyperactive children. *New England Journal of Medicine*, 1974, **291**, 1118–1120.

Krippner, S., Silverman, R., Cavallo, M., & Healy, M. Stimulant drugs and hyperkinesis: A question of diagnosis. *Reading World*, 1974, **13**, 193–222.

Kubany, E. S., Weiss, L. E., & Sloggett, B. B. Good behavior clock: A reinforcement/timeout procedure for reducing classroom behavior. *Journal of Behavior Therapy and Experimental Psychiatry*, 1971, **2**, 173–179.

Lambert, N. M., Windmiller, M., Sandoval, J., & Moore, B. Hyperactive children and the efficacy of psychoactive drugs as a treatment intervention. *American Journal of Orthopsychiatry*, 1976, **46**, 335–352.

McKensie, H. S., Clark, M., Wolf, M. M., Kothera, R., & Benson, D. Behavior modification of children with learning disabilities using grades as tokens and allowance as backup reinforcers. *Exceptional Children*, 1968, **34**, 745–753.

Meichenbaum, D. H. The nature and modification of impulsive children: Training impulsive children to talk to themselves. *Journal of Abnormal Psychology*, 1971, **77**, 115–122.

Meichenbaum, D., & Goodman, J. Training impulsive children to talk to themselves: A means of developing self-control. *Journal of Abnormal Psychology*, 1971, **77**, 115–125.

Mendelson, W. Johnson, N., & Stewart, M. A. Hyperactive children as teenagers: A follow-up study. *Journal of Nervous and Mental Disease*, 1971, **153**, 273–279.

Minde, K., Levin, D., Weiss, G., Laviguerer, H., Douglas, V., & Sykes, E. The hyperactive child in elementary school: A five year, controlled, follow-up. *Exceptional Children*, 1971, **38**, 215–221.

Minde, K., Weiss, G., & Mendelson, W. A 5-year follow-up study of 91 hyperactive school children. *Journal of American Academy of Child Psychiatry*, 1972, **11**, 595–610.

Mitchell, D. W., & Crowell, P. J. Modifying inappropriate behavior in an elementary art class. *Elementary School Guidance and Counseling*, 1973, **8**, 34–42.

Miller, R. G., Palkes, H. S., & Stewart, M. A. Hyperactive children in suburban elementary schools. *Child Psychiatry and Human Development*, 1973, **4**, 121–127.

Novak, H. S. An educator's view of medication and classroom behavior. *Journal of Learning Disabilities*, 1971, **4**, 507–508.

O'Leary, K. D., Pelham, W. E., Rosenbaum, A., & Price, G. H. Behavioral treatment of hyperkinetic children. *Clinical Pediatrics*, 1976, **15**, 510–515.

O'Malley, J. E., & Eisenberg, L. The hyperkinetic syndrome. *Seminars in Psychiatry*, 1973, **5**, 95–103.

Palkes, H., Stewart, M., & Freedman, J. Improvement in maze performance of hyperactive boys as a function of verbal-training procedures. *Journal of Special Education*, 1972, **5**, 337–342.

Palkes, H., Stewart, M., & Kahana, B. Porteus maze performance of hyperactive boys after training in self-directed commands. *Child Development*, 1968, **39**, 817–826.

Patterson, G. R. An empirical approach to the classification of disturbed children. *Journal of Clinical Psychology*, 1964, **20**, 326–337.

Patterson, G. R., Jones, R., Whittier, J., & Wright, M. A. A behavior modification technique for the hyperactive child. *Behaviour Research and Therapy*, 1965, **2**, 217–226.

Patterson, G. R., Shaw, D. T., & Ebner, M. J. Teachers, peers, and parents as agents of change in the classroom. In F. A. Benson (Ed.), *Modifying deviant behaviors in various classroom settings*. Eugene, Oregon, Department of Special Education, Monograph No. 1, 1970.

Pigeon, G., & Enger, A. Increasing assignment completion and accuracy in a hyperactive, first grade student. SALT: *School Application of Learning Theory*, 1972, **4**, 24–30.

Rie, H. E., Rie, E. D., Stewart, S., & Ambuel, J. P. Effects of Ritalin on underachieving children: A replication. *American Journal of Orthopsychiatry*, 1976, **46**, 313–322. (a)

Rie, H. E., Rie, E. D., Stewart, S., & Ambuel, J. P. Effects of methylphenidate on underachieving children. *Journal of Consulting and Clinical Psychology*, 1976, **44**, 250–260. (b)

Risley, T. R. The effects and side effects of punishing the autistic behaviors of a deviant child. *Journal of Applied Behavior Analysis*, 1968, **1**, 21–34.

Rogers, J. M. Drug abuse—just what the doctor ordered. *Psychology Today*, 1971, **5**, 16–24.

Rosenbaum, A., O'Leary, K. D., & Jacob, R. G. Behavioral intervention with hyperactive children: Group consequences as a supplement to individual contingencies. *Behavior Therapy*, 1975, **6**, 315–323.

Sachs, D. A. The efficacy of time-out procedures in a variety of behavior problems. *Journal of Behavior Therapy and Experimental Psychiatry*, 1973, **4**, 237–242.

Safer, D. H., & Allen, R. P. Side effects from long-term use of stimulants in children. *International Journal of Mental Health*, 1975, **4**, 105–118.

Safer, D., Allen, R., & Barr, E. Depression of growth in hyperactive children on stimulant drugs. *New England Journal of Medicine*, 1972, **287**, 217–220.

Sandoval, J., Lambert, N. M., & Yandell, W. Current medical practice and hyperactive children. *American Journal of Orthopsychiatry, 1976*, **46**, 323–334.

Schaefer, J. W., Palkes, H. S., & Stewart, M. A. Group counseling for parents of hyperactive children. *Child Psychiatry and Human Development*, 1974, **5**, 89–94.

Schleifer, M. Weiss, G., Cohen, N., Elman, M., Cvejic, H., & Kruger, E. Hyperactivity in preschoolers and the effect of methylphenidate. *American Journal of Orthopsychiatry*, 1975, **45**, 38–50.

Schnackenberg, R. C. Caffeine as a substitute for schedule II stimulants in hyperactive children.

American Journal of Psychiatry, 1973, **130**, 769–798.

Seitz, S., & Terdal, L. A modeling approach to changing parent-child interactions. *Mental Retardation*, 1972, **10**, 39–43.

Smith, J. A., & Smith, E. P. *Child management*. Ann Arbor: Ann Arbor Publishers, 1964.

Solomans, G. Guidelines on the use and medical effects of psychostimulant drugs in therapy. *Journal of Learning Disabilities*, 1971, **4**, 471–475.

Sprague, R. L., Barnes, K. R., & Werry, J. S. Methylphenidate and thioridazine: Learning, reaction time, activity, and classroom behavior. *American Journal of Orthopsychiatry*, 1970, **40**, 615–627.

Sroufe, L. A. Drug treatment of children with behavior problems. In F. Horowitz (Ed.), *Review of child development research*, IV, 1975.

Sroufe, L. A., & Stewart, M. A. Treating problem children with stimulant drugs. *New England Journal of Medicine*, 1973, **289**, 407–413.

Stableford, W., Butz, R., Hasazi, S., Leitenberg, H., & Peyser, J. Sequential withdrawal of stimulant drugs and use of behavior therapy with two hyperactive boys. *American Journal of Orthopsychiatry*, 1976, **46**, 302–312.

Stewart, M. A., Palkes, H., Miller, R., Young, C., & Welner, Z. Intellectual ability and school achievement of hyperactive children, their classmates, and their siblings. In D. A. Ricks, A. Thomas, & M. Roff (Eds.), *Life history research in psychopathology III*, Minneapolis: University of Minnesota Press, 1974.

Stewart, M. A., Pitts, F. N., Craig, A. G., & Dierof, W. The hyperactive child syndrome. *American Journal of Orthopsychiatry*, 1966, **36**, 861–867.

Strauss, A., & Kephart, N. C. *Psychopathology and education of the brain-injured child*. New York: Grune & Stratton, 1955.

Strauss, A., & Lehtinen, L. B. *Psychopathology and education of the brain-injured child*. New York: Grune & Stratton, 1947.

Sulzbacher, S. I. Psychotropic medication with children: An evaluation of procedural biases in results of reported studies. *Pediatrics*, 1973, **51**, 513–517.

Twardosz, S., & Sajwaj, T. Multiple effects of a procedure to increase sitting in a hyperactive, retarded boy. *Journal of Applied Behavior Analysis*, 1972, **5**, 73–78.

Vance, B. J. Modifying hyperactive and aggressive behavior. In J. D. Krumboltz & C. D. Thoreson (Eds.), *Behavioral counseling: Cases and techniques*. New York: Holt, Rinehart, & Winston, 1969.

Walker, H. M., & Buckley, N. K. The use of positive reinforcement in conditioning attending behavior. *Journal of Applied Behavior Analysis*, 1968, **1**, 245–250.

Weiss, G. The natural history of hyperactivity in childhood and treatment with stimulant medication at different ages: A summary of research findings. *International Journal of Mental Health*, 1975, **4**, 213–226.

Weiss, G., Minde, K., Douglas, V., Werry, J., & Sykes, D. Comparison of the effects of chlorpromazine, dextroamphetamine, and methylphenidate on the behavior and intellectual function of hyperactive children. *Canadian Medical Association Journal*, 1971, **104**, 20–25.

Weiss, G., Minde, K. K., Werry, J. S., Douglas, V. I., & Nemeth, E. Studies on the hyperactive child—VIII: Five-year follow-up. *Archives of General Psychiatry*, 1971, **24**, 409–414.

Werry, J. S. Developmental hyperactivity. In S. E. Chess & A. B. Thomas (Eds.), *Annual progress in child psychiatry and child development*. New York: Brunner-Mazel, 1969.

Werry, J., Weiss, G., Douglas, V., & Martin, J. Studies on the hyperactive child III: The effect of chlorpromazine upon behavior and learning ability. *American Academy of Child Psychiatry*, 1966, **5**, 292–312.

Whitehead, P., & Clark, L. Effect of lithium carbonate, placebo and thioridazine on hyperactive children. *American Journal of Psychiatry*, 1970, **127**, 124–125.

Wiltz, N. A., & Gordon, S. B. Parental modification of a child's behavior in an experimental residence. *Journal of Behavior Therapy and Experimental Psychiatry*, 1974, **5**, 107–109.

Wolf, M. M., Hanley, E. L., King, L. A., Lachowicz, J., & Giles, D. K. The timer-game: A variable interval contingency for the management of out-of-seat behavior. *Exceptional Children*, 1970, **10**, 113–117.

Wunderlich, R. C. Treatment of the hyperactive child. *Academic Therapy*, 1973, **8**, 375–390.

Zrull, J. A comparison of chlordiazepoxide, D-amphetamine, and placebo in the treatment of the hyperkinetic syndrome in children. *American Journal of Psychiatry*, 1963, **120**, 590–591.

6. Psychotropic medication with children: an evaluation of procedural biases in results of reported studies

STEPHEN I. SULZBACHER

Studies of clinical uses of psychopharmaceuticals to change behavior in children published between January 1937 and March 1971 were reviewed. The period from January 1968 until March 1971 was exhaustively reviewed by a MEDLARS)medical Literature Analysis and Retrieval System) search, which retrieved 1,163 English and German citations for that 39-month period. Most of the references published prior to 1968 were obtained from original sources and earlier reviews.[1-4] Finally, several additional references were identified through an on-line query to the Epilepsy Abstracts Retrieval System (EARS), although studies relating specifically to seizure control were excluded from the present survey.

The MEDLARS program sorted the studies into three categories: (1) controlled clinical research, (2) comparative studies, and (3) all others. If a study employed two or more drugs, it was classified as a comparative study. However, if a placebo was employed in addition to two or more drugs, then the study was classified as controlled clinical research. The category of controlled clinical research as defined by MEDLARS as including (but not limited to) studies with a preconceived research design which are double or

triple blind, or have some other reference to control of extraneous variables, such as the use of placebos.

The remaining studies were classified as "other" and included typically reports of change in behavior noticed after the administration of a single dosage level of a drug. The search specifically excluded any studies with animals or with human tissue examined *in vitro*.

RESULTS OF THE SURVEY

A total of 1,359 studies were surveyed, of which 560 were discussions of usages of psychotropic drugs which fell outside of the purview of this study. These included biochemical studies, applications of psychoactive drugs in dentistry, obstetrics and anesthesiology, studies concerned only with seizure control in epilepsy, and reports of drug effects in the neonate or teratogenesis.

Table 6-1 summarized the categories within which studies were tabulated. The first methodological sort identified 548 reports which did not contain the word "placebo" and in which only one drug was assessed. Also included in this category as lacking adequate control for subject or

From *Pediatrics*, Vol. 51, No. 3, March, 1973. Copyright 1973, American Academy of Pediatrics.

The author is grateful to Lawrence Halpern, Ph.D., for access to EARS, a new experimental abstracting service of the National Institute of Neurological Diseases and Stroke; to Nancy Blase, MEDLARS search analyst at the University of Washington; and to Ralph Wedgwood, M.D., for his critical reading of the manuscript. The research was supported by Maternal and Child Health Service Project No. 913.

Table 6-1. Summary of surveyed literature (1937–1971)

	Number	Percentage of total (n = 756)
Total number studies surveyed	1,359	
Studies of unrelated (nonbehavioral) effects of psychoactive drugs	–560	
Unavailable reports	– 43	
Total number studies of drug effects on the behavior of children	756	
Uncontrolled studies (no placebos or double-blind)	548	72.5
Controlled studies categorized by dependent variable:		
"Clinical impression" or professional opinion	34	4.5
Rating scale	99	13.1
Standard psychological tests	46	6.1
Direct measurement of behavior	29	3.8
	756	100.0

experimenter bias were 15 studies which employed placebos but were not double-blind and 39 studies which compared two or more drugs but did not use double-blind conditions.

PLACEBOS

The first serious attention to the use of placebos occurred in the early 1950s and coincided almost exactly with the beginning of widespread use of psychopharmaceuticals. Joyce[5] reported no more than 20 papers a year containing the word "placebo" in the literature abstracts during the period 1952 to 1960. Thus, even though only 27.5 % of the studies in the present review employed double-blind and placebo control methods, such studies appear to be on the increase.

There have been reports of significant placebo effects in hyperactive children for whom dextroamphetamine sulfate (Dexedrine) was prescribed.[6,7] Freed[8] found that a placebo effect of approximately 33% was typical in most drug studies of children. It is common to find studies like that by Knights and Hinton[9] in which the net effect of placebos was greater than the effect of the drug, in this case methylphenidate hydrochloride (Ritalin). Out of a total of 40 children in that study, the teachers rated 88% of the methylphenidate group as improved and rated 67% of the placebo group as improved. In other words,

Knights and Hinton found a net effect of the drug of only 21%, as compared to a remarkable 67% placebo effect. Similar effects, but of lower magnitude, were also obtained with the parent ratings on these children. Many of the studies in the present review which did employ placebo groups showed between 20% and 50% improvement with the inert medication; therefore, it is clear that uncontrolled studies must be viewed as preliminary reports and that any assessment of the efficacy of drug therapy should rely heavily on the results obtained in well-controlled studies.

DOUBLE-BLIND

Just as placebos are needed to control subject bias, double-blind conditions (where neither the experimenter-observer nor the subject are aware when the active medication is being administered) are required to control for experimenter bias. This was clearly shown in a review of 35 studies by Glick and Margolis[10] in which 37.5% of the patients were reported as improved with chlorpromazine treatment under double-blind conditions, whereas 70% of the patients were reported improved in comparable studies in which only "single-blind" (experimenter aware but patient unaware) conditions were employed.

Heaton-Ward[11] demonstrated the importance of completely double-blind procedures and also raised some questions about the use of rating scales, which in his study were filled out by the nursing staff on a ward of 24 children. A crossover design was employed in which one of each matched pair of children received drug A during the first half of the experiment and drug B in the second. The staff doing the rating could not discern one tablet from the other but knew when the switch would occur. During the first half of the study a statistically significant difference was found in the ratings which favored the active medication (Niamid). However, at the time when the children were to be crossed over to the other drug, Heaton-Ward told the staff that the children had been switched from one medicine to the other when, in fact, all children continued to receive the same medication they had been receiving during the first half of the study. Nevertheless, the ratings from the second half of the study were completely reversed and revealed a statistically significant difference favoring the placebo. Clearly, this suggests that the person evaluating behavior change must not only be unaware of which medication contains active drug, but must also be unaware of when drug

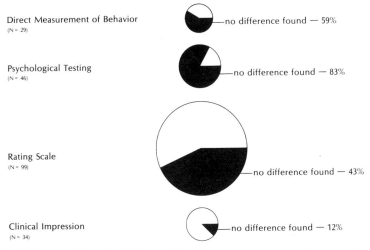

Direct Measurement of Behavior
(N = 29)
no difference found — 59%

Psychological Testing
(N = 46)
no difference found — 83%

Rating Scale
(N = 99)
no difference found — 43%

Clinical Impression
(N = 34)
no difference found — 12%

Figure 6-1. The influence of method of measuring drug response upon the percentage of studies which report significant drug effect. The area of the circles is proportional to the number of studies and the shaded portion of the circles represents the studies which reported no significant effect of medication. Only studies which employed double-blind and placebo controls (total n = 208) are included.

changes occur. Heaton-Ward's results also illustrate the unreliability of rating scales. A more objective measure, in which specific behaviors are counted, might be less susceptible to observer bias.

EXPERIMENTAL DESIGN

As can be seen in Table 6-2, there were totals of 123 studies which employed a between-groups design and 85 studies using a within-subjects, or crossover, design in which each subject served as his own control. The results of the present survey support Kellner's [12] conclusion that there is no difference in likelihood of obtaining a significantly different outcome between these two designs: in the present review 49% of the within-subjects studies found significant differences

compared with 51% of the between-groups studies. However, as Chassan [13] has pointed out, the within-subjects designs typically require fewer subjects to reach the same conclusion.

DEFINING THE DEPENDENT VARIABLE

Criteria for the evaluation of results of psychotherapy have varied from intuitive subjective generalizations of therapists or patients, through rating scales, to objective measures of behavioral change in patients. [14] In Table 6-2, a set of such criterion categories relates the method of response definition to the likelihood of finding statistically significant results. The implication is that an actual count of the frequency of occurrence of an identifiable behavior throughout the course of the treatment is the most accurate mea-

Table 6-2. Analysis of studies by type or design, measurement technique and significance of result

Response measurement technique employed	Significant Difference Favoring the Drug		Results not Significant or Favoring Placebo	
	Within-Subjects Design	Between-Groups Design	Within-Subjects Design	Between-Groups Design
Direct measurement of behavior	8	4	10	7
Standard psychological tests	2	6	12	26
Rating scale	19	37	17	26
"Clinical impression" or professional opinion	13	17	4	0
Totals	42	64	43	59

surement procedure; and that when one is forced to look only at samples of behavior, or make inferences from one sample of behavior to another, one must accept an increasing likelihood of error.[15,16] Therefore, unstructured opinion or "clinical impression" about degree of improvement made before and after treatment is considered to be the least accurate form of measurement of behavior change.

It can be seen that half of the reviewed studies found significant differences favoring a drug, but an equal number did not. In a similar survey of drug studies with neurotic adults,[12] a ratio of about 2:1 was found of significant to nonsignificant results. This trend toward negative results among published studies certainly understates the case for a reinterpretation of the clinical implications for drug treatment, since reports of positive results are much more likely to be published than are studies which fail to find significant differences.

Figure 6-1 illustrates a disturbing inverse relationship between degree of rigorousness in response measurement and percentage of studies finding significant differences. This association between reported significant results and type of measure used to estimate behavioral change is highly significant, both statistically ($X^2 = 42.716$, df = 3, p = .000001) and in its implications for the direction future research should take toward greater use of objective techniques for behavioral measurement.

DISCUSSION

Even though it is overwhelmingly clear that drugs do in fact exert very powerful behavioral influences, the evidence is not very clear as to how this effect is exerted, under what conditions, and on what specific behaviors. Furthermore, even though it is fairly well established that drugs like the amphetamines, and probably others as well, affect children differently from adults,[17–19] there is still no satisfactory explanation of this interaction between age and drug effect.

Another interaction that has not received sufficient attention is that between dosage level and behavioral effect. The failure of most investigators to use standardized dosages (mg/kg of body weight) might account for many of the reported differences in drug response.[4] The intensive study of single subjects, exposing each case to several dosage levels of the drug, appears to be the best methodological approach to this dose-effect problem.[20,21] In fact, the single case design should probably be used for all studies of drug effects, because of the tremendous individual differences known to exist in drug response.

In view of the foregoing considerations, it seems clear that without exercising sustained caution about the influence of procedural biases on the results of studies of the effect of psychotropic medication on children, the practitioner will not find the existing research literature useful or an adequate base from which to make valid judgments about using pharmacologic approaches to learning and behavior disorders in children. Neither the current diagnostic categories nor the global rating scales often used to assess improvement are sufficiently precise to permit any valid conclusions to be reached regarding which patients might benefit in what ways from one or another dose of any given psychotropic medication. Whereas the designs of the more recently published studies show greater attention to experimental rigor, there remains a pressing need for greater objectivity in defining the nature of observed behavioral changes in precise countable terms. Furthermore, it is important that clinically relevant behaviors be used as the criterion for judging the effectiveness of the pharmacologic treatment, since these constitute the therapeutic objective and the only valid reason to consider such medication.

REFERENCES

1. Fish, B.: Methodology in child psychopharmacology. In Edron, D. H., Cole, J. O., Levine, J., and Wittenborn, J. R., eds. Psychopharmacology: A Review of Progress, 1957–1967. Public Health Service Publication 1836:989, 1968.
2. Freeman, R. D.: Drug effects on learning in children: A selective review of the past thirty years. J. Special Education, 1:17, 1966.
3. Millichap, J. G., and Fowler, G. W.: Treatment of "minimal brain dysfunction" syndromes. Pediat. Clin. N. Amer. 14:767, 1967.
4. Sprague, R. L., and Werry, J. S.: Methodology of psychopharmacological studies with the retarded. In Ellis, N. R., ed.: International Review of Research in Mental Retardation. New York: Academic Press, 1971, vol. 5, pp. 148–220.
5. Joyce, C. R. V.: Experiments with control substances. Ann. Rheum. Dis., 20:78, 1961.
6. Holm, V. A., Gode, R. O., Sulzbacher, S. I., and Hedrick, D. L.: A practical strategy for the assessment of drug effects on behavior. Presented at the American Academy of Pediatrics, Chicago, 1968.
7. McDermott, J. F.: A specific placebo effect encountered in the use of dexedrine in a hyperactive child. Amer. J. Psychiat. 121:923, 1965.

8. Freed, H.: The Chemistry and Therapy of Behavior Disorders in Children. Springfield, Ill.: Charles C Thomas, 1962.

9. Knights, R. M., and Hinton, G. G.: The effects of methylphenidate (ritalin) on the motor skills and behavior of children with learning problems. J. Nerv. Ment. Dis., **148**:643, 1969.

10. Glick, B. S., and Margolis, R.: A study of the influence of experimental design on clinical outcome in drug research. Amer. J. Psychiat., **118**:1087, 1962.

11. Heaton-Ward, W. A.: Inference and suggestion in a clinical trial (niamid in mongolism). Journal of Mental Science, **108**:865, 1962.

12. Kellner, R.: The design of drug trials with neurotic patients. Behav. Neuropsychiat. **2**:12, 1970.

13. Chassan, J. B.: Research Design in Clinical Psychology and Psychiatry. New York: Appleton-Century-Crofts, 1967.

14. Jarvik, M. E.: Drugs used in the treatment of psychiatric disorders. *In* Goodman, L. S., and Gilman, A., eds.: The Pharmacological Basis of Therapeutics, ed. 4. New York: MacMillan, 1970, pp. 151–203.

15. Siegel, S.: Non-parametric Statistics. New York: McGraw-Hill, 1956.

16. Stevens, S. S.: Handbook of Experimental Psychology. New York: John Wiley & Sons, Inc., 1951, pp. 1–50.

17. Baker, R. R.: The effects of psychotropic drugs on psychological testing. Psychol. Bull., **69**:377, 1968.

18. Kornetsky, C.: Psychoactive drugs in the immature organism. Psychopharmacologia, **17**:105, 1970.

19. Young, R. D.: Developmental psychopharmacology: A beginning. Psychol. Bull., **67**:73, 1967.

20. Chassan, J. B.: Statistical inference and the single case in clinical design. Psychiatry, **23**:173, 1960.

21. Hollis, J. H., and St. Omer, V. V. Direct measurement of psychopharmacologic response: effect of chlorpromazine on motor behavior of retarded children. Amer. J. Ment. Defic., **76**:397, 1972.

7. Effects of methylphenidate on underachieving children

HERBERT E. RIE   ELLEN D. RIE
SANDRA STEWART   J. PHILIP AMBUEL

It is now generally agreed that methylphenidate hydrochloride (Ritalin) effects behavioral changes in children typically including reduction of activity and distractibility and increase in attention (Conners, 1971; Hoffman, Englehardt, Margolis, Polizoes, Waizer, & Rosenfelt, 1974; Satterfield, Cantwell, Saul, Lesser, & Podosin, 1973; Sleater & von Neumann, 1974; Sroufe, 1975). These observations have led to the use of Ritalin especially with children who are deemed to be "hyperactive." The noted changes are often welcome in the classroom, and the children so treated have been viewed as more amenable to instruction.

Despite this apparent clarity and consensus, significant problems remain. They concern the definition and assessment of activity level, the assumed but uncertain relationships between hyperactivity and organicity and between hyperactivity and achievement, and the assumed but unsubstantiated assumption that Ritalin has a positive effect on scholastic achievement. The present research deals primarily with the last of these and bears implications for the remaining issues.

Hyperactivity—or the hyperkinetic impulse disorder—is not an easily identifiable syndrome (Paine, Werry, & Quay, 1968; Werry, 1968).

There are neither norms nor standard measures of activity in children (Rie, 1975). Current usage often fails to distinguish between hyperkinesis and minimal brain dysfunction, learning disability, and behavior disorder (American Academy of Pediatrics, 1970; Conference Report, 1971; Freeman, 1972; Grinspoon & Singer, 1973; Mackay, Beck, & Taylor, 1973; Sprague & Sleater, 1973). The interchangeability of terms has surely been encouraged by the apparent correlation between hyperactivity and poor school performance. Though the correlation has been questioned (Palkes & Stewart, 1972), learning disability is sometimes viewed as part of the definition of "hyperactivity" (Clements, 1966; Sprague & Sleater, 1973). The sometimes vaguely defined "syndromes" of minimal brain dysfunction and learning disability may or may not be characterized by hyperactivity. The confusion then leads to the use of stimulant medication to contend with problems on which it may not have the same demonstrable effects as it has on activity level.

The use of Ritalin or dextroamphetamine sulfate in the "treatment" of learning disability is a case in point. Such treatment has been encouraged partly by research indicating positive effects on functions such as paired-associate

From *Journal of Consulting and Clinical Psychology*, 1976, *44*, 250–260. Copyright 1976 by the American Psychological Association. Reprinted by permission.

This study and several related studies have been supported by U.S. Health, Education and Welfare Grant MC-R-390065 and are currently supported by Office of Program Evaluation and Research, Ohio Department of Mental Health and Mental Retardation.

learning, continuous performance tasks, orienting response, and concept learning under different reinforcement conditions (Conners, 1971; Conners, Eisenberg, & Sharpe, 1964; Douglas, 1972; Sprague & Sleater, 1973). Yet there seems to be no research on actual scholastic achievement, over an adequate period of time, utilizing a complete achievement test, despite the selection of research subjects by the criterion of learning disability (Spring, Greenberg, Scott, & Hopwood, 1973). In the very limited research reported, the results proved negative (Conners, Taylor, Meo, Kurtz, & Fournier, 1972; Conrad, Dworkin, Shai, & Tobiessen, 1971). Several studies reporting positive effects have relied on screening instruments, from which generalization is hazardous (Finnerty, Soltys, & Cole, 1971; Hoffman et al., 1974). Others appear to have relied solely on teachers' or parents' judgments of achievement or improvement in "performance" that are necessarily influenced by the obvious behavioral changes, if not by biased expectations (Barcai, 1971; Comly, 1971; Conners, Eisenberg, & Barcai, 1967; Denhoff, Davids, & Hawkins, 1971; Sleater & von Neumann, 1974). These changes are suggestive of an attentive, studious task orientation and increase the expectation that learning will occur. A recent study finds neither drug-attributable improvement in acquisition and retention nor evidence of (drug) state-dependent learning, though the tasks were again rather circumscribed (Aman & Sprague, 1974). It is evident that research is badly needed on the effects of stimulant medication on scholastic achievement particularly if it continues to be assumed that learning is contingent on those behaviors that ensue with drug treatment.

Despite doubts cast on the existence of a syndrome of minimal brain dysfunction in hyperactive children and of the necessarily organic etiology of hyperactivity (Minde, Webb, & Sykes, 1968; Werry, 1968; Werry, Minde, Guzman, Weiss, Dogan, & Hoy, 1972; Werry & Sprague, 1970), the use of methylphenidate with organic children has been encouraged. It has even been suggested that among the characteristics distinguishing minimal brain dysfunction children is a common (positive) response to stimulant drugs (Wender, 1971).

Curiously, a recent study comparing the effect of medication on extremely hyperactive and somewhat hyperactive children showed that the former responded *less* favorably (Sleater & von Neumann, 1974). If the grossly hyperactive children can be assumed to be more obviously organic, then organicity would appear to be an inadequate predictor of drug response. Finally, our own observations and those of others (Douglas, 1972) have raised questions about the character of the child's emotional response to Ritalin. These questions remain to be answered.

In summary then, available data are inconclusive at best about the effects of Ritalin on scholastic achievement and about the association between diagnosis and/or etiology on the one hand and drug response on the other. Data are essentially nonexistent on the emotional response to Ritalin.

Our research has been addressed to these issues, seeking to determine the effects of methylphenidate on primary-grade underachieving children with respect to scholastic achievement, behavior, a variety of psychologic functions including affectivity, and medical status. The last two foci, affective response and medical status, are not considered in detail in the present article. All data reported herein derive from a study during the school year of 1972–1973. Additional data from a study during the subsequent school year will enable us to compare hyperactive and nonhyperactive underachievers, and our current study will offer us sufficient data to report on the effects of treatment for the duration of an entire school year.

METHOD

The responses to methylphenidate of underachieving primary-grade children were studied by means of a double-blind, counterbalanced design, with a duration of 12 weeks for each of the two "treatment" conditions—active drug and placebo. Fifteen children received active drug treatment during the first 12 weeks and placebos in the subsequent 12 weeks, and 13 children received the treatments in the reversed order.

Evaluations occurred at the beginning of the study prior to either treatment, after 12 weeks, and again at the end of the study, or 24 weeks after the initial evaluation. At each point, the child was seen by a pediatrician, a psychologist, a psychometrician, and a nurse.

Data obtained included a medical history (with prenatal and perinatal factors), medical and neurological evaluation, assessment of intellectual functioning, scholastic achievement, psychological clinical status, and a variety of other perceptual and cognitive functions (see the Procedure section). A developmental history was obtained, as were ratings of behavior by parent and teacher and a classroom sociogram. On the basis of the child's behavior and performance during each of the evaluations, ratings were made of several functions comprising the organicity-psychogenicity scale and summed to yield an organicity score. This scale (see below) served as a basis for determining whether drug response is elated to initial presumed organicity.

SUBJECTS

The sample consisted of 28 children referred from Children's Hospital, Columbus, Ohio, and local urban and suburban schools. Referral criteria included at least a 6-month deficit in reading achievement; an IQ of 85 or above; enrollment in the primary grades; absence of physical handicap, severe emotional disturbance, and known brain damage; and no prior trials on medication because of underachievement or behavioral problems. The children were also characterized by some attribute such as inattentiveness, distractibility, disruptiveness, or hyperactivity that would presumably be responsive to stimulant medication. Nearly half of the sample (13 of 28) were deemed "hyperactive" by their teacher and/or parent.

The 17 males and 11 females had an initial mean age of 7 years 6 months (range = 6 years 1 month to 9 years 1 month) and an initial mean grade placement of 2 (range = kindergarten to 3 years 4 months). Wechsler Intelligence Scale for Children (WISC) Full Scale IQ ranged from 84 to 124 with a mean of 106.6. Six of the children had been retained in grade, 5 were in special "learning disability" classes, and 9 had tutors while attending regular classes.

The 26 white children and 2 black children were from families whose social status was distributed as follows on the Hollingshead index of social position: Level I = 0%; Level II = 39%; Level III = 39%; and Level IV = 22%. Fathers' and mothers' mean ages were 38.1 and 34.1, respectively, with mean years of education of 14.1 years and 13.1 years, respectively. Four of the children were adopted. Fathers were absent in five families, and family members, in various combinations, were in psychotherapy in six families.

PROCEDURE

On the first visit, following an initial telephone contact, the parents' understanding of the study

was confirmed and their consent for participation obtained. The evaluation included the following: (a) complete history; measurement of height and weight; determination of blood pressure, pulse, and head circumference; visual screening; physical and neurological examination; (b) psychological evaluation; (c) parent conference (clinical child-psychologist and prediatrician); and (d) parental ratings of child's typical behavior.

Medication was prepared and coded by the pharmacy of the University Hospitals of The Ohio State University. The pharmacy assigned each child to active drug or placebo treatment without the knowledge of the project staff. The pharmacy was notified of scheduled reevaluations for "crossover" to the alternate treatment condition.

The initial dose was either 5 or 10 mg per day, depending on the child's size, history of response to medication, and complaints of symptoms likely to occur as side effects of methylphenidate. Based on weekly phone calls and review of side effects, the dose was increased (in the absence of side effects) to no more than 20 mg twice a day, with a few doses being reduced from 10 mg per day to 5 mg per day because of side effects. The mean dose was 21.07 mg per day for a sample with an initial mean weight of 55.65 pounds (25.2 kg). In retrospect, active drug doses were such that seven children received more than 1 mg/kg/day; 15 received .5 to 1.0 mg/kg/day, and 6 received less than .5 mg/kg.

Teachers completed a behavior rating scale and administered a classroom sociogram at each of the three evaluation points. The rating scale was identical to the one completed by parents.

All assessment procedures were repeated after 12 weeks and again after 24 weeks (from the start) except for items or measures that would not be subject to change (e.g., child's history).

After the final (third) assessment of each child, all data were compiled and tabulated and parent conferences were arranged with the clinical child-psychologist. In these extensive and detailed "completion" interviews, the parents were given a report of observed changes during the course of the study; the child's psychological, social and educational status was discussed, and parental understanding and appreciation of his status confirmed; and plans were formulated with the parents for any further care for intervention that was needed. It is noteworthy that no subjects were lost to the study after agreement to participate.

Variables assessed or tests, measures, and

procedures used to generate were as follows: (a) in the medical category or by medical personnel: weight, height, activity (by actometer), neurological signs, Benton Left-Right Discrimination Test, rapid alternating movements, construction task ("tinker toy"), finger twitch, perinatal insults, speech, blood pressure, pulse, side effects, allergies, minor physical anomalies. (b) In the psychological, social, and educational categories: WISC; classroom sociogram (by teacher); Iowa Test of Basic Skills (for achievement); Illinois Test of Psycholinguistic Abilities (four subtests for auditory functioning); Bender Visual-Motor Gestalt Test; Thematic Apperception Test (selected cards for rating by clinical child psychologists on a limited number of dimensions of affectivity); a behavior rating scale, completed independently by parent and teacher; and an organicity-psychogenicity scale completed by the clinical child psychologist.

BEHAVIOR RATING SCALE

The behavior rating scale was developed for use by parents and teachers of children in this and several related studies by the second author. The scale contains 35 items distributed equally among seven subscales intended to elicit judgments of activity level, achievement, attention, disruptiveness, distractibility, need achievement (motivational factors), and sociability. Hence, every subscale contains five items, each of which is rated on a 5-point scale of frequency of occurrence of the behavior to which the item refers. The items are worded so that a high score represents favorable behavior and a low score represents behavior that is generally disapproved in the classroom. For example, a high score on the Activity subscale indicates low activity level (or absence of "hyperactivity"), whereas a high score on the Attention subscale indicates good attentiveness. The sum of the seven subscale scores is the total behavioral score.

Items were selected from countless teachers' reports of children with learning disabilities and classroom behavior problems. All of the negative descriptions were extracted from these reports and grouped by item similarity. Within each group, the most frequently occurring items were selected and five of them ultimately chosen in each category that referred to the most obvious or easily recognizable behavior.

Ratings of children by 43 pairs of parents were obtained for a comparison group—with mothers and fathers rating the same child—as an indication of the reliability of the scale. Despite differences of perspective based on different interactions and relationships with the child, parents constitute the best available judges of a child's typical behavior under more or less comparable conditions.

The mean age and age range of the children and the socioeconomic status of the families were roughly comparable to our experimental sample, although these children were free of behavioral and scholastic problems. For the several subscales and the total behavioral rating, the reliability coefficients were as follows: Activity, .66; Achievement, .65; Sociability, .49; Attention, .63; Distractibility, .71; Need Achievement, .54; Total, .66 ($p < .01$ for all).

Further, "test-retest" reliability was determined for half of the present sample using teachers' ratings prior to treatment and following the initial 12-week placebo period. The other half of the sample received active drug treatment during this period, and hence the behavior (and ratings) was not expected to remain unaltered. Though the correlation between the two ratings might be attenuated somewhat by teachers' awareness that the children were participating in a study, nevertheless, $r = .78$, albeit only with a sample of 13.

ORGANICITY SCALE

The organicity scale is essentially an attempt to quantify clinical judgment about the degree to which certain behaviors occur that are characteristic of organicity and that are most directly related to scholastic performance. They fall in the general category of verbal, symbolic, conceptual, and integrative skills. Since coordination is excluded, this scale of organicity would not reflect presence of cerebral palsy that has not affected mental processes.

Clinical judgments were based on extensive observation of the child throughout a clinical, psychological evaluation involving the assessment of multiple and diverse functions (see Procedure section) by a clinical child-psychologist with approximately 15 years of postdoctoral experience. The total organicity score is the sum of scores on seven items, each with a 5-point range. The items are as follows: (a) *Integrative-synthesizing skills* refer to evidence of the process of organizing, combining, and restructuring data so as to offer the possibility of arriving at a correct solution or conclusion. A high score indicates the presence of these integrative-synthesizing skills. (b) *Perseveration,* in the realm of visually perceived stimuli and verbal expression, refers to evidence of the continued use of a reponse, or of continued response to a stimulus, when it has ceased to be relevant. A high score indicates effective functioning and, hence, little or no evidence of perseveration. (c) *Conceptual shifts* refer to evidence of the child's ability to change his focus from one concept or idea to another, to alter the boundaries or limits of an idea, and to avoid continued preoccupation with a thought which is no longer relevant. A high score indicates ability to shift. (d) *Concrete thinking* refers to evidence that the child is unduly focused or dependent on immediately present stimuli, that he fails to think abstractly or to generalize relative to his age expectation, and that he is excessively literal in his interpretations. A high score indicates absence of these behaviors or evidence of adequate abstract thinking, generalization, and conceptualization. (e) *Word recall* refers to evidence that the child can select and use words with reasonable fluency, that immediate recall of words in a brief interchange is adequate, and that the words the child has available are suitable to the meaning he wishes to convey. A high score indicates adequate word recall, whereas a low score, at the extreme, might be indicative of expressive aphasia. (f) *Word misuse* refers to evidence that the child selects and uses words that are incorrect but bear some irrelevant or tangential relation to the word intended, such as a word having a similar sound or slightly different meaning or one referring to the same general class of objects but to an incorect subgroup (e.g., "Doggie" for animals of different species). A high score indicates no word misuse, whereas a low score indicates frequent misuse. (g) *Compensatory scale* refers to evidence that low scores obtained on the above scales are the consequence of obvious early deprivation, lack of exposure to adequate verbal communication, or emotional and motivational problems. A high score indicates that these nonorganic factors are prominent. This item was included because effects of organic and nonorganic etiologies can appear very similar and, in the absence of a high correlation (coexistence) of these several factors in a given child as an indication of organicity, it is critical to consider the context in which these maladaptive behaviors have developed.

A low total organicity score is therefore indicative of behavior of the kind noted, which is very likely to be the product of neurologic dysfunction. A high score necessarily indicates essential absence of organicity but, in the context of underachievement, implies inadequate exposure, emotional problems, and/or motivational problems. Ilustratively, a score up to perhaps 14 or 15 would imply some degree of organicity (depending on the numerical value); a score in the range of 16 to perhaps 21 or 22 would imply some developmental lag, presence of organic signs that are not pronounced, and difficulty in specifying "organicity"; a score of 23 and above would imply presence of few organic signs, presence of psychosocial problems, and essentially adequate skills of the kind rated in this scale.

A test-retest reliability coefficient of .80 was obtained between behavior ratings 15 weeks apart. For children of this age there is of course some possibility of change in this span of time particularly if symptoms were occasioned by developmental lag. The reliability coefficient is regarded as acceptable.

RESULTS

Correlations were determined among initial (pretreatment) scores of variables falling in the general behavior, achievement, and organicity categories because of the common assumption of coexistence of problems in these areas. Almost all of the correlations among these three categories of variables proved to be of a very low order. There were no indications of other (nonlinear) relationships among the variables in question.

Thus, correlations between parents' ratings of activity, teachers' ratings of activity, arm actometer and leg actometer on the one hand, and total organicity score (as defined in our organicity scale) on the other hand ranged from .07 to .13. A similar pattern was observed in the correlations between the several measures of activity and such "organic indicators" as neurological soft signs, Bender test scores, and left-right discrimination scores. The total organicity score, in turn, showed a moderate, significant relation to several such indices (.47 with perinatal insults; .49 with soft signs; and .39 with left-right discrimination). There is, then, no evidence in this sample of concomitance of hyperactivity and organicity.

Sample selection tended to limit the range of scholastic achievement and hence correlations of achievement with other variables. However, similar low-order and inconsistent correlations between achievement test scores and activity measures are at least suggestive of the absence of a

Table 7-1. Treatment effects on selected dependent variables

	M			
Variable	Pretreat-ment	Placebo	Drug	p
Organicity (total)	19.96	21.22	21.44	
Iowa Test of Basic Skills (grade equivalent)				
Vocabulary	1.14	1.74	1.80	
Word Analysis	.85	1.73	2.17	.001
Reading	.56	1.32	1.44	
Spelling	1.09	1.75	1.77	
Math 1	1.55	2.02	2.09	
Math 2	1.28	1.61	1.82	
Illinois Test of Psycholinguistic Abilities				
Auditory Reception	39.36	37.64	37.12	
Auditory Association	36.96	36.85	39.22	.004
Auditory Sequential Memory	30.48	31.11	32.07	
Auditory Closure	31.89	39.22	38.85	
Bender (deviation)	−1.86	−2.12	−1.64	
WISC				
Verbal IQ	105.79	105.68	105.18	
Performance IQ	106.46	113.57	114.75	
Full Scale IQ	106.64	110.04	110.50	
Comprehension	9.93	10.21	9.64	.019
Behavior scale:Parent ratings				
Activity	17.61	17.79	19.07	.007
Achievement	14.55	15.37	17.32	.003
Attention	17.89	18.21	19.25	.032
Total score	123.18	125.21	132.61	.013
Behavior Scale:Teacher ratings				
Activity	17.14	18.00	19.44	—
Achievement	13.50	14.75	16.71	.008
Attention	15.57	16.68	20.64	
Distractibility	15.64	16.01	18.14	.024
Need achievement	15.72	16.89	18.39	.013
Total score	110.93	117.36	128.12	.047
Classroom sociogram	3.79	4.71	2.89	.067[a]
Activity				
Arm actometer	9.13	9.36	7.38	.017
Leg actometer	8.60	6.38	5.58	.054[a]
Weight	55.65	57.57	56.57	.03
Height	49.73	50.40	50.44	
Pulse	98.64	96.64	102.36	.018
Blood pressure (systolic)	92.07	93.79	97.71	.002
Number of side effects		.93	1.96	.007

Note. Included are all variables showing drug main effect (positive and negative) and additional variables of similar kind or of interest relative to the existing research literature.
[a] Close to but fail to achieve $p < .05$.

strong relation between these two kinds of variables as well.

In sum, at the beginning of the study more active and otherwise behaviorally difficult children and not poorer students (in this sample of underachieving children), nor are they more "organic." The less orgnic children tend to have higher WISC IQs ($r = .52$ for Full Scale IQ and total organicity score). Parents' and teachers' ratings of activity are in reasonable agreement, considering the different conditions under which observation occurs ($r = .58$), though the ratings of achievement by both (with an admittedly small range) show no relation to achievement test scores.

Drug effects were determined by means of analyses of variance with pretreatment scores of the relevant variables and pretreatment organicity scores as covariates. The analyses of covariance were used to preclude the effect on the results of chance differences between the two groups undergoing the two "treatment" conditions in different sequence.

Results are summarized in Table 7-1 indicating which variables were significantly affected by active drug treatment. The several means for placebo and drug treatments were calculated by combining weighted means of the two subgroups of each treatment condition in the counterbalanced design. Variables were included in the table if they showed a drug main effect (positive or negative), if they were of the same general category as a variable showing such effect, or if they confirmed or denied findings and assumptions reported in the literature.

Although the number of variables studied urges caution is interpreting significant effects, there is only a limited number of variables showing such effects, the majority of which fall in the predictable behavioral and physiological categories. These constraints do not apply to the interpretation of the *absence* of positive findings in the critical realm of scholastic achievement.

Among the behavioral effects, measures of *activity* were not entirely consistent. Arm actometer clearly decreased ($p < .017$), leg actometer tended to decrease ($p < .054$), parents' ratings of activity showed significant decrease ($p < .007$), and teachers' ratings failed to reach an acceptable level of significance although teachers' ratings did show a significant order of treatment effect. That is, in contrast to parents, teachers failed to distinguish between treatment groups following the first half of the counterbalanced procedure but did so on final evaluation. Apparently expectation of change in the absence of knowledge about treatment being used initially affected the teachers' (blind) ratings of response to "treatment." Once they observed the contrast between treatments, this apparent bias no longer obtained. The findings support the common observation of drug effect on activity level but raise doubt about the reliability of teachers' ratings under some conditions.

Drug effects were also observed in parents' ratings of increased *attention* ($p < .032$); teachers' ratings of reduced *distractibility* ($p < .024$); and both parents' and teachers' total from the several behavioral ratings, reflecting *general behavioral improvement* ($p < .013$ and $p < .047$, respectively).

Both parents' and teachers' ratings indicated improvement in *scholastic achievement* on active drug treatment. However, there is little support for this conclusion in the achievement test findings that show *no* drug-attributable improvement on vocabulary, reading, spelling, or either math subtest. Only the word analysis subtest showed a significant, positive drug effect ($p < .001$).

Among the several remaining measures, clear drug effects of uncertain meaning were observed on the WISC Comprehension subtest (a *decrease* with $p < .019$), and the Illinois Test of Psycholinguistic Abilities Auditory Association subtest (an *increase* with $p < .004$).

Finally, suggestive drug effects on social behavior were essentially negative. The classroom sociogram indicated a tendency toward less socially acceptable behavior ($p < .067$), whereas teachers' ratings of sociability favored the placebo group after the first course of treatment but not subsequently.

Time effects—or changes that did not occur differentially in response to the treatment conditions—were observed with respect to a small number of variables. Though they may be of little consequence for present purposes, they raise the possibility that such changes might be mistaken for drug effects in the absence of adequate controls.

Among these "time effects" were (a) reduced activity, reflected in arm and leg actometer scores ($p < .038$ and $p < .006$, respectively); (b) less disruptive behavior by parents' ratings ($p < .025$); (c) improvement in all achievement subtest scores except Math 2 (p ranging from $< .001$ to $< .041$); (d) increased WISC Full Scale IQ ($p < .05$); (e) improved Illinois Test of Psycholinguistic Abilities Auditory Association score ($p < .043$); (f) improvement in conceptual shift (organicity scale) ($p < .016$); and (g) less concrete thinking (organicity scale; $p < .003$).

Changes in scores of dependent variables during the active drug treatment periods were correlated with pretreatment scores to determine whether such changes might be predictable from the particular variables studied. Given the large number of correlations relative to the number of subjects, these findings are viewed as suggestive only, requiring future confirmation. Selected correlations are reported in Table 7-2.

The relatively high, significant, negative correlations between a number of pretreatment scores and change in the *same* variables have been omitted. These are viewed as spurious since the opportunity for substantial change was limited to one end of the distribution. In none of the correlations reported in Table 7-2 were the pre-

Table 7-2. Correlations between pretreatment scores and drug response

Drug response	r	Pretreatment score
Activity		
Actometer (arm)	− .46	Actometer (leg)
	− .42	ITPA auditory association
Parent rating	.55*	Organicity total score
	.62*	Word recall
Teacher rating	—	
Attention (parent rating)	.45	WISC
	.48*	Performance IQ
		Full Scale IQ
	.49*	Organicity total score
	.50*	Word recall
	.47	Actometer (leg)
Total behavior rating		Organicity scale
Parent rating	.60*	Total Integrative Ability
	.52*	
	.58*	Word Recall
	.49*	Word Misuse
	.55*	Concrete Thinking
Teacher rating	—	
Achievement (parent rating)	.54*	Organicity total score
	.55*	WISC Object Assembly
Achievement (teacher rating)	—	
IOWA word analysis	.38	Bender deviation score
	.42	Conceptual shifts
ITPA auditory association	− .52*	IOWA Math 1
WISC Comprehension	− .51*	Finger twitch
Sociogram (classroom)	− .44	Parent ratings
	− .51*	Total Achievement
	− .40	Activity
	− .45	Attention

*$p < .01$; for all others, $p < .05$.

treatment scores of the variables in question highly correlated.

As is evident in Table 7-2, there is a tendency for children with initially greater auditory association skills to manifest a greater reduction of arm (actometer) *activity* on medication. Change in *activity* as rated by parents tended to occur in children who were initially viewed as less organic and whose word recall skills were deemed better. Change in *activity* as rated by teachers was not readily predictable from pretreatment measures.

Improved *attention*, as determined by changes in parents' ratings, is somewhat more likely to occur in response to drugs in the brighter and less organic children. The data offer no indication that such change occurs in children who were initially behaviorally more deviant, except to the extent that their leg (actometer) activity tended to be greater.

General *behavioral improvement* during drug treatment, represented by the total parental behavior rating, occurred more often in children who initially functioned more effectively on several items on the organicity scale and who were hence deemed less organic. Similar improvement based on teachers' ratings is moderately correlated only with teacher's pretreatment rating of distractibility. However, the pretreatment scores of these two variables are highly correlated.

Improvement on drug treatment in parentally judged *achievement* tended to occur in children who were regarded initially as less organic. Improvement in teacher-judged *achievement* was related only to pretreatment measures derived from teacher ratings. Since these pretreatment behavioral ratings are relatively highly intercorrelated, none is considered further, for the present, as a predictor of change in the others.

In still greater contrast, changes in standardized tests measures of *achievement* were not significantly correlated with any pretreatment behavioral ratings by parents or teachers. Change in the Word Analysis subtest (the only one affected significantly by drug treatment) tends to be related to two rather circumscribed indexes of organicity that alone do not adequately characterize a child's functioning. The pattern, however, is consistent with the above findings relating to organicity.

Finally, though the classroom sociogram failed to respond significantly to drug treatment, it may be worth noting that those changes that did occur tended to occur in children perceived initially as behaviorally more deviant by parents. In summary, these correlational findings suggest with some consistency that the frequently noted, drug-induced behavioral changes (including improvement in parentally judged achievement) occur somewhat more often in children who are viewed as less organic.

Though the more strictly medical elements will be treated elsewhere, it should be noted that the following drug effects were also observed: suppression (rather than actual reduction) of weight; increase in pulse; increase in systolic blood pressure; and the additional side effects (in order of decreasing frequency) of irritability and lability; loss of appetite; abdominal pain; headache; sleep disturbances; and nausea.

Finally, quite apart from the statistically analyzable findings, our extensive, repeated evaluations permitted some clinical observations as well. Principal among these were the behavioral effects of active drug treatment that we have tentatively subsumed under the heading of "responsivity." Children who were retrospectively confirmed to have been on active drug treatment appeared at the times of evaluation, distinctly more bland or "flat" emotionally, lacking both the age-typical variety and frequency of emotional expression. They responded less, exhibited little or no initiative or spontaneity, offered little indication of either interest or aversion, showed virtually no curiosity, surprise, or pleasure, and seemed devoid of humor. Jocular comments and humorous situations passed unnoticed. In short, while on active drug treatment, the children were relatively but unmistakably affectless, humorless, and apathetic.

DISCUSSION

At the most general level, our findings indicate that one cannot speak meaningfully about the beneficial effects of methylphenidate without specification of the functions affected. Although we observed the commonly reported changes in behavior, we find no support for the assumption

that scholastic achievement ("learning") improves. The contrast between that assumption and our findings may be more apparent than real. With respect to both the duration of study and the measures used to assess achievement, there is no strictly comparable study.

Other studies have relied on impressions of parents and/or teachers and, in a number of cases, on the Wide Range Achievement Test (WRAT). We are compelled to conclude that parents' and teachers' impressions of achievement are not sufficiently reliable and that they may be influenced by more obvious and welcome changes in behavior. In the present study, they are clearly at odds with the more objective findings.

Significant increase has previously been reported in the Reading subtest score of the WRAT in response to stimulant drugs. The subtest is described as a measure of pronunciation and word recognition (Jastak & Jastak, 1965). It is similar to the Word Analysis subtest, which showed improvement in response to methylphenidate in the present study. The skills tapped by these subtests obviously bear little resemblance to reading speed, accuracy, and comprehension, and improvement in these subtests should not be viewed as evidence of general improvement in achievement during drug treatment. Indeed, there is reason to wonder whether the noted WRAT and Iowa Word Analysis changes are not primarily changes in drug-enhanced "performance" rather than the consequence of learning, a question to which some of our current research is addressed.

If Ritalin fails to yield significant improvement in scholastic achievement, it should obviously not be used to "treat" learning disorder. Even when such a problem is accompanied by undesirable behavior that may be affected by the drug, additional intervention is required to contend with the difficulty in learning.

Quite in contrast to the misconception that achievement improves during drug treatment, the drug-attributable relative *decrease* in the WISC Comprehension subtest score may reflect less independent problem solving under the influence of methylphenidate. Although this finding is only suggestive, it is consistent with Sroufe's (1975) observation that no evidence exists to indicate beneficial drug effects on "problem solving, reasoning, (and) non-rote learning." Correlations between the several pretreatment measures of activity and changes in achievement during drug treatment offer no support to the supposition that the more active children show greater improvement on Ritalin. Hence, our essentially negative findings concerning drug effects on achievement do *not* appear to be attributable to the somewhat less hyperactive composition of our sample relative to samples of some other studies.

Our pretreatment correlations lend little support to the presumed coexistence of hyperactivity, minimal brain dysfunction ("organicity"), and learning disorders. The finding is attentuated somewhat by the delimited range of achievement and by the sample size relative to the number of correlations obtained. The initially more active children (by any of the criteria used) prove not to be more organic with respect to verbal, symbolic, conceptual, and integrative skills. Nor are they characterized by more neurologic soft signs, greater Bender deviations, or left-right discrimination problems. A moderate correlation appears only between perinatal insults and one or another criterion of activity level.

However tentatively these findings may need to be expressed, they are consistent with those of Werry (1968) and Paine et al. (1968). The assumption of the coexistence of hyperactivity, minimal brain dysfunction, and learning disability may be the consequence of biased selection and excessive weighting of a few symptoms. Children selected on the basis of *both* hyperactivity and learning problems may unjustifiably be regarded as representative of *either* population. Dramatic changes in one set of functions (e.g., overt behavior) may suggest the inevitability of change in others (e.g., achievement) and encourage the view of general, unspecifie "benefit" or "positive effects." In contrast we found not only an absence of positive drug effect on achievement but the possibility that even the noted behavioral effects are more likely to occur in children who, while initially quite active, are not at the organic end of the continuum.

Though the prior literature offered little reason to study what we have called "responsivity," our clinical observations convince us of the need to do so. The reactions of the children strongly suggest a reduction in commitment of the sort that would seem to be critical for learning. There would then appear to be not only a reduction of the disapproved behaviors that interfere with learning but also of the desirable behaviors that facilitate it. The net effect on learning would presumably be nil, or precisely the findings of the present study.

We are equally concerned about the possible impact of drug-attributable reduction in responsivity on emotional development. It would appear difficult for a child to "learn" to contend with the variety of complex phenomena that are called emotional experiences if there is consistent absence of age-typical impact of such experiences on him. For the present, one can only speculate whether these apparent conditions deprived the child of the opportunity to integrate his emotional experiences and thereby interfere with his ability to adapt to them in increasingly more mature ways.

Finally, we have debated the further study of the effects of Ritalin in light of our results. We necessarily have some misgivings especially about the matter of responsivity. On the other hand, we are cognizant of the continued use of the drug in clinical practice and of our inability, thus far, to speak definitively about the possible negative effects. To be able to do so, or perhaps even to discover that our concerns are unwarranted, would be of greater value. Hence, we have continued our studies, accepting children who, so far as we are able to ascertain, would be treated by the same means in the normal course of events but quite likely without the repeated assessments, careful monitoring, support and guidance, and ultimate interpretation that are a part of our research.

For the present, the issue is clearly not that of the absolute value of methylphenidate hydrochloride, often heatedly advanced or denied, but rather its differential effects on multiple functions. The balance between positive effects on some functions and negative effects on others must determine the use of the drug in any given case, though it is conceivable that the previously emphasized positive effects will, on balance, justify continued use in a much smaller number of children than has been the practice.

REFERENCES

Aman, M. G., & Sprague, R. L. The state-dependent effects of methylphenidate and dextro-amphetamine. *Journal of Nervous and Mental Disease*, 1974, *158*, 268–279.

American Academy of Pediatrics, Committee on Drugs. An evaluation of the pharmacologic approaches to learning impediments. *Pediatrics*, 1970, *46*, 142–146.

Barcai, A. Predicting the response of children with learning disabilities and behavior problems to dextroamphetamine sulfate. *Pediatrics*, 1971, *47*, 73–80.

Clements, S. D. *Minimal brain dysfunction in children: Terminology and identification.* (Phase 1 of a three-phase project, U.S. Department of Health, Education and Welfare, PHS Publication No. 1415)

Washington, D.C.: U.S. Government Printing Office, 1966.

Comly, H. H. Cerebral stimulants for children with learning disorders. *Journal of Learning Disabilities,* 1971, *4,* 484–490.

Conference on the Use of Stimulant Drugs in the Treatment of Behaviorally Disturbed Young School Children. *Journal of Learning Disabilities,* 1971, *4,* 523–530.

Conners, C. K. Drugs in the management of children with learning disabilities. In L. Tarnopol (Ed.), *Learning disorders in children: Diagnosis, medication, education.* Boston: Little, Brown, 1971.

Conners, C. K., Eisenberg, L., & Sharper, L. Effects of Methylphenidate (Ritalin) on paired associate learning and Porteus maze performance in emotionally disturbed children. *Journal of Consulting Psychology,* 1964, *28,* 14–22.

Conners, C. K., Eisenberg, L., & Barcai, A. Effect of dextroamphetamine on children. *Archives of General Psychiatry,* 1967, *17,* 478–485.

Conners, C. K., Taylor, E., Meo, G., Kurtz, M. A., & Fournier, M. Magnesium pemoline and dextroamphetamine: A controlled study in children with minimal brain dysfunction. *Psychopharmacologia,* 1972, *26,* 321–336.

Conrad, W. G., Dworkin, E. S., Shai, A., & Tobiessen, J. E. Effects of amphetamine therapy and prescriptive tutoring on the behavior and achievement of lower class hyperactive children. *Journal of Learning Disabilities,* 1971, *4,* 509–517.

Denhoff, E., Davids, A., & Hawkins, R. Effects of dextroamphetamine on hyperkinetic children: A controlled double blind study. *Journal of Learning Disabilities,* 1971, *4,* 491–498.

Douglas, V. I. Stop, look and listen: The problem of sustained attention and impulse control in hyperactive and normal children. *Canadian Journal of Behavioral Sciences,* 1972, *4,* 259–282.

Finnerty, R. J., Soltys, J. J., & Cole, J. O. The use of d-amphetamine with hyperkinetic children. *Psychopharmacologia,* 1971, *21,* 302–308.

Freeman, R. D. The drug treatment of learning disorders: continuing confusion. *Journal of Pediatrics,* 1972, *81,* 112–115.

Grinspoon, L., & Singer, S. B. Amphetamines in the treatment of hyperkinetic children. *Harvard Educational Review,* 1973, *43,* 515–555.

Hoffman, S., Engelhardt, D. M., Margolis, R. A., Polizoes, P., Waizer, J., & Rosenfelt, R. Response to methylphenidate in low socioeconomic hyperactive children. *Archives of General Psychiatry,* 1974, *30,* 354–359.

Jastak, J. F., & Jastak, S. R. *The Wide Range Achievement Test Manual.* Wilmington, Del.: Guidance Associates, 1965.

Mackay, M. C., Beck, L., & Taylor, R. Methylphenidate for adolescents with minimal brain dysfunction. *New York State Journal of Medicine,* 1973, *73,* 550–554.

Minde, K., Webb, G., & Sykes, D. Studies on the hyperactive child. VI. Prenatal and paranatal factors associated with hyperactivity. *Developmental Medicine and Child Neurology,* 1968, *10,* 355–363.

Paine, R. S., Werry, J. S., & Quay, H. C. A study of minimal cerebral dysfunction. *Developmental Medicine and Child Neurology,* 1968, *10,* 505–520.

Palkes, H., & Stewart, M. Intellectual ability and performance of hyperactive children. *American Journal of Orthopsychiatry,* 1972, *42,* 35–39.

Rie, H. E. Hyperactivity in children. *American Journal of Diseases of Children,* 1975, *129,* 783–789.

Satterfield, J. H., Cantwell, D. P., Saul, R. E., Lesser, L. I., & Podosin, R. L. Response to stimulant drug treatment in hyperactive children: Prediction from EEG and neurological findings. *Journal of Autism and Childhood Schizophrenia,* 1973, *3,* 36–48.

Sleater, E. K., & von Neumann, A. W. Methylphenidate in the treatment of hyperkinetic children. *Clinical Pediatrics,* 1974, *13,* 19–24.

Sprague, R. L., & Sleater, E. K. Effects of psychopharmacologic agents on learning disorders. *Pediatric Clinics of North America,* 1973, *20,* 719–735.

Spring, C., Greenberg, L., Scott, J., & Hopwood, J. Reaction time and effect of Ritalin on children with learning problems. *Perceptual and Motor Skills,* 1973, *36,* 75–82.

Sroufe, L. A. Drug treatment of children with behavior problems. In F. Horowitz (Ed.), *Review of child development research.* Chicago: University of Chicago Press, 1975.

Wender, P. H. *Minimal brain dysfunction in children.* New York: Wiley, 1971.

Werry, J. S. Studies on the hyperactive child. IV: An empirical analysis of the minimal brain dysfunction syndrome. *Archives of General Psychiatry,* 1968, *19,* 9–16.

Werry, J. S., Minde, K., Guzman, A., Weiss, G., Dogan, K., & Hoy, E. Studies on the hyperactive child—VII: Neurological status compared with neurotic and normal children. *American Journal of Orthopsychiatry,* 1972, *42,* 441–451.

Werry, J. S., & Sprague, R. L. Hyperactivity. In C. G. Cotello (Ed.), *Symptoms of psychopathology.* New York: Wiley, 1970.

8. Predicting the response of hyperkinetic children to stimulant drugs: a review

RUSSELL A. BARKLEY

Bradley (1937–1938) is typically credited with being the first to describe the effectiveness of stimulant drugs in the treatment of children's behavior disorders. Since that time, a plethora of research has been conducted on the effects of central nervous system (CNS) stimulant drugs on children, particularly those described as hyperkinetic or minimally brain damaged (MBD). A review of this research (Barkley, 1976a) clearly shows that not all hyperkinetic children respond well to stimulant drugs—indeed the symptoms of some are exacerbated by them. It appears that approximately 75% of hyperkinetic children receiving these drugs respond favorably, while the remaining 25% are unchanged or made worse (Barcai, 1971; Barkley, 1976a; Bradley, 1950; Rapoport, Quinn, Bradbard, Riddle, & Brooks, 1974; Weiss, Minde, Douglas, Werry & Sykes, 1971).

Given that hyperkinetic children respond differentially to the CNS stimulants, it would seem clinically useful to identify those variables which discriminate responders (those who improve) from nonresponders (those who are unchanged or worsened). If this could be done, a clinician would be better able to decide which children should receive stimulant drugs and which should not. Previous attempts at identifying predictors

have focused on a number of variables, several of which appear to have some utility. An overview of these studies is provided in Table 8-1, in which 36 research reports are summarized, covering more than 1,400 children. For each, the authors, the number of subjects, the type of drug studied, the daily dosage administered, and the time the children spent on the drug during the study, as well as information relevant to placebo conditions, are reported. Also noted are the types of experimental designs, the blindness of raters, and the criteria adopted to define improvement. Only those results bearing on the prediction of drug response will be reported. The discussion will be organized according to types of predictor variables investigated in the studies: (1) psychophysiological, (2) neurological, (3) familial, (4) demographic/sociological, (5) diagnostic category, (6) parent/teacher/clinician ratings, (7) psychological, and (8) profile types. The limitations of these studies and of the present review also will be briefly discussed.

PSYCHOPHYSIOLOGICAL PREDICTORS

The most frequently studied psychophysiological variable in the literature dealing with prediction of drug response has been the presence or ab-

From the *Journal of Abnormal Child Psychology*, 1976, *44*, 250–260. Copyright © 1976 Plenum Publishing Corporation. Reprinted by permission.

The assistance of Virginia Douglas, Ph. D., and Douglas G. Ullman, Ph. D., in providing comments on an earlier version of this manuscript is gratefully acknowledged.

Table 8-1. Review of research on predicting stimulant drug response in hyperkinetic children

Authors and Year	Number of children	a. Drug b. Daily dosage c. Time on drug	Use of placebo	Design type[a]	Use of double-blind	Drug response criteria[b]
Arnold et al. (1973)	11	a. l-amphetamine d-amphetamine b. 5–30 mg c. 3 weeks	Yes	Crossed	Yes	Changes in ratings completed by parent, teacher, and psychiatrist.
Barcai (1971)	53	a. d-amphetamine b. 20 mg c. 6 weeks	Yes	Crossed	Yes	Independent staff ratings of response vs. no response based on pre–post drug changes in teacher ratings.
Barkley & Jackson (1976)	14	a. methylphenidate b. 10 mg c. 1 day	Yes	Crossed	Yes	Changes in multiple measures of activity level and attention span from placebo to drug conditions.
Barkley (1976)	18	a. methylphenidate b. 10 mg c. 1 day	Yes	Crossed	Yes	Changes in a variety of measures of activity and attentiveness.
Breitmeyer (1969)	54	a. methylphenidate b. 1.1 and 4.5 mg/kg c. one dose	Yes	Crossed	?	Changes in measures of activity.
Buchsbaum & Wender (1973)	24	a. amphetamine b. 10–20 mg c. 4–8 months	No.	Crossed—on vs. off drugs	No	Clinical judgement of prior drug response.
Burks (1964)	43	a. amphetamine b. ?c c. ?	No	Pre-post drug treatment	No	Changes in teacher ratings
Butter & Lapierre (1975)	32	a. methylphenidate b. 10–30 mg c. 2 weeks	Yes	Crossed	Yes	Improvement in test scores on the Illinois Test of Psycholinguistic Ability and a series of mono-, bi-, and trisensory stimulation detection tests.
Conners (1971)	132	a. methylphenidate d-amphetamine b. 30 mg 15 mg c. 3 weeks	Yes	Uncrossed	Yes	Changes in human figure drawings test.
Conners (1972a)	178	a. stimulant drugs b. ?	?	?	?	?

				records		
(1967)		b. ? c. ?				judged as improved or unimproved.
Denhoff et al. (1971)	42	a. d-amphetamine b. 10 mg c. 3 weeks	Yes	Crossed	Yes	Changes in teacher ratings.
Epstein et al. (1968)	10	a. d-amphetamine b. 10–15 mg c. 2 weeks	Yes	Crossed	Yes	Changes in a variety of medical, psycho-physiological, and psychological dependent measures.
Hoffman et al. (1974)	34	a. methylphenidate b. 20–80 mg c. 12 weeks	No	Pre-post drug treatment	No	Children were judged as "variable" or "consistent" responders using the variability of teacher ratings over the 12 weeks of drug therapy.
Knights & Hinton (1969)	40	a. methylphenidate b. 20–40 mg c. 6 weeks	Yes	Uncrossed	Yes	Judgment of good or poor drug response.
Knopp et al. (1973)	22	a. d-amphetamine b. less than 5 mg c. ?	No	Pre-post drug treatment	No	Changes in electropupillographic responses and ratings made by parents and clinicians.
Loney et al. (1975)	50	a. methylphenidate b. ? c. ?	No	Pre-post drug treatment	No	Psychologist's judgment of drug improvement using parent and teacher reports that all major problems had cleared up.
Lytton & Knobel (1958)	20	a. methylphenidate b. 80–100 mg c. 1 wk. to 4½ mos.	?	Pre-post drug treatment	?	Judged to be good or poor responders based on parental reports, clinician's opinion, and teacher reports.
McConnell et al. (1964)	57	a. d-amphetamine b. 7½ & 15 mg c. 6 days	Yes	Crossed	Yes	Changes in activity level as measured by ballistograph and ward attendants' ratings.
Porges et al. (1975)	16	a. methylphenidate b. 3 mg/kg c. 3 weeks	Yes	Crossed	?	Improvement in reaction time, heart rate variability, and classroom behavior ratings
Rapoport et al. (1971)	19	a. d-amphetamine b. 10 mg c. 3 weeks	Yes	Crossed	No	Changes in a variety of tests and rating scales.
Rapoport et al. (1974)	76	a. methylphenidate b. 30 mg c. 6 weeks	Yes	Crossed	Yes	Psychologist's judgment of improvement.
Rie et al. (1976)	28	a. methylphenidate b. 5–40 mg c. 12 weeks	Yes	Crossed	Yes	Changes in a variety of measures of activity level, achievement skills, intelligence, and parent and teacher ratings.

Table 8-1. Continued

Study	N	Drug / Dose / Duration		Design		Criterion for improvement
Safer & Allen (1975)	84	a. methylphenidate d-amphetamine b. 10–40 mg 4–20 mg c. ?	No	Pre-post drug treatment	No	Children with greater than 50% change in teacher ratings from pre-post drug therapy were judged to be improved.
Satterfield et al. (1972)	31	a. methylphenidate b. ? c. 3 weeks	Yes	Uncrossed	Yes	Judgment of good vs. poor drug response using changes in teacher ratings.
Satterfield et al. (1973)	57	a. methylphenidate b. ? c. 3 weeks	Yes	Uncrossed	Yes	Children with greater than 30% change in teacher ratings from predrug scores were judged as improved.
Schain & Reynard (1975)	98	a. methylphenidate b. 10–60 mg c. 16 weeks	Yes	Uncrossed	Yes	Changes in parent and teacher ratings.
Schleifer et al. (1975)	26	a. methylphenidate b. 2½–20 mg c. 3 weeks	Yes	Crossed	Yes	Changes in a variety of measures of activity level, achievement skills, intelligence, chological tests.
Shetty (1971)	28	a. methylphenidate d-amphetamine b. 20 mg 10 mg c. one intravenous injection then 3 weeks oral ingestion	Yes	Crossed	Yes	Judgment of good vs. poor drug response using changes in subjective and objective measures of activity, impulsivity, performance, and coordination.
Steinberg et al. (1971)	46	a. d-amphetamine b. 10–15 mg c. 4 weeks	Yes	Crossed	Yes	Children whose ratings had changed more than the highest change score from pre-drug to placebo conditions were judged as improved.
Weber & Sulzbacher (1975)	12	a. methylphenidate d-amphetamine b. 12–62 mg/kg	Yes	Crossed	Yes	Changes in classroom behavior ratings.

Study	N	Drug/Dose		Design[a]		Criterion[b]
Weiss et al. (1968)	40		d-amphetamine b. less than 50 mg less than 20 mg c. 4–6 weeks	Yes	Uncrossed	Yes	?
Werry & Aman (1975)	24	a. methylphenidate b. .3 mg/kg c. 3 weeks	Yes	Crossed	Yes	Changes in scores on memory and vigilance tasks.
Werry & Sprague (1974)	37	a. methylphenidate b. .1–1.0 mg/kg c. 4 weeks	Yes	Crossed	Yes	Physician's judgment of good vs. poor drug response.
Zahn et al. (1975)	42	a. methylphenidate d-amphetamine b. ? c. about 2.5 months	No	Pre-post drug treatment	No	Poor responders were children who failed to change a certain amount from pre- to postdrug conditions or whose on-drug ratings were worse than predrug ratings.

[a] The type of experimental design employed in the study. "Crossed" refers to a complete crossover design in which children receive both drug and placebo conditions in a random fashion. "Uncrossed" refers to a design in which children were assigned to either the drug or placebo condition, or the drug or no-drug condition, in the study. "Pre-post drug treatment" refers to a design in which all children were evaluated before receiving drugs and then again while receiving drugs.

[b] This refers to the criterion used in the study to determine whether or not children were good or poor drug responders, or to determine the degree to which the children improved during drug treatment.

[c] A "?" indicates that the information in this column was either not provided in the report or was so ambiguously stated as to be uncertain.

sence of abnormalities in clinical electroen-cephalograms (EEG). The results of research on this variable, however, appear to be equivocal. Satterfield, Cantwell, Saul, Lesser, and Podosin (1973) found that significantly more drug responders had abnormal EEGs as compared to nonresponders. On the other hand, several investigators either have found no relationship between drug response and EEG abnormality (Knights & Hinton, 1969; Lytton & Knobel, 1958; Rapoport et al., 1974; Weiss, Werry, Minde, Douglas, & Sykes, 1968; Weiss et al., 1971) or they report that abnormal EEGs predict poor drug responding (Burks, 1964; Schain & Reynard, 1975). Thus, at this time, there does not appear to be any clearcut evidence of a relationship between EEG abnormality and responsiveness of hyperkinetic children to stimulant drugs.

While not as frequently studied, one aspect of the EEG which has shown a consistent relationship with differential drug responding in hyperkinetic children has been the averaged evoked response (AER). This measure involves recording the effects on the EEG of presenting various patterns of stimuli in one or more sensory modalities. Research with hyperkinetic children has focused on visual and auditory AERs as a neuropsychological means of studying the attentional deficits in these children (Buchsbaum & Wender, 1973). With respect to auditory AERs, research indicates that drug responders have significantly higher baseline (i.e., predrug) AER amplitudes, lower recovery of evoked responses, less change in latency and intensity of AERs with age, and greater variability of AERs as compared to nonresponders (Buchsbaum & Wender, 1973; Satterfield, Cantwell, Lesser, & Podosin, 1972). Furthermore, responders have been shown to have significantly lower off-drug, placebo, and on-drug AER thresholds (Weber & Sulzbacher, 1975) as compared to nonresponders. On visual sine-wave stimulation, both responders and nonresponders show greater right hemisphere occipital AERs but nonresponders and normal children show a decreased hemispheric asymmetry in responding with age. Responders, however, continue to lag behind this developmental pattern and show an increasing right hemisphere predominance of AER with age (Buchsbaum & Wender, 1973). The results of this research indicate that responders show psychophysiological evidence suggestive of an immature central nervous system (Buchsbaum & Wender, 1973; Satterfield et al., 1972). Further

research is necessary, however, before such a conclusion can be drawn safely.

Satterfield et al. (1972) also have examined other aspects of the EEG and found responders to have higher baseline resting EEG amplitudes, range of amplitudes, EEG power, and EEG movement artifacts as compared to nonresponders. On drugs, responders also differed in displaying no increase in resting EEG power whereas nonresponders did show such an increase. Shetty (1971) also studied various aspects of the clinical EEG in hyperkinetic children and found that responders showed an increase in alpha rhythm during drug treatment while nonresponders did not. These results support the notion that responders are somehow psychophysiologically different from nonresponders but do not clearly support any one explanation for this difference.

Another psychophysiological measure examined in this research is the skin conductance response (SCR). Only two studies used this variable and their results were contradictory. Satterfield et al. (1972) found responders to have SCRs which were lower than those of normal children and much lower than those of nonresponders. These findings are consistent with the possibility that the hyperkinetic drug responders are centrally underaroused. Zahn, Abate, Little, and Wender (1975), however, found responders to have lower SCRs as well as slower rises and recovery of SCRs, smaller and longer latency of specific SCRs to tones in a reaction time task, and greater increases in SCR recovery while on drugs. These results suggest that the responders of Zahn et al. (1975) are autonomically overaroused rather than underaroused as found by Satterfield et al. (1972). Thus, with respect to SCR, no conclusions about the level of autonomic arousal of responders or the predictive utility of this measure can be drawn at this time.

Various aspects of heart rate also have been studied for their predictive utility. Porges, Walter, Korb, and Sprague (1975) found that responders had significantly lower baseline heart rate levels, a significantly greater increase in heart rate while on drugs, and a significantly greater reduction in heart rate variability while on drugs as compared to nonresponders. These results suggest that responders are autonomically underaroused in comparison to nonresponders or normal children. However, Barkley and Jackson (1976) obtained just the opposite results when mean predrug heart rate levels were correlated with change scores representing degree of improvement on a variety of measures of activity level and attention span during drug treatment. It was found that mean predrug heart rate correlated significantly with reduction in ankle activity in free play and wrist activity during a testing session. As with measures of skin conductance, these results do not permit any clearcut conclusions to be drawn with respect to the level of automatic arousal of drug responders or the utility of heart rate as a predictor of drug responsiveness.

Two studies were found which examined heart rate deceleration as a predictor of drug responsiveness in hyperactive children. Zahn et al. (1975) found no difference between good and poor drug responders in heart rate deceleration immediately prior to the response signal on a reaction time task. Similarly, Porges et al. (1975) found no relationship between heart rate deceleration on a delayed-reaction time task and response to drug treatment. Heart rate deceleration, then, has yet to prove itself a useful predictor of drug responding in hyperkinetic children.

Using a different psychophysiological measure, Barkley and Jackson (1976) attempted to correlate mean predrug levels of respiration with degree of improvement on a number of measures of activity level and attention span during drug treatment. Results indicated that mean predrug rate of respiration was negatively related to improvement in wrist and seat movement activity during observation of a televised school lesson and to improvement in the amount of time the child did not visually attend to that lesson. However, mean predrug rate of respiration was found to positively correlate with improvement in toy-change activity during a restricted play setting. (Restricted play refers to a setting in which a child is instructed to play in only one part of a large playroom and with only one of a variety of toys available for play.) Results suggested that the higher the predrug rate of respiration, the greater the improvement in toy-change activity during the restricted play period. Thus, depending on which objective measure of activity or attentiveness one uses as a criterion of drug improvement, predrug respiration can be found to be either positively or negatively related to such improvement in hyperactive children.

Another promising psychophysiological measure of drug response is the electropupillogram (EPG). Knopp, Arnold, Andras, and Smeltzer (1973) measured the changes in dark-adapted pupil diameter in response to light in hyperki-netic children both before and after administration of dextroamphetamine. Changes in EPG from predrug to on-drug phases were found to correlate significantly with parental ($r = .59$) and clinician ($r = .41$) ratings of improvement. These children were then categorized into five groups based upon their EPG responses. These five groups differed from each other in the percentage of children showing behavioral improvement as reflected in parental and clinician ratings. Approximately 23% of the hyperkinetic children were found to have high predrug electropupillary contractions suggesting overaroused EPG responses, while 36% had low electropupillary contractions indicating the possibility of underarousal. Both of these groups changed significantly during drug treatment in becoming closer to the mean EPG response of normal children and both were rated as more improved than the other groups of children. Children with normal EPG responses which did not change significantly during drug treatment also did not change significantly in behavioral ratings by parents and clinicians. A fourth group of hyperkinetic children were somewhat underaroused in EPG and changed very little with respect to on-drug EPG. These children were also rated as having worsened behaviorally during drug treatment. The fifth category consisted of only one child whose EPG response was the smallest in deviating from the mean of normal children but whose response became very sensitive or reactive when placed on a CNS stimulant. Little behavior change was reported for this child. Thus, Knopp et al. (1973) appear to have found a method of discriminating between groups of drug responders and nonresponders on the basis of their autonomic arousal levels, as inferred from their EPG responses.

Yoss (personal communication, 1975) and Yoss and Moyers (1971) also have studied the EPGs of hyperkinetic children both on and off CNS stimulant drugs and have found 25% to 35% of these children to have narcoleptic or underaroused EPG responses while off drugs. When they are placed on stimulant drugs, the level of EPG arousal in these children is significantly increased. Coupled with the findings of Knopp et al. (1973), these results suggest two conclusions. First, hyperkinetic children appear to be heterogeneous in their autonomic arousal level as reflected in EPG responses, with those who are either under- or overaroused responding favorably to CNS stimulants. Those children with EPGs approximating normal children appear to respond poorly or not at all to stimulant medication. Second, the EPG, as a measure of arousal and a correlate of attention span (Hakerem, 1970), shows promise as a discriminator of good from poor drug responders.

Related to the research into psychophysiological correlates and drug responding is a study by Epstein, Lasagna, Conners, and Rodriguez (1968) which found that responders have a higher mean percentage of free amphetamine recovery from their urine than do nonresponders. This may account for their finding that responders were able to tolerate higher doses of amphetamine with fewer side effects than nonresponders. The study, however, has yet to be replicated.

Other psychophysiological variables investigated but found to have no discriminative validity in this area are skin temperature, blood pressure, and pulse rate (Epstein et al., 1968; Zahn et al., 1975).

In summary, in the category of psychophysiological predictors, EEG averaged evoked responses, other EEG parameters, heart rate, heart rate variability, EPGs, and free amphetamine recovery from urine have been reported to discriminate good from poor drug responders. Of these variables, all but urine recovery of amphetamine probably bear some relationship to attention span. This relationship between correlates of attention span and drug response in hyperkinesis appears repeatedly throughout this review and is perhaps due to the fact that CNS stimulants seem to have their major effect on the attention span or concentration of hyperkinetic children (Barkley, 1976a; Conners, 1972b; Douglas, 1972; Werry, 1970).

NEUROLOGICAL PREDICTORS

One of the more commonly studied neurological variables has been the number of "soft" signs found during a neurological examination. Satterfield et al. (1972) found that hyperkinetic children with four or more soft signs had a more favorable response to CNS stimulants than those with no soft signs. As noted earlier, they also found a positive relationship between EEG abnormality and drug response. Ranking the hyperkinetic children on the extent of abnormality on both of these measures, Satterfield et al. (1973) found an interaction suggesting a high correlation between degree of "soft" neurological and EEG abnormality and drug response. This evidence was interpreted as indicating a more favorable response to stimulants among those children

with evidence suggestive of organic brain damage. Similar results with respect to neurological soft signs have been found by Steinberg, Troshinsky, and Steinberg (1971) and Conrad and Insel (1967). However, other investigators (Rapoport et al., 1974; Weiss et al., 1968, 1971) have found no association between extent of neurological soft signs and drug response in hyperkinetic children. Thus, the predictive utility of neurological soft signs is uncertain at this time.

Several investigators have categorized hyperkinetic children as "organic" or "nonorganic" using evidence (developmental, neurological, cognitive, historical) suggestive of organic impairment. Epstein et al. (1968) found that "organics" showed greater improvement in Porteus Maze performance, parental evaluations, and psychiatric interview ratings while on stimulants as compared to "nonorganics." These "organics" were the same drug-responding children who had greater free amphetamine recovery from their urine and fewer side effects while tolerating higher drug dosages than "nonorganics." Weiss et al. (1968) also noted a trend for children with a history suggestive of brain damage to have a better drug response. However, Knights and Hinton (1969) found no differences between groups of hyperkinetic children categorized in a manner similar to the Epstein et al. (1968) groups. Further, Rie, Rie, Stewart, and Ambuel (1976) found cognitive measures of organicity to be negatively related to stimulant drug response. That is, children who were less "organic" showed more improvement in parental ratings of activity level, achievement, and general behavior.

It is tempting, though premature, to take these results in conjunction with those for neurological soft signs and abnormal EEGs and suggest that the greater the evidence for neurological impairment, the more likely the hyperkinetic child is to respond favorably to stimulant drugs. Further research is needed, however, to clarify the role of "organicity" in the prediction of drug responsiveness.

Another potentially useful measure of drug response is Barcai's (1971) finger twitch test. In this test, the child is asked to sit with his hands hung between his knees to see how long he can maintain this posture without moving his hands or fingers. His score is the time between test onset and the first brisk finger movement. Coupled with the results of a personality assessment procedure to be reviewed later, Barcai (1971) was able to correctly predict 21 of 23 responders and 15 of 16 nonresponders. Rapoport et al. (1974) also found this simple test to accurately predict response to methylphenidate. If future research continues to replicate this finding, a very simple test may have been discovered which can predict differential responding of hyperkinetic children to stimulant drugs.

At first glance, this simple test appears to be associated with motor inhibition and extrapyramidal signs of neurological impairment. A closer look at the instructions to the child also suggests that it may involve that aspect of attention span known as "maintenance of set." However, whether it is the motor or the attentional aspects of this test which underly its usefulness as a predictor is uncertain at this time.

FAMILIAL PREDICTORS

Several research reports have examined the relationship between familial variables and drug response. Loney, Comly, and Simon (1975) judged the parents of hyperkinetic children as either good or poor managers of their children. They found that good managers had a significantly greater number of drug responders than poor managers. The results of Schleifer, Weiss, Cohen, Elman, Cvejic, and Kruger (1975) appear to contradict this finding in that they found mothers of children who were rated as extremely hyperactive used more physical punishment and were more "frustrated" than mothers of children rated as less hyperactive. Yet, these extreme hyperactive children showed the best response to drugs. In agreement with the findings of Loney et al. (1975), however, Weiss et al. (1971) and Conrad and Insel (1967) noted that hyperkinetic children rated as having better mother-child relationships also had a greater number of drug responders than those with poor relationships. Additionally, Conrad and Insel (1967) found that a group of children living with at least one parent rated as "grossly deviant" or "socially incompetent" had significantly fewer responders than a group of children without such a parent. With the exception of the data reported by Schleifer et al. (1975), these results appear to indicate that a child is more likely to respond favorably to stimulant medication when the parents are competent, good managers, and able to maintain a positive relationship with the child. Just exactly how such variables influence drug responding is uncertain nor is the direction of causality in these relationships very clear. Do drug responders

create better parent-child relationships or is the opposite the case?

DEMOGRAPHIC/SOCIOLOGICAL PREDICTORS

A number of studies have examined demographic and sociological predictors such as age, race, sex, and socioeconomic status for their utility in determining drug responses in hyperkinetic children (Buchsbaum & Wender, 1973; Butter & Lapierre, 1975; Hoffman, Engelhardt, Margolis, Polizos, Waizer, & Rosenfeld, 1974; Safer & Allen, 1975; Schain & Reynard, 1975; Werry & Sprague, 1974; Weiss et al., 1968, 1971). The only variables for which positive results have been found are age at the time the child began drugs and age at time of testing. Contradictory results have been reported for both variables. While not tested for statistical significance, the data reported by Schain and Reynard (1975) were interpreted as suggesting a trend for poor drug responders to be older at the time they began drug treatment. Safer and Allen (1975), on the other hand, found no support for any relationship between drug responsiveness and age at which medication was started.

As for the variable of age itself, Butter and Lapierre (1975) divided their hyperkinetic children into three groups on the basis of chronological age and found that older hyperactives (ages 10.4 to 12.6 years) made significantly fewer errors on a trisensory stimulation test when they were receiving drugs than when they were on placebo. This pattern of results was not observed for younger hyperactives. Buchsbaum and Wender (1973) also found an effect of age on visual AERS for good and poor responders (see section on Psychophysiological Predictors). Thus, the variable of age appears to influence drug response on some measures, although its utility as a predictor is unclear.

DIAGNOSTIC CATEGORY PREDICTORS

Several research reports have looked for differences in responsiveness to drugs among various diagnostic categories. The vast majority of these studies examined differences among the three diagnostic subcategories advocated by Fish (1971). These subcategories are: "unsocialized aggressive," "hyperkinetic," and "overanxious reactions to childhood." In an investigation of drug response to l-amphetamine and d-amphetamine, Arnold, Kirilcuk, Corson, and Corson (1973) compared MBD children diagnosed as unsocialized aggressive with a group composed of both hyperkinetic and overanxious children. They found that the unsocialized aggressive children responded as well to both amphetamine isomers but that d-amphetamine was more effective with the hyperkinetic and overanxious children.

Knopp et al. (1973) studied the response to drugs of children who were assigned to groups using Fish's diagnostic system. They found differences among the three groups on both predrug and on-drug EPGs. Unsocialized aggressives were observed to have predrug electropupillary contractions suggestive of underarousal which were reduced during drug treatment. Hyperkinetic children tended to have smaller than normal predrug electropupillary contractions indicating overarousal, with these contractions being increased or "normalized" by stimulant drugs. Only 14% of the total subject sample were labeled overanxious and these children tended to show normal predrug EPGs with little change in EPG while on drugs. Werry and Aman (1975), however, compared MBD children diagnosed as unsocialized aggressive with those diagnosed hyperkinetic and found no significant differences between them on several memory and vigilance tasks. It appears, therefore, that differences among Fish's diagnostic categories have not been consistently found, although the data of Knopp et al. (1973) and Arnold et al. (1973) are encouraging in that they suggest possible psychophysiological differences among these groups. Further research into the diagnostic categories may prove helpful.

Using a different diagnostic system, Conrad and Insel (1967) divided their hyperkinetic children into three groups according to the presence or absence of emotional pathology (unspecified) and the number of neurological soft signs present. "Organics" were those children with three or more soft signs, while "organic-emotionals" were those with two or more soft signs and emotional pathology, and "emotionals" were those without soft signs but with emotional pathology. The "organic" group contained a significantly greater number of drug responders than the other two groups which suggested that the presence of emotional pathology might predict a poor response to stimulant drugs. This notion, however, has yet to be tested and confirmed by other investigators.

RATING SCALE PREDICTORS

Several studies provided parents, teachers, and clinicians with the opportunity to rate hyperkinetic children on their home and classroom behavior, as well as on other dimensions, and these ratings were subsequently used to predict improvement on CNS stimulants. With respect to parental ratings, the results are equivocal. Hoffman et al. (1974) used the variability in teacher ratings over a 12-week drug-treatment interval to divide hyperkinetic children into "variable" and "consistent" responders. Parents completed the Werry-Weiss-Peters Activity Rating Scale and the Conners Parent Symptom Questionnaire (PSQ). Only the initial predrug scores on five of the PSQ categories discriminated "consistent" from "variable" responders. "Variable" or unstable drug responders were found to have higher scores on the scales of conduct problems, hyperactivity-impulsivity, learning problems, and perfectionism. Other investigators, however, have not found parental ratings to be particularly useful in predicting drug responsiveness (Barkley, 1976b; Rapoport et al., 1971, 1974; Rie et al., 1976; Werry & Sprague, 1974; Zahn et al., 1975).

Similarly, studies using teacher rating scales have not been consistently useful in predicting drug response. Denhoff, Davids, and Hawkins (1971) divided learning-disabled children into groups of "probable" and "nonprobable" hyperkinetic children using scores from the Davids Rating Scale of Hyperkinesis as completed by teachers. The former group had scores of four or more on each of the six subscales of this questionnaire while the latter consisted of the remaining children. Denhoff et al. (1971) found that "probable" hyperkinetics showed significantly greater improvement in teacher ratings that "nonprobable" hyperkinetics. Steinberg et al. (1971) found similar results using children classified in a similar manner. Schleifer et al. (1975) also used teacher ratings to divide hyperactive children into "extreme," "moderate," and "low" groups. Extreme hyperactives tended to show greater on-drug improvement in the frequency with which they were observed to leave their chairs during nursery school as compared to the other two groups of children. However, other researchers (Hoffman et al., 1974; Rapoport et al., 1971, 1974; Rie et al., 1976; Werry & Sprague, 1974) have not found teacher ratings to be useful predictors of drug responding.

A similar state of affairs exists for clinician ratings of children's behavior. Butter and Lapierre (1975) assigned subjects to high, medium, and low hyperactive groups on the basis of ratings made by three psychiatrists using the Davids Rating Scale of Hyperkinesis. "High" hyperactives were found to improve more from drugs than the other two groups on the Illinois Test of Psycholinguistic Ability, on an auditory and visual monosensory stimulation test, and on a simultaneous bisensory stimulation test.

In another study, Barcai (1971) compared good and poor drug responders on clinician ratings of nine personality characteristics which were assessed during a psychiatric interview. Differences were found between the groups in six of nine rated areas. Good responders were rated higher on "excessive body movement" and lower on "ability to abstract and use imagination," "adjustment to societal values," "sense of perspective," "good language ability," and "planning" than poor responders. Coupled with his finger twitch test, Barcai was able to correctly predict 21 of 23 responders and 15 of 16 nonresponders.

A study by Zahn et al. (1975) also found clinician's ratings to be useful in predicting differential drug responsiveness. Hyperkinetic children were rated on a scale intended to measure "acting out," "anxiety," and "inattention." Prior to medication, poor drug responders were rated as having higher anxiety and acting out scores than good responders. This finding is consistent with the previously mentioned results of Conrad and Insel (1967), who found that children with primarily emotional pathology are poorer responders to stimulant drugs than those without such pathology. It is also in keeping with the finding that of the three diagnostic categories defined by Fish (1971), the anxious and aggressive groups tended to be the poor responders. Thus, perhaps highly aggressive and anxious children do not respond as well as inattentive or hyperkinetic children to CNS stimulant drugs. Knopp et al. (1973), as noted earlier, found EPG differences among these diagnostic categories which suggested that a basic physiological difference might mediate the differential response to drugs of hyperkinetic children. While clinician's ratings were found to be of some use in the above studies, other investigators (Hoffman et al., 1974; Lytton & Knobel, 1958; Rapoport et al., 1974; Werry & Sprague, 1974) have not found such relationships.

An obvious flaw in many studies using rating scales is the absence of empirical proof that the scales measure the constructs they purport to assess. Since little research has been conducted to uncover the relationships between rating scales and more objective measures, it is difficult to ascertain what these scales do measure. For instance, while intended to measure some aspect of children's activity level, the Werry-Weiss-Peters Activity Rating Scale has not been found to correlate with more objective measures of activity level (Barkley & Ullman, 1975). Such ambiguity makes it difficult to determine which variable(s) the parents, teachers, and clinicians are using when they judge hyperkinetic children to be improved on drugs. It is also difficult to compare the results of studies which used different rating scales. Thus, the conclusions that can be drawn in this section must be limited to noting that empirical validation of these scales is needed and that parent, teacher, and clinician ratings of behavior have so far proved inconsistent in their ability to predict response to drugs in hyperkinetic children.

PSYCHOLOGICAL PREDICTORS

A substantial amount of research has examined the ability of a variety of psychological measures to predict drug responding in hyperkinetic children. Most of these have not proven useful. These include the *Wechsler Intelligence Scale for Children* (Buchsbaum & Wender, 1973; Hoffman et al., 1974; Knights & Hinton, 1969; Rapoport et al., 1971, 1974; Satterfield et al., 1972; Weiss et al., 1968; Werry & Sprague, 1974; Zahn et al., 1975), *Wide Range Achievement Test of Psycholinguistic Ability* (Satterfield et al., 1972), *Motor inhibition and body boundary tests* (Hoffman et al., 1974), *Goodenough Draw-A-Man Test* (Rapoport et al., 1971, 1974; Satterfield et al., 1972; Weiss et al., 1968; Zahn et al., 1975), *Playroom activity ratings and measures* (Breitmeyer, 1969; Rapoport et al., 1971, 1974; Schleifer et al., 1975), *Self-concept tests* (Rapoport et al., 1974), *Burt Reading Test* (Werry & Sprague, 1974), *Witkin Rod and Frame Test* (Buchsbaum & Wender, 1973; Zahn et al., 1975), *Child's Manifest Anxiety Scale* (Rapoport et al., 1971), *Short-term memory tests* (Weary & Aman, 1975), *Loney Draw-A-Car Test* (Loney et al., 1975), *Motor steadiness and fine motor coordination tests* (Knights & Hinton, 1969), *Lincoln Oseretsky Motor Development Test* (Satterfield et al., 1972; Weiss et al., 1968), the *Primary Mental Abilities Test* (Weiss et al.,

1968), and the *Bender Visual Motor Gestalt Test* (Knights & Hinton, 1969; Rapoport et al., 1971, 1974; Satterfield et al., 1972; Weiss et al., 1968; Zahn et al., 1975).

Exceptions to these findings were observed in a recent study by Rie et al. (1976) in which WISC full-scale and performance IQs were found to be predictive of improvement in parental ratings of attention, WISC object assembly scores were predictive of improvement in teacher ratings of achievement, ITPA scores on auditory association were related to improvement in actometer measures of arm activity, and leg actometer scores were positively related to improvement in parental ratings of attention but negatively related to improvement in arm activity. These tests, then, appear to be inconsistent in their ability to predict drug responses in hyperkinetic children.

However, the following psychological variables were found to have some predictive utility in discriminating good from poor drug responders: number of toy changes in free play (Rapoport et al., 1971), reaction time (Porges et al., 1975; Zahn et al., 1975), Porteus Mazes (Epstein et al., 1968; Rapoport et al., 1971), Kagan Matching Familiar Figures Test (Rapoport et al., 1974), and WISC Verbal IQ (Epstein et al., 1968). With the exception of WISC Verbal IQ, all of these measures found to predict drug response have been regarded as having some relationship to attention span (Barkley & Routh, 1974; Douglas, 1972, 1974; Pope, 1970; Routh, Schroeder, & O'Tuama, 1974; Sroufe, Sonies, West, & Wright, 1973; Zahn et al., 1975). Thus, it seems that those psychological measures associated with attention span have been found to be the most sensitive predictors of differential drug response in hyperkinetic children.

In an attempt to directly address this hypothesis, Barkley (1976b) used a wide variety of measures of activity level and attentiveness or concentration in an effort to predict improvement on these measures during drug treatment. Results indicated that pretreatment levels of activity were positively related to improvement in activity level during drug treatment. That is, the higher the child's initial activity level, the greater the improvement displayed by that child in activity level. This probably resulted from the significant interrelations among these measures of activity level. However, pretreatment levels of attentiveness or concentration were found to significantly predict improvement not only in attentiveness but in activity level as well. Thus, the

more inattentive the hyperkinetic child was initially, the greater was his improvement in attention span or concentration and the greater his reduction in activity level during treatment with methylphenidate. Apparently, then, measures of attention span appear to be the most promising predictors of drug responsiveness in hyperkinetic children.

PROFILE TYPE PREDICTORS

In an attempt to identify those characteristics of hyperkinetic children which predict their favorable response to stimulant drugs, Conners (1971, 1972a) correlated and factor analyzed the results for a substantial number of psychological tests, rating scales, physiological measures, and objective behavior measures. This analysis yielded seven distinct profile patterns that account for a significant amount of drug treatment effects among the large number of hyperkinetic children sampled (See Conners, 1971, 1972a). In general, profiles containing measures of inattentiveness or the inability to concentrate, or the psychophysiological correlates of these abilities, were the best predictors of drug improvement. However, further research is needed to cross-validate these profile patterns before their utility as drug response predictors can be established.

LIMITATIONS OF THIS REVIEW

Before attempting to draw conclusions from the results of research in this area, it is important to briefly mention certain limitations placed upon such conclusions as a result of differences across the studies being reviewed. These limitations appear to be: (1) differences in the definitions used to select hyperkinetic subjects, (2) differences in the drug types, dosages, and time on-drugs, (3) differences in the type of experimental designs and control procedures, (4) differences in the measuring techniques used to assess the same construct, and most importantly (5) differences in the criteria used to define improvement in hyperkinetic children during drug treatment. Obviously, the likelihood of finding a child "improved" on stimulant drugs depends, to some extent, on the manner in which these investigators chose to deal with these limitations. To the extent that differences in their procedures resulted in discrepancies in the results of these studies, the conclusions drawn from these findings are also limited.

CONCLUSIONS

Taking these limitations into consideration, the results of this review indicate that a number of variables are related to the drug responsiveness of hyperkinetic children. In general, those variables which have been consistently found to predict improvement during stimulant drug treatment appear to be those related to attention span or concentration. This is particularly apparent in those research reports utilizing psychophysiological or psychological measures as drug response predictors. The former have found such measures as average evoked responses in the EEG, other EEG parameters, heart rate, heart-rate variability, rate of respiration, and electropupillogram responses to be useful predictors of drug responding. Most of these measures have also been noted to have some relationship to attentional processes in children (Buchsbaum & Wender, 1973; Hakerem, 1970; Knopp et al., 1973; Porges et al., 1975; Satterfield et al., 1972; Sroufe et al., 1973; Yoss & Moyers, 1971). As for psychological predictors, measures of toy-change activity, reaction time, maze coordination, Porteus Mazes, and the Matching Familiar Figures Test appear to have some utility in predicting drug responsiveness. Here, too, such measures have been regarded as measures of attention span or concentration in hyperkinetic children (Barkley & Ullman, 1975; Conners, 1972b; Douglas, 1972, 1974; Pope, 1970; Sroufe et al., 1975). Thus, measures of attention span and its correlates seem to be the most promising predictors of drug responding in hyperactive children.

This conclusion is not surprising given that research on the effects of stimulant drugs and hyperkinesis finds attention span or concentration to be the variable most affected by these drugs (Barkley, 1976a; Barkley, 1976b; Conners, 1972b; Douglas, 1972, 1974). It would be expected, then, that variables related to attention span would also prove the most useful in predicting stimulant drug responding in hyperactive children.

The results of this review have also suggested other avenues which future research might wish to pursue. Further study of the extent to which the presence or absence of organic impairment or emotional pathology contributes to drug responsiveness is needed. The determination of the empirical correlates of the commonly used parental, teacher, and clinician rating scales would be another direction for future research. An additional one would be the cross-validation of the profile types of Conners (1972a) or the diagnostic categories of Fish (1971). Certainly, further research on the ability of measures of attention span to predict the response of hyperactive children to stimulant drugs is also required.

REFERENCES

Arnold, E., Kirilcuk, V., Corson, S., & Corson, E. Levoamphetamine and dextroamphetamine: Differential effect on aggression and hyperkinesis in children and dogs. *American Journal of Psychiatry,* 1973, *130,* 165–170.

Barcai, A. Predicting the response of children with learning disabilities and behavior problems to dextroamphetamine sulfate. *Pediatrics,* 1971, *47,* 73–80.

Barkley, R. A review of stimulant drug research with hyperactive children. *Journal of Child Psychology and Psychiatry,* 1976 (in press). (a)

Barkley, R. *The prediction of differential responsiveness of hyperkinetic children to methylphenidate.* Unpublished doctoral dissertation, Bowling Green State University, Ohio, 1976. (b)

Barkley, R., & Jackson, T. *The effects of methylphenidate on the autonomic arousal, activity level, and attention span of hyperkinetic children.* Unpublished manuscript, Bowling Green State University, Ohio, 1976.

Barkley, R., & Routh, D. Reduction of children's locomotor activity by modeling and the promise of contingent reward. *Journal of Abnormal Child Psychology,* 1974, *2,* 117–131.

Barkley, R., & Ullman, D. A comparison of objective measures of activity and distractibility in hyperkinetic and nonhyperkinetic children. *Journal of Abnormal Child Psychology,* 1975, *3,* 231–244.

Bradley, C. The behavior of children receiving Benzedrine. *American Journal of Psychiatry,* 1937–38, *94,* 577–585.

Bradley, C. Benzedrine and Dexedrine in the treatment of children's behavior disorders. *Pediatrics,* 1950, *5,* 24–37.

Breitmeyer, J. *Effects of thioridazine and methylphenidate on learning and retention in retardates.* Unpublished masters thesis, University of Illinois, 1969. Cited in Werry, J. Some clinical and laboratory studies of psychotropic drugs in children: An overview. In W. L. Smith (Ed.), *Drugs and cerebral function.* Springfield, Illinois: Charles C. Thomas, 1970.

Buchsbaum, M., & Wender, P. Averaged evoked responses in normal and minimally brain dysfunctioned children treated with amphetamine. *Archives of General Psychiatry,* 1973, *29,* 764–770.

Burks, H. Effects of amphetamine therapy on hyperkinetic children. *Archives of General Psychiatry,* 1964, *11,* 604–609.

Butter, H., & Lapierre, Y. The effect of methylphenidate on sensory perception in varying degrees of hyperkinetic behavior. *Diseases of the Nervous System*, 1975, *36*, 286–288.

Cohen, N., Douglas, V., & Morgenstern, G. The effect of methylphenidate on attentive behavior and autonomic activity in hyperactive children. *Psychopharmacologia*, 1971, *22*, 282–294.

Conrad, W., & Insel, J. Anticipating the response to amphetamine therapy in the treatment of hyperkinetic children. *Pediatrics*, 1967, *40*, 96–98.

Conners, C. A teacher rating scale for use in drug studies in children. *American Journal of Psychiatry*, 1969, *126*, 884–888.

Conners, C. The effect of stimulant drugs on human figure drawings in children with minimal brain dysfunction. *Psychopharmacologia*, 1971, *19*, 329–333.

Conners, C. Psychological effects of stimulant drugs in children with minimal brain dysfunction. *Pediatrics*, 1972, *49*, 702–708. (a)

Conners, C. Pharmacotherapy of psychopathology in children. In H. Quay & J. Werry (Eds.), *Psychopathological disorders of childhood*. New York: J. Wiley & Sons, 1972. (b)

Conners, C., & Rothschild, G. Drugs and learning in children. In *Learning disorders* (Vol. 3). Washington, D.C.: Special Child Publications, 1968.

Denhoff, E., Davids, A., & Hawkins, R. Effects of dextroamphetamine on hyperkinetic children: A controlled double-blind study. *Journal of Learning Disabilities*, 1971, *4*, 259–282.

Douglas, V. Stop, look and listen: The problem of sustained attention and impulse control in hyperactive and normal children. *Canadian Journal of Behavioral Science*, 1972, *4*, 259–282.

Douglas, V. Sustained attention and impulse control: Implications for the handicapped child. Psychology and the Handicapped Child, U.S. Department of Health, Education and Welfare; Office of Education, 1974.

Epstein, L., Lasagna, L., Conners, C., & Rodriguez, A. Correlation of dextroamphetamine excretion and drug response in hyperkinetic children. *Journal of Nervous and Mental Diseases*, 1968, *146*, 136–146.

Fish, B. The "one child, one drug" myth of stimulants in hyperkinesis. *Archives of General Psychiatry*, 1971, *25*, 193–203.

Hoffman, S., Engelhardt, D., Margolis, R., Polizos, A., Waizer, J., & Rosenfeld, R. Response to methylphenidate in low socioeconomic hyperactive children. *Archives of General Psychiatry*, 1974, *30*, 354–359.

Kakerem, G. Pupillography as a tool in the assessment of CNS functions and drug effects. In W. L. Smith (Ed.), *Drugs and cerebral function*. Springfield, Illinois: Charles C. Thomas, 1970.

Knights, R., & Hinton, G. The effects of methylphenidate (Ritalin) on the motor skills and behavior of children with learning problems. *Journal of Nervous and Mental Diseases*, 1969, *148*, 643–653.

Knopp, W., Arnold, L., Andras, R., & Smeltzer, D. Predicting amphetamine response in hyperkinetic children by electronic pupilography. *Pharmakopsychiatrie*, 1973, *6*, 158–166.

Loney, J., Comly, H., & Simon, B. Parental management, self-concept, and drug response in minimal brain dysfunction. *Journal of Learning Disabilities*, 1975, *8*, 187–190.

Lytton, G., & Knobel, M. Diagnosis and treatment of behavior disorders in children. *Diseases of the Nervous System*, 1958, *20*, 1–7.

McConnell, T., Cromwell, R., Bialer, I., & Son, C. Studies in activity level: **VII** Effects of amphetamine drug administration on the activity level of retarded children. *American Journal of Mental Deficiency*, 1964, *68*, 647–651.

Millichap, J., & Boldrey, E. Studies in hyperkinetic behavior: **II** Laboratory and clinical evaluations of drug treatments. *Neurology*, 1967, *17*, 467–471.

Pope, L. Motor activity in brain injured children. *American Journal of Orthopsychiatry*, 1970, *40*, 783.

Porges, S., Walter, G., Korb, R., & Sprague, R. The influences of methylphenidate on heart rate and behavioral measures of attention in hyperactive children. *Child Development*, 1975, *46*, 727–733.

Rapoport, J., Abramson, A., Alexander, D., & Lott, I. Playroom observations of hyperactive children on medication. *Journal of the American Academy of Children Psychiatry*, 1971, *10*, 524–534.

Rapoport, J., Quinn, P., Bradford, G., Riddle, D., & Brooks, E. Imipramine and methylphenidate: Treatments of hyperactive boys. *Archives of General Psychiatry*, 1974, *30*, 789–793.

Rie, H., E., Stewart, S., & Ambuel, J. Effects of methylphenidate on underachieving children. *Journal of Consulting and Clinical Psychology*, 1976, *44*, 250–260.

Routh, D., Schroeder, C., & O'Tuama, L. Development of activity level in children. *Developmental Psychology*, 1974, *10*, 163–168.

Safer, D., & Allen, R. Stimulant drug treatment of hyperactive adolescents. *Diseases of the Nervous System*, 1975, *3*, 454–457.

Satterfield, J., Cantwell, D., Lesser, L., & Podosin, R. Physiological studies of the hyperkinetic child: I. *American Journal of Psychiatry*, 1972, *128*, 1418–1424.

Satterfield, J., Cantwell, D., Saul, R., Lesser, L., & Podosin, R. Response to stimulant drug treatment in hyperactive children: Prediction from EEG and neurological findings. *Journal of Autism and Childhood Schizophrenia*, 1973, *3*, 36–48.

Schain, R., & Reynard, C. Observations of effects of a central stimulant drug (methylphenidate) in children with hyperactive behavior. *Pediatrics*, 1975, *55*, 709–716.

Schleifer, M., Weiss, G., Cohen, N., Elman, M., Cvejic, H., & Kruger, E. Hyperactivity in preschoolers and the effect of methylphenidate. *Ameri-*

can *Journal of Orthopsychiatry,* 1975, *45,* 38–49.

Shetty, T. Alpha rhythms in the hyperkinetic child. *Nature,* 1971, *234,* 476.

Sroufe, A., Sonies, B., West, W., & Wright, F. Anticipatory heart rate deceleration and reaction time in children with and without referral for learning disability. *Child Development,* 1973, *44,* 267–273.

Steinberg, G., Troshinsky, C., & Steinberg, H. Dextroamphetamine responsive behavior disorder in school children. *American Journal of Psychiatry,* 1971, *128,* 174–179.

Weber, B., & Sulzbacher, S. Use of CNS stimulant medication in averaged electroencephalic audiometry with children with MBD. *Journal of Learning Disabilities,* 1975, *8,* 300–303.

Weiss, G., Werry, J., Minde, K., Douglas, V., & Sykes, D. Studies on the hyperactive child: V. The effects of dextroamphetamine and chlorpromazine on behavior and intellectual functioning. *Journal of Child Psychology and Psychiatry,* 1968, *9,* 145–156.

Weiss, G., Minde, K., Douglas, V., Werry, J., & Sykes, D. Comparison of the effects of chlorproma-zine, dextroamphetamine, and methylphenidate on the behavior and intellectual functioning of hyperactive children. *Canadian Medical Association Journal,* 1971, *104,* 20–25.

Werry, J. Some clinical and laboratory studies of psychotropic drugs in children: An overview. In W. L. Smith (Ed.), *Drugs and cerebral function.* Springfield, Illinois: Charles C. Thomas, 1970.

Werry, J., & Arman, M. Methylphenidate and haloperidol in children. *Archives of General Psychiatry,* 1975, *32,* 790–795.

Werry, J., & Sprague, R. Methylphenidate in children—effect of dosage. *Australian and New Zealand Journal of Psychiatry,* 1974, *8,* 9–19.

Yoss, R., & Moyers, N. The pupillogram of the hyperkinetic child and the underachiever. Abstracts for 7th Colloquium on the Pupil, The Mayo Clinic, Rochester, Minnesota, 1971.

Zahn, T., Abate, F., Little, B., & Wender, P. Minimal brain dysfunction, stimulant drugs, and autonomic nervous system activity. *Archives of General Psychiatry,* 1975, *32,* 381–387.

9. Hyperactivity and learning disabilities as independent dimensions of child behavior problems

BENJAMIN B. LAHEY   MICHAEL STEMPNIAK
EARL J. ROBINSON   MERLE J. TYROLER

Hyperactivity and *learning disabilities* are two of the most troublesome terms in the field of child behavior disorders. This is evidenced by the controversy surrounding attempts to arrive at an "official" U.S. Office of Education definition of *learning disabilities* (Schaar, 1977), the vagueness and heterogeneity of working definitions of both terms used by researchers (Ross, 1976; Ross & Ross, 1976), and the wide variety of legal definitions adopted by different states in this country (Mercer, Forgnone, & Wolking, 1976). As a result, research on these two ill-defined, putative populations may create more misunderstandings than it dispels, and applied efforts to assess and treat children who are supposed to have such problems may do more harm than good in some instances. Clearly, clarification of definitions and terminology is needed by both researchers and practitioners.

It may be that to effectively attack this problem, we will need to return to the most basic theoretical question, Can a pattern (or patterns) of maladaptive behaviors be identified that characterizes at least some major segment of the children who are currently diagnosed as hyperactive and/or learning disabled? It is quite likely that at the present time, the most defensible, empirically based answer to this question is No. Because learning disabilities are legally defined

(albeit with many variants) largely by exclusion (children with academic learning deficits who are *not* mentally retarded, *not* emotionally disturbed, *not* physically handicapped, and *not* environmentally disadvantaged), it may be that no pattern(s) of behaviors typifies even the majority of these children.

The problems inherent in defining *hyperactivity* are even more serious. Although the psychometric instruments used in assessing learning disabilities have been frequently criticized, they provide a degree of objectivity (at least for administrative-legal purposes) that does not exist for hyperactivity. Although many measures of hyperactivity have been proposed (Lubar & Shouse, 1977), there are few available data to use in selecting between these widely differing methods.

There would appear to be little reason to believe, therefore, that given the current problems of definition, a coherent dimension or dimensions of hyperactivity and learning disabilities can be identified. Still, the clinical impression of common factors amidst diversity exists for both of these populations (Ross, 1976; Ross & Ross, 1976). Perhaps the difficulty lies in the fact that previous investigators have begun with essentially a priori definitions of *hyperactivity* and *learning disabilities* and have worked backwards

From the *Journal of Abnormal Psychology*, 1978, *87*, 333–340. Copyright 1978 by the American Psychological Association. Reprinted by permission.

toward descriptions of the core characteristics of these groups. It would seem more appropriate to work in the opposite direction, by beginning with descriptions of maladaptive child behaviors and working toward definable diagnostic categories through such inductive methods as factor analysis.

Ross (1974) has suggested that the most influential approach to the classification of maladaptive behaviors in children has been the factor-analytic approach. This method analyzes empirically generated descriptions of maladaptive behaviors, such as diagnostic descriptions used in child guidance clinics and descriptions used by teachers in referring students to school psychologists, which are used to form scales on which children are rated by parents or teachers (e.g., Conners, 1969; Peterson, 1961; Ross, Lacey, & Parton, 1965; Walker, 1969). Each item in the scale consists of a description of an aspect of maladaptive behavior, with the full set of items, in theory at least, being representative of the entire range of maladaptive child behaviors. The resulting ratings are then factor analyzed to isolate intercorrelated clusters of maladaptive behaviors.

If one looks at the factor-analytic literature, however, scant and equivocal evidence can be found for learning disabilities or hyperactivity dimensions of behavior. Of the most widely used and researched school behavior rating scales (Arnold & Smeltzer, 1974; Conners, 1969; Miller, 1972; Peterson, 1961; Pimm & McClure, 1967; Quay & Quay, 1965; Ross et al., 1965; Sines, Pauker, Sines, & Owen, 1969; Swift & Spivak, 1968; Walker, 1969), only one scale (Miller, 1972) yielded a factor that could reasonably be labeled *learning disabilities,* and only 3 of 11 scales yielded putative hyperactivity factors (Arnold & Smeltzer, 1974; Miller, 1972; Sines et al., 1969).

In contrast, much stronger support can be found for the two dimensions of maladaptive behavior identified in Peterson's (1961) influential early study: "conduct problems" (aggression, noncompliance, disruption) and "personality problems" (anxiety, fears, somatic complaints, social isolation). Every factor-analytic study cited above has essentially replicated these two factors, although in studies that extracted a large number of factors, these clusters of items may be broken down into two or more smaller clusters.

Therefore, in comparison to the conduct problems and personality problems factors, factor-analytic studies have provided little evidence to

support the notion that there are independent hyperactivity and learning disabilities dimensions of behavior. In fact they argue against it. A closer inspection of these studies, however, reveals several methodological factors that may account for the discrepant results for a learning disabilities and hyperactivity factor(s). The studies differ from one another in the number of factors extracted, the labels applied to clusters of items, and the age and description of the children rated (referred for treatment or nonreferred). But, apparently the most salient difference is in the item pools that were analyzed. The scales that failed to identify a learning disabilities and/or hyperactivity factor simply did not contain many items related to those possible factors, whereas the scales that found such factors, did contain large numbers of relevant items. It may be that few studies have extracted hyperactivity or learning disabilities factors simply because few have put such items into their analyses.

Based on the assumption that inadequately narrow item pools are responsible for the lack of consistency in extracting hyperactivity and learning disabilities factors, an item pool was constructed by combining the items from a number of different scales (Arnold & Smeltzer, 1974; Peterson, 1961; Pimm & McClure, 1967; Ross et al., 1965; Sines et al., 1969; Swift & Spivak, 1968). In addition, items from two scales designed to measure the learning disabilities-hyperactivity dimension that were constructed on an a priori basis (i.e., the items were not empirically determined to be characteristics of learning disabled or hyperactive children) were also included (Meier, 1971; Myklebust, 1973). Redundant items were eliminated and some items were rewritten to make them more descriptive of overt behavior, resulting in a 110-item scale that was more broadly inclusive than that of any other single existing scale. It was hypothesized that a factor analysis of ratings based on this scale would replicate the conduct problems and personality problems factors of previous studies and would yield either a combined hyperactivity-learning disabilities factor or separate factors that might be associated with each term.

METHOD

Subjects

A total of 19 teachers generated 404 ratings of fourth- through eighth-grade children. The students were from two semi-urban school districts in Georgia. In one school system, 84 of the ratings were of children enrolled in a heterogeneous special education program, and 128 of the ratings were of children enrolled in regular classes. In the second school system, all 192 of the rated students were in normal classes, but because the school system used a mainstream special education program, some of the children in each class spent part of each day in special education resource classes. Thus, the population was heterogeneous in respect to deviance and approximated an unselected sample.

Procedure

The scale was given to teachers with written instructions to check all items typical of the child's behaviors that he or she engaged in more often than most other children. Each teacher rated all of the students in his or her class and returned the ratings in 1–4 weeks. The resulting ratings were analyzed using a principal-components method of factor analysis. Four items that were never marked were eliminated from the analysis. The number of factors to be extracted was based on the amount of variance accounted for by each successive factor. The number of factors chosen was rotated using a variance-maximizing rotation procedure. This resulted in a factor structure with the maximum amount of information possible being contained in the minimum number of factors (Tatsuoka, 1971).

RESULTS

Inspection indicated that either a four- or six-factor solution would be appropriate. Because the first four factors accounted for 34.5% of the variance before rotation and the addition of two factors added only a total of 5.9% to the accounted variance, the four-factor solution was chosen according to Cattell's (1966) scree criteria. The eigenvalues for the four factors before rotation were 17.80, 6.07, 5.51, and 2.99, respectively. The percentage of variance accounted for by Factors 1 through 4 was 32.7%, 27.5%, 21.4%, and 18.4%, respectively, of the total variance accounted for by the four factors after orthogonal rotation.

The four factors are presented in Table 9-1. The first and third factors extracted closely replicated the factors that have been labeled *conduct problems* and *personality problems* in previous research. The second and fourth factors closely resembled the factors that have been labeled in a few previous studies *learning disabilities* and *hy-*

peractivity, respectively. As predicted, they are distinct from the conduct problems and personality problems (anxiety-withdrawal) factors. Furthermore, these two factors were found to be independent of one another.

The degree of independence of these four orthogonally rotated factors can be further seen in the intercorrelations presented in Table 9-2. Factors 1 and 3 were found to be significantly correlated ($p < .01$), but such correlations of $r = .13$ or less are probably not large enough to be of practical significance.

DISCUSSION

The results of this study should be viewed as both hypothesis testing and hypothesis generating. In the first sense, they substantiate the hypothesis that factors that might appropriately be labeled *learning disabilities* and *hyperactivity* were infrequently found in previous studies because of essentially *nonsubstantive* reasons (among which may be the size and breadth of the item pool, the particular method of factor analysis used and procedural decisions made, and the use of different subject populations and sampling methods) rather than for more substantial reasons that would argue more strongly against the possible existence of these dimensions of child behavior problems.

More interestingly, these data suggest many hypotheses about the *meaning* of these two factors. Clearly, they suggest that *dimensions of behavior* that appear to be related to the diagnostic categories of learning disabilities and hyperactivity can be included as independent and dependent variables in types of studies that have had to rely solely on diagnostic categories, but the actual applied and theoretical importance of these two factors is still very much open to question.

It may be, for example, that the *diagnostic category* of learning disabilities may be made up of two or more behavioral subtypes. Children who are rated as showing a marked degree of deviance on the learning disabilities dimension are apparently likely to be diagnosed as learning disabled, but since hyperactivity can be assumed to result in academic problems in some cases, it also seems probable that many children who are deviant on this dimension would also be diagnosed as learning disabled. These two subtypes of diagnosed learning-disabled children might differ from one another in significant respects, and might differ from other diagnosed children who are not rated as deviant on either dimension.

Table 9-1. Principal loadings of each item following factor analysis

Item	Factor			
	1	2	3	4
Factor 1: Conduct problems				
1. Speaks disrespectfully to teacher (calls teacher names, treats teacher as an equal)	.762	—	—	—
2. Refuses to admit he is wrong	.701			
3. Becomes upset or angry when he cannot have his way	.684			
4. Lies or evades the truth	.682			
5. Says things that hurt feelings of others	.678			
6. Has to have his way "right now"	.672			
7. Frequently loses his temper	.660			
8. Argues and attempts to have the last word in verbal exchanges	.643			
9. Gets other children into trouble	.630			
10. Often destroys or defaces property	.626			
11. Prone to blame the teacher, the test, or external circumstances when things don't go well	.614			
12. Often uses violent or obscene language	.603	.405		
13. Acts violently (hits, pushes) to other children or adults	.551	.436		
14. Cannot be sent on an errand or given an important task; irresponsible	.545		.325	
15. Won't follow rules, won't wait his turn	.540			.434
16. Associates with group of children continually breaking rules, or "getting into trouble"	.511			
17. He sulks when things go wrong, may refuse to talk to anyone	.486			
18. Interrupts whoever is speaking, frequently demanding the spotlight	.471			.312
19. Avoids work requiring concentrated visual attention	.462			.412
20. Sensitive to criticism or correction about his school work (gets angry, sulks, seems defeated)	.456			
21. Distracts other children by making noises, touching them, talking to them, etc.	.435			.368
22. Plays with matches	.431	.352		
23. Complains of nightmares, bad dreams	.428	.386		
24. Says he doesn't like school or school subjects	.420			
25. Usually doesn't turn in homework	.407		.360	
26. Usually comes to class unprepared (without paper, pencils, etc.)	.403		.358	
27. Seeks attention excessively: asking needless questions	.367			
Factor 2: Learning disabilities				
28. Can't sound out or decode words		.811		
29. Can't follow written directions, which most peers can follow, when he reads them orally or silently		.735		
30. Has trouble telling time		.722		
31. Reads silently or aloud far more slowly than most peers (word by word while reading aloud)		.720		
32. Loses place more than once while reading aloud for one minute		.719		
33. Reads aloud far less accurately (omits, substitutes, inserts words) than most peers		.710		
34. Doesn't pronounce words clearly or clutters words together		.647		
35. Stutters all the time or in stressful situations		.637		
36. Reading ability at least ¾ of a year below most peers		.722		
37. Unable to change from one task to another when asked to do so (has difficulty beginning a new task, may get upset or disorganized)		.597		
38. Frequently gets directions ("right-left" or "up-down") confused		.580		
39. Quick to say work assigned is too hard ("You expect too much," "I can't get it")		.512		
40. Easily frustrated and confused (may "forget" his recitation at slight disturbance)		.507		
41. Slow to complete his work (has to be prodded, takes excessive time)		.494	.378	

Table 9-1. Continued

	Factor			
Item	1	2	3	4
42. Has poor memory for things that happened both short and long time ago		.434		.357
43. Lets other children lead him almost all the time; he is rarely the leader		.425	.345	
44. Copies work of others or cheats on tests	.331	.423		
45. Becomes more active or more talkative in groups, becomes noisy and more excited in a group than alone		.363		
46. Likely to quit or give up when something is difficult or demands more than usual effort		.353	.346	
47. Wants help on things he should do alone		.339		
48. Can do a task well some days, and can't do it on others; variable in his school performance		.337		

Factor 3: Anxiety-withdrawal

49. Does not perform in front of a group; refuses to speak before the class when requested			.651	
50. Often appears miserable, unhappy, lonely, or distressed			.614	
51. Is upset or frightened by test, or gets upset when he doesn't know the correct answer to a question			.580	
52. Won't look you in the eye when talking			.569	
53. Volunteers to answer questions or participate much less frequently than other children		.322	.542	
54. Says nobody likes him, says no one understands him			.520	
55. Is not liked by other children (may be ignored, avoided)			.457	
56. Tends to be absent from school for trivial reasons or is frequently tardy	.350		.455	
57. Doesn't do work when teacher isn't watching	.330		.454	
58. Oblivious to what is going on in class (seems to be in own "private" world, not "with it")			.447	
59. Poor handwriting compared with peers' writing			.440	
60. Has stolen things on one or more occasions			.424	
61. Is slow, lethargic, seems to have little interest or energy in the classroom		.326	.417	
62. Reacts to stressful situations or changes in routine with general body aches, head or stomachaches			.414	
63. Sloppy in his work (his products are dirty or marked up or wrinkled)			.395	.385
64. It is difficult to understand what he is trying to tell you even though his articulation is clear			.391	
65. Will not ask questions even when he doesn't know how to do the work			.388	
66. Doesn't stand up for himself when hit or bossed around			.381	
67. Tries to avoid calling attention to himself (doesn't raise hand even when he knows the answers)			.379	
68. Frequently complains about being ill			.356	
69. Speaks with weak voice, in a monotone, voice "trails off" at the end of sentence, or speaks in a weak, high-pitched voice			.341	
70. Shows muscle twitching, eye blinking, frequent nail biting, hand wringing, "fiddles" with objects, hair			.337	
71. Rarely smiles or seems to be having fun			.316	
72. Is perfectionistic or fussy; details must be exactly right, meticulous			.301	

Factor 4: Hyperactivity

73. Starts working on something before getting the directions right				.638
74. Looks to see how others are doing something before he tries it				.574
75. Rushes through his work and therefore makes unnecessary mistakes				.571
76. Moves constantly, "gets into everything," "fidgets," does not sit quietly at desk except very briefly	.340			.544
77. Answers questions too quickly (before he has had a chance to think)				.500
78. Unable to follow directions given in class (needs precise directions before he can proceed successfully)		.439		.483

Item	Factor 1	2	3	4
79. Jumps from one activity to another, does not finish task (is described as having a short attention span)				.480
80. Has trouble organizing written work (seems scatterbrained, confused)				.443
81. Misinterprets simple statements (doesn't understand many words or sentences)				.418
82. Can recall things told him a long time before, but not a short time before				.408
83. Stumbles, falls easily, throws clumsily, drops things, is awkward			.392	.407
84. Is quickly drawn into talking or noisemaking of others (stops work to listen or join in)	.369	.374		.396
85. Is overtalkative, chatters, keeps talking or interrupting conversation	.386			.395
86. Looks around the room when he shouldn't or leaves seat when he shouldn't	.367			.389
87. Doesn't pay attention when teacher explains something to him (because fidgety, looks away)	.325		.327	.374
88. Says "I can't do it" before trying, especially before a new task				.366
89. Talks, babbles, sings, or hums to himself				.364
90. Cannot relate ideas in logical, meaningful way				.334
91. Cannot remember instructions				.334

Table 9-2. Intercorrelations between the four factors

Factor	Factor 1	2	3	4
1				
2	.001			
3	.130	−.044		
4	−.093	.010	.056	

If so, these results suggest a possible clarification of the heterogeneity in this diagnostic category.

The finding that teachers' evaluations of below-grade-level reading performance weights highly on the factor labeled *learning disabilities* and not on any other scale tentatively suggests a relationship between this factor and the diagnostic category of learning disabilities, but future research will be needed to clarify this relationship. One indirect test of the proposition that the diagnostic category of learning disabilities is composed of at least two independent patterns of deviance can be based on the degree of overlap between the diagnoses of hyperactivity and learning disabilities in actual practice. Since a clinically significant degree of hyperactivity should almost always lead to academic difficulties, a high proportion of individuals diagnosed as hyperactive should also be diagnosed as learning disabled. On the other hand, since the tentative learning disabilities factor identified in the present study is independent of the hyperactivity factor, a smaller proportion of children who are diagnosed as learning disabled should also be diagnosed as hyperactive. This prediction is supported by Safer and Allen (1976), who have estimated in a review of the literature that approximately 80% of children diagnosed as hyperactive are also diagnosed as learning disabled, whereas approximately 40% of those diagnosed as learning disabled are also diagnosed as hyperactive.

The results of the factor analysis may also have significance for questions of the independence of the hyperactivity and conduct problems factors. Previous factor analysis literature did not clearly support the existence of hyperactivity as a separate dimension of behavior. On the contrary, most of the scales that included a few items relating to overactivity and distractibility found that they loaded most heavily on the conduct problems factor (Peterson, 1961; Rodd et al., 1965). In fact, some critics of the use of pharmacological and behavioral means of controlling children's behavior have argued that hyperactivity does not *exist*, as such, and suggest that some children are perceived as hyperactive simply because they do not conform to the rules of the home or classroom (Shrag & Divoky, 1975).

The present results, on the other hand, suggest the existence of an independent dimension of maladaptive behavior that can be labeled *hyperactivity.* The importance of these data may, furthermore, go beyond the question of independence to the topic of the diagnostic definition of hyperactivity. In their review of diagnostic criteria, Ross and Ross (1976) emphasized that overactivity, per se, is not sufficient to warrant the label *hyperactivity*. Rather, most writers restrict that term to children whose activity level is "inappropriate" or "brings them into conflict with their environment" (Ross & Ross, 1976, pp. 11–12). Thus, it may be that by definition, the diagnostic label *hyperactivity* is restricted to only those children who are deviant in *both* dimensions that resemble the hyperactivity and conduct problems factors identified in the present investigation. Although such a two-factor definition may very well be justifiable on clinical grounds, the unknowing confounding of these apparently independent factors will almost certainly lead to confusion.

An example of the possible confusion arising from this confounding of factors may be found in the hyperactivity-treatment literature. Currently, the most widely used dependent variables for clinical studies of both behavioral and pharmacological treatments are the behavior rating scales for hyperactivity developed by Conners (1969), Stewart, Pitts, Craig, and Dieruf (1966), and Werry (1968). Each of these scales confounds items that typically load principally on the conduct problems factor ("disturbs other children," "temper outbursts," "fights," "teases") with items that load principally on the factor labeled *hyperactivity* in this and other studies ("overactive," "can't sit still," "inattentive," "easily distracted"). This fact raises the possibility that behavioral and pharmacological treatments that produce significant changes in behavior ratings on these scales may have had their principal effects on conduct problems rather than on activity problems. There is substantial evidence that behavior therapy can produce changes in conduct-type problems (Kent & O'Leary, 1976), but there are apparently no clinical studies in which hyperactivity was measured in a way that ruled out confounds with conduct problems. The possibility of drugs directly affecting conduct problems has not been directly demonstrated, but it may be that stimulants improve the conduct of hyperactive children in the same way that a nap improves the disposition of sleep-deprived children.

In any case, the ancient caveat that additional research is needed has never been more true. It is clear that until it is known which and how many patterns of deviance are involved, comparison studies of learning disabled, hyperactive, and other deviant children will not be fully interpretable.

REFERENCES

Arnold, E., & Smeltzer, D. J. Behavior checklist factor analysis for children and adolescents. *Archives of General Psychology,* 1974, *30,* 799–804.

Cattell, R. B. The scree test for the number of factors. *Multivariate Behavioral Research,* 1966, *1,* 245–276.

Conners, C. K. A teacher rating scale for use in drug studies with children. *American Journal of Psychiatry,* 1969, *126,* 884–888.

Kent, R. N., & O'Leary, K. D. A controlled evaluation of behavior modification with conduct problem children. *Journal of Consulting and Clinical Psychology,* 1976, *44,* 586–596.

Lubar, J., & Shouse, M. N. Use of biofeedback in the treatment of seizure disorders and hyperactivity. In B. B. Lahey & A. E. Kazdin (Eds.), *Advances in clinical child psychology.* New York: Plenum Press, 1977.

Meier, J. H. Prevalence and characteristics of learning disabilities found in second grade children. *Journal of Learning Disabilities,* 1971, *4,* 7–18.

Mercer, C. D., Forgnone, C., & Wolking, W. D. Definitions of learning disabilities used in the United States. *Journal of Learning Disabilities,* 1976, *9,* 376–386.

Miller, L. C. School behavior checklist: An inventory of deviant behavior for elementary school children. *Journal of Consulting and Clinical Psychology,* 1972, *38,* 134–144.

Myklebust, H. R. The pupil rating scale: Screening for learning disabilities. *Journal of Special Education,* 1973, *7,* 311–320.

Peterson, D. R. Behavior problems of middle childhood. *Journal of Consulting Psychology,* 1961, *25,* 205–209.

Pimm, J. B., & McClure, G. A screening device for early detection of emotional disturbances in a public school setting. *Exceptional Children,* 1967, *33,* 647–648.

Quay, H. C., & Quay, L. C. Behavior problems in early adolescence. *Child Development,* 1965, *36,* 215–220.

Ross, A. O. *Psychological disorders of children: A behavioral approach to theory, research and therapy.* New York: McGraw-Hill, 1974.

Ross, A. O. *Psychological aspects of learning disabilities and reading disorders.* New York: McGraw-Hill, 1976.

Ross, A. O., Lacey, H. M., & Parton, D. A. The development of a behavior checklist for boys. *Child Development,* 1965, *36,* 1013–1027.

Ross, D., & Ross, S. *Hyperactivity: Research, theory, action.* New York: Wiley, 1976.

Safer, D. J., & Allen, R. P. *Hyperactive children:*

Diagnosis and management. Baltimore, Md.: University Park Press, 1976.

Scharr, K. "Learning disabilities" captures increased congressional attention. *APA Minitor,* July 1977, pp. 10–16.

Shrag, P., & Divoky, D. *The myth of the hyperactive child*. New York: Pantheon Books, 1975.

Sines, J. O., Pauker, J. D., Sines, L. K., & Owen, D. R. Identification of clinically relevant dimensions of children's behavior. *Journal of Consulting and Clinical Psychology,* 1969, *33,* 728–734.

Stewart, M. A., Pitts, F. N., Craig, A. G., & Dieruf, W. The hyperactive child syndrome. *American Journal of Orthopsychiatry,* 1966, *36,* 861–867.

Swift, M., & Spivack, G. The assessment of achievement-related classroom behavior. *Journal of Special Education,* 1968, *2,* 137–154.

Tatsuoka, M. M. *Multivariate analysis: Techniques for educational and psychological research*. New York: Wiley, 1971.

Walker, H. M. Empirical assessment of deviant behavior in children. *Psychology in the Schools,* 1969, *11,* 93–97.

Werry, J. S. Developmental hyperactivity. *Pediatric Clinics of North America,* 1968, *15,* 581–599.

10. Relationships between symptomatology and SES-related factors in hyperkinetic/MBD boys

CARL E. PATERNITE   JAN LONEY
JOHN E. LANGHORNE, JR.

Over the course of the past 30 to 40 years, the relationship between socioeconomic status (SES) and such factors as prevalence of psychological disorders, symptom patterns within disorders, organicity and mental retardation, and childhood socialization and cognitive development have been widely studied and reviewed.[4,5,8,12,13,17,21,24] A variety of definitions of SES are represented within the existing work. These various conceptualizations of SES have included global and vague descriptions,[7,10] single-variable indices (e.g., paternal or head-of-household education or occupation),[14,21] and more complex indices based on empirically determined weightings for multiple variables.[11,17]

As Lorion[20] has pointed out, traditional SES conceptualizations generally do not reflect the profound educational, economic, and social changes of the last two decades. This shortcoming is especially evident in the virtually uniform neglect of maternal education, maternal occupation, and family income (paternal plus maternal income) in definitions of SES. However, the recent work of Rossi et al.[26] among others, addresses this problem by considering both paternal and maternal variables.

Deutsch[6] has also been quite critical of much of the work that has been done, noting that in most instances SES has been viewed as a unitary variable—a stable, specific, and homogeneous entity. She argues that SES can be viewed as a shorthand label for a conglomerate of complexly interrelated factors that should be studied both singly and in combination.

In his view of class and ethnic influences on socialization, Hess[8] also stressed the appropriateness of considering SES as a multidimensional concept. Hess sees family and parental styles, attitudes, and practices as a potentially important subset of factors from among the conglomerate of SES-related influences. The relationships of both parenting variables and traditionally measured SES to child development and psychopathology have been extensively studied and critically reviewed.[1,2,8,9,15,30]

So far as we know, the suggestion to examine thoroughly multiple SES and SES-related influences has not been systematically followed in the study of the Hyperkinetic/Minimal Brain Dysfunction (HK/MBD) syndrome. Instead, parental occupation, education, and income have been either ignored or controlled for by using clinical samples that are homogeneous for these or other SES variables.[7,10,16] Further, there have been only a few isolated attempts to examine the effects of parenting on HK/MBD children. For example, Conrad and Insel[3] found that poor outcome of children in drug treatment was

From the *American Journal of Orthopsychiatry*, 1976, 46, 291–301. Copyright © the American Orthopsychiatric Association, Inc. Reproduced by permission.
   Research was supported in part by NIMH grant MH-22659 to Dr. Loney.

significantly related to parental "gross deviance" and "social incompetence."

In addition, Loney, Comly and Simon[19] reported a significant positive relationship between quality of parental management and response to drug treatment. They also reported findings suggesting a positive relationship between quality of parental management and self-esteem inferred from a projective test, whereas no relationship was found between parental management and similarly-inferred impulse control. We are aware of no systematic attempts to examine the relationships between parenting variables and more directly assessed symptom patterning in HK/MBD children.

In summary, there are many unanswered questions about SES and SES-related influences on HK/MBD children. The present study examines the relationships among HK/MBD child symptomatology at the time of referral, an SES measure derived from both paternal and maternal information, and a subset of presumably SES-related parenting influences.

CLINICAL POPULATION

As the initial part of an ongoing comprehensive study of HK/MBD children, we have recently created an extensive information resource concerning boys initially seen for outpatient evaluation at the Child Psychiatry Service of the University of Iowa from January 1967 to September 1972. Pre-treatment data have been compiled on a multitude of family, perinatal, developmental, psychiatric, neurological, and educational variables for 135 nonretarded HK/MBD boys, ages four to twelve, all of whom were placed on central nervous system stimulants following their outpatient evaluation.

The mean age at referral of the 135 boys was 8.2 years; their IQs ranged from 71 to 133, with a mean of 99.5. The group included boys from rural and more urban areas of Iowa and a few surrounding states, and was 98% white (as is the Iowa general population). The remainder of this report will focus on those 113 of the 135 boys who were living with intact families at the time of referral (that is, both a mother and father figure were present in the household), and who were subsequently given a clinical trial of Ritalin.

SES MEASURE

Five pieces of information contained within the case records served as the basis for classifying

the sample into SES groups. These five variables were patient pay status at the Child Psychiatry Service, maternal education, paternal education, paternal occupation, and family income. Three payment categories (private or full-fee, clinic or reduced-fee, and state—i.e., indigent—or no-fee) constituted the patient pay status variable. At the time of the out-patient evaluation, the parents collaborated with a clinic social worker to choose one of these three payment scales. The choice was based primarily on a consideration of family financial factors from the parents' point of view. The education and occupation variables were obtained from a direct application of the seven-point scales originally developed by Hollingshead and Redlich[11] and elaborated by Lesser, Fifer and Clark.[17] The family-income variable consisted of the combined paternal and maternal incomes as reported on intake forms.

Because the cases in our sample were referred during a period of generally rising income and increasing educational and occupational opportunities, it was necessary to attempt to control for the problem of changing SES criteria over time. Therefore, the sample was divided into three separate subsamples of cases drawn from consecutive two-year periods (1967–68, 1969–70, 1971–72), and the derivation of the three SES groups was accomplished for each of these subsamples separately. Within each subsample, trichotomous divisions were made for the patient pay status variable, and median divisions were made for the maternal and paternal education, paternal occupation, and family income variables. Patient pay status full-fee was coded as 1, reduced-fee as 0.5, and no-fee as 0. For the family-income variable, values above the median were coded as 1, and values below the median were coded as 0. For the other three variables, values below the median were coded as 1, and values above the median were coded as 0.

Sixteen of the 113 cases had missing data on one or more of the SES-defining variables. Specifically, a value for mother's education was missing for 3.6% of the 113 cases, father's education for 5.3%, father's occupation for 5.3%, and family income for 12.4%. Rather than discard useful information and perhaps introduce nonrandom error by deleting the sixteen cases, replacement scores were generated. For each instance of a missing value, the replacement score was computed by prorating on the basis of the summed codings for all nonmissing variables within a given case.

Following the coding of values and the replacement of missing scores for each of the five SES-defining variables, a combined SES score was computed by summing across variables for each case. Within each two-year subsample the cases were then divided into three SES levels (high, middle, and low) by separating the cases into three approximately equal groups based on the combined SES scores. Thus, the final SES designation for each family was relative to all other families seen during the same two-year period. Considering the three two-year subsamples together, the resultant SES groups (high, middle, and low) contained 38, 37, and 38 cases, respectively.

SYMPTOM SEVERITY MEASURES

Among the psychological variables that we have compiled are ratings of each child by two independent judges on the severity of nine HK/MBD symptoms. Consistent with recent trends to discriminate between primary or core hyperkinetic symptoms and secondary or resultant symptoms,[18,22,23,28,29] each judge independently reviewed each child's staff, medical, and social summaries and psychological and educational test reports, and then rated on a six-point scale the severity of each of six primary and three secondary symptoms. The primary symptoms were *hyperactivity, fidgetiness, inattention, judgment deficits (impulsivity), negative affect (excitability/irritability),* and *uncoordination.* The secondary symptoms were *aggressive interpersonal behavior, impulse control deficits,* and *self-esteem deficits.* (A more detailed discussion of the rating scales is already available.[18]) The effective rater reliabilities[25] for the symptom ratings ranged from .72 to .80, with all correlations significant at $p < .001$.

Due to the lack of sufficient information upon which to base ratings, two children from the high SES group were not rated on the severity of primary and secondary symptoms. These cases were eliminated from subsequent analyses involving the symptom ratings.

PARENTING MEASURES

Among the family variables we have compiled are ratings of each parent by two independent judges on nine parenting dimensions. The same set of chart summaries and reports was used to make both the parent ratings and the symptom severity ratings, but the judges were a different pair. The nine parent-rating variables included

separate seven-point ratings along both the *love-to-hostility* and *autonomy-to-control* parenting style dimensions (with the variables adapted from the Parent Attitude Research Instrument[27]), separate five-point ratings of parental *firmness, consistency, simplicity,* and *placidity,*[19] and separate dichotomous ratings of parental *gross deviance, social incompetence,* and *poor parent-child relationship.*[3] The effective rater reliabilities[25] for the nondichotomous parenting ratings ranged from .36 to .85, with all correlations significant at $p < .05$.

Additional sources of information about parenting styles were the mother and father intake forms, which were completed separately by each parent during the period between the child's initial referral and his outpatient evaluation. In addition to other information, these forms yielded checklist type data on whether each parent saw himself or herself, and his or her spouse, as being *too busy, too demanding, too short-tempered, too easygoing* and *too strict* as a parent. Four further variables consisted of the total number of self- or spouse-reported checklist responses for each parent. These variables, with possible scores ranging from 0 to 5, were labeled *self-reported father shortcomings, spouse-reported father shortcomings, self-reported mother shortcomings,* and *spouse-reported mother shortcomings.*

Because the raters did not find enough relevant information in the case records, 5.2% of the rating data for fathers and 4.7% of the rating data for mothers was missing. For variables from the parent intake forms the amounts of missing information for mothers and fathers were 4.5% and 5.3%, respectively. The statistical procedures most appropriate for subsequent analyses necessitated complete data for all cases. This requirement could have been met either by eliminating cases with any missing data or by replacing missing values. Again, we chose to replace missing values rather than to eliminate cases totally. Within each SES group the replacement scores for each variable were randomly assigned, with the restriction that the probability of assignment of a specific score depended on the relative frequency of that score value in the distribution of nonmissing values.

RESULTS

As expected, the three SES groups were statistically separable on each of the five SES-defining variables. All *t*-test differences except one between all possible pairs of SES groups were significant at the $p < .001$ level for each variable. The exception was the family income difference between middle and low SES groups, which was significant at the $p < .01$ level. Comparing the high and low SES groups, the mean family income for the high SES cases ($14,100) was more than twice that of the low SES cases ($6,800). Further, the mean paternal and maternal education for the high SES cases was at the college level, whereas the mean for the low SES cases was at the tenth to eleventh grade level. The mean paternal occupation for the high SES cases was above the semiprofessional level, whereas the mean for the low SES cases was between the skilled and semiskilled levels. Regarding patient pay status, 94% of the private or full-fee patients were in the high SES group, and 89% of the state or no-fee patients were in the low SES group.

While the three SES groups clearly varied on each of the five SES-defining variables, they did not differ significantly in the age of the boys at the time of outpatient evaluation. The mean ages of the high, middle, and low SES boys were 8.5, 8.0, and 8.2 years, respectively. Recent and complete WISC IQ data were available for 63% of our 113 boys. There were no significant differences in either WISC Verbal or Performance

IQ between any pair of SES groups (high vs. middle, high vs. low, middle vs. low). For the WISC Full Scale IQ data, there were no significant differences between the high vs. middle or the middle vs. low SES groups. The WISC Full Scale IQ difference between 21 of the 38 high SES group and 30 of the 38 low SES group reached significance at the $p < .05$ level. However, the magnitude of that one difference (high SES IQ = 105.9; low SES IQ = 97.3) is neither numerically nor clinically impressive.

A series of t-test analyses was performed to compare the high vs. low SES groups on the severity of each rated symptom. The means of the high and low SES groups for each rater are shown in Table 10-1. There are significant differences between SES groups for both raters in the severity of all three secondary symptoms at referral, with boys from high SES homes showing less severe symptomatology. In contrast there are no consistently significant differences between SES groups in the six primary symptoms at referral. The fact that this interaction between SES and symptom severity emerges, in general, for both raters separately can be considered a within-sample replication of the findings.

In addition to the pattern of differences between SES groups for symptom severity ratings, a number of SES-related differences emerged for

Table 10-1. Mean ratings of primary and secondary symptom severity for high and low SES boys

Symptoms	Rater	SES		t
		High[a]	Low[b]	
Primary				
Hyperactivity	1	3.38	3.18	0.64
	2	2.97	3.05	0.27
Fidgetiness	1	2.50	2.58	0.28
	2	2.72	2.59	0.43
Inattention	1	3.21	3.10	0.39
	2	2.62	2.83	0.79
Judgment deficits	1	3.22	3.40	0.57
(Impulsivity)	2	2.47	2.70	0.78
Negative affect	1	2.65	3.26	1.89
(Excitability/Irritability)	2	2.58	3.24	2.24[c]
Uncoordination	1	2.44	2.25	0.73
	2	2.01	1.87	0.79
Secondary				
Aggressive interpersonal behavior	1	2.50	3.45	3.16[d]
	2	2.16	3.18	3.52[e]
Impulse control deficits	1	3.53	3.95	2.95[d]
	2	3.54	3.92	2.41[c]
Self-esteem deficits	1	3.47	3.82	2.02[c]
	2	3.54	3.87	2.39[c]

[a] N = 36 for rater 1 and 37 for rater 2; [b] N = 38 for raters 1 and 2.
[c] p < .05; [d] < .01; [e] < .001.

Table 10-2. Mean ratings of parenting variables for high and low SES mothers and fathers

| | | Ratings of mother | | | Ratings of father | | |
| | | $High^a$ | Low^a | | $High^a$ | Low^a | |
Variable	Rater	SES	SES	†	SES	SES	†
Love-to-hostility	1	2.84	3.84	3.67^d	3.03	3.82	2.41^b
	2	1.97	3.05	3.41^c	2.18	3.21	2.52^b
Autonomy-to-control	1	4.37	3.82	2.28^b	4.00	3.24	3.18^c
	2	4.26	4.26	0.00	3.95	3.90	0.16
Firmness	1	3.24	2.79	2.92^c	3.24	2.60	3.57^d
	2	3.26	2.32	4.32^d	3.24	2.29	3.86^d
Consistency	1	2.90	2.34	3.36^c	2.87	2.40	2.76^c
	2	3.05	2.18	3.91^d	3.00	2.18	3.39^c
Simplicity	1	2.92	2.47	2.41^b	2.90	2.29	3.05^c
	2	2.87	2.68	.80	2.92	2.66	1.06
Placidity	1	2.74	2.34	2.34^b	3.08	2.61	2.82^c
	2	2.92	2.10	3.25^c	3.16	2.76	1.60

^{a}N = 38; ^{b}p < .05; ^{c}p < .01; ^{d}p < .001.

parenting ratings and mother and father intake form variables. The means of the high and low SES groups for the parenting ratings (excluding those based on the work of Conrad and Insel[3]) are presented in Table 10-2. As was the case for the symptom-severity ratings, the consistency between raters for several of the variables can be considered a within-sample replication. The variables for which consistent SES group differences did not result (e.g., *mother autonomy-to-control*) tended to be those with the lowest effective rater reliabilities (e.g., .36).

When Chi Square analyses were carried out for each of the 12 dichotomous Conrad and Insel[3] parenting ratings (three variables for two parents rated by two raters), no significant

($p < .05$) differences between SES groups emerged.

Differences between the SES groups for the dichotomous checklist variables from the parent intake forms are shown in Table 10-3. Chi Square analyses revealed significant SES-related differences in whether mothers and fathers were considered *too easygoing* according to both their own and their spouses' reports, and whether mothers were called *too demanding* by their husbands. The four *too easygoing* variables showed a rather consistent pattern, with 8%–16% of high SES parents responding *yes*, and 37%–42% of low SES parents responding similarly. The majority of the fathers responding *yes* for the mother *too demanding* variable were in the high SES

Table 10-3. Percent of mothers and fathers responding "Yes" to dichotomous checklist items from the parent intake forms

| | Reported by mother | | Reported by father | |
	$High^a$ SES	Low^a SES	$High^a$ SES	Low^a SES
Mother too busy	26.3%	31.6%	18.4%	15.8%
Father too busy	50.0	39.5	52.6	28.9
Mother too easygoing	10.5	39.5^c	15.8	39.5^b
Father too easygoing	15.8	42.1^b	7.9	36.8^c
Mother too strict	18.4	7.9	15.8	7.9
Father too strict	18.4	10.5	13.2	5.3
Mother too short-tempered	65.8	47.4	52.6	34.2
Father too short-tempered	50.0	36.8	42.1	36.8
Mother too demanding	26.3	15.8	28.9	5.3^b
Father too demanding	10.5	15.8	23.7	15.8

^{a}N = 38.
^{b}Difference statistically significant (p < .05) based on Chi Square analyses.
^{c}Difference statistically significant (p < .01) based on Chi Square analyses.

group. Examination of Table 10-3 also suggests rather consistent agreement between parental reports by self and by spouse. A series of Chi Square analyses was conducted within SES groups to examine the differences between self and spouse reports; none of the twenty resulting Chi Square values approached significance at the $p < .05$ level. In addition, there were no significant differences between the high and low SES groups for the *self-* or *spouse-reported shortcomings* variables.

When the SES-related differences for parenting rating and parent intake variables are considered together, substantial agreement is apparent between the raters and the parents. For example, the differences between SES groups for the ratings on parental *firmness* and *consistency* and for the four *too easygoing* intake variables are in the same direction. The general picture that emerges from the parenting data is of low SES parents who are more lax, easygoing, and inconsistent than are the high SES parents. These patterns correspond with much of the parenting research literature.

In summary, then, data obtained from research staff ratings and from self- and spouse ratings uniformly suggest that the attitudes and styles of these parents of HK/MBD boys vary as a function of SES. Having demonstrated differences between SES groups for secondary symptom severity ratings and for a number of parenting variables, we performed a series of stepwise multiple regression analyses to examine the relative contributions of SES and parenting to the symptom severity ratings. For the symptom *aggressive interpersonal behavior*, the seven predictors making statistically significant independent contributions to the regression equation, in decreasing order of magnitude, were *father's love-to-hostility*, the *spouse-reported mother too short-tempered* variable, *mother's consistency*, *spouse-reported mother shortcomings*, SES, the *self-reported mother too easygoing* variable, and *mother's autonomy-to-control*. For the symptom *impulse control deficits*, three significant predictors resulted, including *mother's consistency*, *father's placidity*, and the *spouse-reported mother too short-tempered* variable. The four significant predictors for the symptom *self-esteem deficits* were *father's consistency*, the *self-reported mother too strict* variable, *mother's firmness*, and the *spouse-reported mother too easy-going* variable.

For all three of the secondary symptoms, parenting variables contributed much more to the prediction equation than did the SES index. For the symptom *aggressive interpersonal behavior*, however, the addition of the SES variable did add significantly to the prediction.

Limiting consideration to those variables which contribute significantly to each of the three regression equations, the resultant multiple correlations, while based on only two general sources of information (parenting and SES), were quite high (.64, .52, .42). All three regression analyses involved the combination of a small number of parenting rating and parent intake-variables, the majority of which concerned mothers. In fact, no self- or spouse-reported father intake variables were involved. However, the apparent importance of father information was indicated by the fact that staff ratings of father's *love-to-hostility* and *consistency* made the single greatest contributions to the regression equations for two of the three symptoms. Research staff-rated parental consistency (twice maternal and once paternal) contributed significantly to all three regression equations. Further, for both analyses in which *mother's consistency* contributed significantly, the *spouse-reported mother too short-tempered* variable from the intake forms also contributed significantly.

DISCUSSION

Although the need for systematic replication and refinement of our findings is plain, the results do suggest that traditional SES and parenting styles are related to the HK/MBD syndrome in potentially important ways. Specifically, children who differ very little in age, IQ, or primary symptomatology (e.g., hyperactivity, inattention), do differ in secondary symptomatology, depending upon the nature and quality of parenting styles and upon SES.

Our interpretation would be that parental attitudes and styles and other SES-related variables have a considerable impact on the expression and severity of secondary or resultant symptoms in children who do not differ in the primary symptoms of the HK/MBD syndrome at referral and who may not have differed in constitutional predispositions either. Among the possible implications would be that research samples of HK/MBD children from different clinics might be systematically quite different in impulse control, self-esteem, etc., depending upon the socioeconomic characteristics of the patient population.

Further, such symptom differences might well

affect the children's responses to various forms of treatment and their ultimate condition at follow-up. Regarding drug treatment specifically, these findings suggest that the relationships between parenting and response to medication may be a function of differential parenting (or other SES-related influences) having produced systematic differences in children. Our findings would provide support for those who point out the inappropriateness of static diagnostic formulations and monolithic treatment plans for the HK/MBD syndrome.

Not surprisingly, it is the secondary or resultant symptoms that seem to vary with SES and parenting influences; variance in the commonly-accepted primary or core symptoms is apparently not associated with differences in the SES-related variables measured in this study. It may be that parenting characteristics do not strongly affect the severity of children's hyperactivity, inattention, judgment deficits, etc.—and, conversely, that the severity of the children's hyperactivity, etc., does not substantially influence the parents' attitudes and styles.

Considerable distance lies between these initial findings and more firm conclusions. What implications these findings may have for studies of genetic-familial factors in the HK syndrome is especially unclear. Primary symptomatology may occur more or less at random, and some children may develop additional secondary symptomatology through the action of adverse environmental factors, among them poor parenting. It does not seem likely that the adverse parental behavior is solely the result of frustrations with a constitutionally difficult child, since the parental behaviors express themselves differentially across SES, whereas the primary child behaviors do not.

If the primary symptoms of the HK syndrome are in fact unrelated to SES and parenting variables, it may be because they are not familial. It does seem clear that definitions of the HK syndrome which mix primary and secondary symptoms make it difficult to study etiology and course with the necessary precision. We need to know, for example, if the familial linkage is between paternal sociopathy and primary child symptoms such as hyperactivity, or whether it is simply between paternal sociopathy and secondary child symptoms that are essentially early indicators of sociopathy. Making a clear distinction between primary and secondary symptoms in follow-up studies should also allow us to determine if the severity of childhood hyperactivity

per se is linked to later aggressive behavior—or if, instead, the association is between childhood forms of aggression and adolescent and adult manifestations.

REFERENCES

1. Becker, W. and Krug, R. 1965. The parent attitude research instrument: a research review. Child Devlpm. 36:329–365.
2. Bell, R. 1968. A reinterpretation of the direction of effects in studies of socialization. Psychol. Rev. 75:81–95.
3. Conrad, W. and Insel, J. 1967. Anticipating the response to amphetamine therapy in the treatment of hyperkinetic children. Pediatrics 40:96–98.
4. Davis, A. 1941. American status systems and the socialization of the child. Amer. Sociol. Rev. 6:345–354.
5. Derogatis, L., Yevzeroff, H. and Wittelsberger, B. 1975. Social class, psychological disorder, and the nature of the psychopathologic indicator. J. Consult. Clin. Psychol. 43:183–191.
6. Deutsch, C. 1973. Social class and child development. In Review of Child Development Research: Child Development and Social Policy, B. Caldwell and H. Ricciuti, eds. University of Chicago Press, Chicago.
7. Fleming, J. and Sabatino, D. 1973. A study of two sociocultural variables. Academic Ther. 8:295–301.
8. Hess, R. 1970. Social class and ethnic influences upon socialization. In Carmichael's Handbook of Child Psychology, Vol. II, P. Mussen, ed. John Wiley, New York.
9. Hetherington, E. and Martin, B. 1972. Family interaction and psychopathology in children. In Psychopathological Disorders of Childhood, H. Quay and J. Werry, eds. John Wiley, New York.
10. Hoffman, S. et al. 1974. Response to methylphenidate in low socioeconomic hyperactive children. Arch. Gen. Psychiat. 30:354–359.
11. Hollingshead, A. 1957. Two Factor Index of Social Position. 1965 Yale Station, New Haven, Connecticut.
12. Hollingshead, A. and Redlich, F. 1958. Social Class and Mental Illness. John Wiley, New York.
13. Hollingshead, A. and Redlich, F. 1953. Social stratification and psychiatric disorders. Amer. Sociol. Rev. 18:163–169.
14. Jacob, T. 1974. Patterns of family conflict and dominance as a function of child age and social class. Devlpm. Psychol. 10:1–12.
15. Kagan, J. and Moss, H. 1962. Birth to Maturity: A Study in Psychological Development. John Wiley, New York.
16. Lauffer, M. 1971. Long term management and some follow-up findings on the use of drugs with minimal cerebral syndromes. J. Learning Disabil. 4:56–68.

17. Lesser, G., Fifer, G. and Clark, D. 1965. Mental abilities of children from different social-class and cultural groups. Monogr. Society Res. Child Devlpm. 30:Serial No. 102.

18. Loney, J. 1974. The intellectual functioning of hyperactive elementary school boys: a cross-sectional investigation. Amer. J. Orthopsychiat. 44:754–762.

19. Loney, J., Comly, H. and Simon, B. 1975. Parental management, self-concept, and drug response in minimal brain dysfunction. J. Learning Disabil. 8:187–190.

20. Lorion, R. 1973. Socioeconomic status and traditional treatment approaches reconsidered. Psychol. Bull. 79:263–270.

21. McDermott, J., Jr. et al. 1967. Social class and mental illness in children: the diagnosis of organicity and mental retardation. J. Amer. Acad. Child Psychiat. 6:309–320.

22. Mendelson, W., Johnson, N. and Stewart, M. 1971. Hyperactive children as teenagers: a follow-up study. J. Nerv. Ment. Dis. 53:273–279.

23. Palkes, H. and Stewart, M. 1972. Intellectual ability and performance of hyperactive children. Amer. J. Orthopsychiat. 42:35–39.

24. Petras, J. and Curtis, J. 1968. The current literature on social class and mental disease in America: critique and bibliography. Behav. Sci. 13:382–398.

25. Rosenthal, R. 1974. Estimating effective reliabilities in studies that employ judges' ratings. J. Clin. Psychol. 30:342–345.

26. Rossi, P. et al. 1975. Measuring household social standing. Unpublished paper.

27. Schaefer, E. 1965. Children's reports of parental behavior: an inventory. Child Devlpm. 36:413–424.

28. Stewart, M., Mendelson, W. and Johnson, N. 1973. Hyperactive children as adolescents: how they describe themselves. Child Psychiat. Hum. Devlpm. 4:3–11.

29. Wender, P. 1971. Minimal Brain Dysfunction in Children. Wiley-Interscience, New York.

30. Yarrow, M., Campbell, J. and Burton, R. 1968. Child Rearing: An Inquiry into Research and Methods. Jossey-Bass, San Francisco.

11. Early identification of handicapped children through a frequency sampling technique

LARRY A. MAGLIOCCA   ROBERT T. RINALDI
JOHN L. CREW   HAROLD P. KUNZELMANN

A top priority of congressional action for the promotion of programs for handicapped children is termed "child find." The child find concept is based on at least two major conclusions about children who are disabled. First, many handicapped children are not detected until their late primary years in the second or third grade. Second, when the children are found and diagnosis is completed, much of the information is not directly related to daily instructional plans of remediation.

The roots of the delivery of special education services are founded in the early detection of any form of handicapping condition, rapid remedial assistance in learning, and return to or placement in the least restrictive educational environment. The referral process available for teachers becomes the initiation point for causing special education services to become operational.

The early childhood program is a key area from which a child find concept may evolve. As part of the project entitled Baltimore Early Childhood Learning Continuum, project personnel selected three classes in early childhood education to determine if children who had learning problems could be identified and assisted while remaining in a regular program placement.

CHANNELS OF INVESTIGATION

It was determined that at least three channels of identification were open to investigation:

Alternative 1. Children would be identified when the teacher felt the child could profit from special education services. This meant waiting until the teacher had enough interaction with each child to feel comfortable in the referring process to initiate the referral actions.

Alternative 2. A second means of identification considered was ability testing either through an achievement test or a battery of standardized instruments. The two factors that were considered obstacles to this approach were (a) that such testing was prohibitive in terms of cost and (b) that there are serious questions as to the cultural free aspects of tests that are available. In addition, the norming processes used to standardize the

From *Exceptional Children*, 1977, *43*, 414–420. Reprinted by permission of The Council for Exceptional Children. Copyright 1977 by The Council for Exceptional Children, 1920 Association Drive, Reston, Virginia 22091.

The research reported herein was supported in part by Grant No. OEG-0-74-2709 from the Bureau of Education for the Handicapped, US Office of Education. Contractors undertaking such projects under Government sponsorship are encouraged to express freely their professional judgment in the conduct of the project. Points of view or opinions stated do not, therefore, necessarily represent official Office of Education position or policy.

ability tests for young children are highly questionable.

Alternative 3. The third identification alternative was to devise a screening process that has the following characteristics: (a) it should be easily administered by classroom teachers, (b) it should provide the earliest possible means of inschool identification of at risk children with a high correlation to teacher identification of at risk children at the end of the school year, and (c) it should have direct instructional relevance for remedial actions.

While each of the above was a viable alternative for early identification of handicapping conditions, it was determined that alternatives 1 and 3, teacher referral and screening process, would be combined to produce a pilot project. The conclusion was based on a review of the available literature relating to the identification of handicapping conditions in young children.

REVIEW OF THE LITERATURE

An Educational Resources Information Center search of related literature based on descriptors such as *Identification, Preschool Programs,* and *Education* revealed 32 current studies. The primary mode of identification within these studies was equally distributed over academic, social behaviors, developmental patterns, language development, and visual motor development categories. Not only does the mode differ, but as Glidewell and Swallow (1969) pointed out, the screening methods vary considerably from the interview, to full diagnostic batteries, to symptom surveys. However, only a small number of studies addressed themselves to the crucial issue: predictive validity. Keeping this deficiency in mind, there still remain significant guidelines currently in the literature to assist in the development of early identification instruments and procedures.

Bradley (1974) reported that when a team approach to learning-problem identification was used for devising a learning profile and modifying kindergarten curriculum, a degree of difference was found favoring the experimental groups for more child improvement. The implication is that some form of identification will be slightly better than relying solely on the referral process.

A contrasting view was given by Keogh and Becker (1973). They have raised questions concerning the relevancy of any identification procedures depending upon criteria from outside the actual school environment. Their questions serve as cautions in the development of identification instruments: (a) How valid are the identifying or predictive measures? (b) What are the implications of diagnostic data for remediation or educational intervention? (c) Do benefits of early identification outweigh possible damaging or negative efforts of such recognition?

The validity question cited in this critique is the most important in the development of early identification procedures but remains unanswerable. There are few clear corresponding relationships between the identification of learning disabilities from screening procedures and subsequent school achievement. The reasons for a lack of successful progress in educational programs on the part of some children are complex. In addition, as Haring and Ridgway (1967) have indicated, a failure to progress satisfactorily in learning may be as much the fault of the learning environment as a function of the organism. However, Keogh and Becker (1973) postulated a most important guideline: Predictive validity will increase when the screening material is relevant to the immediate school environment in which the child will function.

The above studies conclude contrasting views which may be interpreted to mean that some combination of teacher identification and screening with materials of immediate consequence to the school environment is the best means of finding handicapping conditions and effecting instructional change.

The two predictive validity studies reviewed yielded one correlational design and one longitudinal study. The correlational study (Amundson, 1972) was based on the Metropolitan Readiness Test and the Wizard of Oz Preschool Screening Program (Amundson, 1972) and showed $r = .90$ with an N of 23 pupils. The longitudinal study (Rubin & Krus, 1974) indicated the School Behavior Profile found the same identified problem kindergarten pupils in the fourth grade 42% of the time. Both studies tended not to use acceptable predictive criteria. However, it can be concluded that a need exists for identification instruments which have firm predictive validity.

Generally, the research literature indicates consensus on some important points: (a) Teachers of preschool children should be the basic identification agent of finding handicapping conditions of children in their charge, (b) any means of finding children who may need learning assistance that avoids standardized testing should be considered, and (c) no child should be labeled as "at risk" based on any previously administered standardized test in light of the inadequate reliability and validity of such instruments (Dykstra, 1967; Severson, 1972; Proger, 1972). The remaining potential seems to lie in some procedure that insures teacher agreement and predictive outcome of immediate program change.

Based on a pragmatic approach, the administration and staff of the Baltimore Learning Continuum Project, which provided comprehensive special services to young handicapped children within regular preschool and first grade classrooms, designed and field tested a screening instrument. The instrument attempted to identify children 4 and 5 years of age early in the school year while having a high correlation with teacher referrals of children needing some type of special education service.

PROCEDURES

The basic measurement used for the investigation of the screening device was frequency. Frequency is defined as counts per unit time. The counts were academic performances, such as writing letters and numbers and saying names, words, and letters. The fixed time unit was 1 minute. The frequency score was the correct number of responses per minute. The consistent measurement plan insured complete reliability when counts were accurate. The staff of the project did the counting and timing to insure high reliability.

Children were individually screened on 5 consecutive days. Screening stations were manned by two project staff members in an area adjacent to the early education classroom. During the first day of screening, children received assistance in relational and directional concepts such as *alike* or *different* and *top* or *bottom*. The actual 1 minute timing of the task began when the child started the task rather than on the signal of "go" by the tester.

The selected population was based on children enrolled in an early education program within a lower socioeconomic area of the City of Baltimore. The population included children from three classrooms, 35 females and 30 males for a total of 65 children.

Table 11-1 includes the subtests that were used and the purpose of each subtest. Also included are descriptions of the materials used, task descriptions, and scoring.

The screening procedures were initiated in February, which was somewhat late in the school year. However, this was a pilot effort in preparation for the coming school year in the fall. Teachers' classification of their children into at risk and low risk categories was completed in May.

The most useful reference in the literature involving a frequency sampling procedure in early identification was the *State of Washington Screening Booklets* (Kunzelmann, 1972). Under this system several subtests are similar to their procedures: the X's in Circles, the See-Say Letters, the See-Say Numbers and the See-Write Letters. However, in the present study several changes were initiated. First, several subtests were added to reflect a younger population of pupils: Naming Pictures, Naming Number Sets, Color Matching and Hear-Touch (body parts). Secondly, to reduce the typical great variability of performance at this early age, children were tested individually on all subtests rather than including a mixture of group and individual sessions. Finally, subtests were eliminated from consideration that did not have immediate curricular implications of performance for the child.

RATIONALE FOR SUBTEST SELECTIONS

Subtest design was based on several factors. Measures were developed on the basis of their face validity to the immediate school environment in which the child functioned; that is, the content of the measure reflected an important curricular goal or performance skill that the child was expected to exhibit. The frequency score yielded the child's relative proficiency in the performance of each specific task. In addition, the visual, auditory, and kinesthetic modalities were all tapped in the design of various subtests. The first seven subtests were administered to the 3- and 4-year-olds; all nine subtests were administered to the 5-year-olds.

The first two subtests represented a measure of proficiency with the child's basic tool in the early education program, the primary pencil. The X's in Circles provided the opportunity to assess eye-hand coordination with the primary pencil within the spatial requirements of a small circle. In the second subtest, *XO* Pattern, the child's developing skill with the pencil was employed in the reproduction of patterns of visual stimuli. This subtest was included after behavioral analy-

Table 11-1. Subtest selections

Subtests	Purpose	Task	Materials	Scoring
X's in Circles	Test eye-hand coordination when using a pencil	Mark X in each circle	40 ¾-inch circles on grid	Total no. of X's inside circles
XO Pattern	Test ability to produce and imitate a pattern	Continue XO pattern	Paper divided into 88 squares	Total no. of X's and O's in correct pattern
Counting Number Sets	Test ability to count	Count objects on each card	20 cards; Objects 1 to 10	Total no. of correct counts
See-Say Letters	Test ability to name letters	Name letters	Chart with upper and lower case letters (114)	Total no. of letters named
Matching Colors	Test ability to match colors	Match colored blocks to colored boxes	46 blocks and 6 matching boxes	Total no. of blocks matched
Naming Pictures	Test ability to name picture symbols of objects	Name pictures objects	77 pictures mounted on a chart	Total no. of pictures named
Hear-Touch (body parts)	Test auditory discrimination and locating body parts	Touch body parts named	Audiotape with 40 cues	Total no. of responses
See-Write Letters	Test ability to reproduce letters	Reproduce letters underneath samples	Paper with upper case letters	Total no. of letters copied
See-Say Numbers	Test ability to name numbers	Name random numbers from 1 to 20	78 numbers on a chart	Total no. of numbers named

Note: Time = 60 seconds.

sis of the mainstream classroom revealed an increasing emphasis on the child's skill to reproduce visual patterns via the chalkboard, overhead projector, and practice worksheets.

Counting in sequence is viewed in many early childhood programs as a primary mathematics skill. Within this particular program, children also identified the counted objects as a set. In the Counting Number Sets subtest, a chart of objects and geometric shapes in sets of 1 to 10 was developed. The child was to count the number of objects or shapes on the card and specify the number in the set.

The names of the letters of the alphabet were emphasized as a preliminary activity to reading. In this school environment, both upper case and lower case letters were used. The See-Say Letters subtest measured the child's facility at naming upper and lower case letters from a chart.

Colors were an important learning task not only in simple discrimination of one color from

another but also as cues to learning other instructional tasks. The Matching Colors subtest involved the matching of blocks of six different colors with a colored box of the same color. The child was not required to name the color.

A child's expressive language within any educational program is critical to most learning activities, especially prereading instruction. The Naming Pictures subtest was devised to measure a child's verbal facility in naming simple object drawings without any background to distract from the object. Special consideration was given to selecting objects for the drawings that were in high frequency use in the classrooms and appropriate to the children's background of experiences.

The last subtest administered to the 3- and 4-year-olds was the Hear-Touch. In this subtest, a voice on a prerecorded tape named a part of the body every 1.5 seconds as the child listened and touched the correct part of the body. The specific body parts were derived from curricular objectives: head, ear, eye, nose, neck, shoulder, elbow, hand, waist, knee, ankle, and foot.

Two additional subtests were administered only to the 5-year-olds. Both subtests reflect the cognitive emphasis of this specific curriculum on proficiency in letters and numbers. In the See-Write Letters, the child copied randomized alphabet letters (upper and lower case) in a box directly beneath the model letters. The last subtest was the See-Say Numbers. The child named randomized numbers from 1 to 20 from a number chart.

RESULTS

Upon completion of the screening, a mean score was computed for the 5 days of frequency scores per each subtest yielding seven scores for 4-year-olds and nine scores for 5-year-olds.

The frequency scores for each subtest were ranked from highest to lowest score for each age group. Children were identified as at risk when three or more of the subtest scores fell below a certain cutoff level. Initially, three different cutoff levels were established. However, as shown in Table 11-2, the 25% cutoff level was verified later as possessing the highest predictive value. Applying the 25% criteria as the cutoff for ranked scores, 15 children were identified as possible at risk learners.

Table 11-2. Comparison of three cutoff levels to year end teacher identification of at risk children

Cutoff criteria	Number of children identified
37.5%	17 (13% overidentified)
25 %	15 (1% underidentified)
10 %	12 (8% underidentified)

Study of the cumulative records of the 65 children following the screening found that 8 of the 15 children identified by the screening instrument had already been referred for special instructional assistance by the classroom teacher. One child had been referred for assistance whose frequency scores were above the cutoff domain.

The issues raised from the research literature indicated predictive validity as the most critical outcome of an early identification procedure. Teacher judgment is cited as one of the most reliable means of identifying at risk children when teachers have sufficient time to observe their children (usually a minimum of 4 months or more). Predictive validity of an early identifica-

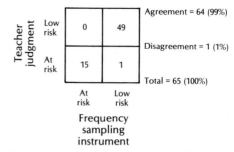

Figure 11-1. Comparison of identification by teacher judgment to results of instrument identification.

tion procedure can be established, therefore, by comparing the results of early identification screening with teacher judgment.

Near the completion of the school term (third week in May), the three classroom teachers participating in this study were interviewed. On the basis of their judgment, the 65 children were classified as either at risk or low risk for the upcoming school year. The teachers indicated that in addition to the 9 children previously referred, there were 7 other children who, in the teachers' opinions, could be classified as at risk. Using teacher judgment as the criteria for accuracy, Figure 11-1 summarizes the findings. At the 25% cutoff level, there is a high correlation between teacher judgment and identification through the frequency sampling technique as to the classification of 65 children into low risk or at risk categories.

While the results of this screening are strong, it should be noted that only 65 children were included in this pilot study. The power of the screening device is questionably high. There is a need to repeat the procedures with a larger population.

ADMINISTRATION OF HIGH PREDICTIVE SUBTESTS

Although subtests were designed to represent major instructional emphases and performance skills within the extant early education program, the nine subtests did not function equally well at discriminating at risk learners from low risk learners. In Table 11-3, the nine subtests are ranked by their predictive value. Each subtest's predictive value was established by correlating teachers' judgment of at risk learners at the end of the year with each child's position in the ranking of the mean scores per each subtest. A brief

Table 11-3. Ranking of subtests by highest predictive value

Subtest	4-year-olds	5-year-olds
X's in Circles	1	3
XO Pattern	2	2
Counting Number Sets	4	6
See-Say Letters	5	1
Matching Colors	3	4
Naming Pictures	6	8
Hear-Touch (body parts)	7	9
See-Write Letters	–	7
See-Say Numbers	–	5

perusal of Table 11-3 indicates that the see-write subtest and see-say subtests seem to have the most predictive value.

There were a number of empirical findings that improved test administration reliability. First, administration of the subtests should be on an individual basis. It is generally agreed that children at this age level do not perform consistently in most testing situations. Factors such as attending to directions, on task behaviors, and motivation are school related skills beginning to develop during kindergarten and first grade; it is difficult to obtain reliable results in a group administration situation. To accommodate these developmental factors, three screening stations, with furniture suitable to the children's age, were used to test individual children.

Second, children should receive a practice session for all subtests on the first day of screening. It was found that some children needed assistance with making marks such as X or did not understand key directional and relational concepts used in the screening procedures.

Third, although children are started on the subtest with the traditional "Ready, get set, go" type of direction, timing should not begin until the child actually begins the task. This procedure makes the stopwatch a necessity during testing.

Careful preparation of subtest materials also insures reliable results. A packet of subtest materials for each child should be kept in a large envelope with a cover sheet stapled to the front to record identification data and all subtest scores for the 5 days of screening. Practice sheets may be covered with laminating material so that they are reusable; confusion of practice materials with scored materials is also prevented in this way. To design standard charts, press type letters and numbers were used. In this way the materials were prepared with a standard appearance without requiring the services of a draftsman.

CONCLUSIONS

Three major conclusions have evolved from this pilot study: (a) The amount of instructional months of savings for children by using screening is critical, (b) the teacher variable was not an issue in the screening, and (c) the predictive validity of screening through a frequency sampling technique is high.

The first conclusion is the most critical to the children who may be identified by teachers during a school year. Given that teacher referrals are the best means of identification when teachers know the children, any means of speeding the process is advantageous to the children. By waiting for teacher referrals to evolve, many instructional months are lost. From the pilot study reported here, it is estimated that over 144 months of needed instruction were wasted because of not identifying children earlier in the year.

The second conclusion (the teacher variable issue), which is found in most testing, is not a factor based on the independent judgments of three project staff members. Table 11-4 indicates the ranking of the three classroom teachers from the sample screening classes on various instructional issues. The teachers are clearly different in their approach to instruction. Without question they agreed with the screening results when the 25% cutoff level was used.

Table 11-4. Teacher instructional strategies

Area observed	Teacher		
	A	B	C
Class control	2	3	1
Attention to children	2	3	1
Individual testing	2	1	3
Group work	2	3	1
Noise level	2	3	1
Class organization	2	3	1
Curriculum materials	2	3	1
Extra activities	3	2	1
Student motivation	2	3	1
Teacher motivation	2	3	1
Use of school resources	3	2	1

Note: Scale of 1 to 3, with 3 as highest.

The third conclusion (high predictive validity) must be replicated because of sample size of this study; however, the predictive validity of the screening is a guarded conclusion on which the above two conclusions are based. Based on the findings in this pilot study, the early identification techniques described here will be expanded to six elementary schools for the 1975–1976 school year with a total student population of approximately 800 students in kindergarten and first grade classrooms. If the predictive validity holds at or above .90, then it will be recommended that the screening techniques be implemented systemwide.

REFERENCES

Amundson, M. S. *A preliminary screening program to identify functioning strengths and weaknesses in preschool children.* ERIC ED 071743, August, 1972.

Berger, S., & Perlman, E. *A model for prevention: A kindergarten screening program.* ERIC ED 085083, 1973.

Bradley, E. *Identification of Learning Problems—Adjustment in kindergarden curricula.* ERIC ED 095995, 1974.

Dykstra, R. The use of reading readiness tests for diagnosis and prediction: A critique. In T. C. Barrett (Ed.), *The evaluation of children's reading achievement.* Newark DE: International Reading Association, 1967.

Glidewell, J. C., & Swallow, C. S. *The prevalence of maladjustment in elementary schools: A report prepared for the Joint Commission on the Mental Health of Children.* Chicago: University of Chicago Press, 1969.

Haring, N. G., & Ridgway, R. W. Early identification of children with learning disabilities. *Exceptional Children,* 1967, *33,* 387–395.

Keogh, B. K., & Becker, L. D. Early detection of learning problems: Questions, cautions and guidelines. *Exceptional Children,* 1973, *40,* 5–11.

Kunzelmann, H. *Child service demonstration project.* State of Washington: Department of Public Instruction, 1972.

Proger, B. E. Test review no. 9: Tests of basic experiences. *Journal of Special Education,* 1972, *6,* 179–184.

Rubin, R. A. & Krus, P. H. *Predictive validity of a school behavior rating scale.* ERIC ED 090276, April, 1974.

Severson, R. A. Early detection of children with potential learning disabilities: A seven year effort. *Proceedings, 80th Annual Convention, American Psychological Association,* 1972, *7,* 561–562.

12. Attention and distractibility during reading in hyperactive boys

DAVID A. BREMER   JOHN A. STERN

Hyperactivity, or hyperkinesis, has been considered to be an important clinical syndrome found in children described as overactive, inattentive, and distractible (Burks, 1960; Chess, 1960; Stewart, Pitts, Craig, & Dieruff, 1966). Experimental research has resulted in the seemingly contradictory findings that hyperactive children are less attentive, yet not more distractible, than nonhyperactive children. According to Douglas (1973), one should be "cautious about treating failures of attention and distractibility as identical problems, as clinicians and teachers almost invariably seem to do." Although being inattentive to a task may appear to be synonymous with being distracted from it, operational definitions of attention and distractibility have tended to differ with regard to the type of stimulus being studied.

Attention has been defined in terms of efficiency of reactions to signal stimuli on laboratory tasks under constant background conditions. Evidence of attentional deficits among hyperactive children has been found on reaction time and vigilance tasks. Slower and more variable reaction times of hyperactive children compared to normal children (Cohen & Douglas, 1972) are thought to result from lapses in attention. Hyperactive children respond to fewer signal stimuli on vigilance tasks (Sykes, Douglas, Weiss, &

Minde, 1971; Sykes, Douglas, & Morgenstern, 1973), and failure to detect such signals is suggestive of inattention. Sykes et al. (1971) recommended that "future research must examine behaviors that are more closely related to the actual attentional demands placed on the child in the school setting."

Distractibility has been measured by decrements in task performance as the result of presentation of extraneous, "distracting" stimuli. Sykes et al. (1971) found no deleterious effect of intermittent white noise on hyperactive children's vigilance performance. Distracting color backgrounds in a discrimination task had no differential effect on reaction times of hyperactive and normal children (Sykes et al., 1973). Decreases in speed of color naming in the presence of contradictory cues were no greater among hyperactive children than in controls (Campbell, Douglas, & Morgenstern, 1971). These results are difficult to reconcile with statements by clinicians that distractibility is a cardinal symptom of hyperkinesis (Eisenberg, 1966).

Sykes et al. (1973) did find significantly more glances off-task among hyperactive children than among controls. This finding suggests an alternative measure of distractibility in terms of visual responses to distracting stimuli.

The present study was designed to determine

From the *Journal of Abnormal Child Psychology*, 1976, *4*, 323–334. Copyright © 1976 Plenum Publishing Corporation. Reprinted by permission.

(a) if attentional deficits of hyperactive children previously demonstrated on laboratory tasks generalize to a typical school task, i.e., reading and (b) if differences between hyperactive and normal children are found in visual attention to distracting stimuli.

METHOD

Subjects

Fifteen 9- to 12-year-old hyperactive boys were selected from outpatient mental health services on the basis of three criteria: (a) an impression of overactivity as a prominent symptom, derived from clinical records and/or referral statements, (b) parental ratings of "overactivity" and "always on the move" plus any 6 symptoms from a list of 18 other hyperactive symptoms according to the method of Stewart et al. (1966), and (c) an IQ above 80 on the Peabody Picture Vocabulary Test and a Reading Grade Placement of at least 3.0 on the Wide Range Achievement Test (WRAT). Two boys who met the above criteria were excluded from the sample because of lack of cooperation and another due to equipment failure.

The hyperactive boys were matched closely with nonhyperactive boys on the basis of age (hyperactive and control $\bar{X} = 10$ years, 7 months), Peabody IQ (hyperactive $\bar{X} = 97.5$, control $\bar{X} = 96.0$), WRAT Reading Grade (hyperactive $\bar{X} = 5.3$, control $\bar{X} = 5.4$), and socioeconomic background (predominately low-income families, 3 pairs were black and 12 white).

Apparatus. Stories at the second (300 words), fourth (500 words), and sixth (900 words) grade levels were selected from materials published by Science Research Associates (1960) and pica typed in uniform style at 20 lines per page. The reading materials were placed on a stand attached to a comfortable chair.

Distracting stimuli consisted of (a) a telephone ringing (65db) with flashing lights on the telephone or (b) a sinusoidal oscilloscope display accompanied by a 75-db sound of a Monroe electromechanical calculator performing multiplication operations. Auditory stimuli were taped in random order with 5-second stimulus duration and variable intertrial intervals from 10 to 20 seconds. A sound-sensitive relay activated the corresponding visual stimulus on each trial.

Horizontal and vertical electroculograms were recorded on magnetic tape for subsequent processing by a PDP-12 computer programmed for analysis of eye movements during reading (Hawley, Stern, & Chen, 1974). Onset and offset of distracting stimuli were recorded on a third channel of the magnetic tape. The recording equipment was enclosed in a recording booth equipped with a one-way mirror situated at an angle to the reading chair to eliminate the child's reflection as a distraction.

Procedure. Each S was tested individually on one occasion. E explained the recording procedure and reassured the child as electrodes were applied. After electrodes were in place and equipment turned on, E administered the PPVT and WRAT according to standard instructions.

Then E said, "I have some stories for you to read silently to yourself." E explained that he would be in the recording booth and could see when S was finished via the one-way mirror. The first story was at the second grade level. After S finished the story, E removed the material, asked S some questions about the story, and presented another second grade story for S to read. Following the initial story, one story at each of the three levels was presented for S to read silently under quiet background conditions. However, Ss whose reading speed on the second grade story was less than 80 words per minute (wpm) were not given a sixth grade level story and Ss who read at 33 to 50 wpm received a short version of the fourth grade story.

After S completed the stories in the quiet condition, a similar procedure was followed using an alternate set of second, fourth, and sixth grade stories and the distraction tape was activated while S was reading.

RESULTS

Reading speeds in the two groups were similar. One boy (hyperactive) read less than 33 wpm and received only second grade level stories; five hyperactive boys and four of the nonhyperactive boys read more than 80 wpm. Differences between the two groups in average time to read a page and average time to read a line were not significant.

It had been predicted that as the result of inattentiveness the electrooculograms of hyperactive boys would differ from those of nonhyperactive boys in a number of respects, but no significant differences were found prior to the distraction periods. Variables considered were durations of fixation pauses, variance of fixation pause duration, incidence of exceptionally long or short fixations, variability in reading speed, eye-blink frequency, head movement artifacts, and horizontal eye movements away from the printed page, i.e., off-task. In the last comparison it was found that more than half of the nonhyperactive boys were on-task all the time while less than a third of the hyperactive boys were consistently on-task; however, this difference was not statistically significant.

The hyperactive group was found to be significantly more reactive to the distracting stimuli than was the nonhyperactive group. Responses to the first 15 distraction stimulus presentations were considered since all Ss were exposed to at least 15 stimuli and some Ss finished reading before the 16th trial.

All but one of the boys in each group responded visually (by looking toward the stimulus display) to at least one distraction presentation. The number of stimuli eliciting a response was highly correlated with the total time distracted (rho = .98 in the hyperactive group, rho = .80 in the control group). The number of responses on odd stimulus trials correlated with responses on even trials (rho = .91 for hyperactive, rho = .82 for controls). The telephone and the oscilloscope also were responded to similarly (hyperactive rho = .78, control rho = .60).

The median number of stimuli eliciting a response was five in the hyperactive group and four in the control group. This numerically small difference was reliable ($p<.05$, Wilcoxon matched-pair, signed-ranks test). In terms of the duration of responses to distractions, the median time distracted during the entire series of stimuli was 18 seconds in the hyperactive group and 5 seconds in the control group ($p<.05$, Wilcoxon matched-pair, signed-ranks test).

The average number of children responding per stimulus for three blocks of five stimulus trials is presented in Table 12-1. Trends toward habituation of responses to the distracting stimuli were evaluated by the Friedman two-way analysis of variance by ranks, and the tests were significant ($p<.001$) for both hyperactive and control groups. Differences between the two groups

Table 12-1. Mean number of children distracted per trial

| Group | Trial blocks | | |
	1–5	*6–10*	*11–15*
Hyperactive	10.6	6.0	3.8
Control	8.2	3.0	1.8

in rate of habituation were assessed by the Wilcoxon test for significance of interactions which was not significant. Though hyperactive boys were significantly more responsive to the distractors, such distractors did not interfere with the aspects of task performance measured.

Hyperactive children, under conditions of no distraction, could not be discriminated from their matched controls on any of our measures of eye movements during reading. We therefore conducted a post hoc analysis of one other aspect of reading behavior on the five boys who were most responsive to the distracting stimuli used in this experiment. All five of these boys were members of our "hyperactive" group. The aspect of reading behavior evaluated consisted of indicants that the child had skipped lines during reading. Since each page consisted of 20 typewritten lines, we expected the normal reader to make 19 large regressive eye movements per page to reposition the eyes from the end of one line to the beginning of the next. Eye movement data for all children in the hyperactive group and the five matched controls for the most distractible hyperactive children were evaluated for this analysis. This analysis revealed that four of these five highly distractible boys had skipped at least one-fourth of the reading material presented (prior to the distracting condition). None of their matched controls appeared to have skipped lines. Fisher's exact probability test indicated that the difference between the five distractible boys and their controls was statistically significant ($p<.05$, one-tailed). Fisher's test of the difference between the five most distractible and the remaining hyperactive boys, only one of whom had skipped material, was also significant ($p<.05$).

DISCUSSION

The hypothesis that hyperactive boys have, on the average, more lapses in attention during reading than is true of normal children was not supported by our data. If groups are matched on the basis of age, intelligence, and reading skill level (as measured by the WRAT), no differences in how they go about the task of reading under either nondistracting or distracting conditions are found. In other words, on-task behavior does not discriminate between groups.

The hypothesis that hyperactive boys are more readily distracted by extraneous stimuli was supported. Hyperactive boys were more often distracted by the extraneous stimuli used, spent more time looking toward or at the distractors, and the degree of distraction, as rated by an observer (on a 6-point scale), was greater than that of normal boys.

Our data thus generally indicate that hyperactive children (matched for age, IQ, and reading skill level) show no attentional deficits while engaged in a reading task where distractors are kept to a minimum. They were, however, significantly more responsive to distractors while reading. We must agree with Douglas (1973) that failure in attention and distractibility are not identical problems. Our hyperactive children demonstrated their *ability* to attend; this of course has been reasonably well documented in studies which have manipulated motivation and demonstrated dramatic improvement in the performance of hyperactive children so manipulated (Worland, North-Jones, & Stern, 1973). Thus in the present study it is not their ability to attend but their ability to inhibit responding to other environmental events that discriminates hyperactive from normal children.

If we restrict our analysis to a "select" group of hyperactive boys, namely those most responsive to the distracting stimuli used in phase 2 of our experiment, we do find these boys to be less attentive to the reading task under nondistracting conditions than are either the other hyperactive boys or their matched controls. We thus have at least suggestive evidence that children who are readily distracted are also more inattentive on tasks where there are no external (or at least no obvious external) distractors, inattentiveness here being manifested by the fact that they skipped more lines during reading of text than did less distractible boys.

We would concur with the Cromwell, Baumeister, and Hawkins (1963) suggestion that so-called hyperactive children are not necessarily overactive but that their apparent hyperactivity is due principally to their lack of persistence and shifting of activities. Thus, for some authors, especially clinicians, distractibility is an important component of the hyperactive child syndrome. They see hyperactivity as the principal symptom; inferred as a variable important in the manifestation of this behavior is distractibility (Clarkson & Hayden, 1971; Eisenberg, 1966; Fish, 1971; Stewart, Thach, & Freidin, 1970). Unfortunately, much of the experimental literature finds distractors not producing differential effects on normal and hyperactive children. Sykes et al. (1971), for example, found intermittent white noise to have no differential effect on the performance of a vigilance task; Campbell et al. (1971) found irrelevant peripheral figures to produce no differential effect on a primary task involving color naming. From our study it appears that if one utilizes a well-practiced skill, such as reading, that distractors are differentially responded to by the two groups, with hyperactives responding more than control children. Our findings of nondifferential effects between the two groups on our measures of reading can be attributed to the fact that we selected our control group so that it was matched on reading level with the hyperactive group. Though we had hoped to find differences in processing strategies (as inferred from eye movement data) between the groups, this did not occur.

REFERENCES

Burks, H. F. The hyperkinetic child. *Exceptional Children,* 1960, *27,* 18.

Campbell, S. B., Douglas, V. I., & Morgenstern, G. Cognitive styles in hyperactive children and the effect of methylphenidate. *Journal of Child Psychology and Psychiatry,* 1971, *12,* 53–67.

Chess, S. Diagnosis and treatment of the hyperactive child. *New York State Journal of Medicine,* 1960, *60,* 2379–2385.

Clarkson, F. E., & Hayden, B. S. A developmental study of perceptual, conceptual, motivational and self-concept differences between and within hyperactive and normal groups of preadolescent boys, Project No. 5-0414, Washington, D.C., U.S. Office of Education, Bureau for the Handicapped, 1971.

Cohen, N. J., & Douglas, V. I. Characteristics of the orienting response in hyperactive and normal children. *Psychophysiology,* 1972, *9,* 238–245.

Cromwell, R. L. Baumeister, A., & Hawkins, W. F. Research in activity level. In N. R. Ellis (Ed.), *Handbook of mental deficiency.* New York: McGraw-Hill, 1963.

Douglas, V. I. Sustained attention and impulse control: Implications for handicapped children. In J. A. Swets & L. L. Elliott (Eds.), *Psychology and the handicapped child,* Washington, D.C., U.S. Office of Education, 1973.

Eisenberg, L. The management of the hyperkinetic child. *Developmental Medicine and Child Neurology,* 1966, *8,* 593–598.

Fish, B. The "one child, one drug" myth of stimulants in hyperkinesis, importance of diagnostic categories in evaluating treatment. *Archives of General Psychiatry,* 1971, *25,* 193–203.

Hawley, T. F., Stern, J. A., & Chen, S. C. Computer analysis of eye movements during reading. *Reading World,* 1974, *13,* 307–317.

Stewart, M. A., Pitts, F., Craig, A., & Dieruff, W. The hyperactive child syndrome. *American Journal of Orthopsychiatry,* 1966, *36,* 861–867.

Stewart, M. A., Thach, B. T., & Freidin, M. R. Accidental poisoning and the hyperactive child syndrome. *Diseases of the Nervous System,* 1970, *31,* 403–417.

Sykes, D. H., Douglas, V. I., & Morgenstern, G. Sustained attention in hyperactive children. *Journal of Child Psychology and Psychiatry,* 1973. *14,* 213–220.

Sykes, D. H., Douglas, V. I., Weiss, G., & Minde, K. K. Attention in the hyperactive child and the effect of methylphenidate (Ritalin). *Journal of Child Psychology and Psychiatry,* 1971, *12,* 129–139.

Worland, J., North-Jones, M., & Stern, J. A. Performance and activity of hyperactive and normal boys as a function of distraction and reward. *Journal of Abnormal Child Psychology,* 1973, *1,* 363–377.

13. Current medical practice and hyperactive children

JONATHAN SANDOVAL   NADINE M. LAMBERT
WILSON YANDELL

A growing number of studies dealing with children variously diagnosed as hyperkinetic, minimally brain damaged, hyperactive, or learning disabled are available to the physician in child practice.[4] The results of these studies offer a wide variety of information, some of it contradictory, to those who are responsible for diagnosis and treatment of children with these problems. As yet, very little has been done to assess the impact of this information on physicians or to validate it against medical practice. This report presents the results of a survey of physicians who treat children in a California metropolitan area. The survey's aim was to elicit from physicians 1) opinions about the value of diagnostic procedures used in identifying conditions which include symptoms of hyperactivity, 2) preferences for several commonly used diagnostic labels, and 3) preferred treatment procedures for children with these conditions. The investigators further attempted to determine whether the medical diagnosis and treatment of children with hyperactive symptoms was influenced by factors such as the child's family and home environment, the child's school environment, and other aspects of the child's personal and social functioning. In addition, the study investigated the attitudes of a representative sample of physicians toward the several treatment regimens commonly

recommended for children who exhibit symptoms including hyperactivity.

There is perhaps no other area in contemporary pediatric diagnosis where the practitioner must sift through a more confused set of opinions and research findings. Most often, the designation of "hyperkinesis," "minimal cerebral dysfunction," or other preferred terms used to label this complex of behavioral and medical difficulties, is defined by the *presence* of hyperactive behavior patterns and by the *absence* of other conditions such as cerebral palsy, epilepsy, gross brain damage, psychosis, or mental retardation. Regardless of the label applied to such children, the common denominator is the presence of behavior that is inappropriately and excessively active. While there is no expert consensus about the etiology or etiologies of this syndrome of medical and behavioral findings, the practicing physician is, nevertheless, expected to treat these children when they appear in his office. We hoped, by documenting the procedures followed by physicians, to be able to provide baseline information on what diagnostic information is most valuable to physicians, information on which types of diagnostic labels physicians consider to be most appropriate, and information on the range of recommended treatments.

From the *American Journal of Orthopsychiatry*, 1976, 4, 381–387. Copyright © The American Orthopsychiatric Association, Inc. Reproduced by permission.
  Research was supported by NIMH grant MH–20756–01.

METHOD

The survey was conducted in the two East Bay counties of the San Francisco-Oakland Metropolitan Area. The two counties embrace inner city, rural, and suburban areas and in many respects are a microcosm of California, if not North American environments.

The Alameda-Contra Costa Medical Association printed an announcement of the study in its monthly bulletin and provided the investigators with a roster of its members from which to draw the survey sample. The population of physicians surveyed included those whose practices might include children with hyperactive symptoms—the pediatricians, neurologists, psychiatrists, and general or family practice physicians. Since the number of physicians within each specialty varied, each group was randomly sampled until a number of members of each specialty was selected in proportion to the number of such specialists in the two counties. As those sampled declined to participate, they were replaced when possible by another physician with the same specialty. The final number of respondents differs slightly from the ideal proportions because most of the small number of practitioners in the child psychiatry and the neurology specialty cooperated, while a large number of general practitioners stated they did not treat children and declined to participate. Table 13-1 presents the number of respondents by specialization, sex, and year graduated from medical school; all were white, except for one black psychiatrist and one Oriental pediatrician. A check of the location of the practices of the respondents indicated that the two counties were proportionately represented and distributed through the rural, suburban, and urban locales in the geographic region. About half of the respondents stated they had no regular contact with schools, whereas the other half had served schools in some consultative capacity.

Each physician sampled was contacted by mail and offered an honorarium of $30 for completing the questionnaires. There was a telephone follow-up with those who indicated they did not wish to participate, as well as those who did not respond to the mailing.

Physician cooperation. A total of 120 sets of questionnaires was sent out. We received 67 replies and ultimately 48 completed forms. Pediatricians, child psychiatrists, and neurologists were the most cooperative in agreeing to complete the questionnaires (see Table 13-1). When we questioned the physicians who did not complete the forms, 35 (or 29.1% of total sampled group) said they declined to participate because they saw only adults. Other reasons given by those who did not wish to participate included being too busy to complete the forms (13, or 10.8% of total), being no longer in practice (13, or 10.8% of total), and objecting to the questions on a philosophical basis (8, or 6.6% of total). We regard our sample as reasonably representative of the physicians in the two-county area who treat children who are referred to them for problems which include symptoms of hyperactivity.

SURVEY INSTRUMENTS

Any survey of medical practice must present a comprehensive set of symptoms, diagnostic procedures, and treatment options rather than listing items associated with a specific label with its accompanying implied etiology. In the construction of the instruments in this study, we consulted the available research literature on the topic and presented review copies of the questionnaire to a panel of ten prominent specialists representing the fields of child psychiatry, neurology, and pediatrics. Each panelist held a somewhat different expert opinion about hyperactivity in children.

Table 13-1. Characteristics of physicians surveyed (N = 48)

Medical practice	Sex		Year graduated	
	Male	Female	Before 1950	After 1950
Child Psychiatry	5	1	3	3
Psychiatry	4	1	3	2
Neurology[a]	7	0	1	6
Pediatrics	21	2	10	12[b]
General Practice	6	1	6	1
Total[b]	43	5	23	24

[a] Includes one psychiatrist-neurologist.
[b] One pediatrician did not state year of graduation.

We asked each consultant to be sure that our questionnaire reflected his concerns. The resulting instruments were a comprehensive collection of items identified both from research studies and from the nominations of our expert panel of physicians. We believe that the items, as a consequence, represent standard good medical practice.

Diagnostic information check list. This form listed a sequence of information a physician might obtain and use in the evaluation of a child having symptoms of hyperactivity. The items were collected from lists of symptoms that writers in the field considered to be characteristic of hyperactive children.[6,7] These items were collated and reviewed by the consultants. The checklist included the following types of information: 1) History: Presenting Complaints and Symptomatic Behavior (36 items); II) Personal Medical History (41 items); III) Family History (15 items); IV) School History (12 items); V) Physical Examination (21 items); and VI) Laboratory Findings (7 items). For each diagnostic indicator, the sampled physicians were asked to indicate the extent to which they judged the item to have diagnostic significance for hyperactivity on a three-point scale: of critical importance, important, and of no consequence in evaluating hyperactive children. In the event a respondent considered the list of items incomplete, he was invited to add diagnostic signs he considered useful to each section of the questionnaire. few respondents made additions.

Preference for diagnostic labels associated with hyperactivity. This part of the questionnaire contained nine diagnostic labels that have been associated with symptoms of hyperactivity. The respondents were to mark those diagnostic categories that they normally used, and indicate how often they assigned each label to hyperactive children in their practice.

Treatment recommendations. This section contained a list of the most commonly prescribed drugs for hyperactivity, summarized from articles on the topic.[1,2,5] In addition the several other treatment options were listed: "neurological consultation or follow-up care," "referral for counseling or psychotherapy for child," "referral for counseling or psychotherapy for parents," "consultation with school authorities," "referral for physical (motor skills) remediation or therapy," and "referral for special educational remediation." In this section, as in the others, we

asked physicians to add to the list any treatment recommendations which were not listed. However, there were only a few additional suggestions.

The physicians used a three-point rating scale to indicate the frequency with which they have prescribed each treatment for patients they have diagnosed as hyperactive. We realized that some physicians might selectively prescribe one or another treatment depending on the diagnostic label he had assigned to a case. Since this was an observational study, we did not attempt to analyze potential relationships between diagnostic label and treatment program. We focused our attention instead on defining variability or uniformity of medical opinion about these problems of children.

Attitudes toward treatment alternatives. In order to assess the influence of specific factors on treatment, we designed a standard set of case history vignettes describing cases which varied with respect to age of child, severity of problem, and flexibility of school and family response to the child. For each case vignette, we asked the physician to rank-order his preference for the treatment alternatives which have been commonly associated with the management of hyperactive children with learning and behavior disorders. The instrument intentionally left the definition of hyperactivity to the responding physician, since we were primarily interested in assessing preference for individual treatment options relative to characteristics of the child and his environment. The treatment alternatives were: cerebral stimulants, mild tranquilizers, phenothiazines, antidepressant medication, anticonvulsant medication, counseling, or psychotherapy for the child; counseling or psychotherapy for the parents; consultation with school authorities; and recommendation of tutoring or recreational therapy.

Appropriateness of treatment interventions. On this questionnaire, the physicians indicated the extent of their agreement with eight value statements about the many conventional treatments for children with problems of hyperactivity. They rated each statement on a five-point scale from "strongly agree" to "strongly disagree."

RESULTS

Importance of diagnostic signs. The first column of Table 13-2 lists the diagnostic indicators that 80% or more of the physicians judged to be im-

Table 13-2. Physicians' judgments of importance of diagnostic signs

I. History: presenting complaints and symptomatic behavior

A. General Activity Level

Important	*Marginal*	*Not important*
1. Inability to sit still[a]	5. Restlessness in MD's waiting room	10. Spills food often
2. Destructive of toys and furniture[a]	6. Talks too much	
3. Overuses, careless with toys, furniture	7. Gets into things	
4. Doesn't play with games; nomadic play	8. Accident prone	
	9. Reckless	

B. Habit Disturbances

1. Inability to delay gratification	3. Irregular sleep pattern	6. Irregular hunger pattern
2. Doesn't complete projects	4. Hard to get to bed	7. Irregular excretion pattern
	5. Adapts slowly to changes in environment	8. Enuresis

C. Interpersonal Attitudes and Behavior

1. Inattentive; doesn't listen	6. Unpredictable show of affection	14. Constant demand for candy, etc.
2. Temper tantrums	7. Can't accept correction	15. Withdraws from new objects or persons
3. Unresponsive to discipline	8. Teases other children	
4. Unusually aggressive in behavior	9. Defiant	
5. Difficulty in obeying commands	10. Doesn't follow directions	
	11. Lies	
	12. Unpopular with peers	
	13. Plays so as to provoke adult intervention	

D. Affect Mood

1. Unable to tolerate frustration[a]	2. Irritable	
	3. Negative in mood	

II. Personal medical history

A. Prenatal and Perinatal Status, Infancy

1. Early infancy feeding (bottle or breast) problems	4. Extended labor	12. Mother's age at birth
2. Early infancy sleep patterns	5. Fetal distress during labor	13. History of maternal miscarriages
3. Early infancy responsiveness	6. Birth weight	14. Incompatible RH factor
	7. Difficult training for urinary control	15. Over six previous pregnancies
	8. Difficult training for bowel control	16. Operative delivery
	9. Special problems of dependency or anxiety about separation from mother in infancy	17. Infant late in raising head
		18. Late in smiling
	10. Sleep disturbance in infancy	19. Late in turning over
		20. Late in sitting
	11. Withdrawal from affective relating in first two years	21. Late in crawling
		22. Late in walking
		23. Late in talking
		24. Colic of the newborn
		25. Delayed speech development
		26. Night terrors in infancy
		27. Skin disorders in infancy

Table 13-2. Continued

B. Problems in Later Childhood Development

Important	*Marginal*	*Not important*
1. Little capacity for problem-solving in life situations	5. Excessive dependence upon mother	12. Happy and outgoing personality configuration
2. Indications of psychopathology in mother-child relationship	6. Indications of psychopathology in father-child interaction	13. Normal visual acuity
3. Indications of psychopathology in sibling relationships	7. Happy but isolated personality configuration	14. Impression of dexterity
4. Unhappy but taking initiative towards others; may be so intrusive as to antagonize others	8. Unhappy and withdrawn personality configuration	
	9. Provocative and hostile toward others	
	10. Lack of skill in catching a ball	
	11. Awkward use of body skills	

III. Family history

1. Recognized personality disturbance or learning disability in family[a]	3. Marriage of parents considered unhappy	7. Mental illness present
2. Disagreement in response to patient regarding affection and/or discipline	4. Divorce considered	8. Exceptional intellect and achievement present
	5. Discord in marriage open	9. Child born early in marriage
	6. Discord in marriage covert	10. Open display of affection in marriage
		11. Child born late in marriage with other siblings older
		12. Child close in age to another siblings (9 mo. to 2 yrs.)
		13. Child's birth order position
		14. Convulsive seizures in family
		15. Mental deficiency or mental retardation in family

IV. School history

1. Leaves class without permission	10. Factors suggesting presence of mental retardation
2. History of fights	11. Immature speech
3. Repeated grade in school	12. Problems in articulation (dysarthria)
4. History of discipline problems[a]	
5. Moves from one activity to another in class[a]	
6. Difficulty in learning to read	
7. Current work below grade level	
8. Uneven or irregular academic performance	
9. Referral to school psychologist	

V. Physical examination

Important	Marginal	Not important
1. Evidence of disturbance in mental status[a]	3. Impaired sensorium	11. Head circumference
2. Disturbed or hyperactive general behavior in exam[a]	4. Cranial nerve #8; hearing and balance	12. Cranial nerve #1; olfactory sense
	5. Major reflexes normal	13. #2 visual acuity and visual fields, pupillary response
	6. Cerebellar damage (problems of coordination, balance, etc.)	14. #3, 4, 6 extra-ocular movements
	7. Sensation (touch, pain position, vibratory, stereognosis)	15. #5 trigeminal nerve impairment
	8. "Soft" neurological signs: asymmetries	16. #7 facial muscle control
	9. "Soft" neurological signs: twirling of self or objects	17. #9 swallowing, gag reflex, deviation of uvula
	10. Toe walking without evidence of contractures	18. #10 voice quality
		19. #11 head rotation, shoulder movement
		20. #12 tongue control and movement
		21. Peripheral nerve damage (weakness, sensory loss, deformity, contractures)

VI. Laboratory findings

	Marginal	Not important
	1. EEG abnormalities—focal or generalized	4. Blood studies—positive findings
	2. EEG abnormalities—"epileptic"	5. Urinalysis—albuminurria; infection; PKU
	3. Abnormal response to hyperventilation or photic stimulation	6. EEG abnormality—slow
		7. EEG abnormality—fast

[a] Majority of physicians judging item "Of Critical Importance"

portant or critically important in their diagnosis of the syndrome. The third column itemizes the diagnostic indicators that 50% or more of the physicians rated as being of no consequence in a diagnosis of hyperactivity. The middle column lists the remainder of the items, those judged on the whole neither to be important nor of no importance.

Of the presenting complaints and symptomatic behavior, physicians reported looking for evidence in the child's record or behavior of constant physical activity that changes its focus continually (items IA: 1, 2, 3, 4; IC: 1, 4); impatience with goal-directed activities (items IB: 1, 2; ID: 1); and poor relationships with parents around disciplinary matters (items IC: 2, 3, 5). In the patient's medical history, the physicians considered as important disturbed feeding and sleep patterns during infancy (ITEMS IIA: 1, 2); evidence of psychopathology in any of the family interactions (items IIB: 2, 3); and inappropriate attempts to gain attention (items IIB: 1, 4).

In the family history, the physicians ascribed diagnostic significance to a recognized personality disturbance or learning disability (item III: 1), and parental disagreement around the discipline of the child (item III: 2). School history items which were considered to be of diagnostic value were a background of academic failure (items IV: 3, 6, 7, 8, 9); an inability to cope with the movement restrictions of the classroom (items IV: 1, 5); and conflicts with peers and teachers (items IV: 2, 4). There was little consensus among physicians regarding the significance of findings from the physical examination of the child. The child's general behavior during the examination seemed to be the most important characteristic in physician judgments. Surprisingly, no laboratory findings were considered important in diagnosis by a large proportion of our sample.

The items considered by most of the physicians to be of no importance in the diagnosis of the syndrome are also of interest. Most of these items were included to fill out the questionnaire to offer a complete diagnostic record. In general the physicians did not consider developmental lateness, factors surrounding the timing of the child's birth, specific neural impairment, or fast and slow EEG abnormalities to be related to hyperactive conditions.

Items where physicians disagree, where there was no majority consensus, represent either differences in viewpoint about the condition or items of marginal importance. To differentiate these two possibilities we looked to see if physicians with different training (i.e., training in psychiatry, in neurology, and in pediatrics) viewed the importance of the items differently. Although we had a relatively small number of neurologists, in general there were no significant patterns. Physicians with the same training do not necessarily hold the same opinion about the hyperactive conditions. There were expections in two areas, however. Physicians with psychiatric training felt that interpersonal attitudes and behaviors were more important to a diagnosis than did other physicians, placing more importance on the presence of unpredictable shows of affection, defiance, lying, and unpopularity with peers. Physicians with pediatric training tended to place less importance on "soft" neurological signs involving asymmetries and on focal or generalized EEG abnormalities than did physicians with training in neurology or psychiatry. On the whole, items in column two of Table 13-2 represent items which few physicians thought were critically important or of no importance in making their diagnosis.

Preferences for diagnostic labels for hyperactive children. Table 13-3 indicates the extent to which physicians assign any of the several diagnostic labels to children they see in their practices with problems of hyperactivity. The most frequently used diagnostic label was "hyperactive-learning-behavior disorder, etiology unknown." Next most frequent was "minimal brain damage-hyperkinesis," and the third and fourth in order of frequency were "hyperactive behavior syndrome as derivation of anxiety" and "organic brain damage due to birth injury, infection, trauma or unknown etiology." These results suggest that the children that physicians evaluate most often with symptoms of hyperactivity are seen as having disorders with an unknown etiology, perhaps because the most salient diagnostic findings are behavioral indicators rather than physical examination and laboratory data.

Frequency of treatment recommendations for hyperactive children. We were able to gather from the questionnaire an estimate of the frequency of recommended treatment programs, including medication, psychotherapeutic intervention, or educational management. The cerebral stimulants were most often prescribed, with Ritalin and Dexedrine far and away the most popular among these (70% reported prescribing Ritalin frequently). Although Dilantin was frequently prescribed by 20%, so were mild tranquilizers and Phenothiazine tranquilizers such as Mellaril. Antidepressants and anticonvulsants other than Dilantin were not in widespread use.

Follow-up recommendations for a neurological examination were frequent. Two-thirds of the physicians reported recommending consultation with school authorities. Half the physicians polled indicated that they frequently made referrals for psychotherapy or counseling for the

Table 13-3. Frequency of physicians' assignment of diagnostic labels to children referred for hyperactivity, behavior or learning problems

Diagnosis	Rare	Occasional	Frequent
Minimal brain damage-hyperkinesis	16%	32%	52%
Hyperactive behavior syndrome as derivation of anxiety	18	55	27
Organic brain damage due to birth injury, infection, trauma, or unknown etiology	18	57	25
Focal cortical brain lesion	60	35	5
Hyperactive-learning-behavior disorder, etiology unknown	9	20	71
Extreme disorder of temperament	56	32	12
Character disorder	46	42	12
Psychoneurosis	49	37	14
Psychosis	59	27	14

parents and for the children. Referrals for special education or remedial instruction were common recommendations. These findings suggest, contrary to many publicly held views, that physicians in private practice consider multiple, rather than single treatment recommendations for hyperactive children as being most appropriate.

Attitude toward treatment alterantives. In an effort to assess attitudes toward different treatment approaches each physician ranked a comprehensive list of treatment recommendations in terms of their appropriateness for several hypothetical case vingettes of hyperactive children. Here the objective was to determine whether the age of the child, his school, and his family situation were variables which would affect the physician's recommendations. From this questionnaire we inferred that physicians viewed the cerbral stimulant drugs as being of great value in ameliorating the symptoms associated with the hyperactive syndrome regardless of age or other factors. However, it is of great importance in this study of treatment alternatives that physicians ranked highly recommendations for psychotherapy for parents and for children (often considered next after cerebral stimulants). Consultation with school authorities was also a highly valued intervention. In spite of the value assigned by these physicians to psychotherapy and school collaboration, there is little evidence that families follow through on these.[3]

Physicians did not consider as very useful drugs other than cerebral stimulants. They would least often recommend mild tranquilizers, phenothiazine tranquilizers, antidepressants and anticonvulsants, in that order, for the hypothetical cases presented. There was essentially no difference between treatment recommendations for eight-year-olds and eleven-year-olds except for a consistent trend in physician responses which suggests that noncerebral stimulant drugs may be more frequently recommended for older children.

Consultation with school authorities was the recommendation with the highest rank in most of the questionnaire examples, especially where the school was having difficulty with the child and where the school and parents showed evidence of concern. In the cases where the child was not anxious about his behavior or completely unaware of his behavior, the physician respondents often assigned a high rank to counseling or psychotherapy for the child. Counseling or psychotherapy for the parent was deemed more appro-

priate for the sample case which described the parents as desperate for help in coping with the child. Tutoring or recreational therapy as an intervention was suggested for the child who was described as failing, and strongly suggested for a child simply behind but making progress in school.

Prescription of a cerebral stimulant was ranked highly for most of the cases, and was preferred over consultation with school authorities in a majority of the eleven-year-old examples. It received highest rankings in cases of children described in the vingettes who were making an effort already to overcome their handicap.

Attitudes about the efficacy of treatment philosophies. The results of the attitude questionnaire are shown in Table 13-4. The findings indicate that physicians are divded in their opinion of the effectiveness of psychotherapy for hyperactive children, as well as of the effectiveness of amphetamines and amphetaminelike drugs. More than half of the physicians were positive about the value of medication in treatment of the syndrome. The majority of the physician sample was undecided as to whether the parent's ability to tolerate and accept a child's hyperactive behavior had any influence on the child's development of self control. Although there was no consensus, the majority agreed that psychotherapy is warranted when a child is unaware that his behavior is hyperactive. While there was a range of opinion, many physicians agreed with the statement that ''depriving a hyperactive child of Ritalin is similar to depriving a diabetic of insulin.'' Physicians did not generally accept the belief that hyperactivity is an extreme of normal temperament rather than a medical problem. There was strong agreement with the statement that successful children in schools are seldom considered to be hyperactive, although they share many symptoms with children who are so classified.

SUMMARY

The results of this survey indicate that physicians who treat children referred to them because of their hyperactive behavior view hyperactivity in different ways. Some generalizations emerge regarding the diagnostic importance praticing physicians ascribe to the many medical and behavioral signs that have been associated with hyperactivity. Physical trauma and disease are not judged consistently to be related to the condition, although the presence of a similar condition in

Table 13-4. Physician agreement with questions about interventions for hyperactivity (N = 48)

Questionnaire item	Strongly agree	Agree	Undecided	Disagree	Strongly disagree	Blank
Psychotherapy is a very effective tool for many children with the hyperactive syndrome.	29%	8%	38%	13%	0%	12%
Amphetamine and amphetaminelike drugs are successful in treating most children with the hyperactivity syndrome.	35	13	33	2	0	17
His parents' ability to tolerate and accept his hyperactive behavior does not influence the child's development of self-control.	6	8	63	23	0	0
Little can be done in a child's classroom to accommodate his hyperactive behavior.	6	0	63	31	0	0
If a child is unaware that his behavior is unusually hyperactive, psychotherapy is strongly warranted.	27	21	33	13	0	6
Depriving a hyperactive child of Ritalin (or other medication) is similar to depriving a diabetic of insulin.	27	8	38	21	0	6
Hyperactivity in children is simply an extreme of normal temperament and is not really a medical problem.	5	8	48	31	0	8
Successful children in schools are seldom considered to be hyperactive, although they share many symptoms with children who are so classified.	55	8	23	6	0	8

another member of the family is considered to be an important correlate of hyperactivity in the child. Practically none of the routinely gathered physical examination findings, nor the evidence from the laboratory studies were judged to be important in making a diagnosis of hyperactivity. Behavioral indicators, information from the child's personal medical history, as well as evidence from the family history constitute the group of medical findings which most of the randomly sampled physicians cited as being important in making the diagnosis of hyperactivity. Consistently there was a rejection of the importance of positive neurological findings in making a diagnosis of a hyperactive syndrome. The physicians view the disorder as a behavioral condition rather than one with a neurological basis; it follows, therefore, that the most commonly employed diagnostic label was "Hyperactivity-Learning-Behavior Disorder-Etiology Unknown."

Consistent with the inference that physicians apparently respond to the condition not as a uniquely defined syndrome, but as a group of syndromes, is the fact that recommendations of several treatment regimens are common. Although as the popular press reminds us, Ritalin and other cerebral stimulants seem to be a preferred treatment, phsyicians frequently recommend other interventions, many centered on efforts to effect changes in the child's environment at school and at home. The survey did not allow conclusions regarding differential treatment for different kinds of presenting problems. The data from the physician sample do suggest, however, that while medication may frequently be the treatment prescribed, recommendations are very often made for follow-up consultation or interventions other than drug therapy, or in combination with the prescription of one of the preferred drugs.

The findings from this investigation suggest

that, although physicians respond to behavioral rather than medical indicators, many different diagnostic labels can be associated with the presenting problems of hyperactivity. When physicians indicate that they select from among several diagnostic labels appropriate to the presenting problems of children with hyperactive behavior patterns, each implying etiological or behavioral correlates, it follows that their practice includes multiple, comprehensive recommendations. A variety of treatment programs for children with presenting problems of hyperactivity, rather than drug therapy as the single preferred treatment, characterizes medical practice. It was not clear from the survey how many physicians were of the opinion that the condition has multiple causes and how many physicians were of the opinion that there was one predominant cause, however, one particular physician's approach may be quite different from another's.

An important research effort would be to determine whether groups of medical findings can be found to be consistently associated with or consistently absent in a particular diagnosis, thus defining sets of typologies for the several syndromes. Additional study of the indicators in the patient's diagnostic record which direct the physician to select one or another treatment alternative would add important information to our understanding of problems of hyperactivity and the appropriateness of varying treatment regimens. The authors are undertaking such an investigation by examining variations in school environments, individual differences in cognitive development, and individual variations in affective status as they are associated with medical diagnosis and treatment interventions.

REFERENCES

1. Eisenberg, L. 1971. Principles of drug therapy in child psychiatry with special reference to stimulant drugs. Amer. J. Orthopsychiatry. 41:371–379.
2. Freeman, R. 1966. Drug effects on learning in children: a selective review of the past thirty years. J. Special Ed. 1:17–44.
3. Lambert, N. et al. 1973. Report of Pilot Project, Factors Associated With the Identification and Treatment of Children With Hyperactive-Learning-Behavior Disorders. Grant No. 1 ROI MH20756-01, National Institute of Mental Health. University of California, Berkeley.
4. Lambert, N. et al. 1975. Hyperactive children and the efficacy of psychoactive drugs as a treatment intervention. Amer. J. Orthopsychiat. In press.
5. Minde, K. and Weiss, G. 1970. The assessment of drug effects in children as compared to adults. J. Amer. Acad. Child Psychiat. 9:124–133.
6. Stewart, M. et al. 1966. The hyperactive child syndrome. Amer. J. Orthopsychiat. 36:861–867.
7. Werry, J. et al. 1966. Studies on the hyperactive child. V: the effect of chlorpromazine upon behavior and learning ability. J. Amer. Acad. Child Psychiat. 5:292–312.

Behavior intervention strategies

Section III contains nine chapters that deal with a variety of approaches to the behavioral treatment of hyperactivity and learning disabilities. While the previous section cast considerable doubt on the effectiveness of traditional treatment approaches to these disorders, the chapters on behavioral strategies are consistently positive. There are a number of methodological problems with this body of evidence too, however, and each chapter must be evaluated with this in mind. No "definitive" studies have yet been done from the behavioral or any other perspective.

The chapter by O'Leary, Pelham, Rosenbaum, and Price (Chap. 14) deals with the training of parents to control high rates of inappropriate behavior in children diagnosed as hyperactive. Using behavior ratings by parents, the training program was found to be successful. A similar training program reported by O'Leary and Pelham is included in Section IV of this volume (Chap. 24). As noted in the Introduction, however, there are disadvantages as well as advantages inherent in the use of parent ratings as a dependent variable.

Douglas, Parry, Marton, and Garson (Chap. 15) and Bornstein and Quevillon (Chap. 16) report on evaluations of cognitive training programs for hyperactive children. Both show positive results, but the positive findings of the larger study by Douglas and her associates were rather limited. Further research will be needed before such methods are put into widespread use. Similar encouraging but tentative early findings by Lubar and Shouse (Chap. 17) suggest that EEG biofeedback may be an effective treatment method for some hyperactive children.

The chapters by Lahey, Busemyer, O'Hara, and Beggs (Chap. 18), Stromer (Chap. 19) Lovitt and Hansen (Chap. 20), and Smith and Lovitt (Chap. 21) suggest that direct behavioral intervention can be used to improve the academic behaviors of diagnosed learning disabled children in the same manner as modifying any other behaviors. As noted in the Introduction, adequately designed long-term studies of the effectiveness of such methods have not been conducted, but those data that are avilable suggest strong and positive academic gains can be obtained.

Closing out this section is a key chapter by Ayllon, Layman, and Kandel (Chap. 22). In this study, they demonstrate the possibilities of simultaneously controlling both hyperactive behavior and improving academic performance in children who have been diagnosed as both hyperactive and learning disabled by structuring and reinforcing academic performance only. This study uses only three subjects over a limited period of time. The consistency of the data are very impressive, however, and the study has been successfully replicated many times using children who presented serious learning and behavior problems, but were not given the labels of hyperactivity and learning disabilities (see Introduction).

14. Behavioral treatment of hyperkinetic children: an experimental evaluation of its usefulness

K. DANIEL O'LEARY   WILLIAM E. PELHAM
ALAN ROSENBAUM   GLORIA H. PRICE

Pharmacologic treatment of children diagnosed as hyperkinetic has been shown repeatedly to alter teacher ratings of hyperactivity and classroom disruption.[1] However, physicians have expressed concern over side effects associated with stimulant medication, which is the preferred drug therapy for hyperkinesia. Suppression of growth,[2] increased heart rate, or blood pressure elevations[3-5] have been described with stimulant drugs. Moreover, in 30 to 50 percent of the cases, central stimulants are not effective even on a short-term basis.[6,7] Consequently, it has become apparent that alternatives or supplements to pharmacologic treatment of hyperkinetic children are needed.

Several behavior therapy procedures have been shown effective in reducing excessive seat movements and disruption in special classrooms for retarded, hyperactive children.[8,9] The incidence of hyperkinesia is such that it is likely that there is one hyperkinetic child in almost every elementary school classroom.[10] We have carried out a controlled evaluation of a behavior treatment program for hyperkinetic children attending normal or nonremedial classes.

GENERAL DESIGN AND MEASURES OF CHANGE

Teachers of children referred for hyperactivity were asked to use the Abbreviated Conners' Teacher Rating Scale (TRS), and children who received extreme scores (≥ 15) were taken into our study. The children thus referred were assigned randomly to the behavioral treatment group (N = 9), or a control group (N = 8). Those in the control group were not contacted until later.

The treatment given lasted for a ten-week period. Treatment effectiveness was assessed by the standardized TRS and by an individualized Problem Behavior Rating (PBR) established for each child. The TRS, shown to be sensitive to drug effects, has been widely used as a standardized measure of change in studies with hyperkinetic children.[11] The PBR consisted of an eight-point target rating of the severity of four or five problem behaviors for each child (0 = no problem; 1,2,3 = mild or infrequent problem; 4,5,6 = serious or frequent problem; 7 = severe problem). All children referred for hyperkinesia were compared with randomly selected same-sex peers.

SUBJECT SELECTION

The children all came from the same large elementary school, grades 3–5, in a lower middle-class area. Teachers who referred children to us were told that our program would involve parents, and they were asked to refer parents who they thought might be cooperative and who

From *Clinical Pediatrics*, 1976, *15*, 274–279. Reprinted by permission of J. B. Lippincott Company.

This research was supported by Office of Education Grant OEG–0–71–28–72. The opinions expressed herein, however, do not necessarily reflect the position or policy of the U.S. Office of Education.

had telephones. Actually, one parent of a treated child did not have a phone but was reached via ham-radio contact with a neighbor.

The children ranged in age from 8 years, 11 months to 10 years, 11 months; their average age was 10 years. As mentioned earlier, in order to be selected for the study a child had to have a score ≥ 15 on the TRS.[11] The average score in the current sample of hyperkinetic children was 19.7, whereas a sample of randomly selected same-sex peers in the same rooms as our hyperkinetic children had an average score of 5.1 ($p < .001$).

In order to obtain some independent validation of the teacher ratings, observations of hyperactivity were made of the referred children ($N = 17$) and of randomly selected same-sex peers ($N = 17$) in the same classrooms. Each referred child and his randomly selected classmate were watched for simultaneous ten-minute classroom periods by trained observers who scored in 20-second intervals the presence of three behaviors symptomatic of hyperkinesis: locomotion, fidgeting, and not attending to task. (The observers had been trained to a reliability criterion of .85 before making these observations.) The children referred for hyperkinesia had significantly higher scores based on the average of these three behaviors than control subjects ($p < .025$).

To allow normative comparison of our treated subjects with other previously published studies on hyperkinesia, the following assessments were made: Wechsler Intelligence Scale for Children, Wide Range Achievement Test (WRAT), NIMH Physical and Neurologic Examination for Soft Signs (PANESS), and the Werry-Weiss-Peters Activity Scale.[12]

All the children were of average intelligence, and seven of the nine were below average in achievement (≥ 1 grade in math, spelling, or reading on WRAT). All of the children were above average on the activity scale completed by the parents ($\bar{X} = 20$); this average is more than double the scores obtained from nine-year-old normal controls.[13] On the PANESS, treated subjects had an average of 1.5 Soft Signs (range 0–4) as indicated by extreme scores on PANESS items. None of the children were receiving medication for hyperkinesia, although two of the treated children had been given Ritalin during the previous school year.

No behavior-control drugs were administered during any of these periods of experimental observation.

In sum, using standardization ratings, the children we selected for the program were deemed by both teachers and parents as being hyperkinetic. They were of average intelligence but lagged academically. When observed critically for hyperactivity, they were significantly different from randomly selected peer-classmates.

MANAGEMENT

The primary treatment consisted of a home-based reward program. This program had five components: 1) specification of each child's daily classroom goals; 2) praising the child for efforts to achieve those goals; 3) end-of-day evaluation of the child's behavior relevant to the specified goals; 4) sending the parents a daily report card on their child's daily progress; and 5) rewarding of the child by the parent for progress toward his goals.

The program began with a conference between the therapist and the parents. In this, the therapist obtained information about the child's behavior at home, and explained the parents' role in the program, including the selection of suitable rewards for the child. The therapist also met with the child's teacher for approximately one hour to choose the behavioral goals for the child. Throughout the program, the therapist maintained weekly contact with the parents by telephone and with the teachers through visits.

Selection of the child's school goals was a crucial aspect of the management program. Examples of the goals chosen were: completing assigned math, helping neighbor with class project, not fighting, bringing in homework. We did not reinforce the children directly for sitting still, attending, or not fidgeting. Instead, academic and prosocial goals were given priority as most salient behaviors to be changed.

During the program period, the teacher advised the parents on their child's progress by means of a daily report card (Table 14-1). At the end of each day, the teacher completed the daily report, to be taken home by the child to his parents. They, in turn, rewarded him every time he had met his goals for the day, as indicated by the teacher's report. When more than one goal was established, the teacher used his or her judgment in deciding whether a child should get a reward from his parents. This judgment was based on an impression of overall improvement or lack thereof.

Perhaps the most critical element of the program was the selection of appropriate rewards

Table 14-1. Daily report card (submitted daily by teacher to parents)

	Name of Child_____	
	Yes	No
1. Finished math asignment	____	____
2. 80 percent correct in spelling	____	____
3. Cooperated with others	____	____
Should get reward	____	____
Date: _____	Teacher's Signature: _____	

for the children. Care and ingenuity were exercised in selecting maximally motivating rewards. Several examples of frequently used rewards were:1) 30 minutes extra television, 2) a special dessert, 3) spending time with either parent playing a game such as checkers, and 4) money to spend. In addition to those daily rewards, the children were given weekly rewards when four out of five daily report cards indicated improvement. Among the weekly rewards were a fishing trip with father, a dinner at a favorite aunt's, and a family meal at a "fast-food" restaurant.

Only in two cases, where the parents did not consistently reward their children, was it necessary to establish an in-school reward program. These rewards consisted of a piece of candy per day for one child and "free-time" in the school library for the other.

Just as no single drug or dose is appropriate for all hyperkinetic children, no single type of reward program can suffice for all cases. When one type of reward program fails to produce significant behavioral improvement, the therapist should consider modifying the program. The wide range of possible reward programs, limited only by environmental constraints and the ingenuity of the therapists, makes it likely that a behavioral program can be individually tailored for each child.

OBSERVATIONS MADE

The PBR and the TRS were the two primary measures utilized. These provided complementary information regarding behavior change—the PBR is individualized for each child, whereas the TRS is a standardized measure of a number of behaviors thought to be present in the hyperkinetic syndrome.

With the PBR, treatment and control groups did not differ significantly at the beginning of treatment, but they were significantly different by the end of treatment ($p<.012$) (Fig. 14-1). Both groups showed some decline, but only the change in the treatment group was significant ($p<.005$). Seven of the treated subjects improved ≥ 25 percent on the PBR, whereas only two of the control subjects evidenced such improvement.

With the TRS, also, both groups were essentially equivalent prior to treatment (Fig. 14-2). During the treatment period, both groups improved significantly ($p<.005$), but at the end of the period the treated children's scores were significantly lower than the control ($p<.066$). Eight of the nine treated subjects showed improvement. In seven of these, the gains ($\geq 25\%$) with the TRS were quite substantial. Only one of the control subjects made gains of that magnitude. The changes on the TRS were generally comparable to the changes reported with stimulant drugs.[14]

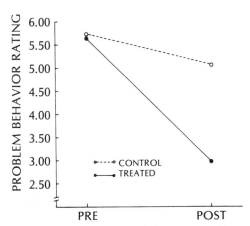

Figure 14-1. Comparison of the mean problem behavior ratings of nine hyperkinetic children treated with behavior therapy, and of eight similar controls.

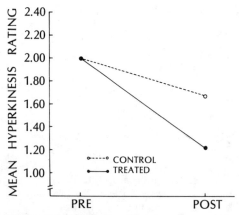

Figure 14-2. Mean hyperkinesia ratings of the same children, obtained from the Teacher Rating Scale (TRS). The data reflect the mean item ratings (range 0.0–3.0) on the ten-item TRS.

DISCUSSION

These results relate critically to the most commonly used treatment for hyperkinetic children, namely, stimulant drugs such as methylphenidate (Ritalin) and dextroamphetamine.

First, stimulant therapy is quite effective with many hyperkinetic children (50% to 70% do respond), but not all will respond.[6,7] When a pediatrician takes care of a child who fails to improve with medication, he should be aware of alternative modes of treatment. In our experience, behavior therapy can be an effective alternative for some hyperkinetic children.

Although early reports indicated that the adverse side effects of stimulant therapy were of limited duration, controllable by adjusting dosage, and thus of relatively small concern, different conclusions have been reached in recent studies. Safer and Allen[2] reported suppression of growth in weight and height in some treated children. Other physiologic changes have been discovered which are attributed to the central effects of the drug while it is being administered.[3,5] Obviously more research is needed, such as that of Sleator and von Neumann,[11] to assess the minimal dosages required for cognitive and social changes. It may be feasible to obtain desired results by combining lower and presumably safer dosages of stimulants with behavior therapy.

It is curious that, although stimulant drugs such as Ritalin are recommended "as adjunctive therapy to other remedial measures" in the treat-ment of hyperkinesis,[15] an all-too-common practice seems to be that of medicating these children to the exclusion of other remedial measures. Yet a number of recent reviews and discussions have stressed the importance of combining drug therapy with other forms of intervention for hyperkinesis.[16–19] Unfortunately, however, the effectiveness of other treatment and remedial measures has not been well documented, so that the pediatrician has the dilemma of not knowing which adjunctive therapy to utilize. On the basis of other controlled case studies and our own observations, behavior therapy appears to be an effective adjunct.

Drug therapy alone may be helpful with hyperkinesia in the short term, but there is little evidence that drug therapy achieves any long-term change in the hyperkinetic child's social and academic behavior.[17] We have seen a number of children who, after having been on stimulant medication for a year or more, have reverted to their original behavior patterns immediately upon discontinuance of the medication. For, as Eisenberg[16] has noted, drugs do not produce social or academic learning; they merely make it possible. Consequently, unless the calming effects of medication are associated with adjunctive educational and psychologic management, any improvement in the child's behavior will not be lasting.

Finally, one other aspect of the effectiveness of drug treatment of hyperkinesia merits consideration. What effects do drugs have on a hyperkinetic child's problems at home? Therapy directed toward the home problems is as important as therapy directed toward school problems. Unfortunately, because of the anorexic and insomnious effects of the drugs, these often cannot be given in the late afternoon. As a consequence, their action may not continue into the evening. This is where adjunctive therapy dealing with home problems of hyperkinetic children becomes clearly desirable and often critical. Because of practical considerations we did not work with behavior in the home setting in this study, but we feel quite strongly that, because of its emphasis on parental involvement, behavior therapy is uniquely suited for use as adjunctive therapy in the home, during the evenings. In our every day clinical management of such children, we routinely and quite successfully utilize parent training as part of family therapy.

SUMMARY

Although drug therapy is helpful in the control of many children with hyperkinesia, alternative and adjunctive therapies are needed also, for a number of reasons: 1) not all of these children improve with medication; 2) the drugs may have adverse physiologic effects which at the least dictate caution in their use; 3) medication alone does not always return responding children to normal functioning; and 4) drug action cannot often be used to help with problems occurring in the children's home setting after school hours.

The data here presented suggest strongly that behavior therapy can be effective for hyperkinesia.

Since other therapeutic resources may be available in his community also, we urge the pediatrician to investigate and to make use of these resources as adjunctive or alternative approaches to the management of children diagnosed as being hyperkinetic.

We urge the pediatrician to investigate the therapeutic resources available in his community and to make use of these resources as adjunctive or alternative therapy for children diagnosed hyperkinetic.

REFERENCES

1. Conners, C. K.: Pharmacotherapy of psychopathology in children. In H. C. Quay and J. S. Werry, Eds.: Psychopathological Disorders of Children. New York, John Wiley and Sons, 1972, p. 316.
2. Safer, D. J., and Allen, R. P.: Factors influencing the suppressant effects of two stimulant drugs on the growth of hyperactive children. Pediatrics 51: 660, 1973.
3. Cohen, N., Douglas, V., and Morganstern, G.: The effect of methylphenidate on attentive behavior and autonomic activity in hyperactive children. Psychopharmacologia 22: 282, 1971.
4. Knights, R., and Hinton, G.: The effects of methylphenidate (Ritalin) on motor skills and behavior of children with learning problems. J. Nerv. Ment. Dis. 148: 643, 1969.
5. Rapoport, J. L., Quinn, P. O., Bradbard, G., Riddle, D. and Brooks, E.: Imipramine and methylphenidate treatments of hyperactive boys. Arch. Gen. Psychiatr. 30: 789, 1974.
6. Wender, P. H.: Minimal Brain Dysfunction in Children. New York, Wiley Interscience, 1971.
7. Fish, B.: The "one child, one drug" myth of stimulants in hyperkinesis. Arch. Gen. Psychiatr. 25: 193, 1971.
8. Patterson, G. R., Shaw, D. A., and Ebner, M. J.: Teachers, peers, and parents as agents of change in the classroom. In F. A. M. Benson, Ed.: Modifying Deviant Social Behaviors in Various Classroom Settings. Eugene, Oregon, Department of Special Education Monographs, 1969, p. 13.
9. Christensen, D. E., and Sprague, R. L.: Reduction of hyperactive behaviors by conditioning procedures alone and combined with methylphenidate (Ritalin). Beh. Res. Ther. 11: 331, 1973.
10. Department of Health, Education and Welfare. Office of Child Development: Report of the Congerence on the Use of Stimulant Drugs in the Treatment of Behaviorally Disturbed Young School Children. Washington, D.C., U.S. Government Printing Office, January, 1971.
11. Sleator, E. K., and von Neumann, A. W.: Methylphenidate in the treatment of hyperkinetic children. Clin. Pediatr. 3: 19, 1974.
12. Werry, J. S., and Sprague, R. L.: Hyperactivity. In C. G. Costello, Ed.: Symptoms of Psychopathology. New York, John Wiley and Sons, 1970, p. 397.
13. Routh, D. K., Schroeder, C. S., and O'Tuama, L. A.: Development of activity level in children. Dev. Psychol. 10: 163, 1974.
14. Conners, C. K.: Psychological effects of stimulant drugs in children with minimal brain dysfunction. Pediatrics 49: 702, 1972.
15. Physicians Desk Reference. Oradell, N.J., Medical Economics Company. 1973, p. 682.
16. Eisenberg, L.: Behavior modification by drugs. III. The clinical use of stimulant drugs in children. Pediatrics 49: 709, 1972.
17. Sroufe, L. A., and Stewart, M. A.: Treating problem children with stimulant drugs. N. Engl. J. Med. 289: 407, 1973.
18. O'Malley, J. E., and Eisenberg, L.: The hyperkinetic syndrome. Seminars Psychiatr. 5: 95, 1973.
19. Sroufe, L. A.: Drug treatment of children with behavior problems. In F. Horowitz, Ed.: Review of Child Development Research 4: 347, 1975.

15. Assessment of a cognitive training program for hyperactive children

VIRGINIA I. DOUGLAS   PENNY PARRY
PETER MARTON   CHRYSTELLE GARSON

Although the stimulant drugs have become extremely popular in the treatment of hyperactivity and related disorders in children (Gallagher, 1970; Greenspoon & Singer, 1973; Krager & Safer, 1974), an increasingly active search is under way to develop cognitive and behavioral approaches aimed at improving these children's problem-solving skills and eliminating their disruptive behavior. Part of the impetus for the search for alternatives to drug treatment has come from growing concern about the indiscriminate use of the stimulants, from questions regarding their long-term effectiveness and safety and from concern about the social and psychological consequences of informing children that drugs are required to control their behavior (Safer & Allen, 1975; Sroufe, 1975; Weiss, Kruger, Danielson, & Elman, 1973; Whalen & Henker, in press).

In the past few years, contingency management techniques have been used in several attempts to eliminate troublesome and disruptive behaviors of hyperactive children at home and in the classroom and to encourage observable behaviors thought to accompany attention and learning (Christensen & Sprague, 1973; Doubros & Daniels, 1966; O'Leary, Pelham, Rosenbaum, & Price, 1976; Patterson, 1965; Patterson, Jones, Whittier, & Wright, 1965; Pihl, 1967;

Quay, Sprague, Werry, & McQueen, 1967; Rosenbaum, O'Leary, & Jacob, 1975). Implicit in most of these studies is the usually untested assumption that if nonattending, nonwork-oriented behaviors can be reduced and "attendinglike" behaviors increased, the child will learn more efficiently and perform better academically (Ferritor, Buckholdt, Hamblin, & Smith, 1972; Ross, 1976). In a few recent studies, however, a more direct approach, involving the use of operant techniques to reward task achievement, has been successful in improving academic performance (Ayllon, Layman, & Kandel, 1975; Ayllon & Roberts, 1974; Ferritor et al., 1972).

Thus, there is evidence that several kinds of disruptive behavior can be brought under control and some kinds of academic performance improved, so long as parents and teachers continue to apply contingencies consistently.

Nevertheless, several considerations suggest that it would be unwise to rely solely on operant techniques to train hyperactive children. Thus far, there have been few attempts to document resistance to extinction or to establish the long-term effectiveness of these methods. Our own concern about the exclusive use of contingency management was also raised by investigations in which the first author and her colleagues studied the effect of several different reinforcement para-

From the *Journal of Abnormal Child Psychology*, 1976, *4*, 389–410. Copyright © 1976 Plenum Publishing Corporation. Reprinted by permission.

This reasearch was supported by Canada Council Grant #S74-0750, principal investigator, Virginia I. Douglas.

meters on the performance of hyperactive children on a variety of tasks. The findings suggest that these children respond to reinforcement contingencies in unique ways. Their performance is more disrupted than that of normal children by partial and noncontingent reinforcement and by extinction. It also appears that positive reinforcement may increase impulsivity and attract their attention away from the task and toward the reinforcement or the reinforcing adult (Cohen, 1970; Douglas, 1975; Firestone, 1974; Firestone & Douglas, 1975; Freibergs & Douglas, 1969; Parry, 1973; Parry & Douglas, in press).

These findings support the argument that approaches emphasizing self-reinforcement and the development of self-control, as opposed to control by outside agents (Goldfried & Merbaum, 1973; Thoresen & Mahoney, 1974), should be incorporated into training programs for these children. Cognitive approaches, such as those employed by Meichenbaum and Goodman (1971) and Palkes, Stewart, and Freedman (1972) with hyperactive children and by Debus (1970), Egeland (1974), Nelson (1968), and Ridberg, Park, and Hetherington (1971) with impulsive children, have the additional advantage of offering training in aspects of problem solving that have been shown to be deficient in hyperactive children. In previous reports, Douglas (1972, 1974) has reviewed several studies designed to discover the kinds of cognitive deficits which accompany childhood hyperkinesis. Measures that have discriminated between hyperactive and normal children include errors of omission and commission on vigilance tasks (Sykes, Douglas, & Morgenstern, 1972, 1973); mean reaction time, variability of reaction times, and impulsive responses on delayed reaction time tasks (Cohen, Douglas, & Morgenstern, 1971; Firestone & Douglas, 1975); scores on the Porteus mazes test (Parry, 1973); response latency and errors on Kagan's (1966) Matching Familiar Figures test of Reflection-Impulsivity (Campbell, Douglas & Morgenstern, 1971; Parry, 1973); and responses to frustration as measured by a story completion technique (Douglas, 1965; Parry, 1973). The performance of hyperactive children also deteriorated more quickly over time than that of controls on several of these measures. Douglas (1972, 1974) has argued that this pattern of deficits points to an attentional-impulsivity problem, or an inability to "stop, look, and listen." Douglas (1975, 1976) also has reviewed the evidence regarding two other symptoms, activity level and distractibility, which are often emphasized in clinical descriptions of hyperactive children, and concludes that the importance of these problems is, at most, secondary to the attentional-impulsivity deficit.

If these assumptions are correct, it follows that training methods should focus on the development of inhibitory control and the teaching of strategies for deploying and sustaining attention more effectively. Efforts to reduce the child's movement or to guard him against distractions would be emphasized only if these problems interfere seriously with the primary goals of training. The study to be described was an attempt to use modeling and self-instructional techniques to improve attention and reduce impulsivity in a group of hyperactive children.

METHOD
SUBJECTS

Because of the prevalence of hyperactivity in males, only boys were included in the study. All of the boys in both the training and control groups were referred to the training project by staff psychologists from the Department of Psychology of the Montreal Children's Hospital or by principals and special education personnel in schools in the greater Montreal area. Both the child's parents and his teacher had to agree that he demonstrated, in serious and persistent form, symptoms associated with the hyperactive syndrome, including excessive activity level, attentional problems, and impulsivity. Parents were interviewed, as well, regarding the history of the child's symptoms and the emotional climate in the home and an attempt was made to exclude any child whose symptoms were caused by conflict or emotional problems in the home or by inconsistent child training practices. In all cases, parents reported that the child had demonstrated his symptoms from infancy or early childhood.

Parents and teachers were required to complete the short form of the Conners Rating Scale for Hyperactivity (Conners, 1969) and each child was administered Kagan's Matching Familiar Figures Test of Reflection-Impulsivity (Kagan, 1966). To be included in the study, a child had to receive a mean rating above 1.5 (out of a possible 3.0) on either the parent or teacher form of the Conners scales, and he also had to have a mean latency score below 10 sec on the MFF Test. The cutoff point for the MFF was derived from norms reported by Campbell and Douglas (1972).

Most of the children in both the training and

control groups were from middle-class or upper-lower-class homes. Parents of children in both groups had to agree not to seek pharmacological or other treatment for their child during the 6-month period of the project. Excluded from the study were children whose IQ was below 80.

The *training group* consisted of 18 boys. Their mean age was 7 years, 9 months (range 6 years, 1 month to 10 years, 11 months) and their mean IQ, as assessed by the Wechsler Intelligence Scale for Children (Wechsler, 1949), was 102.94 (range 89–120). On the Connors Rating Scale for Teachers, the mean score of the training group was 1.7 (range 1.2–2.7); mean score on the Parents' Scale was 2.0 (range 1.2–2.8).

The *control group* consisted of 11 boys. Their mean age was 8 years, 5 months (range 7 years, 1 month to 10 years, 2 months) and their mean IQ was 102.00 (range 80–115). Mean score on the Connors Rating Scale for Teachers was 1.7 (range 1.1–2.5); mean score on the Parents' Scale was 2.0 (range 1.0–2.8).

The training and control groups did not differ significantly on age, $t(27) = 1.17$ n.s.; IQ, $t(27) = .25$ n.s.; or on the Teachers', $t(27) = 0$, n.s.; or Parents', $t(27) = 0$, n.s., scales.

It was not possible to include all children in all of the statistical analyses to be reported because some children were too young for some tests and because many Parent and Teacher Rating Scales were not returned because of a mail strike. Whenever part of the sample was used in an analysis, separate checks were made to make certain that children in the trained and control groups did not differ on age, IQ, or Conners Ratings. In no case was a significant difference found.

THE TRAINING PROGRAM

The training program covered a 3-month period in which the children were seen for two 1-hour sessions per week, for a total of 24 sessions. A minimum of 6 consultation sessions with the child's teacher and 12 sessions with one or both parents also were held.

The training and consultation sessions were conducted by four trainers, three female and one male. One had a Ph.D. in psychology, two were graduate students, and one was a bachelor's graduate. At least two staff members were involved in the training and consultation sessions for each child.

Consultation sessions with parents and teachers. The consultation sessions with parents and teachers were directed toward familiarizing them with the training techniques and helping them implement them at home and at school. Whenever possible, the parents and teachers observed and participated in the training sessions with the children. The trainer then discussed with them ways of encouraging the children to use the strategies being taught while doing their schoolwork, while engaging in tasks and responsibilities at home, and while interacting with peers and siblings. Parents and teachers were given a brief introduction to contingency management techniques and used them, to a limited extent, to bring seriously disruptive behaviors under control and to reinforce the children for verbalizing and using the strategies. Heavier emphasis was placed, however, on the importance of helping them become self-controlling, self-monitoring, and self-reinforcing individuals. Thus, for example, teachers were asked to provide answer sheets for work assigned and to encourage the children to check their own work carefully.

Training sessions with children. The major goal of the training sessions was to teach the children to cope more effectively and independently with cognitive problems and social situations in which care, attention, and organized planning are required; closely related to the goal was the need to help them achieve better inhibitory control. Modeling, self-verbalization, and strategy training techniques, based on the work of Meichenbaum and Goodman (1969, 1971) were the major training methods employed, although when a child was particularly unmanageable, contingency management techniques, similar to those of Patterson (1965) and O'Leary et al. (1976) also were used. Relatively minor emphasis was placed on limiting the child's movement or protecting him from distraction, unless these problems seriously interfered with training. Thus, although other approaches were used occasionally, we believe that the "essential ingredients" of our program were training in the self-regulated use of more effective problem-solving strategies and in the suppression of impulsive responding.

The modeling and self-verbalization procedures used followed the basic approach of Meichenbaum and Goodman (1969, 1971). The trainer worked on a task while verbalizing aloud a clear statement about the nature of the problem and the strategies he was using. The child was then asked to do the same; as sessions progressed, he was told to verbalize less and less loudly and finally, to "talk to himself." Some tasks also were included in which the trainer and the child took turns giving each other very explicit instructions about how to proceed.

An attempt was made to assure generalization of the strategies being taught to visual, auditory, and tactual processes and to academic and social situations. A wide range of tasks and games was employed, including academic work assigned by each child's teacher. In later sessions, pairs of children were trained together in an attempt to make the environment more similar to the classroom and to provide an opportunity for training in peer interactions. Periods also were provided in which the children were required to work alone, using strategies previously modeled for them.

A prearranged schedule of activities for the 24 sessions was established so that all of the children received fairly comparable experience with the various materials and types of tasks. If a child did well on a particular task, however, the trainer moved on to more complex games or activities of the same type.

Before training began, we told each child we were sure, from what we had learned about him, that he was a bright, intelligent boy, but that he was getting into difficulty at home and at school because he was not taking advantage of certain strategies or "tricks" that we could teach him. It was emphasized that these strategies would "work" with many kinds of problems and in many situations.

The general strategies emphasized included: stopping to define a problem and the various steps within it; considering and evaluating several possible solutions before acting on any one; checking one's own work throughout and calmly correcting any errors; sticking with a problem until everything possible had been tried to solve it correctly; and giving oneself a "pat on the back" for work well done. Verbalizations modeled by the trainer to support these strategies included: "I must stop and think before I begin." "What plans could I try?" "How would it work out if I did that?" "What shall I try next?" "Have I got it right so far?" "Gee, I made a mistake there—I'll just erase it." "Now, let's see, have I tried everything I can think of?" "I've done a pretty good job!"

Modeling and, occasionally, direct instruction, also were used to give the children training in specific search, focusing, and attention deployment strategies. Emphasis was placed on teaching them how to scan and explore visual, auditory, and tactual stimuli for essential similarities and differences and how to sort, arrange, and classify stimuli possessing particular features. Examples of verbalizations accompanying a (visual) task might be: "This one has two lines going across this way, so this one can't be right because it has lines going the other way. I'll put the wrong one over here." "I haven't looked at them all yet. I'd better keep going until I'm really sure." "What I need here is one that has one door, two windows, and a chimney on this side. Oh, oh! This one has all those things but it's still not quite right because it doesn't have a roof with marks like this." "Now I think I've got it, but let's check once more." An example of a verbalization for a tactual task would be: "I feel a long, flat part. It feels like a handle. Then there are a lot of pointy things on the end. I bet I am holding a fork." For an auditory task the trainer might say: "I heard two long taps and then a short one. That matches the letter k in our secret code."

Emphasis also was placed on planning ahead and thinking sequentially and on learning strategies for organizing ideas and work materials. Verbalizations modeled by the trainer included: "I'm going to need paper, a red and a green pencil, and scissors." "To get this right I have to think of different things that have wings." "I am going to make a list of everything I need for this school assignment. Then I'll mark each part off as I get it ready."

Some training also was given in encouraging the children to note carefully and then rehearse important facts or features to be remembered. The trainer and child played "remembering games," like "I packed my bag," and card games that required remembering cues about which card the opponent was holding. Sometimes, child and trainer took turns trying to remember all the essential parts of a picture or of a set of instructions. An appropriate verbalization during a card game might be: "He's asking me for all of my threes, so I'll have to remember that he has threes in his hand." When the task was to remember the essential parts of a picture, the model might say: "I'll have to look at the main things in this picture carefully so I can remember what I saw. The most important things I see are. . . ."

Finally, strategies were taught for playing games or cooperating on a task with a peer. Emphasized were the importance of taking turns, trying to figure out the strategy one's opponent was using, and becoming sensitive to the other child's motives and emotional state. Here the trainer modeled relevant thoughts and suggested that the child keep them in mind. Examples are: "I'd like to make my move now but I have to wait my turn." "I bet that Harry is risking everything to get the aces again. I'll try to block him." "I guess Tom wants to win as much as I do. He'll be unhappy if he loses too many times." "It looks like I'm making John mad by teasing him so much. I guess I'd better stop."

Tasks and materials used in training. The following criteria were observed in choosing the tasks and materials used to teach the strategies: (1) The materials used in training should overlap as little as possible with the tests and measures used to assess the effects of training; (2) they should be varied and interesting and should facilitate generalization of the strategies taught to problems in the visual, auditory, and tactual modes; and (3) there should be several examples of each type of task and these should be arranged in ascending order of difficulty.

One example of the materials used to train in the areas of visual discrimination and visual memory was the designs from the Hereward Observation Test Matching Tablets (J. Noel Publications). These were used in several matching games in which the child was required to sort pictures and designs on the basis of similarities and differences. The number of cards to be sorted and the subtlety of the differences among them were gradually increased from session to session. Also popular was a set of plastic forms representing a variety of shapes and colors which could be used to play a game called "dominoes." The player's task was to match the pieces on one or more dimensions. In another game, played with colored blocks, participants had to reproduce a pattern depicted on a card, either with the card present or after it had been removed. In a final example, the Raven Progressive Matrices (Raven, 1958), participants had to describe all of the essential qualities of each missing pattern before looking at the alternatives from which the correct choice was to be made.

An example of a task used to teach sequencing was a series of pictures which were placed before the child in random order; his task was to rearrange them so that they depicted the various episodes of a story in logical order. An auditory form of a sequencing task involved carrying out a series of verbal instructions in an assigned order.

A general teaching aid that was used throughout the training sessions was an ordinary kitchen timer. The children were told that they would be expected to work on each activity for only a set period; as sessions progressed, the periods were extended. Another aid, used in tasks in which explicit instructions were to be given by both trainer and child, was a tape recorder; it provided unassailable evidence as to whether all the essential directions had, in fact, been included.

THE ASSESSMENT BATTERY

Effectiveness of the training program was assessed by a battery of measures administered to the experimental group prior to training, at the end of the 3-month training period, and after a further period of 3 months in which there was no contact between the training staff and the child, his parents, or the teacher. The tests were given in random order. Children in the control group were administered the same tests at the same intervals.

Testing was done by three (female) psychologists, one master's and two bachelors' graduates. Individuals who participated in a child's training did not take part in the assessment of that child.

Tests and measures used to assess effects of training. Measures used to assess training effects were selected to meet one or more of the following criteria: (1) The measure had successfully differentiated between normal and hyperactive subjects in previous studies; (2) it had been proven sensitive to treatment with the stimulant drugs; (3) it was widely used in clinical practice as a diagnostic instrument for children demonstrating hyperactivity and related symptoms; or (4) it was closely related to academic achievement. The following measures were included in the assessment battery:

Matching Familiar Figures Test of Reflection-Impulsivity (Kagan, 1966). This test was developed to measure the cognitive styles of reflection and impulsivity. It is a visual matching task consisting of 12 items. A standard and 6 alternatives are presented simultaneously and the child is asked to select the item identical to the standard. Measures scored are latency to the first response and total number of errors.

The MFF has been shown to differentiate between hyperactive and normal children and to be sensitive to the effects of drug treatment in hyperactives (Campbell et al., 1971; Parry, 1973).

Story Completion Test (Parry, 1973). This test is a modification of a story completion technique developed by Douglas (1965) and is designed to tap a child's response to frustrating events. The test consists of nine stories which portray situations in which a boy is blocked from achieving a goal by the action of another child. The child taking the test is asked to choose among three endings: (1) an *aggressive* response which involves direct, uncontrolled expression of aggression; (2) *withdrawal,* a response in which the protagonist retreats, usually in tears, and (3) *realistic problem solving,* a response that reflects realistic acceptance of the disappointment, usually accompanied by some attempt to make the best of the frustrating situation.

This technique has demonstrated significant differences between hyperactive and normal children (Parry, 1973), as well as showing developmental changes (Douglas, 1965).

Porteus Mazes (Porteus, 1969). This test consists of a series of mazes, graded in difficulty. The test quotient (TQ) used in the present study is thought to reflect planning, judgment, and attention (Stroufe, 1975).

This measure has shown differences between normal and hyperactive subjects (Parry, 1973) and has, as well, demonstrated its sensitivity to the effects of stimulant drug treatment (Conners, 1972; Conners, Eisenberg, & Barcai, 1967).

Bender Visual-Motor Gestalt Test (Bender, 1938). This test requires the child to copy geometric figures. It is considered a measure of perceptual-motor ability. Two scores were recorded: a time score, which reflects the time taken to copy all the figures, and an error score, derived from norms developed by Koppitz (1964).

The Bender has repeatedly demonstrated differences between hyperactive and normal children (Douglas, 1972, 1974; Parry, 1973), but drug studies in which the Bender has been used to measure drug effects have not yielded consistent evidence of improvement (Stroufe, 1975).

Memory tests from the Detroit Tests of Learning Aptitude (Baker & Leland, 1967). Two subtests, one measuring auditory attention span for related words and the other, auditory span for unrelated words, were included from the Detroit Tests. The score used on the unrelated words test was total number of words correctly recalled; on the test for related words, standard scoring procedure was used.

Although these tests have failed to show differences between hyperactive and normal children (Douglas, 1974), they were included in the assessment battery because of their apparent relevance to academic achievement.

Durell Analysis of Reading Difficulty (Durrell, 1955). Four tests from the Durrell were used: oral reading, oral comprehension, listening comprehension, and spelling. Grade levels, as described in the test manual, were used in scoring the first three tests. The score used on the spelling test was number of errors (out of a possible 20).

The Durrell was included in the test battery because of its relevance to academic achievement and because hyperactive children are known to have academic problems (Douglas, 1972, 1974; Minde, Lewin, Weiss, Lavigueur, Douglas, & Sykes, 1971).

Wide Range Achievement Test-Arithmetic Subtest (Jastak, 1946). This is a widely used achievement test measuring arithmetic ability. The score used was the total raw score, as described in the test manual. Reasons for including this test in the assessment battery are similar to those mentioned (above) for the Durrell.

Conners Rating Scales for Parents and Teachers, Short Form (Conners, 1969). This is a 10-item scale on which parents or teachers are asked to rate a child on behaviors associated with the hyperactive syndrome. It is scored on a 4-point (0–3) scale.

The scale has been used successfully as a diagnostic instrument (Sprague, Christensen, & Werry, 1974) and has been shown to be sensitive to stimulant drug treatment (Sleator, von Neumann, & Sprague, 1974).

STATISTICAL ANALYSES

There were 10 variables on which all test scores were available for the 18 children in the training group and the 11 children in the control group. A multivariate analysis (Anova Repeated Measures Design) was used to test for overall group X treatment interactions on the pretest and posttest scores and a second multivariate analysis was performed on the pretest and follow-up scores. Individual analyses of variance were then computed to test for groups X treatment interactions on each of the 10 variables for the pretest-posttest and pretest–follow-up comparisons. T-tests (two-tailed) were used to study pretest-posttest and pretest–follow-up changes within the training and control groups.

In the case of the remaining six variables, scores were available on only part of the sample because of postal strikes and because some of the measures were not suitable for younger children in the sample. For these variables, individual analyses of variance were computed to test for groups X treatment interactions on the pretest-posttest and pretest–follow-up comparisons. T-tests (two-tailed) were then used to compare within group changes on the pretest-posttest and pretest–follow-up scores.

RESULTS

PRETEST-POSTTEST COMPARISONS

A multivariate analysis (Anova Repeated Measures Design) was performed on pretest and posttest scores on 9 of the 10 variables[1] on which complete data were available[2] for the training ($N = 18$) and control ($N = 11$) groups. A significant groups X treatment interaction was obtained, $F (9, 19) = 3.53, p < .009$.

Individual analyses of variance were then performed on each of the 10 variables. The groups X treatment interactions thus obtained are reported in Table 15-1. Variables on which the interactions were significant ($p < .05$) include: error and time scores on the MFF, aggressive and realistic coping responses on the story completion test, and the time measure on the Bender-Gestalt test. Three other variables, withdrawal responses on the story completion test, test quotient on the Porteus Mazes, and memory for unrelated words (Detroit Tests of Learning Aptitude), approached significance ($p < .10$). Interactions on the error score on the Bender-Gestalt test and the memory test for related words were nonsignificant.

T tests (two-tailed) comparing pretest and posttest scores on each of the 10 variables within the group receiving training revealed significant improvement on 9 out of the 10 measures; the only exception was the error score on the Bender-Gestalt test. Similar comparisons for the control group yielded a significant pretest-posttest difference on only one measure, the Detroit memory test for related words.

Individual analyses of variance also were performed on the six variables on which there were missing data for some subjects. The results appear in Table 15-2. A significant groups X treatment interaction ($p < .05$) was found on the lis-

Table 15-1. Pretest-posttest comparisons: group × treatment interactions for measures included in multivariate analysis[a]

Variable	Trained group		Control group		G ×T interactions	
	Pre X	Post X	Pre X	Post X	F	P
MFT						
Errors	22.72	14.33	19.36	21.82	13.34	.001
Latency	6.08	17.89	4.94	5.48	4.69	.04
Stories						
Aggression	2.94	1.44	3.00	3.27	7.36	.01
Withdrawal	2.50	1.72	2.18	2.54	3.66	.07
Realistic	3.55	5.83	3.82	3.18	16.28	.0004
Porteus Mazes	105.61	115.06	101.73	100.82	3.49	.07
Bender-Gestalt						
Time	250.72	319.11	306.36	250.82	11.22	.002
Errors	8.38	7.61	6.72	7.18	1.00	.32
Detroit Tests of Auditory Memory						
Unrelated Words	36.61	40.94	36.54	36.72	3.73	.06
Related Syllables	40.11	47.89	38.63	43.18	2.09	.16

[a] $N = 29$; $df = 1,27$.

Table 15-2. Pretest-posttest comparisons: group × treatment interactions for measures not included in multivariate analysis

Variable	N	Trained group		Control group		$G \times T$ interactions	
		Pre X	Post X	Pre X	Post X	F	P
Durrell Analysis of Reading Difficulty							
Oral reading	13	3.09	3.61	1.16	1.16	1.47	.25
Oral comprehension	13	3.42	4.42	1.71	1.71	4.20	.06
Listening comprehension	13	2.57	3.57	1.33	1.00	4.73	.05
Spelling	12	10.33	13.33	17.33	16.83	3.23	.10
WRAT							
Arithmetic	22	21.27	23.63	24.40	27.20	.40	.83
Teacher Rating Scale	21	1.71	1.25	1.73	1.60	.99	.33

Table 15-3. Pretest–Follow-up comparisons: group × treatment interactions for measures included in multivariate analysis[a]

Variable	Trained group		Control group		$G \times T$ interactions	
	Pre X	Post X	Pre X	Post X	F	P
MFF						
Errors	22.72	13.27	19.63	18.63	14.03	.0009
Latency	6.08	13.52	4.97	6.47	4.03	.05
Stories						
Aggression	2.94	1.38	3.36	3.27	3.55	.07
Withdrawal	2.50	1.50	1.90	2.45	6.59	.02
Realistic	3.55	6.11	3.72	3.27	12.54	.001
Porteus Mazes	105.61	111.94	100.81	109.18	.06	.79
Bender-Gestalt						
Time	250.72	326.94	303.81	292.36	3.04	.09
Errors	8.38	8.11	7.09	6.63	.01	.90
Detroit Tests of Auditory Memory						
Unrelated Words	36.61	41.50	36.36	42.63	.38	.54
Related Syllables	40.11	50.16	34.09	44.18	.01	.99

[a] $N = 29$; $df = 1,27$.

tening comprehension subtest of the Durrell and trends ($p < .10$) were obtained on the oral comprehension and spelling subtests. The interactions on the remaining measures were not significant.

Two-tailed t tests comparing pretest and posttest scores on each of the six variables within the training group revealed significant improvement on the oral comprehension and listening comprehension subtests of the Durrell and on the Conners Teacher Rating Scale. There were no significant pretest-posttest differences within the control group.

PRETEST–FOLLOW-UP COMPARISONS

A multivariate analysis (Anova Repeated Measures Design) was performed on pretest and follow-up scores on 9 of the 10 variables[1] on which complete data were available[2] for the training and control groups. The significance level for the groups X treatment interaction closely approached significance ($F(9, 19) = 2.36, p < .055$).

Individual analyses of variance were then performed on each of the 10 variables. The groups X treatment interactions appear in Table 15-3. Variables on which the interactions were significant ($p < .05$) include: MFF latency and error scores, and withdrawal and realistic coping responses on the story completion test. Trends ($p < .10$) were obtained on aggressive responses on the story completion test and on the time measure on the Bender-Gestalt test. Interactions on the Porteus Mazes test quotient, the Bender-Gestalt error score, and the two memory tasks of the Detroit Test were nonsignificant.

T tests, (two-tailed) comparing pretest and follow-up scores on each of the 10 variables within the training group revealed significant improvement ($p < .05$) on all measures except the Porteus Mazes and the error score of the Bender-Gestalt test. Pretest–follow-up comparisons within the untrained group yielded a significant change on only the memory test for related words.

Individual analyses of variance, performed on the remaining six variables, are reported in Table 15-4. Significant groups X treatment interactions were obtained on the oral reading and oral comprehension subtests of the Durrell. Interactions on the listening comprehension and spelling subtests of the Durrell, the Conners Teacher Rating Scale, and the Arithmetic Test of the Wide Range Achievement Test were not significant.

Two-tailed t tests comparing pretest and follow-up scores on the six variables revealed significant improvement ($p < .05$) on all six variables in the group that received training. Only the Conners Teacher Rating score showed improvement within the control group.

DISCUSSION

The findings offer substantial evidence for the efficacy of cognitive training with hyperactive chil-

dren. In a review paper on attempts to modify children's information processing behaviors, Denney (1973) emphasizes the importance of the true acquisition of generalized cognitive functions; he stresses that the child must have developed "cognitive representations" of the new behaviors, not just task-specific response sets. Denney argues that, if this is accomplished, the child should: comprehend the basic nature of the behaviors being trained; develop symbolic mediators of those behaviors; use these symbolic mediators to regulate his overt behavior; and be able to provide an explanation of his posttraining performance and the general principles behind it. If these goals are achieved, the new behaviors should persist over time and should generalize to tasks other than those used in training. He reasons that modeling techniques, direct instruction, and self-rehearsal procedures are particularly well suited to ensure the necessary mediation of general principles.

In the present study, the children who received training in techniques of this kind showed significant improvement on several criterion measures, both immediately following training and after three months in which they had no contact with personnel from the training project. Thus, Denney's criterion of persistence over time has been at least modestly met. An attempt also was made to use different materials in the assessment battery and the training sessions. The degree to which we were successful in achieving this, however, could be debated. In the case of the Matching Familiar Figures Test of Reflection-Impulsivity, for example, rather large improvements occurred on both the latency and error measures and these changes held up well over the 3-month follow-up period. These findings

Table 15-4. Pretest–Follow-up comparisons: group × treatment interactions for measures not included in multivariate analysis

Variable	N	Trained group		Control group		$G \times T$ interactions	
		Pre X	Post X	Pre X	Post X	F	P
Durrell Analysis of Reading Difficulty							
Oral reading	13	3.09	4.23	1.16	1.16	6.96	.02
Oral comprehension	13	3.42	5.14	1.71	1.85	7.26	.02
Listening comprehension	13	2.57	4.00	1.33	2.66	.01	.92
Spelling	12	12.00	9.83	17.33	16.67	1.46	.25
WRAT							
Arithmetic	21	20.08	24.41	23.81	24.63	2.67	.12
Teacher Rating Scale	23	1.77	1.29	1.70	1.36	.42	.52

match, or surpass, several previous attempts to improve MFF scores through modeling, self-instruction, and strategy training methods (e.g., Egeland, 1974; Meichenbaum & Goodman, 1969, 1971; Ridberg et al., 1971; Zelnicker, Jeffrey, Ault, & Parsons, 1972). One could argue, however, that the training and assessment materials used resembled each other in essential ways in all of these studies. This is equally true of our own investigation, in spite of the fact that we chose materials like the Hereward Matching Tablets and the Raven Progressive Matrices because they differed from the MFF in format and content. This problem would probably arise with most materials that provide practice in the focusing and search strategies we wished to emphasize. Obviously, some generalization was required to produce the obtained improvements on the MFF, but the degree of that generalization remains a matter of opinion.

On the other hand, there do not appear to be any materials or activities in our training methods that directly teach the kinds of response to frustration tapped by the story completion test. Thus, it would appear that the training we gave in considering consequences of events and of one's own actions had a generalized effect on the ability of the children to cope less aggressively and more effectively with frustration, at least when it is portrayed in story form. It is possible, too, that our sessions in which two children were helped to work and play together more constructively contributed to the generalization obtained on these measures.

The improvements on some of the reading measures also offer evidence of generalization. Although no attempt was made to train the children in the mechanics of reading, the trained group had improved significantly on the oral reading test at the time of follow-up testing. The significant improvements on listening comprehension and oral comprehension also suggest that some generalization may have resulted from our attempts to encourage the children to read written instructions and to listen to oral instructions more carefully. These results agree with those of Egeland (1974), who trained a group of impulsive children in effective search strategies and found improvement 2 months later on Gates-MacGinitie Reading Test scores.

The results on the remainder of the measures are somewhat less encouraging. Although the training was successful in helping the experimental group take more time to work on the Bender figures, there was not an accompanying improvement in their scores on the Bender-Gestalt Test. Douglas (1972, 1975) has reported evidence of poor performance by hyperactive children on tests of eye-hand coordination and gross motor coordination and has suggested that this could reflect either a genuine perceptual-motor problem or a careless, undisciplined approach to these tasks. The fact that the children's performance in the present study did not improve, even though they devoted more time to the task, provides some evidence for the former explanation. A similar interpretation could be drawn from an attempt by Parry (1973) to motivate hyperactive children to produce better Bender-Gestalt drawings by promising them a 25¢ incentive; although the children apparently tried to work more carefully, their drawings did not significantly improve. Also of interest is the fact that drug studies have failed to show consistent effects on Bender-Gestalt performance (Sroufe, 1975).

Our findings on the Porteus Mazes appear, at first glance, to be weaker than those of Palkes, Stewart, and Kahana (1968) and Palkes et al. (1972). It is impossible, however, to make an adequate comparison between their studies and ours because of differences in the statistical analyses used. Our trained group improved by 9.5 points on the test quotient measure in the pretest-posttest comparisons as compared with a change of 7.7 in the verbal training group in the Palkes et al. (1968) study. Also, the comparison of pretest and posttest quotients within our trained group was significant ($p < .01$) while there was no significant change in the control group. In a slightly different analysis, Palkes et al. compared posttraining test quotients of their experimental and control groups and also found a significant difference ($p < .02$). We took the further step of computing an analysis of variance to test for significance of the treatment X groups interaction, which yielded a p of .07. Since Palkes et al. did not report interaction effects in their 1968 study, it is impossible to compare the two investigations in this regard. In their later study, Palkes et al. (1972) did not find significant effects on the Porteus test quotient as a result of their training, although significant differences were obtained on the qualitative score. We did not calculate qualitative scores because of reliability problems with scoring this measure and because we tend to agree with Sroufe's (1975) interpretation that it is strongly influenced by motor ability.

The results on the two memory tests from the Detroit Tests of Learning Aptitude suggest that training had little effect on short-term memory, although the children were given considerable practice in rehearsal techniques in our training sessions. Douglas (1974) has reported that hyperactive children showed no evidence of a short-term memory deficit on several measures, including the two tests used in the present study. This may account for the finding that both trained and untrained hyperactives improved on later administrations of the test. We now have evidence, however, of problems with long-term memory in hyperactive children and it may well be that measures of this kind would prove more sensitive to training effects.

There also is little evidence for effects of training on the arithmetic test of the Wide Range Achievement Test. It seems likely that training specifically geared to arithmetic computations would have to be added to our training program in order to produce significant change on achievement test measures. It should also be stressed that similar advice is in order in the area of reading skills. Although the trained group improved on some tests of the Durell Analysis of Reading Difficulty, the lack of improvement on the remaining Durell comparisons suggests that training in specific reading and spelling skills should be added to the programs of children who have difficulties in these areas.

The failure to find significant training effects on the Conners Teacher Rating Scale is somewhat surprising. It could be argued that the abbreviated, 10-item form of the scale used in the present study is less sensitive than the longer (39-item) version. We did observe that teachers found that some items (e.g., "cries easily and often" and "temper outbursts, explosive and unpredictable behavior") did not apply to several children, although they insisted that these youngsters had serious problems with hyperactivity, concentration, and impulse control. On the other hand, this scale has demonstrated both its value as a diagnostic instrument and its sensitivity to the effects of treatment with the stimulant drugs (Sleator et al., 1974; Sprague et al., 1974). A more likely explanation for our negative findings on this measure is that our training program stressed internal thought processes and the development of inner controls far more heavily than outwardly observable behaviors. Possibly, with more time, the effects of the cognitive changes produced by the training would become more observable to teachers who must deal with the hyperactive child as one of many pupils in a large classroom. But in the short term, it seems likely

that a teacher would be more sensitive to a decrease in disruptive behaviors and increased conformity to classroom demands. It is also possible that our individualized training did not generalize to the classroom situation. Since contingency management techniques have been shown to produce positive changes on the Conners scales (O'Leary et al., 1976; Rosenbaum et al., 1975) it might be advantageous to combine a cognitive approach with greater emphasis on these techniques than was used in the present study.

It is always difficult, in any "multi-push" program, to isolate the factors that produced the achieved effects, and the present study does not escape this problem. We were not able to include an attention-control group because of the ethical and practical factors inherent in such a design in a long-term study. It seems unlikely, however, that attention alone would have produced the changes obtained, particularly since several of the improvements were maintained 3 months after training ended. It is unlikely, too, that the children were trained simply toward test-taking ability. The assessment battery was not administered by the person who trained the child and there were substantial differences between the materials and procedures used in testing and training. Indeed, several children expressed considerable anger when a new individual arrived and insisted that they work on tests rather than "play games" with their familiar training therapist.

Ross (1976) raises an interesting point regarding Douglas's (1972, 1974) analysis of the essential nature of the hyperactive child's deficits which has important implications for the "essential ingredients" issue in training programs. He questions whether it is necessary to hypothesize both impulsivity and attentional problems in these children and suggests that a conceptualization dealing with attention alone may be sufficient. We would argue, however, that it would be unwise to ignore the impulsive aspects of the hyperactive child's behavior. Several of the measures on the diagnostic instruments which differentiated between hyperactives and controls in our early studies revealed problems with inhibitory control. It is true that these problems appear to occur together with attentional deficits and that factor analytic studies show the two kinds of measures loading on a single factor (Douglas, 1972). Our experience in training suggests, however, that it often is necessary to bring the child's tendency to respond impulsively under control before training in focusing and search strategies can begin. Sometimes we have been forced to accomplish this by directing the child to sit on his hands until he has organized and verbalized his strategies for approaching a task.

Questions also have been raised recently about the effectiveness and practicality of the verbalization aspects of self-instructional techniques (Higa, 1973; Robin, Sandi, & O'Leary, 1975). Our own experience suggests that the problems discussed by these authors are more likely to arise if self-verbalization is taught in a mechanical, rote-learning, way. We learned to avoid this, at least partially, by encouraging each child to verbalize strategies in his own words and by accepting reasonable strategies produced by him, even if they diverged from the preferred strategy of the trainer. Thus, although we modeled specific strategies, we also reinforced a more general "set," which involved producing and evaluating the probable effects of several possible strategies. We still believe, therefore, that so long as this caution is observed, self-verbalization should accompany modeling, strategy training, and self-reinforcement techniques.

The present investigation, unfortunately, afforded no opportunity to compare the effectiveness of cognitive training with other approaches to the treatment of hyperactive children. Our positive findings suggest, however, that large-scale studies should now be undertaken to evaluate the relative effectiveness of cognitive training, contingency management, and pharmacological treatment. Studies evaluating combinations of these methods would also be extremely valuable.

Certain cautions should be observed, however. It is important that the individuals providing each kind of treatment be knowledgeable and committed to that particular approach, and it is important, as well, that measures used to assess improvement have established relevance to the social and academic adjustment of children. Treatment effects also should be evaluated over a period sufficiently long to be meaningful for the child's home and school adjustment.

It is essential, too, that research designs allow for the assessment of effects a reasonable period after treatment has been terminated. This requirement is seldom observed in studies of the stimulant drugs and becomes particularly cogent if the recent findings by Swanson and Kinsbourne (1976) on stimulant-related, state-dependent learning in hyperactive children prove to be replicable and validly interpreted.

The study by Swanson and Kinsbourne also points to the need for some investigations in which treatment is continued and evaluated over very long periods. If their conclusions about state-dependent effects are accepted, we are likely to see an increasing number of children maintained on drug treatment indefinitely. Although few individuals would make a similar recommendation regarding cognitive training or conditioning techniques, most proponents of both of these approaches would agree on the value of reinstating training from time to time in order to encourage the child and significant people in his environment to maintain the learned cognitions and behaviors. Thus, if research in this area is to become more applicable to actual clinical practice, we must be prepared to mount studies which compare and combine a variety of treatment approaches and assess their cost and effectiveness over extended periods of time.

NOTES

1. Because the three scores on the story completion test were interdependent, only two scores—aggression and realistic problem solving—were included in the multivariate analyses.
2. As mentioned in the "statistical analyses" section, some data were missing on six of the variables because of a mail strike and because some of the tests were inappropriate for younger children. One measure, the Parent Rating Scale, had to be dropped from the analyses completely because of the mail strike.

REFERENCES

Ayllon, T. Layman, D., & Kandel, H. A behavioral-educational alternative to drug control of hyperactive children. *Journal of Applied Behavior Analysis,* 1975, *8,* 137–146.

Ayllon, T., & Roberts, M. Eliminating discipline problems by strengthening academic performance, *Journal of Applied Behavior Analysis,* 1974, *7,* 71–76.

Baker, H. J., & Leland, B. *Detroit tests of learning aptitude.* Indianapolis: Bobbs Merrill, 1967.

Bender, *A visual motor gestalt test and its clinical use.* American Psychiatric Assoc., New York, 1938.

Campbell, S. B., & Douglas, V. I. Cognitive styles and responses to the threat of frustration. *Canadian Journal 972, 4,* 30–42.

Campbell, S. B., Douglas, V. I., & Morgenstern, G. Cognitive styles in hyperactive children and the effect of methylphenidate. *Journal of Child Psychology and Psychiatry,* 1971, *12,* 55.

Christensen, D., & Sprague, R. Reduction of hyperactive behavior by conditioning procedures alone and combined with methylphenidate. *Behavior Research and Therapy*, 1973, *11*, 331–334.

Cohen, N. J. *Physiological concomitants of attention in hyperactive children*. Unpublished doctoral dissertation, McGill University, 1970.

Cohen, J. J., Douglas, V. I., & Morgenstern, G. The effect of methylphenidate on attentive behavior and autonomic activity in hyperactive children, *Psychopharmacologia (Berlin)*, 1971, ·*22*, 282–294.

Conners, C. A teacher rating scale for use in drug studies in children. *American Journal of Psychiatry*, 1969, *126*, 884–888.

Conners, C. Psychological effects of stimulant drugs in children with minimal brain dysfunction. *Pediatrics*, 1972, *49*, 702–708.

Conners, C., Eisenberg, L., & Barcai, A. Effect of dextroamphetamine on children. *Archives of General Psychiatry*, 1967, *17*, 478–485.

Debus, R. Effects of brief observation of model behavior on conceptual tempo of impulsive children. *Developmental Psychology*, 1970, *2*, 22–32.

Denney, D. R. Modification of children's information processing behavior through learning. *Child Study Monographs*, 1973, *1*, 1–22.

Doubros, S. G., & Daniels, G. T. An experimental approach to the reduction of overactive behavior. *Behavior Research and Therapy*, 1966, *4*, 251–258.

Douglas, V. I. Children's responses to frustration. A developmental study. *Canadian Journal of Psychology*, 1965, *19*, 161–171.

Douglas, V. I. Stop, look and listen: The problem of sustained attention and impulse control in hyperactive and normal children. *Canadian Journal of Behavioral Science*, 1972, *4*, 259–281.

Douglas, V. I. Sustained attention and impulse control: Implication for the handicapped child. In J. A. Swets & L. L. Elliott (Eds.), *Psychology and the handicapped child*. Washington, D.C.: U.S. Office of Education, 1974.

Douglas, V. I. Are drugs enough? To train or to treat the hyperactive child. *International Journal of Mental Health*, 1975, *5*, 199–212.

Douglas, V. I. Perceptual and cognitive factors as determinants of learning disabilities: A review paper with special emphasis on attentional factors. In R. M. Knights & D. J. Bakker (Eds.), *Neuropsychology of learning disorders: Theoretical approaches*. Baltimore: University Park Press, 1976 (in press).

Durell, D. D. *Durrell analysis of reading difficulty*. New York: Harcourt, Brace & World, 1955.

Egeland, B. Training impulsive children in the use of more efficient scanning techniques. *Child Development*, 1974, *45*, 165–171.

Ferritor, S. E., Buckholdt, D., Hamblin, R. L., & Smith, L. The noneffect of contingent reinforcement for attending behavior on work accomplished. *Journal of Applied Behavior Analysis*, 1972, *5*, 7–17.

Firestone, P. *The effects of reinforcement contingencies and caffeine on hyperactive children*. Unpublished doctoral dissertation, McGill University, Montreal, 1974.

Firestone, P., & Douglas, V. I. The effects of reward and punishment on reaction times and autonomic activity in hyperactive and normal children. *Journal of Abnormal Child Psychology*, 1975, *3*, 201–216.

Freibergs, V., & Douglas, V. I. Concept learning in hyperactive and normal children. *Journal of Abnormal Psychology*, 1969, *74*, 388–395.

Gallagher, C. C. *Federal involvement in the use of behavior modification drugs on grammar school children*. Hearing before a subcommittee of the Committee of Government operations, House of Representatives, September 29, 1970.

Goldfried, M. R., & Merbaum, M. *Behavior change through self-control*. Holt, Rinehart & Winston, 1973.

Greenspoon, S., & Singer, S. Amphetamines in the treatment of hyperkinetic children. *Harvard Educational Review*, 1973, *43*, 515–555.

Higa, W. R. *Self-instructional versus direct training in modifying children's impulsive behavior*. Unpublished doctoral dissertation, University of Hawaii, 1973.

Jastak, J. *Wide range achievement test*. Wilmington: C. L. Story Co., 1946.

Kagan, J. Reflection-impulsivity: The generality of conceptual tempo, *Journal of Abnormal Psychology*, 1966, *36*, 609–628.

Koppitz, E. *The Bender-Gestalt test for young children*. New York: Grune & Stratton, 1964.

Krager, J., & Safer, D. Type and prevalence of medication used in treating hyperactive children. *New England Journal of Medicine*, 1974, *291*, 1118–1120.

Meichenbaum, D., & Goodman, J. Reflection impulsivity and verbal control of motor behavior. *Child Development*, 1969, *40*, 785–797.

Meichenbaum, D., & Goodman, J. Training impulsive children to talk to themselves: A means of developing self-control. *Journal of Abnormal Psychology*, 1971, *77*, 115–126.

Minde, K., Lewin, D., Weiss, G., Laviqueur, H., Douglas, V. I., & Sykes, D. The hyperactive child in elementary school: A 5-year controlled follow-up. *Exceptional Children*, 1971, *38*, 215–221.

Nelson, T. *The effects of training in attention deployment of observing behavior in reflective and impulsive children*. Unpublished doctoral dissertation, University of Michigan, Ann Arbor, 1968.

O'Leary, K. D., Pelham, W. E., Rosenbaum, A., & Price, G. H. Behavioral treatment of hyperkinetic children: An experimental evaluation of its usefulness. *Clinical Pediatrics*, 1976, *15*, 275–279.

Palkes, H., Stewart, M., & Freedman, J. Improvement in maze performance of hyperactive boys as a function of verbal-training procedures. *Journal of Special Education*, 1972, *5*, 337–342.

Palkes, H., Stewart, M., & Kahana, B. Porteus maze performance of hyperactive boys after training in self-directed verbal commands. *Child Development*, 1968, *39*, 817–826.

Parry, P. *The effect of reward on the performance of hyperactive children.* Unpublished doctoral dissertation, McGill University, Montreal, 1973.

Parry, P., & Douglas, V. I. The effect of reward on the performance of hyperactive children. *Journal of Abnormal Child Psychology,* in press.

Patterson, G. An application of conditioning techniques to the control of a hyperactive child. In L. Ullman and L. Krasner (Eds.), *Case studies in behavior modification.* New York: Holt, Rinehart, & Winston, 1965.

Patterson, G., Jones, R., Whittier, J., & Wright, M. A. A behavior modification technique for the hyperactive child. *Behavior Research and Therapy,* 1965, *2*, 217–226.

Pihl, R. Conditioning procedures with hyperactive children. *Neurology,* 1967, *17*, 421–423.

Porteus, S. D. *Porteus maze tests: Fifty years' application.* Palo Alto: Pacific Books, 1969.

Quay, H. L., Sprague, R. L., Werry, J. S., & McQueen, M. M. Conditioning visual orientation of conduct problem children in the classroom. *Journal of Experimental Child Psychology,* 1967, *5*, 512–517.

Raven, J. C. *Standard progressive matrices.* London: H. K. Lewis, 1958.

Ridberg, E., Park, R., & Hetherington, E. Modification of impulsive and reflective cognitive styles through observation of film-mediated models. *Developmental Psychology,* 1971, *3*, 369–377.

Robin, A., Sandi, A., & O'Leary, K. The effects of self instruction on writing deficiencies. *Behavior Therapy,* 1975, *6*, 178–187.

Rosenbaum, A., O'Leary, K. D., & Jacob, R. G. Behavioral intervention with hyperactive children: Group consequences as a supplement to individual contingencies. *Behavior Therapy,* 1975, *6*, 315–323.

Ross, A. O. *Psychological aspects of learning disabilities and reading disorders.* New York: McGraw-Hill, 1976.

Safer, D., & Allen, R. Stimulant drug treatment of hyperactive adolescents. *Diseases of the Nervous System,* 1975, *3*, 454–457.

Sleator, E. K., von Neuman, A., and Sprague, R. L. Hyperactive children: A continuous long-term placebo-controlled follow-up. *Journal of the American Medical Association,* 1974, *229*, 316–317.

Sprague, R. L., Christensen, D. E., & Werry, J. S. Experimental psychology and stimulant drugs. In C. K. Conners (Ed.), *Symposium on the clinical use of stimulant drugs in children.* Amsterdam: Excerpta Medica, 1974.

Sroufe, L. A. Drug treatment of children with behavior problems. In F. Horowitz (Ed.), *Review of child development research* (Vol. 4). Chicago: University of Chicago Press, 175.

Swanson, J. M., & Kinsbourne, M. Stimulant related state-dependent learning in hyperactive children, *Science,* 1976, *192*, 1354–1356.

Sykes, D. H., Douglas, V. I, & Morgenstern, G. The effect of methylphenidate (Ritalin) on sustained attention in hyperactive children. *Psychopharmacologia (Berlin),* 1972, *25*, 262–274.

Sykes, D. H., Douglas, V. I., & Morgenstern, G. Sustained attention in hyperactive children. *Journal of Child Psychology and Psychiatry,* 1973, *14*, 213–220.

Thorensen, C. E., & Mahoney, M. J. *Behavioral self control.* New York: Holt, Rinehart & Winston, 1974.

Wechsler, D. *Wechsler intelligence scale for children.* New York: Psychological Corporation, 1949.

Weiss, G., Kruger, E., Danielson, V., & Elman, M. *The effect of long-term treatment of hyperactive children with methylphenidate.* Paper presented at the 13th Annual Meeting of the American College of Neuropsychopharmacology, Palm Springs, California, 1973.

Whalen, C., & Henker, B. Psychostimulants in children: A review and analysis. *Psychological Bulletin,* 1976 (in press).

Zelniker, T., Jeffrey, W., Ault, R., & Parsons, J. Analysis and modification of search strategies of impulsive and reflective children on the Matching Familiar Figures Test. *Child Development,* 1972, *43*, 321–335.

16. The effects of a self-instructional package on overactive preschool boys

PHILIP H. BORNSTEIN   RANDAL P. QUEVILLON

The widespread use of behavioral principles with children has led to the development of several effective procedures for decreasing disruptive behavior and increasing attention in school settings. Aversive stimulation (Hall, Axelrod, Foundopoulos, Shellman, Campbell, & Cranston, 1971; Risley, 1968), response cost (Wolf, King, Lachowicz, & Giles, 1970), timeout (Carlson, Arnold, Becker, & Madsen, 1968; Kubany, Weiss, & Sloggett, 1971; Wahler, 1969), group contingencies (Barrish, Saunders, & Wolf, 1969; Harris & Sherman, 1973), and contingency management approaches (Hall, Lund, & Jackson, 1968; O'Leary & Drabman, 1971; Walker & Buckley, 1968) are among the procedures that have been shown to improve the behavior of "hyperactive" and disruptive children. However, these effects have been limited in two areas. First, some procedures have simply failed to affect significantly the behavior of a percentage of the subjects treated (Kazdin, 1973; Madsen, Becker, & Thomas, 1968). Second, lack of response maintenance at the cessation of intervention and failure to obtain transfer of training effects have been noted (Bornstein & Hamilton, 1975; Kazdin & Bootzin, 1972; O'Leary & Kent, 1973).

Kazdin (1975) has proposed training subjects in self-control (Bolstad & Johnson, 1972; Drab-

man, Spitalnik, & O'Leary, 1973; Meichenbaum, 1973) and the programming of generalization (Blanchard & Johnson, 1973; Walker & Buckley, 1972) as solutions to these problems. Within the former approach, verbally mediated self-control training would seem to have implication and utility in both problem areas defined above. That mediational processes exist in human learning has been amply demonstrated (Cole & Medin, 1973; Mahoney, 1974). In addition, the interaction between verbal and nonverbal behavior has received considerable attention (Luria, 1961; Vygotsky, 1962). Blackwood (1972) described speech as verbal chaining that produces discriminative stimuli and conditioned reinforcers. Self-produced verbalizations may therefore modify motor responses by mediating between stimulus situation and target behavior. The effects of verbal operants on motoric responses have been investigated (Bem, 1967; Lovaas, 1964; Meichenbaum & Goodman, 1969). Verbally mediated self-control training has been effective in eliminating lunchroom disruptions (MacPherson, Candee, & Hohman, 1974), and reducing rule-breaking behavior (Monahan and O'Leary, 1971), and the approach holds promise of reducing yet other forms of childrens' misbehavior (Blackwood, 1970). Additionally, since the individual is the source of behavioral control within the verbal mediation paradigm, response maintenance and transfer of training effects should be facilitated (Meichenbaum & Cameron, 1973).

One technique for training verbally mediated self-control is that of cognitive self-instruction (Meichenbaum & Cameron, 1974). This procedure consists of fading a set of prompts and instructions from an overt (spoken aloud), external (verbalized by a model) condition to a covert, self-produced target response. The effectiveness of the self-instructional package with school-age, "impulsive" children has been demonstrated (Meichenbaum & Goodman, 1971). Results have indicated that self-instructional guidance programs effectively modified the behavior of impulsive children relative to attentional and assessment control groups on several performance measures. Although improvement was maintained on a one-month follow-up assessment, no significant treatment effects were obtained on two indices of classroom behavior.

The present investigation sought to explore the functional utility of a self-instructional program for preschool, impulsive children and to demonstrate transfer of training effects from the experimental tasks to the actual classroom environment. Additionally, an observer-expectancy control condition was utilized such that treatment effects that arose were solely attributable to manipulations of the independent variable.

A multiple-baseline design was used in an attempt to demonstrate explicitly and reliably behavioral control within the self-instructional procedure. Thus, any ensuing behavioral changes within individual subjects were more readily apparent than in the more traditional group designs.

METHOD

SUBJECTS AND SETTING

The three subjects were concurrently enrolled in one classroom of a preschool Head Start program. Children were systematically selected on the basis of teacher and aide reports of highly disruptive and undesirable classroom behavior. Accordingly, only these three children were chosen to participate in the present research. Their parents were of lower- to middle-class social standing and average yearly income did not exceed $5000.

Subject 1 (Scott) was a 4-yr-old white male described as "a disciplinary problem because he is unable to follow directions for any extended length of time." He had been unable to complete standard tasks within the preschool classroom setting and often experienced violent outbursts of temper for no apparent reason. In addition, those working closely with him agreed that compliance and cooperation appeared to be minimal.

Subject 2 (Rod) was a 4-yr-old white male described by teachers as "being out of control in the classroom." Major problems and behavioral deficits included short attention span, aggressiveness in response to other children, and a general overactivity.

Subject 3 (Tim) was a 4-yr-old white male reported to be highly distractible both at home and in preschool. Anecdotal reports indicated that most of his classroom time was spent walking around the room, staring off into space, and/or not attending to task or instruction.

DEPENDENT VARIABLE

The dependent variable was on-task behavior, defined as those subject behaviors directed toward the assigned tasks. During teacher instruction it was expected that the child would be attentive and silent. When asked to participate during a word period (e.g., figure drawing exercises, story reading), on-task behaviors included performing the prescribed and accepted classroom activity. Off-task behaviors included engaging in unassigned activity: movement about the room, playing with toys, shouting, fighting, kicking, and leaving the classroom without permission.

OBSERVATION AND RECORDING

Behaviors were observed and categorized as either on-task or off-task by two independent judges naive as to the design of the study. Judges had been trained for two weeks before baseline and had achieved interrater reliabilities exceeding 80% for four consecutive days.

During the study, rates of on-task and off-task behaviors were obtained for the selected children twice daily, four days per week. Thirty-minute observations were conducted in the morning and afternoon when class activities were more structured, to provide a clear indication of the presence or absence of appropriate behavior.

The measures of on-task performance were determined on a 10-sec observe, 10-sec record basis. That is, both observers would watch the first child on the list for 10 sec, then take 10 sec to record his behavior as "+" (on-task) or "0" (off-task). For the behavior to be coded as "+", the child had to be observed as on-task for the entire 10-sec interval. Behavior was considered off-task if the subject did not meet the above requirements. Subjects were observed in a random order that varied daily.

Both observers sat in the rear of the room (although not within view of each other), avoided all forms of physical and/or verbal contact with the children, and remained relatively unobtrusive throughout the study.

Reliability of observations. Since two observers were present during each phase of the investigation, continuous interobserver agreement data could be generated. The two records were, therefore, compared interval by interval for each child, and a measure of agreement obtained by calculating the number of observer agreements divided by the total number of agreements plus disagreements. Agreement was scored when both observers recorded the same behavior during the same 10-sec observation interval. Disagreement was scored when one observer recorded a behavior code that the other had not.

In addition, further checks on the reliability of the observers were made by the experimenter approximately every eight days, resulting in a total of 10 experimenter-calculated reliability sessions. These 10 sessions were covert in nature; the observers were not informed that a reliability assessment was being performed. This was accomplished simply by having the experimenter positioned out of view of either observer.

GENERAL PROCEDURE

Baseline. During the first eight days of the investigation, behavioral observations were made but were no experimental manipulations.

Self-instruction. Subjects were seen individually for a massed self-instruction session lasting 2 hr. The child worked with the experimenter for about 50 min, was given a 20-min break, and then resumed work for another 50 min. The self-instructional training was similar to that described elsewhere (Meichenbaum & Goodman, 1971) and proceeded as follows: (1) the experimenter modelled the task while talking aloud to himself, (2) the subject performed the task while the experimenter instructed aloud, (3) the subject then performed the task talking aloud to himself while the experimenter whispered softly, (4) the subject performed the task whispering softly while the experimenter made lip movements but

no sound, (5) the subject performed the task making lip movements without sound while the experimenter self-instructed covertly, and (6) the subject performed the task with covert self-instruction.

The verbalizations modelled were of four types: (a) questions about the task (e.g., "What does the teacher want me to do?"), (b) answers to questions in the form of cognitive rehearsal (e.g., "Oh, that's right, I'm supposed to copy that picture"), (c) self-instructions that guide through the task (e.g., "OK, first I draw a line here . . ."), and (d) self-reinforcement (e.g., "How about that; I really did that one well").

It should also be noted that, in numerous tasks, the experimenter consciously erred and then corrected his error without hesitation. In addition, since initially the children did not seem motivated to work, the experimenter paired self-praise with material reward (M&Ms) as a means of creating incentive. This reward was quickly leaned out as the children found they could complete the tasks successfully. Lastly, the entire training session was presented in a storylike manner. In each situation, the subject was told that the teacher (not the experimenter) had asked him to complete the task in question. When using self-instructions, then, the subject would respond as if he were in the classroom (e.g., "Mrs. B wants me to draw that picture over there. OK, how can I do that?").

More specifically, the self-instructional protocol consisted of the experimenter initially instructing the child "——— (child's name), watch what I do and listen to what I say". Immediately on gaining his attention, an M&M was placed in the child's mouth. When the first trial was completed, and if the child's attention had not shifted away from the experimental task, he was again given a candy reinforcer. The experimenter then said to the child, "——— (child's name), this time *you* do it while I say the words". Contingent on correct performance, the experimenter dispensed an M&M to the child paired with self-praise at the conclusion of this second trial. Candy reinforcers were then leaned out quite rapidly and given only at the close of a trial. No more than 10 reinforcers were given to any one child during a training session. Later in the training sequence, when the child was asked to verbalize on his own, acceptable responses were those that included correct performance and the four elements outlined above (i.e., questions about the task, answers, self-instructions, and self-reinforcement). If the child did not produce an acceptable response, the experimenter again modelled the task while talking aloud to himself. Following such demonstrations, the child was then returned to that part of the sequence where his error had been committed. If the child refused to comply, the experimenter merely reiterated his instructions and again modelled an appropriate response. When the child successfully completed a trial, he was given instructions for the next step in the training sequence. When all six steps in the sequence had been completed, the experimenter presented a new task and again modelled its performance while talking aloud to himself (i.e., step one).

A wide variety of tasks were employed in the 2-hr training sessions, with difficulty level increasing over time. These tasks varied from situations tapping simple sensorymotor skills (e.g., copying of lines and figures) to more complex problem-solving situations (e.g., block design and conceptual grouping tasks). In all instances, subjects were required to verbalize the nature of the task and their problem-solving strategy. All tasks were modified slightly from those on the Stanford-Binet, Wechsler Intelligence Scale for children or the McCarthy Scales of Children's Abilities.

Expectancy control. In an attempt to control for any nonspecific effects of treatment (e.g., attention, interaction with stimulus materials) and observer-expectancy effects, all three children were given 2-hr training sessions with the experimenter on the day self-instruction was to be initiated. However, since treatment was sequentially administered in a multiple-baseline fashion across subjects, only one subject received the actual self-instruction training. The other two children were taken from the room in an identical manner and exposed to the same stimulus materials, but did not receive the self-instruction training at that time. Rather, in the expectancy-control condition, the experimenter modelled appropriate responses for the child without verbalization. More specifically, the experimenter initially instructed the child, "——— (child's name), watch what I do". Immediately upon gaining his attention, as in self-instructional training, an M&M was dispensed to the child. If the child remained attentive through the first trial, he was given a second candy reinforcer. The experimenter then said to the child, "——— (child's name), this time *you* do it while I watch." At the conclusion of this trial, reinforcement was again dispensed and then

leaned out rapidly. No more than 10 reinforcers were given to any child during each expectancy-control condition. The procedure was then repeated a second time before presenting a new task. A second presentation was provided to equate across experimental and control conditions the amount of time spent with individual stimulus materials. The sequence in which the subjects were to be given the self-instruction training was randomly determined, and observers were thus kept naive as to the nature of the treatment and the order in which it was to be presented to subjects.

RESULTS

RELIABILITY

The levels of agreement between observers across experimental conditions for all subjects were: Subject A, 96%; Subject B, 92%; Subject C, 93%. Overall observer-observer reliability was 94% agreement. Comparable experimenter-calculated reliabilities for Observer A were: Subject A, 92%; Subject B, 93%; Subject C, 91%. Experimenter-calculated reliabilities for Observer B were: Subject A, 94%; Subject B, 90%; Subject C, 92%. Overall experimenter-observer reliability was 92% in both cases, indicating a difference between observer and experimenter-calculated reliabilities of 2%. A subsequent analysis of variance from raw data demonstrated that reliabilities calculated by observers were not significantly different from those determined by the experimenter ($F < 1$, df = 2/81, $p > 0.10$).

ON-TASK BEHAVIOR

Figure 16-1 represents the daily percent on-task behavior scores for each subject across experimental conditions. The mean rate of on-task behavior during the baseline condition for Scott, Rod, and Tim was 10.4%, 14.6%, and 10%, respectively. Following the 2-hour training in self-instruction, there was an immediate and dramatic increase in on-task behavior. Posttreatment means for the three experimental subjects were Scott, 82.3%; Rod, 70.8%; Tim, 77.8%. Postchecks were instituted on the sixtieth and ninetieth observation days after baseline was initiated, and results indicate that treatment gains were maintained. Percentage of postcheck on-task behaviors for the three subjects were: Scott, 70% and 77%; Rod, 64% and 67%; Tim, 70% and 68%. It should again be noted that observations

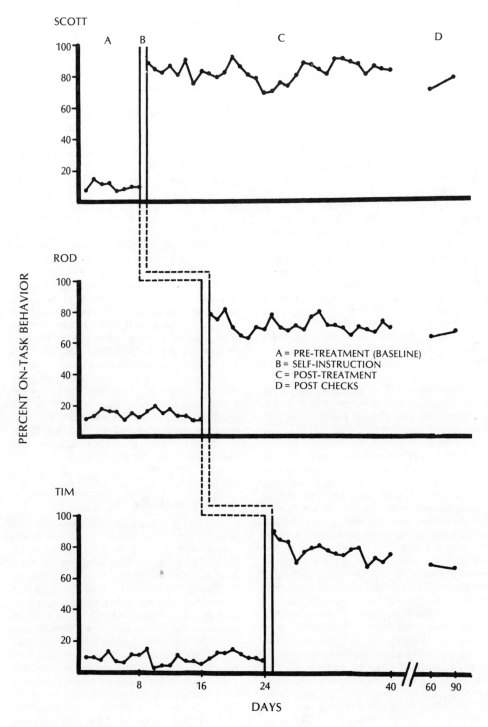

Figure 16-1. Daily percent on-task behaviors for Scott, Rod, and Tim across experimental conditions.

occurred only four days per week. Thus, the final follow-up data collected (i.e., observation day 90) are a sample of classroom behavior 22.5 weeks after baseline was initiated.

DISCUSSION

The present results demonstrate the utility of a self-instructional package as a means of increasing on-task behavior in preschool boys. Moreover, through the use of a multiple-baseline design across subjects and an observer-expectancy control manipulation, the results are made even more compelling. Specifically, the successive application of the self-instructional procedure and the corresponding increase in targeted subject's on-task behavior, as compared to nontargeted subject's baseline stability, unequivocally support the demonstration of a causal relationship. Since observers had no knowledge as to the timing of treatment effects, results cannot be attributed to expectation biases in the observational process. The present investigation was intended not only to demonstrate the utility of a self-instructional program for preschoolers, but also to extend treatment effects and behavioral improvement beyond the experimental situation. Results indicated that behavioral gains transferred to the classroom setting and were maintained for a considerable period of time.

These findings are superior to those found in previous work with verbal mediation and self-instructional training. For example, whereas Meichenbaum and Goodman (1969) obtained control of nonverbal responding in first graders through self-instruction, minimal effects were obtained with kindergarten subjects. The disparity between these findings and the present results may be due to the fact that Meichenbaum and Goodman (1969) used a minimal training, self-instructional method, in which their subjects did not totally fade verbal operants to the covert level. In addition, it is conceivable that their target behavior (i.e., tapping speed) may have interacted with developmental variables related to psychomotor skills. It thus seems likely that self-instructional training may lend itself more readily to the modification of certain classes of behavior rather than others. More specifically, while qualitative task errors related to task approach have been shown to be modifiable by self-direction, performance related to task ability has not been similarly affected (Palkes, Stewart, & Freedman, 1972). Using writing deficiencies as target behavior, Robin, Armel, and O'Leary

(1975) found self-instruction superior to direct training following an extensive and task-specific training package. The authors noted, however, that while motor control deficiencies may have been affected by self-instruction training, other abilities such as spatial-representation were not. Therefore, it would appear that behaviors accompanied by stable ability factors may not be as responsive to alterations in self-control strategies. Moreover, behaviors not directly affected by the demands of the task, such as resistance to temptation (Hartig & Kanfer, 1973), rule following (O'Leary, 1968), and on-task behavior may, in turn, be more influenced by self-instructional training. Certainly, further research is needed to explicate the classes of behavior most amenable to modification via self-instruction.

Despite the obtained results indicating strength, durability, and generalizability of treatment effects, one is unable to acknowledge firmly the treatment components responsible for initial behavioral change or transfer within the present therapeutic package. The present self-instructional program involved a wide variety of procedures, including instruction, self-instruction, verbal modelling, prompts, reinforcement, and fading. Future investigations might therefore include a component analysis as a means of separating the effects of self-instruction from the full therapeutic package. With regard to the issue of transfer of behavioral improvement, Meichenbaum and Goodman (1971) reported a lack of generalization using a similar self-instructional program. Since the present research differed from the Meichenbaum and Goodman (1971) investigation in four major respects (i.e., preschool versus school-age children, massed versus spaced practice, brief use of material rewards, and "storylike" self-instructional training), isolation of individual procedural contributions becomes impossible. Any one of the above components, singly or in combination, may have been responsible for the observed effects. In terms of practical considerations, future studies should therefore also attempt to uncover the "active" agents of change responsible for generalization of treatment effects.

The maintenance of behavioral improvement following treatment intervention was quite remarkable. The authors suggest, however, that such dramatic transfer from the experimental setting to the classroom was a function of two factors: (1) The preschool environment has been described as a "behavioral trap" (Baer and Wolf, 1970) which, upon entry, shapes and maintains an ever-increasing repertoire of appropriate behaviors in children. As a result of such "trapping," changes in the boys' behavior may have produced changes in the teacher's behavior, leading to maintenance of treatment gains. (2) Children in the present investigation were asked to imagine, in the presence of the experimenter, that they were performing tasks assigned by their classroom teacher. The use of such specific covert rehearsal may thus facilitate development and maintenance of appropriate classroom behavior. Although these hypotheses remain to be tested, future investigators attempting to implement the self-instructional package should be forewarned that generalization may not occur without consideration of the above issues.

The present study used several techniques to increase the likelihood of reliable and accurate assessment of behavior. This research differs from past investigations (Romanczyk, Kent, Diament, & O'Leary, 1973) in that here both observers were aware that overt assessment was constantly being performed and only a two-category code was in effect. These differences, no doubt, force observers to record behaviors more reliably at all times (Reid, 1970). Despite the reliability results obtained and the precautions taken to ensure accurate data collection, the phenomenon of observer drift (O'Leary & Kent, 1973) remains a potential source of bias. While constant, overt reliability checks led to high rates of interobserver agreement, these assessments may have been inflated due to consensual observer drift (Lipinski & Nelson, 1974). That is, both observers may have drifted from accurate recording as a highly reliable, though inaccurate, pair.

As a check on such possibility, observers were not aware that on 10 occasions during the investigation, covert assessment was also being performed by the experimenter. This strategy was an attempt to approximate comparison to a "pure" calibrator or constant criterion (Johnson & Bolstad, 1973). In this regard, it may be argued that the experimenter's knowledge of predicted effects would, no doubt, influence his recording and thereby further compound the potential consensual observer drift. Recent evidence, however, has indicated that even when observers have knowledge of predicted results, this is not apt to influence behavioral recording (Kent, O'Leary, Diament, & Dietz, 1974). The present results indicated that covert, experimenter-calculated reliability assessments were comparable to the overt, observer-calculated levels of agreement. Such findings therefore argue against observer drift within this particular observer pair. In addition, Kent et al. (1974) stated that if reliability assessment is to reflect routine data-collection characteristics, assessment must be covert in nature. Present results suggest that accurate reliabilities can also be obtained by means of constant overt reliability assessment.

In conclusion, the positive results obtained in the present research indicate that further investigation of the treatment package is warranted. Future studies should attempt to demonstrate therapeutic effectiveness across a wide variety of situations, subjects, and behaviors. In addition, it appears that the role of self-instruction in the modification of children's behavior demands greater exploration. Behavior modifiers have for some time ignored the study of such "mediational" variables due to the problems they present in empirical investigation. The present research attempted to demonstrate, in part, that an experimental analysis of behavior can be equally applied to this topical domain with a comparable degree of confidence in the reliability of the findings.

REFERENCES

Baer, D. M. and Wolf, M. M. The entry into natural communities of reinforcement. In R. Ulrich, T. Stachnik, and J. Mabry (Eds.), *Control of human behavior: from cure to prevention*. Glenview, Illinois: Scott, Foresman, 1970. Pp. 319–324.

Barrish, H. H., Saunders, M., and Wolf, M. M. Good behavior game: effects of individual contingencies for group consequences on disruptive behavior in the classroom. *Journal of Applied Behavior Analysis*, 1969, **2**, 119–124.

Bem, S. Verbal self-control: the establishment of effective self-instruction. *Journal of Experimental Psychology*, 1967, **74**, 485–491.

Blackwood, R. O. The operant conditioning of verbally mediated self-control in the classroom. *Journal of School Psychology*, 1970, **8**, 251–258.

Blackwood, R. O. *Mediated self-control: an operant model of rational behavior*. Akron, Ohio: Exordium Press, 1972.

Blanchard, E. and Johnson, R. Generalization of operant classroom control procedures. *Behavior Therapy*, 1973, **4**, 219–229.

Bolstad, O. and Johnson, S. Self-regulation in the modification of disruptive classroom behavior. *Journal of Applied Behavior Analysis*, 1972, **5**, 443–454.

Bornstein, P. H. and Hamilton, S. B. Token rewards and straw men. *American Psychologist*, 1975, **30**, 780–781.

Carlson, C. S., Arnold, C. R., Becker, W. C., and Madsen, C. H. The elimination of tantrum behavior of a child in an elementary classroom. *Behaviour Research and Therapy,* 1968, **6,** 117–119.

Cole, M. and Medin, D. On the existence and occurrence of mediation in discrimination transfer: a critical note. *Journal of Experimental Child Psychology,* 1973, **15,** 352–355.

Drabman, R. S., Spitalnik, R. S., and O'Leary, K. D. Teaching self-control to disruptive children. *Journal of Abnormal Psychology,* 1973, **82,** 10–16.

Hall, R. V., Axelrod, S., Foundopoulos, M., Shellman, J., Campbell, R., and Cranston, S. The effective use of punishment to modify behavior in the classroom. *Educational Technology,* 1971, **4,** 24–26.

Hall, R. V., Lund, D., and Jackson, D. Effects of teacher attention on study behavior. *Journal of Applied Behavior Analysis,* 1968, **1,** 1–12.

Harris, V. W. and Sherman, J. A. Use and analysis of the "good behavior game" to reduce disruptive classroom behavior. *Journal of Applied Behavior Analysis,* 1973, **6,** 405–417.

Hartig, M. and Kanfer, F. H. The role of verbal self-instructions in children's resistance to temptation. *Journal of Personality and Social Psychology,* 1973, **25,** 259–267.

Johnson, S. M. and Bolstad, O. D. Methodological issues in naturalistic observation: some problems and solutions for field research. In L. Hamerlynck, L. Handy, and E. Mash (Eds.), *Behavior change: methodology, concepts, and practice,* Champaign, Illinois: Research Press, 1973. Pp. 7–67.

Kazdin, A. E. The failure of some patients to respond to token programs. *Journal of Behavior Therapy and Experimental Psychiatry,* 1973, **4,** 7–14.

Kazdin, A. E. *Behavior modification in applied settings.* Homewood, Illinois: Dorsey Press, 1975.

Kazdin, A. E. and Bootzin, R. R. The token economy: an evaluative review. *Journal of Applied Behavior Analysis,* 1972, **5,** 343–372.

Kent, R., O'Leary, K., Diament, C., and Dietz, A. Expectation biases in observational evaluation of therapeutic change. *Journal of Consulting and Clinical Psychology,* 1974, **42,** 774–780.

Kubany, E., Bloch, L., and Sloggett, B. The good behavior clock: reinforcement/timeout procedure for reducing disruptive classroom behavior. *Journal of Behavior Therapy and Experimental Psychiatry,* 1971, **2,** 173–174.

Lipinski, D. and Nelson, R. Problems in the use of naturalistic observation as a means of behavioral assessment. *Behavior Therapy,* 1974, **5,** 341–351.

Lovaas, O. I. Cue properties of words: the control of operant responding by rate and content of verbal operants. *Child Development,* 1964, **35,** 245–256.

Luria, A. R. *The role of speech in the regulation of normal and abnormal behavior.* New York: Liveright, 1961.

MacPherson, E. M., Candee, B. L., and Hohman, R. J. A comparison of three methods for eliminating disruptive lunchroom behavior. *Journal of Applied Behavior Analysis,* 1974, **7,** 287–297.

Madsen, C. H., Becker, W. C., and Thomas, D. R. Rules, praise, and ignoring: elements of elementary classroom control. *Journal of Applied Behavior Analysis,* 1968, **1,** 139–150.

Mahoney, M. J. *Cognition and behavior modification.* Cambridge, Massachusetts: Ballinger, 1974.

Meichenbaum, D. H. Cognitive factors in behavior modification: modifying what clients say to themselves. In R. D. Rubin, J. P. Brady, and J. D. Henderson (Eds.), *Advances in behavior therapy,* Vol. 4. New York: Academic Press, 1973. Pp. 21–36.

Meichenbaum, D. and Cameron, R. Training schizophrenics to talk to themselves: a means of developing attentional controls. *Behavior Therapy,* 1973, **4,** 515–534.

Meichenbaum, D. and Cameron, R. The clinical potential of modifying what clients say to themselves. In M. J. Mahoney and C. E. Thoresen (Eds.), *Self-control: power to the person.* Belmont, California: Wadsworth, 1974. Pp. 263–290.

Meichenbaum, D. and Goodman, J. The developmental control of operant motor responding by verbal operants. *Journal of Experimental Child Psychology,* 1969, **7,** 553–565.

Meichenbaum, D. and Goodman, J. Training impulsive children to talk to themselves: a means of developing self-control. *Journal of Abnormal Psychology,* 1971, **77,** 115–126.

Monahan, J. and O'Leary, K. D. Effects of self-instruction on rule-breaking behavior. *Psychological Reports,* 1971, **29,** 1059–1066.

O'Leary, K. D. The effects of self-instruction on immoral behavior. *Journal of Experimental Child Psychology,* 1968, **6,** 297–301.

O'Leary, K. D. and Drabman, R. Token reinforcement programs in the classroom: a review. *Psychological Bulletin,* 1971, **75,** 379–398.

O'Leary, K. D. and Kent, R. Behavior modification for social action: research tactics and problems. In L. Hamerlynck, L. Handy, and E. Mash (Eds.), *Behavior change: methodology, concepts, and practice.* Champaign, Illinois: Research Press, 1973. Pp. 69–96.

Palkes, H., Stewart, M., and Freedman, J. Improvement in maze performance of hyperactive boys as a function of verbal-training procedures. *Journal of Special Education,* 1972, **5,** 337–343.

Reid, J. B. Reliability assessment of observation data: a possible methodological problem. *Child Development,* 1970, **41,** 1143–1150.

Risley, T. R. The effects and side effects of punishing the autistic behaviors of a deviant child. *Journal of Applied Behavior Analysis,* 1968, **1,** 21–34.

Robin, A. L., Armel, S., and O'Leary, K. D. The effects of self-instruction on writing deficiencies. *Behavior Therapy,* 1975, **6,** 178–187.

Romanczyk, R., Kent, R., Diament, C., and O'Leary, K. Measuring the reliability of observational data: a reactive process. *Journal of Applied Behavior Analysis,* 1973, **6,** 1975–184.

Vygotsky, L. *Thought and language*. New York: Wiley, 1962.

Wahler, R. G. Oppositional children: a quest for parental reinforcement control. *Journal of Applied Behavior Analysis*, 1969, **2,** 159–170.

Walker, H. M. and Buckley, N. K. The use of positive reinforcement in conditioning attending behavior. *Journal of Applied Behavior Analysis*, 1968, **1,** 245–250.

Walker, H. M. and Buckley, N. K. Programming generalization and maintenance of treatment effects across time and across settings. *Journal of Applied Behavior Analysis*, 1972, **5,** 209–224.

Wolf, M. M., Hanley, E. L., King, L. A., Lachowicz, J., and Giles, D. K. The timer game: a variable interval contingency for the management of out-of-seat behavior. *Exceptional Children*, 1970, **37,** 113–117.

17. Use of biofeedback in the treatment of hyperactivity

JOEL F. LUBAR   MARGARET N. SHOUSE

During the past fifteen years, considerable basic research and applied effort has been directed toward developing methods for controlling internal physiological processes. These processes include autonomic functions, both unit and gross (summated) neuromuscular activity, and central neural electrophysiological responses, all of which may be modifiable through the application of behavioral methods. Psychophysiology is the discipline most concerned with this type of research. A relatively new applied branch of psychophysiology, now known as *biofeedback,* is undergoing rapid development to fulfill basic research and clinical needs related to the control of physiological processes.

DEFINITIONS OF BIOFEEDBACK AND BRIEF HISTORICAL OVERVIEW

Biofeedback is a methodology for acquiring learned control over internal processes. Essen-

tially, biofeedback is operant conditioning of autonomic, electrophysiological, and neuromuscular responses. The procedure usually involves making an extroceptive stimulus contingent upon some clearly delineated change of an internal response, resulting in control of the targeted response. This process may take place with or without awareness on the part of the organism as to exactly what manipulations must be performed to bring about such control. Feedback-mediated control of physiological activity has been demonstrated in a variety of species, including rats, cats, monkeys, and humans. The target responses are usually of the following types: (1) electromyographic activity (EMG) representing activity of specific muscles; (2) autonomic activity that can be detected in a variety of organ systems; or (3) electrophysiological activity, that is, brain waves, evoked potentials, and possibly even slow potential shifts within the nervous system. The extroceptive stimulus is usually a light

This chapter is an edited version of a chapter (by the same authors) that appears in B. B. Lahey and A. E. Kazdin (Eds.), *Advances in Clinical Child Psychology* (Vol. 1). New York: Plenum, 1977, pp. 204–265. Copyright © 1977 Plenum Publishing Corporation. Reprinted by permission of the authors and publisher.

The authors would like to acknowledge Ms. Renee Culver and Mr. Tom Curlee of Biotechniques Incorporated and the ORTEC Corporation, for the development of the instrumentation used in this research, and Ms. Charlotte Gasker for the preparation and typing of this manuscript. We gratefully acknowledge Dr. Ted Mott, Department of Nuclear Engineering of the University of Tennessee, for the use of their facilities and for their kind technical assistance. We would like to acknowledge Dr. Hammond Pride and Dr. Robert Crawford, for referring subjects, and the teachers of the hyperkinetic subjects for nominating the control children and for cooperating with the classroom observation team. We also acknowledge John Maltry and Bret Boring for technical assistance in the laboratory; and Jack Dryden, Steven Soaf, and other undergraduate assistants, who helped in the behavioral observations required for the hyperkinesis research. The research reported here is based on a doctoral dissertation by M. E. Shouse, University of Tennessee, 1976.

or a tone that provides the subject with information about the internal response. It tells the subject that the internal response has taken place and may even provide information dealing with the magnitude of the response, that is, its amplitude or frequency or some other parameter. The extroceptive stimulus can also act as a primary or secondary reinforcer in that its contingent presentation can change the probability that the internal response will occur.

Whereas psychophysiology is primarily concerned with the problem of how autonomic, electrophysiological, or neuromuscular responses are learned, clinical biofeedback is directed at taking advantage of mediating responses in order to increase the rate of learning. Hence, the client might be trained to think "relaxed thoughts" and to try to remain as rested as possible in order to lower his EMG activity and blood pressure, to decrease his heart rate, to increase his gastrointestinal motility, or to bring about a variety of other autonomic responses that are part of the general parasympathetic profile.

A major concern in current biofeedback research is eliminating or accounting for the possibility of placebo effects that may account for desired results. In the studies presented here dealing with epilepsy and hyperkinesis, control procedures are discussed in detail. One of the most potent control procedures is the use of the ABA design, a variety of which is illustrated in our hyperkinesis work. In this type of design, data are collected systematically across several conditions. First, there is a baseline or pretreatment condition, then treatment intervention, and finally a return to the baseline condition. As Blanchard and Young (1974) have pointed out, "if changes in the target symptom occur in going from A to B and then revert when going from B to A . . . this constitutes a very strong evidence that B is the casual variable for changes in that symptom" (p. 575).

Other control procedures involve the introduction of *noncontingent* reinforcement either before treatment is undertaken or at some time during the treatment regimen. It is essential that the patient or subject not be aware that any change in contingencies has occurred. Other procedures involve the use of yoked controls or no-feedback controls, who are observed throughout the period of treatment along with the experimental group and compared on their target responses. This procedure is also exemplified in the hyperkinesis research to be discussed later.

AREAS OF BIOFEEDBACK APPLICATION

These are currently a number of areas in which clinical applications of biofeedback are being explored. These include the management of systolic and diastolic blood pressures (Schwartz & Shapiro, 1973; Elder, Ruiz, Deabler, & Dillenkoffer, 1973), cardiac arrhythmias (Bleecker & Engel, 1973), and the control of stress-related conditions, including tension and migraine headache, anxiety, and lower-back pain. Also, initial controlled studies of tension headache have been carried out by Budzynski, Stoyva, Adler, and Mullaney (1973), as have studies of both migraine and tension headaches by Sargent, Green, and Walters (1973).

Biofeedback has been applied to the rehabilitation of patients who have suffered from neuromuscular disease, stroke, or spinal-cord injury. Considerable effort here has been exemplified in the work of Basmajian (1972) and Brudny, Korein, Levidow, Brynbaum, Liberman, and Friedmann (1974). The interest in this area is currently expanding, so that many physical therapists have learned to integrate electromyographic-feedback techniques as part of their methodology for the rehabilitation of patients with neuromuscular dysfunction.

A recent area of feedback research and application involves the control of the gastrointestinal tract. Engel, Nikoomanesh, and Schuster (1974) have shown that it is possible to operant-condition the rectosphincteric response for the control of fecal incontinence. A more widespread application is the use of biofeedback for the management of ulcerative conditions in various portions of the intestinal tract (Welgan, 1974).

Many systems can also be monitored from the control of brain-wave (EEG) activity. For example, there has been a great deal of interest in the behavioral control of alpha rhythms. Kamiya (1969), Lynch, and Paskewitz (1971), and Beatty (1973) have shown that alpha rhythms (8–13 Hz recorded from the occipital regions of the human scalp) can be manipulated when feedback or reward is provided for changes in the density of this activity. Although the evidence is far from clear, alpha-feedback training has been linked with states of relaxation that may also be associated with low levels of arousal. Other types of electroencephalographic control seem to be much more specific. In the ensuing discussion, emphasis is placed on the behavioral control of a rhythm (sensorimotor rhythm) that is recorded over the sensorimotor cortical regions of the human or mammalian brain. This activity of 12–15 Hz is associated with the inhibition of motor responses and perhaps the generation of spindles during sleep. Current applications of sensorimotor-rhythm (SMR) conditioning include epilepsy (Sterman & Friar, 1972; Sterman, MacDonald, & Stone, 1974; Finley, 1975, 1977; Seifert & Lubar, 1975; Lubar, 1975, 1977; Lubar & Bahler, 1976) and specific types of insomnia in which cerebral mechanisms involved in the generation of Stage 2 sleep spindles might be deficient (Hauri, 1976). The newest application of SMR conditioning, which is described here in detail for the first time, is the management of the hyperkinetic syndrome in children.

It is important to leave the impression that there is *not* a specific biofeedback treatment for every type of functional, psychosomatic, or medical disorder for which biofeedback has been tried. Perhaps the most powerful effects can be obtained when several modalities of feedback are combined within a treatment program that may also include psychotherapy. Schwartz (1975) has effectively argued that many autonomic and electrophysiological responses that are highly correlated are also involved in a particular altered state. For example, the state of deep relaxation appears to be correlated with theta brain-wave activity (4–7 Hz) or the alpha rhythm (8–13 Hz) and also decreased levels of frontalis muscle EMG and EMG recorded from limb flexors. Also, increased peripheral skin temperature, slow and even respiration, and perhaps lowered heart rate and blood pressure occur in deep relaxation. This is what Gellhorn (1968) has called the "state of parasympathetic dominance." In those psychogenic or physiological conditions for which stress levels are high, it appears to be desirable to shift the balance toward the parasympathetic to a considerable extent. In order for a patient to accomplish this and maintain such control in stressful life situations, the combination of multiple feedback for several modalities plus desensitization techniques appears to offer the most potent approach.

HYPERKINESIS: GENERAL CONSIDERATIONS

DEFINITION OF THE DISORDER

The lack of agreement on the identifying features of hyperkinesis is reflected in estimates of its prevalence, which currently range from 5% to 22% of all elementary-school children (e.g.,

Minskoff, 1973). Nevertheless, a uniform set of research criteria may be derived from those characteristics most frequently agreed on by researchers. These include:

1. Consensus of parents, teachers, and pediatricians on the coincidence of the two fundamental symptoms: undirected, ceaseless motor activity and abbreviated attention span (American Psychiatric Association, 1968).
2. The gender of the hyperkinetic population, which is predominaly male.
3. The course of the syndrome, which typically spans the 6-year to 12-year age range (Menkes, Rowe, & Menkes, 1967).
4. The absence of specific sensorimotor deficients and other functional or physical handicaps (e.g., mental retardation), through which the syndrome's manifestations may be simulated.

Adopting such criteria not only appears justified on the basis of the available normative data (Wender, 1971) but should also yield incidence estimates of hyperkinesis in a more conservative and manageable range. Nevertheless, even these prerequisites are infrequently employed in a systematic fashion, and the resulting confusion has especially applied to organic interpretations of the hyperkinetic syndrome (Werry & Sprague, 1970; Omenn, 1973).

HYPERKINESIS AS A BRAIN-DAMAGE SYNDROME

Despite the diversity of opinion on the disorder's etiology, an organic substrate has been customarily assumed for hyperkinesis, and chemotherapy has been the preferred treatment. Historically, attention to hyperkinesis as a brain-damage syndrome emanated from the frequency with which overactivity characterized early postencephalitic cases (Hohman, 1922). The disorder's traditional association with brain damage is exemplified by frequent allusions in the medical literature to minimal brain dysfunction (MBD) and hyperkinesis as interchangeable labels for the syndrome. This practice may be attributed to the following findings relating hyperkinetic subjects to the normal population:

1. A higher coincidence between hyperkinetic behavioral manifestations and a specific history of generalized brain damage, particularly encephalitis (Hohman, 1922)
2. A higher probability for hyperkinesis to be

diagnosed in males (Wender, 1971), suggesting sex-linked holandric transmission
3. A higher coincidence between a history of pre- and perinatal birth complications and subsequent diagnosis of hyperkinesis (Stewart, Pitts, Craig, & Dierak, 1966)
4. Reliable differential MBD diagnoses on the Reitan battery relative to normal children and children with severe cases of brain damage (Reitan & Boll, 1973).

Nevertheless, a number of factors militate against a brain-damage theory of origin. For example, even though a significantly higher percentage of hyperkinetic subjects display specific neurological diseases and "soft neurological signs" than do nonhyperkinetics (Satterfield, 1973), the coincidence of hyperkinesis and other disorders such as encephalitis (Bond & Smith, 1935) and epilepsy, or pre- and perinatal incidents such as accidental poisoning during early childhood (Stewart, et al., 1966), has rarely accounted for a very large proportion of the children diagnosed as hyperkinetic. In addition, the empirical basis on which hereditary estimates are based is extremely meager. No studies, for example, have been reported on the frequency of the disorder in first-degree relatives; also, only 14 sets of siblings participated in the adoption study cited above (Omenn, 1973; Wender, 1971), and the single twin-study available (Lopez, 1965) is inconclusive because a disproportionate number of the fraternal twins were of unlike sex. Finally, although Reitan and Boll (1973) have successfully identified hyperkinetic symptoms with moderate but significant deficits on Reitan's battery, they failed to include a control group of children displaying a history of disruptive behavior problems that are not typically associated with neurological origins. Knights and Tymchuk (1969) were unable to differentiate two such groups on the Halstead categories test, which is a highly reliable diagnostic subtest of the Reitan examination. Until some clarification of these data is provided, only an insubstantial case can be made for brain damage as a necessary or even likely concomitant of hyperkinesis.

TREATMENT OF HYPERKINETIC CHILDREN

The equivocal basis for brain damage as a causal factor in hyperkinesis further obscures the puzzling outcomes reported with chemotherapy. The fact that sedatives exacerbate symptoms in hyperkinetic subjects apparently contradicts the somnolent effects otherwise obtained with these drugs. In contrast, the unprecedented therapeutic success of stimulant drugs, such as methylphenidate and the amphetamines, is contrary to the presumed excitatory nature of the disorder (e.g., Millichap, 1968). On the other hand, the paradoxical stimulant-drug effect does not appear to be a completely generalized phenomenon in the disorder, since moderate therapeutic benefits with tranquilizing agents have been reported in hyperkinetic children to whom stimulant drugs were either not administered or were unsuccessfully applied (e.g., Millichap, 1973).

Such evidence on the disorder's nature, symptoms, and treatment hardly yields a uniform profile of the syndrome. Although few would speculate that all diagnosed cases of hyperkinesis are properly admissible under the same rubric, one recently identified moderator variabler, CNS arousal level, may clarify many of the controversies.

CNS AROUSAL AS AN INTEGRATIVE MECHANISM IN THE HYPERKINETIC DISORDER

In the past decade, evidence has accumulated to suggest two meaningful subgroups of hyperkinetic subjects, one having reduced CNS arousal and the other displaying heightened CNS arousal (Satterfield, Cantwell, Lesser, & Rodesin, 1972). Excessive overactivity in low-arousal subjects is presumed to reflect the overcompensatory behavior of an otherwise sluggish organism. The selective effectiveness of stimulant medication in reducing these subjects' overactivity may therefore be explained by drugs' enhancing their physiological arousal level. In contrast, high-arousal subjects, whose excessive motor activity is presumably commensurate with the excitable state of the nervous system, should respond most favorably to CNS depressants. Establishing CNS arousal level as a moderating influence in the disorder may therefore account for the paradoxical calming effects associated with stimulant-drug administration in some hyperkinetic children and may permit more reliable predictions about the successful clinical application of both stimulants and depressants.

Low- and high-arousal children have been separated on the basis of three CNS-arousal indices taken individually (Satterfield, 1973; Satterfield, Lesser, Saul, & Cantwell, 1973; Satterfield & Dawson, 1971; Stevens, Sachdeo & Milstein,

1968) or in concert (Satterfield et al., 1972). Generally speaking, low-arousal subjects are characterized by excessive synchronized slow-wave activity in the waking EEG (e.g., Stevens et al., 1968), which suggests low arousal because alertness is typified by a faster, low-amplitude EEG (e.g., Penfield & Jasper, 1954); reduced GSR Conductance (e.g., Satterfield et al., 1972), which indicates reduced sympathetic and reticular arousal (Duffy, 1962); and enhanced auditory evoked-response amplitudes (Satterfield et al., 1972), which indicate relaxation, reduced alertness (Guerrero-Figuera & Heath, 1964), and possibly abbreviated attention span (Satterfield, 1965). Subjects differing from controls in the low-arousal direction also displayed more severe disruptive-behavior symptoms (Stevens et al., 1968; Satterfield et al., 1972 and benefited most from stimulant-drug therapy (Satterfield & Dawson, 1971; Satterfield et al., 1972). Finally, medication produced moderate changes toward increased arousal in conjunction with substantial decreases in behavior problems.

High-arousal subjects, on the other hand, displayed less slow-wave activity, higher GSR conductance, and lower-amplitude evoked cortical responses. They also showed the least behavioral disturbance, and although there is no direct evidence that they selectively benefit from CNS depressants, these subjects responded less well, if not unfavorably, to stimulant-drug therapy. Posttreatment data indicated either unchanged or exacerbated behavioral disturbance combined with exceedingly reduced CNS arousal (Satterfield et al., 1972).

These data are consistent with the rate-dependency findings in human and animal subjects in demonstrating that stimultant-drug treatment may affect motor activity either by increasing relatively low base-rates or by decreasing relatively high base-rates (e.g., Millichap, 1973; Stretch & Dalrymple, 1968). Furthermore, analogous drug effects on GSR and EEG base-rates in human subjects indicate levels of CNS arousal as a physiological mediator for the differing drug effects on hyperkinetic behavior.

SMR BIOFEEDBACK AS AN INDEPENDENT TEST OF THE AROUSAL HYPOTHESIS AND A POTENTIAL TREATMENT MODALITY

Even if stimulant drugs were demonstrably more effective for hyperkinetic children with reduced arousal, the role of arousal would remain uncertain since these drugs are known to affect both arousal (reticular) and motor systems concurrently (e.g., Millichap, 1968). A more conclusive assessment of CNS arousal functions in hyperkinesis has been investigated in our laboratory by the conditioning of increases in SMR, which, as shown in epileptics, is an EEG activity associated first with enhanced peripheral motor inhibition and second with changes in CNS arousal measures.

Because of its association with these two characteristics of hyperkinetic children, SMR biofeedback training should provide a convenient test of the arousal hypothesis. Contingent increases in SMR should result in reduced motor activity in all hyperkinetic subjects, increased physiological arousal in low-arousal subjects, and decreased physiological arousal in high-arousal children. This outcome would strengthen the arousal hypothesis. On the other hand, the exclusive display of training effects in either arousal level or motor activity would contraindicate the relevance of arousal as a primary factor in the disorder. In either case, a favorable outcome would provide a set of therapeutic procedures independent of the drug issue and perhaps of independent value when the use of drugs is contraindicated.

PROJECT DESCRIPTION
Goals

The goals of our project were:

1. to subdivide hyperkinetic subjects on the basis of CNS arousal level;
2. to demonstrate more severe pretreatment overactivity and better treatment effects with stimulant drug (Ritalin) medication in subjects with *reduced* CNS arousal level than in subjects with *elevated* CNS arousal levels;
3. to show greater treatment effects in low-arousal hyperkinetic subjects with drugs and SMR training than can be obtained with medication alone;
4. to demonstrate that positive treatment effects can be maintained with SMR training after medication is withdrawn.

Subjects

Hyperkinetic Subjects. In order to participate in all phases of the research (see Table 17-1), hyperkinetic subjects (total sample $n = 12$) had to meet a dual set of criteria. First, a uniform set of

Table 17-1. Number of laboratory and classroom observation sessions conducted during six experimental phases

| | | | Experimental phases | | | |
| | | | *Baseline sequence* | | *Biofeedback sequence* | |
	Exp. subjects	*I No drug*	*II Drug only*	*III Drug & 12–14+ 4–7 Hz– feedback*	*IV Drug & 12–14 Hz– 4–7 Hz+ feedback*	*V Drug & 12–14+ 4–7 Hz– feedback*	*VI No drugs & 12–14 Hz+ 4–7 Hz– feedback*
Behavioral sessions	1	6	6	78	38	30	24
	2	6	6	60	30	24	24
	3[a]	6	6	74	—	—	6
	4	6	6	68	26	24	26
Laboratory sessions	1	15	15	45	15	15	15
	2	15	15	30	15	15	15
	3[a]	15	15	30	—	—	15
	4	15	15	30	15	15	15
Laboratory sessions	Hyperkinetic (5–12) & Normal (1–12) Control Subjects	6	6	—	—	—	6
Behavioral sessions		15	15	—	—	—	15

[a] Training was discontinued in this subject following Phase III; nevertheless, at the end of the training period for the other subjects (Phase VI), additional baseline sessions were obtained for this subject.

diagnostic criteria were required for admission to the initial baseline study. A child was considered an acceptable representative of the hyperkinetic population if he was:

1. Male
2. Within the age range of 6–12 years
3. Diagnosed as hyperkinetic by a pediatrician who considered the case severe enough to warrant medication
4. Regularly taking methylphenidate (Ritalin)
5. Diagnosed as hyperkinetic according to the Stewart teacher questionnaire, requiring definite indication of at least six symptoms, including overactivity and short attention span (Stewart et al., 1966)
6. Without specific sensory deficits or any other functional or physical illness (e.g., mental retardation or epilepsy) that might contribute to or otherwise be confounded with the target syndrome.

Second, participation in the SMR training sequence (training $n = 4$) was dependent upon pretraining arousal and behavioral profiles to be described later. The remaining eight subjects who did not participate in the SMR training sequence served as hyperkinetic control subjects.

Normal Control Subjects. Twelve normal (non-hyperkinetic) control subjects were also selected

from a group of children nominated by the teachers of each hyperkinetic subject. At least two children from each class were nominated, and the final selection was based on the relevant matching characteristics (age, sex, IQ). In addition, the absence of criteria 3, 4, and 5 above for hyperkinetic subjects was required for each normal control.

Experimental Designs

Initial baseline sessions (hyperkinetic $n = 12$) under no-drug (I) and drug-only (II) conditions were conducted in the absence of EEG biofeedback. Reference to these pretraining data permit assessments of the training procedure's therapeutic effects whether the drug regimen was sustained or withdrawn. The same dosage levels were maintained during all phases (II–V) employing chemotherapy.

The feedback contingency implemented in Phase III (training $n = 4$) required the production of 12-Hz to 14-Hz EEG activity and the inhibition of 4-Hz to 4–7-Hz activity. A contingent increase in SMR production (12–14 Hz +; 4–7 Hz –) was followed by a contingency reversal (12–14 Hz –; 4–7 Hz +) in Phase IV. If pretraining performance levels under the drug-only condition (II) were resumed, the feedback manipulation used in training was assumed to produce whatever changes were evidenced during that time. The original contingency (12–14 Hz + ; 4–7 Hz −) was reinstated during Phase V. In the final training phase (VI), the same EEG contingency was maintained after medication was withdrawn.

At the end of the training sequence, baseline measures under the no-drug condition (VI) were reassessed in all hyperkinetic subjects ($n = 12$). Baseline measures were also obtained from all 12 normal children before and at the end of the training period as indicated in Table 17-1.

Classroom and laboratory procedures

Classroom and laboratory apparatus and procedures have been described in detail elsewhere (Shouse, 1976; Lubar & Shouse, 1976). In addition to the 6 stimulus categories, 13 behavior categories selected as indices of overactivity and short attention span have been adapted, largely intact from a larger sample described in detail by Wahler, House, and Stambough (1975).

The following physiological responses were monitored in the laboratory:

1. 4-Hz to 7-Hz events; each 4-Hz to 7-Hz signal above 12.5 μV;
2. SMR events; each 12-Hz to 14-Hz signal above 5 μV in the absence of 4-Hz to 7-Hz events;
3. SMR bursts: 6 cycles of SMR within 0.5 sec;
4. Background EEG;
5. Auditory evoked cortical responses;
6. EMG criterions: each set of 50 integrated EMG signals of predetermined amplitude between Hz 30 and 300 Hz;
7. GSR: basal skin resistance in response to 18 μA constant current read at 30-sec intervals and converted to conductance units (μmhos).

RESULTS

PRETAINING DATA

No-drug comparisons of hyperkinetic and normal subjects

Overall differences between hyperkinetic and normal children on questionnaire, behavioral, and physiological measures during the no-drug condition are provided in Table 17-2. Hyperkinetic subjects differed significantly from normal ones in producing a higher frequency of parent- and teacher-reported developmental problems and symptoms of overactivity and distractibility. They also exhibited fewer desirable behaviors and more frequent undesirable and social behav-

iors in the classroom setting. In contrast to the questionnaire and behavioral findings, differences between the two groups in laboratory performance were confined to the relative dearth of SMR anticipated in hyperkinetic subjects. This statistically significant result was consistent with the EEG rhythm's noted correlation with behavioral immobility (Shouse, 1976).

Arousal differences during the no-drug condition

A rank ordering of hyperkinetic and normal subjects as a function of physiological arousal level is presented in Figure 17-1. The distribution of these data demarcates the four hyperkinetic subjects who consistently showed reduced-arousal characteristics relative to normal control subjects and to the remainder of the hyperkinetic population. In the absence of high-arousal characteristics, the latter were labeled *hyperkinetic control subjects* to reflect extensive overlap with normal children on physiological measures.

Table 17-2 summarizes the performance of the three groups on all questionnaire, behavioral, and physiological measures during the no-drug condition. The statistical analyses presented confirmed advance predictions that the low-arousal subjects would display more severe symptom profiles than hyperkinetic control subjects. According to qualitative assessments of questionnaire items, low-arousal subjects were more likely to be characterized as overactive, extraverted, and oppositional but were less likely than hyperkinetic control subjects to show severe attentional deficits. Also, although low-arousal subjects exhibited fewer parent-reported developmental problems than hyperkinetic control subjects, they were more likely to display problems in sensorimotor development (e.g., deficient large-muscle coordination, speech and hearing impediments) and to have experienced more medical problems at an early age (poor health in the first year, accidental injuries requiring emergency-room visits).

No-drug and drug-only comparisons

An analysis of change scores (no-drug versus drug-only) following the administration of Ritalin is presented in Table 17-3. As expected, low-arousal subjects benefited more by stimultant-drug medication than did control hyperkinetics, whose performance did not significantly differ from that in unmedicated normal subjects. Finally, although low-arousal subjects exhibited

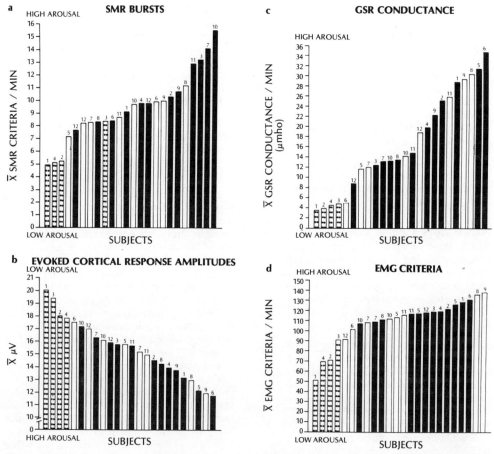

Figure 17-1a–d. Phase I (no .drug) laboratory results: hyperkinetic versus normal children as a function of arousal level. □ Low arousal hyperkinetic subjects, □ hyperkinetic control subjects, ■ normal control subjects.

significant change toward increased physiological arousal level and improved classroom conduct, they still displayed fewer desirable and more undesirable behaviors than did either control group.

TRAINING DATA
Laboratory findings

Figure 17-2 presents evidence supporting the notions that contingent EEG feedback can produce orderly changes in SMR production relative to daily and pretraining baselines and that corresponding changes in EMG occur in the opposite direction as training progresses. SMR and EMG values during the training sequence represent the following ratio:

$$\frac{\overline{X} \text{ criterions per minute during initial 15-min feedback period}}{\overline{X} \text{ criterions per minute during initial 5-min feedback period}}$$

Comparable values are provided for pretraining baseline sessions, when no feedback was presented.

Acquisition of the SMR task was demonstrated in three of four subjects. After six months of unsuccessful training, Subject 3's training was terminated. In Subjects 1, 2, and 4, negligible training effects occurring during early SMR training sessions were successively replaced by substantial increases in SMR ratios. Pretraining performance levels were temporarily resumed following a three-week lapse in SMR training for

Table 17-2. Phase I (no-drug) differences in laboratory questionnaire and behavioral indices as a function of subjects' arousal level

	Low-arousal[b] hyperkinetics (n = 4)	Hyperkinetic controls (n = 8)	Normal controls (n = 12)
Laboratory data[a]			
Mean amplitude evoked cortical response			
(P2 μV)	19.8	15.2	14.5
Mean GSR conductance (μmhos)	4.7	17.5	19.5
Mean no. SMR bursts per minute	5.9	9.1	11.23
Mean no. EMG criterions per minute	70.12	113.1	118.2
Stewart questionnaire data			
Mean no. parent-reported symptoms (n = 47)	24.25	14.125	4.17
Mean no. parent-reported developmental			
anomalies (n = 30)	9.75	11.0	2.25
Mean no. teacher-reported symptoms (n = 37)	19.0	10.05	2.05
Behavioral data			
Mean no. undesirable behaviors (n = 6)	31.35	21.28	14.41
Mean no. desirable behaviors (n = 3)	12.39	27.28	50.83
Mean no. social behaviors (n = 4)	28.75	14.25	15.3

[a] Laboratory and behavioral data were assessed over days; consequently, the degrees of freedom were 5 and 14, respectively, for dependent t tests.
[b] Low-arousal versus hyperkinetic controls: *Evoked response amplitudes: t = 3.53, df = 5, p < 0.05. GSR conductance: t = -3.53, p < 0.05. EMG: t = 3.25, df = 5, p < 0.05. SMR: t = 3.72, df = 5, p < 0.05. Undesirable behaviors: t = 3.38, df = 14, p < 0.05. Desirable behaviors: t = 1.86, df = 14, p < 0.05. Social behaviors: t = 2.62, df = 14, p < 0.05. Parent-reported developmental problem: t = -6.7, df = 10, p < 0.05. Parent-reported symptoms: t = 2.95, df = 10, p < 0.05. Teacher-reported symptoms: t = 4.4, df = 10, p < 0.05.*

Subject 1 and the contingency-reversal phase in all three subjects. Original training effects were recovered when the SMR contingency was reinstated and were sustained following some variability in Phase VI, when medication was gradually withdrawn (5 mg/week). Finally, the inverse

relationship between SMR and EMG is supported by moderate but statistically insignificant outcomes in the brief pretraining phases and by statistically significant ones during the three SMR training phases.

Power spectral analyses similar to those re-

Table 17-3. Phase I (no-drug) versus Phase II (drug-only) changes on laboratory, questionnaire, and behavioral indices as a function of subjects' arousal level

	Low-arousal[a] hyperkinetic	Hyperkinetic control	Normal control
Laboratory data			
Mean amplitude evoked cortical			
responses	Subjects	Subjects	Subjects
(P2 μV)	-3.0	+.9	+.35
Mean GSR conductance (μmhos)	+2.9	+.9	+1.25
Mean no. SMR bursts per minute	+4.42	+1.52	-1.6
Questionnaire data			
Mean no. teacher-reported symptoms	-5.75	-1.97	+2.25
Behavioral data			
Mean no. undesirable behaviors (n = 6)	-7.36	-2.24	+.51
Mean no. desirable behaviors (n = 3)	4.68	1.69	-.94
Mean no. social behaviors (n = 4)	-14.0	-.25	+.75

[a] Low-arousal versus hyperkinetic controls: *evoked responses: t = -2.12, df = 5, p < 0.05. GSR conductance: t = 0.99, df = 5, p < 0.1. EMG: t = 2.5, df = 5, p < 0.05. SMR: t = 5.9, df = 5, p < 0.05. Undesirable behaviors: t = -4.15, df = 14, p < 0.05. Desirable behaviors: t = 1.98, df = 14, p < 0.05. Social behaviors: t = 5.8, df = 14, p < 0.05. Teacher-reported symptoms: t = 3.28, df = 19, p < 0.05.*

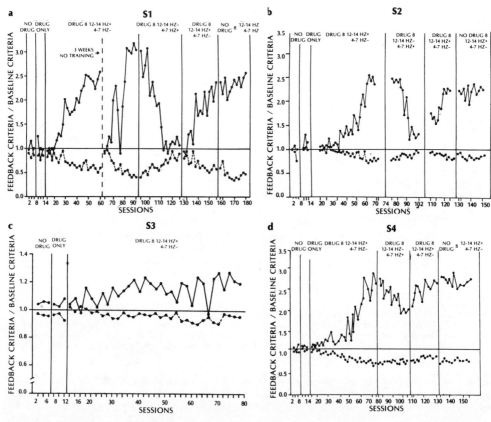

Figure 17-2a–d. SMR and EMG ratios over time for the four training subjects. ●——● 12–14 Hz, ●--● EMG.

ported earlier for our epileptic patients were conducted during initial 5-min baseline periods for the four low-arousal hyperkinetics. The results of these analyses showed the following trends. Relative to the no-drug condition, there was a decline in slow-wave activity between Hz and 4–7 Hz during the drug-only phase for all subjects. This change was not accompanied by a noticeable increase in the 12-Hz to 14-Hz activity range, although slight to moderate increases in the 12-Hz to 18-Hz activity subsequently appeared in the three subjects who responded to the feedback procedure. A temporary reversal in the latter trend during SMR counterconditioning (Phase IV) confirmed that the observed redistribution of power reflects treatment influences above and beyond those expected to accompany maturation alone. Finally, these changes were sustained during SMR conditioning in the absence of medication (Phase VI), thus supporting the effectiveness of the training procedures. As in the case of our epileptics, a baseline shift in the EEG appears to be reasonable if valid extrapolations from the laboratory to general experience are to be made.

Although the changes observed in the feedback-to-baseline ratios and in the spectral analyses were in the predicted direction, the disparity in the spectral analyses were in the predicted direction, the disparity in the magnitude of effects shown in the two types of data is significant. One reason for this difference is that all three of the successfully trained children gritted their teeth during the initial 5-min baseline period. This action resulted in the spurious reduction of initial SMR base-rates. In addition, since EMG electrodes were attached to the chin, artificially high levels of baseline EMG also occurred. Since monetary rewards were based on SMR production during feedback relative to the initial baseline only, this practice tended to assure not only training success but also a highly negative correlation between SMR and EMG on a daily basis. Although monetary rewards were suspended following ostensible signs of the artifact in the EEG, verbal reports at the end of the training indicated that subjects continued to supplement their performance in a similar, if more subtle, fashion. The persistence of the artifact no doubt accounts for the remarkable appearance of the learning curves as well as for the modest changes found in the EEG spectra. Nevertheless, the fact that some evidence of a baseline shift in the EEG occurred in spite of teeth gritting strengthens our basis for postulating a carry-over effect from the laboratory setting.

Classroom observations

Figures 17-3 through 17-6 present the average number of daily events scored per week for eight categories under six conditions in Subjects 1, 2, 3, and 4, respectively. Reliabilities were computed for two independent observers in half the sessions of each condition. Using the formula:

$$\frac{\#\text{categories of agreement}}{\#\text{categories of agreement and disagreement}}$$

the average reliabilities per session for Subjects 1, 2, 3, and 4 were greater than 80 percent.

Combining medication and SMR training was intended to enhance the level of improvement already achieved with drugs alone. The eight behaviors included in Figures 3 through 5 exhibit

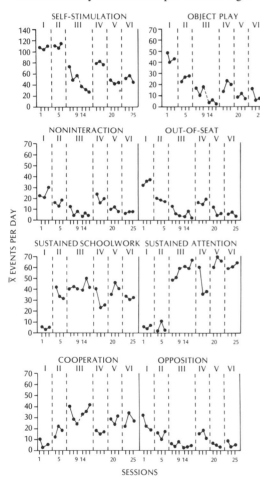

Figure 17-3. Changes in eight behaviors during SMR training: Subject 1. I No drug, II drug only, III drug and 12–14 Hz$^+$ 4–7 Hz$^-$, IV drug and 12–14 Hz$^-$ 4–7 Hz$^+$, V drug and 12–14 Hz$^+$ 4–7 Hz$^-$, VI no drug and 12–14 Hz$^+$ 4–7 Hz$^-$.

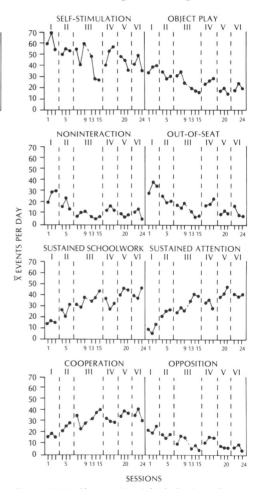

Figure 17-4. Changes in eight behaviors during SMR training: Subject 2. I No drug, II drug only, III drug and 12–14 Hz$^+$ 4–7 Hz$^-$, IV 12–14 Hz$^-$ 4–7 Hz$^+$, V drug and 12–14 Hz$^+$ 4–7 Hz$^-$, VI no drug and 12–14 Hz$^+$ 4–7 Hz$^-$.

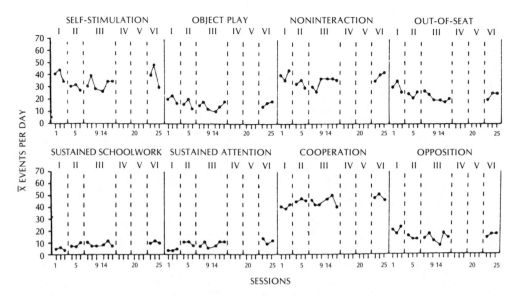

Figure 17-15. Absence of change in eight behaviors during ineffective SMR training: Subject 3. I No drug, II drug only, III drug and 12–14 Hz+ 4–7 Hz−, IV drug and 12–14 Hz−, 4–7 Hz+, V drug and 12–14 Hz+ 4–7 Hz−, VI no drug and 12–14 Hz+ 4–7 Hz−.

the predicted changes during SMR training. Relative to the no-drug phase, improvement in at least six of those categories was displayed during the drug-only phase in all four subjects. Generally, decreases in undirected activities, out-of-seat, and oppositional behaviors were accompanied by increased cooperation and schoolwork. When drugs and effective SMR training were combined (Subjects 1, 2, and 4), even further improvement occurred in the behaviors benefited by medication, and substantial changes were evidenced in those that were not. As expected, Subject 3, who failed to demonstrate SMR task acquisition, also failed to show further improvement in classroom conduct following the inception of biofeedback training (Figure 5).

Five behaviors omitted in the figures failed to change in the predicted direction during SMR training. One undirected activity (self-talk) and all four social behaviors occurred at moderate or high frequencies during the no-drug phase. Uniform decreases in them following drug-only were reversed during SMR conditioning in Subjects 1, 2, and 4, although the pretraining levels under no-drug were not resumed.

Changes in stimulus categories are also omitted. Positive and negative instructions as well as negative social attention from both teachers and peers occurred infrequently during the study regardless of the experimental condition. However, relative to the no-drug phase, positive social attention from peers decreased in the drug-only condition in all subjects and during both treatment conditions in Subjects 1, 2, and 4. Although this reduction varied inversely with improvement in the child's hyperkinetic behaviors in general, it varied most often as a direct function of reductions in self-initiated social approaches to peers. The correlation between the two events was fairly consistent in each subject across conditions, despire overall reductions in their frequency following the no-drug phase. It would be difficult, then, to conclude that changes in peer reinforcement contributed directly, or even positively, to the observed changes in the target indices of hyperactivity. Rather, it would appear that treatment-related reductions in subject-initiated social approaches stimulated the decline in this reinforcement category.

Pretraining versus posttraining analyses

An analysis of the training data suggested not only that combining medication and SMR conditioning leads to more desirable changes in hyperkinetic behaviors than the changes resulting from

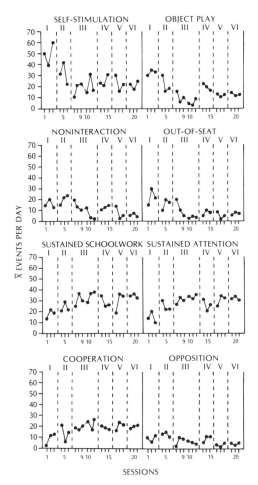

Figure 17-6. Changes in eight behaviors during SMR training: Subject 4. I No drug, II drug only, III drug and 12–14 Hz⁺ 4–7 Hz⁻, IV drug and 12–14 Hz⁻ 4–7 Hz⁺, V drug and 12–14 Hz⁺ 4△ Hζ⁻, VI no drug and 12–14 Hz⁺ 4–7 Hz⁻.

the use of drugs alone but also that these benefits are sustained following the withdrawal of medication. These contentions are supported and extended by the data presented in Figures 17-7 and 17-8, which show physiological and behavioral changes during the no-drug (I), drug-only (II), and no-drug-and-SMR training (VI) phases in all subjects and in Table 17-4, which presents the mean change in all dependent measures between the drug-only (II) and the no-drug-and-SMR training (VI) phases. Physiological and behavioral benefits associated with SMR training are indicated by the following findings:

1. A greater degree of improvement shown by low-arousal subjects during SMR training alone (Phase VI) than during medication alone (Phase II)
2. A better treatment outcome by the end of training (Phase VI versus Phase II) in low-arousal subjects than in hyperkinetic control subjects who did not participate in training and whose physiological and behavioral profile remained relatively stable regardless of the administration or withdrawal of medication
3. The increasing resemblance between the post-training profiles of SMR-trained and control subjects for many of the measures.

All training-related changes in low-arousal subjects were in the predicted direction and were statistically significant relative to their own drug-only performance and to the performance of hyperkinetic controls during Phases II and VI, shown in Table 6. Additionally, relative to normal controls, the absolute posttraining values in low-arousal subjects showed incomplete normalization only in GSR conductance and desirable behaviors (Figures 17-7 and 17-8). Otherwise, SMR-trained subjects could not be differentiated physiologically or behaviorally from normal subjects by the end of the study.

The greatest improvement appears to have occurred in undesirable behaviors, which primarily reflected motor disturbance. This finding is supported both by the selective normalization of undesirable behaviors in the classroom and by the tendency for teachers to continue complaining only of attentional deficits in Phase VI, even though improvement in both overactivity and distractibility were reported. In contrast, desirable behaviors, which primarily reflected attention span, showed incomplete remission by the end of training. These findings suggest a greater relative role for motor functions in a successful training outcome.

CONCLUSIONS

The effectiveness of the biofeedback technique in dealing with hyperkinesis is supported by the fact that the combined effects of drug administration and SMR training resulted in substantial improvement above and beyond the effects of drugs alone. Further support derives from the maintenance of positive treatment effects with SMR training after medication was withdrawn. The loss of improvement following SMR countercon-

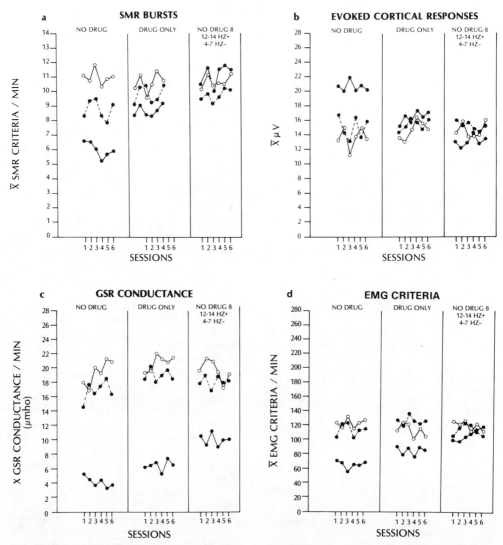

Figure 17-7a–d. Daily changes in four laboratory measures during Phase I (no drug, left panel), Phase II (drug only, center panel), and Phase VI (no drug and SMR training, right panel) in low-arousal and control hyperkinetic subjects and normal control children. Low-arousal hyperkinetic versus normal control during Phase VI: *EMG: t* = 0.11 *df* = 0.5, *p* > 0.1: *Evoked response amplitude: T* = 1.11, *df* = 5, *p* > 0.1: *SMR bursts: t* = 1.57, *df* = 5, *p* = 0.1: *GSR: t* = 6.8, *df* = 5, *p* < 0.05. ●—● Low arousal, hyperkinetic subjects, ●--● hyperkinetic control subjects, ●—● normal control subjects.

ditioning tends to minimize the role of extraneous influences (e.g., maturation) on treatment outcomes. Finally, the fact that the subject who failed to acquire the SMR task also failed to develop associated physiological and behavioral changes lends additional credence to these assertions.

These findings clearly implicate both CNS arousal level and central motor-system functions in the development of the hyperkinetic syndrome and its treatment. However, since SMR acquisition, normalization of CNS arousal indices, and behavioral improvement appear to have emerged concurrently, it is difficult to determine whether

Table 17-4. Phase II (drug only) versus Phase VI (no drug and SMR training) changes on laboratory, questionnaire, and behavioral indices as a function of subjects' arousal level

	Low-arousal hyperkinetics (n = 3)[a]	Hyperkinetic controls (n = 8)	Normal controls (n = 12)
Laboratory data			
Mean-amplitude-evoked cortical response (P2 μV)	−3.9[b]	+4.5[c]	+.27[d]
Mean GSR conductance (μmhos)	+3.6	−.15	−.10
Mean no. SMR bursts per minute	+2.97	−0.3	−.24
Mean no. EMG criterions per minute	+14.07	−2.25	+1.8
Questionnaire data			
Mean no. teacher-reported symptoms	−6.25	+2.0	−.16
Behavioral data			
Mean no. undesirable behaviors	−8.3	+1.3	−.22
Mean no. desirable behaviors	+9.58	+.52	+1.58
Mean no. social behaviors	+4.25	+2.0	+.75

[a] The low-arousal subject (3) who failed to acquire the SMR task is not included in the statistical analyses.
[b] DRUG alone versus SMR alone in low-arousal subjects: Evoked-response amplitudes: t = 2.8, $df = 5, p < 0.05$. GSR: t = 2.27, $df = 0.05, p < 0.05$. SMR bursts: t = −2.96, $df = 5, p < 0.55$. EMG: t = 2.8, $df = 5, p < 0.05$.
[c] Low-arousal versus hyperkinetic controls: Evoked-response amplitude: t = 2.0, $df = 5, p < 0.05$. GSR: t = 2.27, $df = 5, p < 0.05$. SMR bursts: t = 2.96, $df = 5, p < 0.05$. Teacher-reported symptoms: t = 3.0, $df = 2, p < 0.05$. Undesirable behaviors: t = 4.5, $df = 14, p < 0.05$. Desirable behaviors: t = 3.48, $df = 14, p < 0.05$. Social behaviors: t = 2.37, $df = 14, p < 0.05$.
[d] Low-arousal versus normal controls: Evoked response: t = 0.87, $df = 6, p > 0.1$. GSR: t = 0.96, $df = 6, p > 0.1$. SMR bursts: t = 0.86, $df = 6, p > 0.1$. EMG: t = 0.77, $df = 6, p > 0.1$. Teacher-reported symptoms: t = 1.99, $df = 6, p < 0.05$. Undesirable behaviors: t = 1.10, $df = 14, p > 0.1$. Desirable behaviors: t = 1.6, $df = 14, p > 0.1$. Social behaviors: t = 1.41, $df = 14, p > 0.1$.

the observed behavioral outcomes reflect primary changes in CNS arousal or whether the arousal changes represent a secondary effect from enhanced motor control.

An analysis of individual differences in laboratory and classroom performance suggests a greater relative role for enhanced motor control than for arousal level in training success. Two interrelated factors in the no-drug condition may have influenced susceptibility to treatment in the four training subjects. First, pertreatment laboratory data indicated a greater relative dearth of SMR in the subjects who responded most favorably both to medication and to SMR training (Subjects 1, 4, 2, and 3, respectively). Although SMR has also been considered here as a CNS arousal index, the other, more traditional physiological measures of arousal were consistently less effective in predicting treatment outcomes. Second, the interview and behavioral assessments designate excessive overactivity as the dominant problem area in children with reduced SMR production. In contrast, the subject who failed to demonstrate acquisition of the SMR task not only produced the highest pretreatment level of SMR but also displayed abbreviated attention span rather than overactivity as his principal behavioral deficit.

Pretreatment levels of SMR, then, most conveniently and reliably indexed both the severity of the original motor deficits and the subsequent success of both treatments in mitigating those symptoms. These findings not only reconfirm the relationship between SMR and behavioral immobility but also suggest the EEG rhythm's potential value as a diagnostic and prognostic tool in the disorder, especially when overactivity is a central feature. These findings are also consistent with recent research linking reduced production of the Rolandic rhythm in epileptics who have a primary motor symptomatology to a higher probability of successful treatment outcomes during SMR biofeedback training (Sterman, 1976).

Despite these promising findings, a cautious interpretation is particularly warranted in view of the heterogenous symptom profiles typically included in MBD diagnoses, the specificity of the physiological- and behavioral-symptom profiles considered here, and the inability to produce feedback-related changes in one of the four subjects. The possibility exists that short attention span, although partially controlled by medication, may have interfered with successful training in the one negative case. This outcome could restrict the procedure's therapeutic utility on a larger scale since some degree of reduced atten-

a

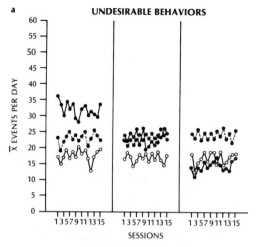

b

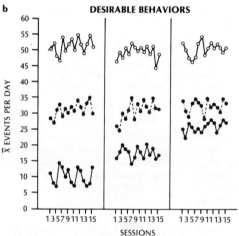

c

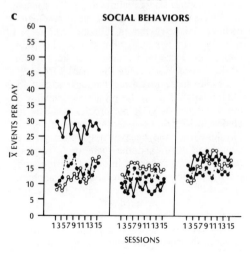

Figure 17-8a–c. Daily changes in (a) desirable, (b) undesirable, and (c) social behaviors during Phase I (no drug, left panel), Phase II (drug only, center panel), Phase VI (no drug and SMR training, right panel) in low-arousal and control hyperkinetic subjects and normal control children. Low-arousal hyperkinetic versus normal control children during Phase VI: *Undesirable behaviors:* $t = 0.93$, $df = 14$, $p > 0.1$; *Desirable behaviors:* $t = 2.72$, $df = 14$, $p < 0.05$; *Social behaviors:* $t = 0.16$, $df = 14$, $p > 0.1$. ●—● Low-arousal, hyperkinetic subjects, ●--● hyperkinetic control subjects, ○—○ normal control subjects.

tion span is symptomatic of the disorder. A considerable increase in the subject population is necessary before adequate evaluation is possible either of the procedure's general application to hyperkinesis or of its basis in CNS mechanisms of arousal or control.

REFERENCES

American Psychiatric Association. *Diagnostic and statistical manual of mental disorders, No, D-SM-11, 1968.*

Basmajian, J. V. Electromyography comes of age. *Science,* 1972, *176,* 603–609.

Beatty, J. Similar effects of feedback signals and instructional information on EEG activity. *Physiology and Behavior,* 1973, *9,* 151–154.

Bickford, R. G., & Fleming, N. *EDAS-1 data analysis system.* San Diego: School of Medicine, University of California, 1970.

Blanchard, E. B., and Young, L. D. Clinical applications of biofeedback training. *Archives of General Psychiatry,* 1974, *30,* 573–589.

Bleecker, E. R., & Engel, B. T. Learned control of ventricular rate in patients with atrial fibrillation. *Psychomatic Medicine,* 1973, *35,* 161–170.

Brazier, M. A. B. The problem of periodicity in the electroencephalogram: Studies in the cat. *Electroencephalography and Clinical Neurophysiology,* 1963, *15,* 287–95.

Budzynski, T. H., Stoyva, J. M., Adler, C. S., & Mullaney, D. J. EMG biofeedback and tension headache: A controlled outcome study. *Psychosomatic Medicine,* 1973, *35,* 484–496.

Denhoff, E. The natural life history of children with minimal brain dysfunction. *Annals of the New York Academy of Sciences,* 1973, *205,* 188–205.

Duffy, E. *Activation and behavior.* New York: Wiley, 1962.

Eccles, J. C., Ito, M., & Szentagothai, J. *The cerebellum as a neuronal machine.* New York: Springer, 1967.

Efron, R. The consitional inhibition of uncinate fits. *Brain,* 1957, *80,* 251–262.

Elder, S. T., Ruiz, Z. R., Deabler, H. L., & Dillenkoffer, R. L. Instrumental conditioning of diastolic blood pressure in hypertensive patients. *Journal of Applied Behavior Analysis*, 1973, *6*, 377–382.

Engel, B. T., Nikoomanesh, P., & Schuster, M. M. Operant conditioning of rectosphincteric responses in the treatment of fecal incontinence. *New England Journal of Medicine*, 1974, *290*, 646–649.

Feldman, S. M., & Waller, H. K. Dissociation of electrocortical activation and behavioral arousal. *Nature*, 1960, *196*, 1320–1322.

Fischer, K. C., & Wilson, W. P. Methylphenidate and the hyperkinetic state. *Diseases of the Nervous system*, 1971, *32*, 695–698.

Forster, F. M. Conditioning in sensory evoked seizures. *Conditional Reflex*, 1966, *1*, 224–134.

Gazzaniga, M. S. Brain theory and minimal brain dysfunction. *Annals of the New York Academy of Sciences*, 1973, *205*, 89–92.

Gelhorn, E. Central nervous system tuning and its implications for neuropsychiatry. *Journal of Nervous and Mental Disease*, 1968, *147*, 148–162.

Greenfield, N. S., & Sternbach, R. A. (Eds.). *Handbook of psychophysiology*. New York: Holt, Rinehart, and Winston, 1972.

Guerrero-Figueroa, R., & Heath, R. G. Evoked responses and changes during attentive factors in man. *Archives of Neurology*, 1964, *10*, 74–84.

Hallgreen, B. Specific dyslexia. *Acta Psychiatry Scandanavica Supplement*, 1950, *65*, 83.

Harper, R. M., & Sterman, M. B. Subcortical unit activity during a conditioned 12–14 Hz sensorimotor EEG rhythm in the cat. *Federation Proceedings*, 1972, *31*, 404.

Hauri, P. Biofeedback as a treatment for insomnia. *Proceedings of the Biofeedback Research Society*, seventh annual meeting, Colorado Springs, 1976, p. 34.

Hohman, L. B. Post-encephalitic behavior disorders in children. *Johns Hopkins Hospital Bulletin*, 1922, *380*, 372.

Jovanovic, U. J. *Psychomotor epilepsy: a polydimensional study. Springfield, Ill.: Charles C. Thomas, 1974.*

Kamiya, J. Operant control of the EEG alpha rhythm of some of its reported effects on consciousness. *In* C. T. Tart (Ed.), *Altered states of consciousness*. New York: Wiley, 1969, pp. 507–517.

Kaplan, B. J. Biofeedback in epileptics: Equivocal relationship of reinforced EEG frequency to seizure reduction. *Epilepsia*, 1975, *16*, 477–485.

Knights, R. M., & Tymchuk, A. J. An evaluation of the Halstead-Reiton category tests for children. *Cortex*, 1969, *4*, 403–414.

Kuhlman, W. N., & Allison, T. EEG feedback training in the treatment of epilepsy: Some questions and some answers. *Pavlovian Journal of Biological Science*, 1977, *In press*.

Lopez, R. E. Hyperactivity in twins. *Canadian Psychiatric Association Journal*, 1965, *10*, 421.

Lubar, J. F. Behavioral management of epilepsy through sensorimotor rhythm EEG biofeedback conditioning. *National Spokesman*, 1975, *8*, 6–7.

Lubar, J. F. Electroencephalographic biofeedback methodology and the management of epilepsy. *Pavlovian Journal of Biological Science*, 1977, *In press*.

Lubar, J. F., & Bahler, W. W. Behavioral management of epileptic seizures following EEG biofeedback training of the sensorimotor rhythm. *Biofeedback and Self-Regulation*, 1976, *1*, 77–104.

Lubar, J. F., & Shouse, M. N. EEG and behavioral changes in a hyperkinetic child concurrent with training of the sensorimotor rhythm (SMR): A preliminary report. *Biofeedback and Self-Regulation*, 1976, *1*, 293–301.

Lynch, J. J., & Paskewitz, D. A. On the mechanisms of the feedback control of human brain wave activity. *Journal of Nervous and Mental Disease*, 1971, *153*, 205–217.

Masland, R. L. Epidemiology and basic statistics on the epilepsies: Where are we? Paper presented at the Fifth National Conference on the Epilepsies, Washington, D.C., 1976.

Menkes, M. M., Rowe, J. S., & Menkes, J. H. A 25-year follow-up study on the hyperkinetic child with minimal brain dysfunction. *Pediatrics*, 1967, *39*, 393.

Millichap, J. G. Drugs in the management of hyperkinetic and perceptually handicapped children: Council on drugs. *Journal of the American Medical Association*, 1968, *206*, 1527–1530.

Millichap, J. G. drugs in the management of minimal brain dysfunction. *Annals of the New York Academy of Sciences*, 1973, *205*, 321–334.

Minskoff, J. G. Differential approaches to prevalence estimates of learning disabilities. *Annals of the New York Academy of Sciences*, 1973, *205*, 139–145.

Omenn, G. S. Genetic approaches to the syndrome of minimal brain dysfunction. *Annals of the New York Academy of Sciences*, 1973, *205*, 212–311.

Penfield, W., & Jasper, H. H. *Epilepsy and the functional anatomy of the human brain*. Boston: Little, Brown, 1954.

Reitan, R. M., & Boll., T. J. Neuropsychological correlates of minimal brain dysfunction. *Annals of the New York Academy of Sciences*, 1973, *205*, 65–88.

Sargent, J. D., Green, E. E., & Walters, D. Preliminary report on the use of autogenic feedback training in the treatment of migraine and tension headaches. *Psychosomatic Medicine*, 1973, *35*, 129–135.

Satterfield, J. H. Evoked cortical response enhancement and attention in man: A study of responses to auditory and shock stimuli. *Electroencephalography and Clinical Neurophysiology*, 1965, *19*, 470–475.

Satterfield, J. H. EEG issues in children with minimal brain dysfunction. *Seminars in Psychiatry*, 1973, *5*, 35–46.

Satterfield, J. H., Cantwell, D. P., Lesser, L. I., & Rodesin, R. L. Physiological studies of the hyperkinetic child: I. *American Journal of Psychiatry*, 1972, *128*, 1418–14.

Satterfield, J. H., & Dawson, M. E. Electrodermal correlates of hyperactivity in children. *Psychophysiology*, 1971, *80*, 191–197.

Satterfield, J. H., Lesser, R. I., Saul, R. E., & Cantwell, D. P. EEG aspects in the diagnosis and treatment of minimal brain dysfunction. *Annals of the New York Academy of Science*, 1973, *205*, 274–282.

Schwartz, G. E. Biofeedback self regulations and patterning of physiological processes. *American Scientist*, 1975, *63*, 314–324.

Schwartz, G. E., & Shapiro, D. Biofeedback and essential hypertension: Current findings and theoretical concerns. *Seminars in Psychiatry*, 1973, *5*, 493–503.

Seifert, A. R., & Lubar, J. F. Reduction of epileptic seizures through EEG biofeedback training. *Biological Psychology*, 1975, *3*, 81–109.

Sharpless, S., & Jasper, H. H. Habituation of the arousal reaction. *Brain*, 1956, *79*, 555–680.

Shouse, M. N. The role of CNS arousal levels in the management of hyperkinesis: Methylphenidate and EEG biofeedback training. Doctoral dissertation, University of Tennessee, 1976.

Sterman, M. B. Effects of brain surgery and EEG operant conditioning on seizure latency following monomethylhydrazine intoxication in the cat. *Experimental Neurology*, 1976, *50*, 757–765.

Sterman, M. B. & Wywricka, W. A. EEG correlates of sleep evidence for separate forebrain substrates. *Brain research*, 1967, *6*, 143–163.

Stevens, J. R., Milstein, V. M., & Dodds, S. A. Endogenous spike discharges as conditioned stimuli in man. *Electroencephalography and Clinical Neurophysiology*, 1967, *23*, 57–66.

Stevens, J. R., Sachdeo, K., & Milstein, V. Behavior disorders of childhood and the electroencephalogram. *Archives Neurology*, 1968, *18*, 160.

Stewart, M. A. Hyperactive children. *Scientific American*, 1970, *222*, 94–98.

Stewart, M. A., Pitts, F. N., Craig, A. G., & Dieruf, W. The hyperactive child syndrome. *American Journal of Orthopsychiatry*, 1966, *36*, 861–867.

Stewart, M. A., Thack, B. T., & Freidin, M. *Diseases of the Nervous System*, 1970, *31*, 403–407.

Stretch, R., & Dalrymple, D. *Psychopharmacologia*, 1968, *13*, 49–64.

Vanderberg, S. G. Contributions of twin research to psychology. *Psychological Bulletin*, 1966, *66*, 327.

Vanderberg, S. G. Possible hereditary factors in minimal brain dysfunction. *Annals of the New York Academy of Sciences*, 1973, *205*, 223–230.

Wahler, R. G., House, A. E., & Stambaugh, E. E. *Ecological Assessment of Child Problem Behavior*. New York: Pergamon Press, 1975.

Welgan, P. R. Learned control of gastric acid secretions in ulcer patients. *Psychosomatic Medicine*, 1974, *36*, 411–419.

Wender, P. H. *Minimal brain dysfunction in children*. New York: Wiley-Interscience, 1971.

Werry, J. S., & Sprague, R. L. Hyperactivity. *In* C. G. Costello (Ed.), *Symptoms of psychopathology*. New York: Wiley, 1970, pp. 397–417.

Wyler, A. R. Operant conditioning of single epileptic neurons and its application to human epilepsy. *Pavlovian Journal of Biological Science*, 1977, *In press*.

Wywricka, W, & Sterman, M. B. Instrumental conditioning of sensorimotor cortex EEG spindles in the walking cat. *Physiology and Behavior*, 1968, *31*, 703–707.

18. Treatment of severe perceptual-motor disorders in children diagnosed as learning disabled

BENJAMIN B. LAHEY   MARY KAY BUSEMEYER
CHRISTIANE O'HARA   VICKI E. BEGGS

Psychologists are being called upon with increasing frequency to design remedial programs for children who have been diagnosed as learning disabled. The psychologist who turns to the research literature for assistance, however, will find no clear guidelines. Recent research reviews have suggested that many widely used remedial procedures may be ineffective in producing beneficial changes when compared to untreated control groups. These include methods of training visual perception (Hammill, 1972), perceptual-motor skills (Goodman & Hammill, 1973; Hammill, Goodman, & Wiederholt, 1974), and psycholinguistic processes (Hammill & Larsen, 1974). An alternative to these approaches is the behavior modification approach. It differs from traditional theories in the meaning it assigns to the inefficient learning characteristics of low achievement children. Instead of viewing these deficits as "symptoms" of underlying disorders in organic functioning, or functional disorders of perceptual, perceptual-motor, or psycholinguistic processes, such deficits are viewed simply as characteristics that must be changed.

This study was designed to provide a test of this approach using positive reinforcement. The focus of the investigation was on severe perceptual-motor disturbances in handwriting. This disability was chosen because of the important theoretical role it plays in organic, perceptual, and perceptual-motor models of learning disabilities and because it has often proved refractory to traditional methods of treatment (e.g., Gallagher, 1960).

Several previous studies have evaluated the effects of reinforcement procedures on disorders of handwriting. Smith and Lovitt (1973), Hasazi and Hasazi (1972), and Stromer (1975) showed effective positive change, but they worked with children with very mild problems that were restricted to a few letter and number reversals. In addition, only the single subject of Smith and Lovitt (1973) could be identified as learning disabled. The others were young enough to be exhibiting minor developmental lags. The present study will evaluate a direct instructional procedure with children who show severe and widespread perceptual-motor disorders. A major focus will be on the degree to which changes in behavior generalize to other responses under conditions of no reinforcement. The treatments used in the following two experiments were essentially the same, but were evaluated using different design strategies.

EXPERIMENT I

METHOD

Subjects

Students A and B were chosen by asking school officials to refer students who had serious and pervasive perceptual problems and by pretesting on tasks similar to those used in the baseline phase. Both students were diagnosed by a school psychologist as learning disabled. Both were black males, aged 8 years, 4 months and 7 years, 1 month, respectively, but neither was from a disadvantaged background. They were chosen on the basis of a high frequency of errors of orientation and sequence in copying words, often referred to as "mirror writing" or "reversals." Psychometric data were not made available by the school system on these students.

Student A was disruptive in the classroom but not clinically deviant in his behavior. He appeared to be of normal intelligence but was very distractible and accomplished little school work. He had to be reminded frequently to carry out instructions during treatment and argued with the experimenter about the number of reinforcers to be given for each correct response.

Student B's behavior in the classroom and treatment situation was more friendly and cooperative than average. He brought his school work to the treatment sessions to show the experimenter and was uniformly attentive to the task. Except for his obvious perceptual-motor and learning problems, he was considered to be a perfectly normal child.

Setting

Both students attended the same suburban public elementary school in South Carolina. They were brought individually to a quiet room where they sat facing a female experimenter.

Response definition and reliability

In each session, the students were asked to copy their first name five times, five different simple four-letter words made up mostly of asymmetrical letters, and five different geometric figures similar to those found on tests of perceptual abilities. These stimuli were presented in a repeating name-figure-word order for a total of 15 stimulus presentations per session. In all phases of the experiment, a correct response was defined as one

in which all letters were legible, were in the proper left to right sequence, and did not deviate from normal orientation by more than 20 degrees. For responses in which geometric figures were copied, a correct response was one in which the figure was clearly recognizable and did not deviate from the proper orientation by more than 20 degrees. The entire response was counted as incorrect if any feature violated the rules. Correct and incorrect responses are illustrated in Figure 18-1, in which the last baseline trial and the eighth trial of the treatment phase for Student A are presented.

The students made each response in pencil on a separate 5 x 8 card. A second experimenter who was not aware of which phase the responses came from later scored these cards independently to assess interrater agreement. Checks were made on all of the responses from three sessions and one probe session during each phase, for a total of eight reliability checks per student. Interrater agreement was calculated by dividing the total number of agreements that the response was correct or incorrect (according to stated criteria) by the total number of agreements plus disagreements. Agreement for Students A and B ranged from .87 to 1.00, with a mean of .94.

Procedure

The procedure was divided into two phases, a baseline and a treatment phase. Subjects were taken to the experimental room four days each week. Two sessions were carried out in sequence each day. Each session lasted 15 to 30 minutes for a total of 30 to 60 minutes of participation per experimental day. To control for time-related confounds (such as familiarization with the task), Student A's baseline phase lasted four sessions, while Student B's lasted 12 sessions (multiple baseline design across subjects).

Baseline

Prior to the first session, the students were told that the experimenter wanted to help them with their printing. During the first baseline trial, the students were asked in a straightforward way to practice on the items being presented and to do the best they could. No elaborate explanation of the task was given. The task was to make the 15 copying responses per session; no feedback or reinforcement of any kind was given after either correct or incorrect responses. Following each

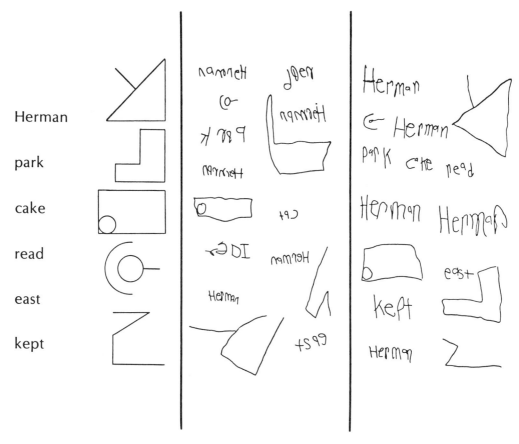

Figure 18-1. Sample handwriting for Student A. Stimuli presented to students are on the left. The sample in the middle shows the last baseline session and the sample on the right shows the eighth treatment session.
(Published originally in Lahey, 1976. Reprinted with permission of Academic Press, Inc.)

session, the students were thanked for their co-operation.

Treatment

During the treatment phase, all conditions remained the same except the subjects were told "right" and given a token after each correct response (as defined above) or were told "wrong" and given corrective feedback after incorrect responses. The students were informed that they could keep the tokens until the end of the session, when they could "trade them in" for pen-

nies that they could keep. Corrective feedback consisted of a brief explanation of why the response was incorrect, with an illustration on a separate sheet of paper (e.g., "These letters are backwards. Watch me; they should go like this"). Tokens were exchanged at the end of the daily sessions for pennies at the rate of three tokens per penny. The same contingency was applied to all three responses during this phase.

As is typical of applications of these methods by the authors in such settings, no serious problems were encountered in treatment. Student A needed to be prompted to respond in baseline and argued a few times over the reinforcers, but

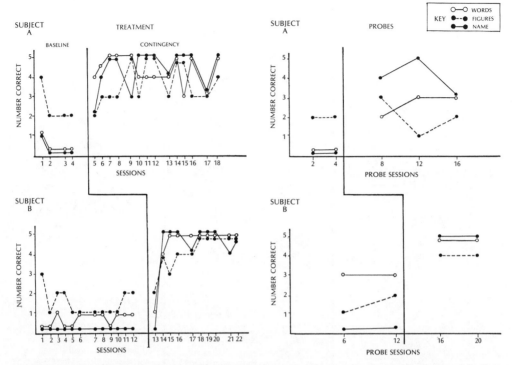

Figure 18-2. The frequency of correct handwriting responses per session for Students A and B. Data are presented separately in each graph for copied words, geometric figures, and first names. The graphs on the left present data for items used in the training sessions. The graphs on the right present data for items in the probe sessions.
(Published originally in Lahey, 1976. Reprinted with permission of Academic Press, Inc.)

none of these behaviors presented any real problem.

Probe sessions

Probe sessions were interspersed throughout the baseline and treatment phases, as indicated in Figure 18-2, for the purpose of assessing degree of generalization during training. On these trials, the subjects were asked to copy five new words and five new geometric figures and to copy their first name five times. These stimuli were presented in the same manner as the original set for a total of 15 trials. No feedback or reinforcement was given during the probe sessions.

RESULTS

As shown in Figure 18-2, baseline performance was basically stable for all three response sets for Students A and B. Performance during the baseline probe sessions was also stable. The number

of correct responses increased, however, after the introduction of reinforcement and corrective feedback. The frequency of correct responses on geometric figures for Student A is an exception to these results. No change from baseline to treatment was found.

DISCUSSION

These data suggest that even severe perceptual-motor disorders in handwriting can be effectively remediated using direct instruction methods. Using reinforcement and corrective feedback, errors of orientation and sequence were modified in two learning disabled boys. Moreover, these changes generalized to other unreinforced handwriting responses in the experimental setting. It is perhaps significant that the only exception to these results occurred because, for one student, the copying of abstract forms such as are found on tests of perceptual-motor ability was not correlated with the important direct measures of handwriting. The teachers were asked to keep all of the written work done by the students throughout the experiment so that generalization to the classroom could be assessed. This was not done, however. One teacher kept only the students' "best" work, and the other teacher did not keep any of the classroom work.

EXPERIMENT II

The second experiment was designed to replicate the first, using different design strategies and using children whose academic and behavior problems were more severe than Students A and B.

METHOD

Subjects

Subjects C and D were enrolled in classes for learning disabled children at the Georgia Retardation Center, a treatment and research facility affiliated with the University of Georgia. The center serves children whose problems are too severe to be handled by local school systems and agencies in a catchment area serving approximately half of the State of Georgia. They were selected from this class because their handwriting problems were more severe than Students A and B and because their teachers judged their handwriting problems to be major obstacles to classroom learning.

Subject C was a white male, 9 years, 11 months of age, from a middle-income family. Because of severe speech and fine motor problems, he was not considered testable using appropriate standardized measures of intelligence. Because of his general behavior, however, his teachers considered him to be of at least average intelligence. His classroom behavior was characterized by noncompliance with requests, little social interaction, and low rates of academic output. Several of his typical behaviors reduced his desirability as a social stimulus, particularly holding his mouth open, picking his nose, yawning, and rarely making eye contact. When he did make eye contact, it was not direct, but involved his peripheral vision. Because he also often looked at academic work peripherally, an opthalmological evaluation suggested the possibility of foveal deterioration due to anoxia. Although it was not recorded in this experiment, his tendency to look directly at academic stimuli in-

creased dramatically after the introduction of reinforcement.

Student D was a white male, 8 years, 10 months of age, from a middle-income family. His Verbal IQ was tested to be 80 on the Wechsler Intelligence Scale for Children, Revised Form (WISC-R); his Performance IQ was 46. He was described as seriously disruptive in class and he completed little academic work. He was very verbal and interacted well socially, but stuttered noticeably, especially in difficult academic situations. His eye-hand coordination was poor on both a fine and gross level, leading him to have serious difficulties in play and sports. Much of his social interaction gave the appearance of serving the purpose of "avoiding" academic and gross motor situations. He appeared to talk about "anything he could think of" in such situations, as long as his conversation prohibited participation in tasks that were difficult for him. After his extraneous verbalizations were extinguished by meeting with responses from the experimenter that redirected his attention (e.g., "Let's not worry about that, let's do the next word"), he presented no further serious problems, particularly after treatment began.

Setting

Students C and D were brought individually to a quiet room where they sat facing different female experimenters.

Response definition and reliability

Student C was asked to copy his first and last name and 14 four- to six-letter words once each during each session for a total of 15 responses per session. Student D was asked to copy 10 four- to ten-letter words and his first name twice each session for a total of 32 responses per session. Correct responses were defined and reliability was assessed in the same way as in Experiment 1. A second experimenter who was not aware of which phase the responses came from scored two sessions each from the baseline and treatment phases. Interrater agreement ranged from .83 to 1.00 with a mean of .93 for Student C, and from .91 to 1.00 with a mean of .96 for Student D.

Procedure

The general procedures were similar to Experiment 1, with sessions lasting from 15 to 60 minutes. Subject C was studied in a withdrawal design using a baseline-treatment-baseline-treatment sequence. Baseline and treatment procedures were carried out as in Experiment 1, except that raisins were substituted for pennies. Throughout the experiment, the classroom teacher was asked to keep all written work performed in the classroom, which was later scored by the experimenters on a letter-by-letter basis using the same criteria as in the experimental sessions.

Subject D was studied in a multiple baseline design across responses. Shoe-tying was chosen as the second behavior in this design for two reasons. First, it was a behavior that he had not yet mastered and that appeared to cause him embarrassment, and second, it was believed to be independent enough of handwriting to meet the requirements of the design. Following baselines of varying length, treatment was introduced first for handwriting and then for shoe-tying. Treatment for handwriting was initially identical to Experiment 1. One penny per correct response was given, but following seven trials of treatment for handwriting monetary reinforcement was discontinued to investigate its role in the treatment package. Since no change in handwriting occurred, pennies were not reintroduced during the remainder of the study. Following 10 trials of treatment for handwriting a second set of 10 words was used, and following four additional trials a third new set of 10 words was introduced. On trial 28, the conditions of the first baseline were reintroduced for five trials for both handwriting and shoe-tying. All classroom handwriting was also collected for Student D and in the same way as in the experimental sessions.

During baseline, Student D was asked to tie his shoe four times per session. During treatment, this behavior was taught using a standard six-step backward chaining procedure beginning with pulling the loops tight, with praise given after each correct chained response, and one penny given for every three correct chained responses. Following every third chaining trial, shoe-tying was modeled and he was asked to tie the shoe by himself. Twenty-seven chaining trials were carried out during the first four treatment trials for shoe-tying, but since he soon began tying his shoes completely by himself, the chaining procedure was discontinued and only three chaining trials were interspersed among the remaining trials. From the fourth treatment trial for shoe-tying, the response was modeled and requested 12 times per session. One penny and praise were given after each completely correct

shoe-tying response, and corrective feedback was given after incorrect attempts. Reliability was assessed by a second observer twice each during baseline and treatment sessions, with complete agreement obtained on all trials.

Student C showed very little disruptive behavior during the treatment sessions and complied with nearly all requests when first stated. Subject D's behavior was very disruptive and noncompliant during the early sessions. He frequently asked to leave and initiated extraneous conversations, which the experimenter ignored or passed over with a comment such as "Let's do the next one." In addition, Student C frequently slid under the table and had to be physically replaced in his chair without comment or eye contact.

RESULTS

As shown in Figures 18-3 and 18-4, baseline handwriting performance was consistently at zero for Student C, but rose rapidly when treatment was introduced. The frequency of correct handwriting responses fell when treatment was discontinued in the second baseline, but rose again when treatment was reintroduced.

Figure 18-5 shows the data on handwriting and shoe-tying for Student D. The frequency of correct handwriting responses was consistently at zero for Student D, but rose rapidly when treatment was introduced and was maintained when pennies were dropped from the treatment package. When the second and third sets of words were introduced, initial accuracy was higher than on the first set and rose quickly to asymptotic level. Shoe-tying was initially at a consistent level during baseline, but rose when treatment was introduced. The first completely correct shoe-tying response occurred during the first session, when only one of the six steps of the backward chaining procedure had been completed. No change in performance was found during the second baseline phase.

The data gathered in the classrooms of these students are shown in Table 18-1. It suggests that generalization to another situation is variable. The evidence for generalization for Student C is weak, increasing slightly from baseline to treatment, while a marked and useful degree of generalization is shown for Student D. The percentage of correct handwriting more than doubled for Student D. The independent teacher's impressions of improvement in the students' handwriting confirmed these findings.

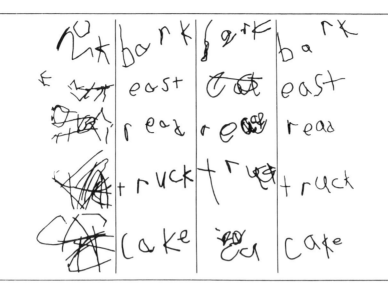

Figure 18-3. Sample handwriting for Student C. From left to right, typical responses are presented from the first baseline, first treatment, second baseline, and second treatment phases.

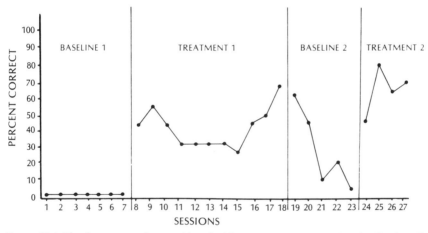

Figure 18-4. The frequency of correct handwriting responses per session for Student C.

The results further suggest individual differences in the durability of improvements in perceptual-motor skills after the reinforcement contingency was discontinued. Rapid extinction occurred in Student C, but no change was found for Student D during the second baseline.

Student D was retested on the WISC-R following the completion of treatment. Interestingly, he showed no improvement on the perceptual-motor areas of the test in spite of his marked and generalized improvement in handwriting and shoe-tying. The new WISC-R scores were V = 80 and P = 45. The skills of handwriting and performing in perceptual-motor tests of the WISC-R apparently were independent in this subject.

DISCUSSION

These data suggest that even severe perceptual-motor disorders in handwriting can be effectively remediated using behavior modification methods.

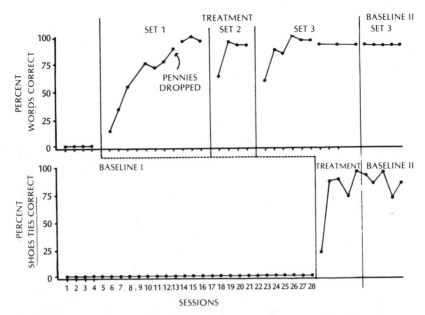

Figure 18-5. The frequency of correct handwriting responses (upper panel) and percent correct shoe ties for Student D.

Using reinforcement and corrective feedback, errors of orientation and sequence were modified in four learning disabled boys. Moreover, these changes generalized to other unreinforced handwriting responses within the experimental sessions for two students, and to the classroom in one other. As such, the results support efforts to develop and evaluate direct instruction methods for learning disabled children as described in somewhat different versions by Haring and Phillips (1972), Lovitt (1967), and Hammill (1972). Individual differences were found among these subjects that must be taken into account during application of the procedures, but they were not serious enough to contraindicate the methods.

Most interestingly, perhaps, these results raise the question of why these children still had these problems after several years of schooling. The techniques used to modify their problem behaviors were very simple, yet produced rapid improvement. Teachers certainly could provide re-

inforcement and corrective feedback without extensive training or cost. Why, then, had these children not received help? The answer is that, contrary to our idealized view of teaching, teachers rarely provide any type of usable feedback to students. In our observations, we saw teachers only put marks and smiling faces on entire pages of written work, with very little explanation as to why the work was good or not. It seems very likely that the problems of all of these students could have been eliminated or prevented if adequate, systematic response consequences had been provided.

Future research will need to focus on the implementation of such procedures by the teachers themselves in the classroom. Generalization from tutorial treatments cannot be relied upon. Therefore, the treatments should be delivered where the change is most desired. There will be many problems with this strategy, however, since none of the teachers we worked with were

Table 18-1. Percentage correct handwriting performed in classroom

Dates: Student C					2/2–2/16	2/18–3/30	4/1–4/29
	—	—	—	—	33*	48	57
Dates: Student D	9/1–9/30	10/1–10/20	10/22–12/15	1/3–1/30	2/1–2/27	3/2–3/30	4/3–4/22
	32*	22*	56	78	77	71	80

*Data taken in classroom during first baseline.

willing to use these techniques on an independent basis. They were simply viewed as too time consuming. On the one hand, we will need to look for more time-efficient methods, but on the other hand, we must become better at convincing teachers to adopt the technology that we now possess. After all, society would not allow a heart surgeon to ignore a better operative procedure just because it was "inconvenient." Can we allow educators to do the same thing? This does not mean that the fault is not our own. We must simply become better persuaders.

REFERENCES

Gallagher, J. J. *The tutoring of brain-injured mentally retarded children.* Springfield, Ill.: Charles C Thomas, 1960.

Goodman, L., & Hammill, D. D. The effectiveness of Kephart-Getman activities in developing perceptual-motor and cognitive skills. *Focus on Exceptional Children,* 1973, 4, 1–9.

Hammill, D. D. Evaluating children for instructional purposes. In D. D. Hammill & N. R. Bartel (Eds.), *Educational perspectives in learning disabilities.* New York: John Wiley, 1971.

Hammill, D. D. Training visual perceptual processes. *Journal of Learning Disabilities,* 1972, 5, 552–559.

Hammill, D. D., & Larsen, S. C. The effectiveness of psycholinguistic training. *Exceptional Children,* 1974, 41, 5–14.

Hammill, D. D., Goodman, L., & Wiederholt, J. L. Visual-motor processes: Can we train them? *The Reading Teacher,* February 1974, 469–478.

Haring, N. G., & Phillips, E. L. *Analysis and modification of classroom behavior.* Englewood Cliffs, N.J.: Prentice-Hall, 1972.

Hasazi, J. E., & Hasazi, S. E. Effects of teacher attention on digit-reversal behavior in an elementary school child. *Journal of Applied Behavior Analysis,* 1972, 5, 157–162.

Lahey, B. B. Behavior modification with learning disabilities and related problems. In M. Hersen, R. Eisler, & P. Miller, *Progress in behavior modification,* Vol. 3. New York: Academic Press, 1976.

Lovitt, T. C. Assessment of children with learning disabilities. *Exceptional Children,* 1967, 34, 233–239.

Smith, D. D., & Lovitt, T. C. The educational diagnosis of written *b* and *d* reversal problems: A case study. *Journal of Learning Disabilities,* 1973, 6, 20–27.

Stromer, R. Modifying number and letter reversals in elementary school children. *Journal of Applied Behavior Analysis,* 1975, 8, 211.

19. Remediating academic deficiencies in learning disabled children

ROBERT STROMER

Children described as having a learning disability show specific behavioral deficits when learning to read and write. These children are characterized by letter reversals, digit reversals, and academic performance that is quite variable from day to day (Waugh & Bush, 1971). These problems are not particularly uncommon among young children learning to read and write. However, the learning disabled child is distinguished by problems that persist beyond the early grades and traditional remediation approaches (Eisenberg, 1966).

Academic difficulties associated with learning disabilities have seldom been dealt with at the behavioral level. Rather, it is hypothesized that some organic abnormality is responsible for the child's problem. The child may be thought to lack the appropriate visual perceptual skills necessary for success in reading and writing, and remediation is directed toward the underlying perceptual processes (Frostig & Horne, 1966; Kephart, 1960). Indirect remediation techniques such as this have been criticized by learning disability specialists, and there appears to be little evidence that they alter specific academic deficiencies (Fisher, 1971; Kelm, 1970; Mann, 1970; Wingert, 1969).

More recently, however, research indicated that behaviors identified with learning disabled children may be effectively modified via a direct behavioral analysis. Hasazi and Hasazi (1972) clearly demonstrated that children's written two-digit reversals were controlled by the attention and special help they received from the teacher. When teacher attention was contingent upon correct formation of numerals, reversals were reduced to a low level. Smith and Lovitt (1973) successfully decreased written *b-d* reversal errors by using a flash card and social reinforcement procedure in a tutorial setting. Similarly, Stromer (1975) employed flash card modeling and social reinforcement to alter a variety of letter and number reversal problems in both regular and special education children.

This series of three experiments was designed to extend the above research by (a) assessing behavioral tutoring procedures with a child showing multiple letter errors, (b) evaluating the generalization of number discrimination training to a regular classroom activity, and (c) investigating the use of modeling and social reinforcement with a small group of children showing letter discrimination difficulties.

EXPERIMENT 1

The purpose of this experiment was to assess the effects of a flash card and differential feedback

From *Exceptional Children*, 1977, *43*, 432–440. Reprinted by permission of The Council for Exceptional Children. Copyright 1977 by The Council for Exceptional Children, 1920 Association Drive, Reston, Virginia 22091.

training procedure upon the letter naming and letter dictation errors of an elementary school child.

METHOD

Subject and Target Behaviors

The subject was a 7 year, 2 month old boy spending his second year in the first grade. The teacher reported that the child could not make simple letter discriminations and had difficulty remembering what he had learned from day to day. Based upon these observations, the teacher referred the student to the experimenter for a suspected learning disability. At an informal screening, the boy was asked to name lower case letter flash cards and to write the letters from dictation. In this screening, he showed the following types of letter errors: reversals (e.g., saying or writing *b* for *d*, or *p* for *q*), substitutions (e.g., saying *a* for *u*), and omissions (e.g., no response, or saying "I don't know").

SETTING AND DATA RECORDING

Individual tutorial sessions (15 to 20 minutes long) were conducted three or four times per week in an office at the subject's school. The letter exercises described below were used to evaluate the frequency of the three types of letter errors stated above.

Letter dictation. All letters of the alphabet were verbally presented by the experimenter in random order twice during each session. The experimenter dictated the 52 letter names from a different dictation list for 5 successive days, then the sequence of lists was repeated. The subject was instructed to write only lower case letters in response to the verbal cues. If the subject did not respond within 5 seconds, the name of the letter was repeated. The next letter was presented if no response occurred within another 5 seconds. Failure to respond was defined as an omission error. After the session the experimenter scored the written responses as correct, substituted, omitted, or reversed.

Letter naming. Immediately following the dictation exercise, the subject was asked to read a random list of the 52 lower case letters appearing on a mimeographed sheet. Five versions of the letter naming sheets were constructed using a primary style (Olympic) typewriter. As the subject read the letters, the experimenter scored

each response on a copy of the naming sheet. Responses were scored as correct, reversed, omitted, or substituted. Several cassette tape recordings were made to allow for interobserver reliability checks at another time.

Reliability of observation. The data recorded by the experimenter were judged by an outside observer once during each experimental phase. The second observer scored the subject's written and verbal responses in the same manner as the experimenter using the appropriate dictation and naming lists and cassette tapes. Interobserver reliability was computed by dividing the number of observer agreements by the total number of possible agreements. Agreement ranged from 98% to 100% for all conditions.

Procedure

A variation of the standard single subject experimental design (ABAB) was used. The sequence of conditions was baseline 1; letter training phases 1, 2, and 3; baseline 2; and letter training phase 4.

Baseline 1. The subject was exposed to a 5 day baseline period in which the letter dictation exercise was followed by the letter naming activity. No experimenter feedback was delivered during this condition.

Letter training phases 1, 2, and 3. Each session during treatment phases 1 through 3 was characterized by a 5 to 10 minute period of presession letter training and by differential feedback during the subsequent letter dictation and letter naming exercises in the form of praise for all correct responses and no scheduled consequences for errors. A description of the pretraining follows.

Presession letter training for each phase involved a select group of the 26 lower case alphabet letters. To arrive at the list of letters for each phase, the letters missed during baseline 1 were divided into roughly three equal groups. The remaining letters were then randomly assigned between the three groups. Phase 1 included eight letters, and nine letters each were assigned to phases 2 and 3. Presession training was composed of a timed dictation exercise involving the letters assigned to that phase (and letters from previous training when phases 2 and 3 were in effect). The letters were printed on 3×5 flash cards and were mixed by the experimenter to determine a random presentation of dictated cues.

The subject was instructed to see how fast he could write the group of training letters from dictation. A stopwatch was placed in view of the child and was used to time his performance. The subject's time was occasionally written on his practice sheet and he was praised for rapid and accurate responding. Any hesitation of more than 1 to 2 seconds following a dictated letter resulted in a brief exposure of the appropriate flash card. Without experimenter prompting, the subject quickly wrote the letter when shown the card.

Presentation of all letters for that training phase defined a trial. Pretraining consisted of two trials, followed by the previously described letter dictation and letter naming exercises. During these exercises, the child was instructed to "get as many right as possible and work quickly." Each correct response resulted in verbal approval from the experimenter while incorrect responses were ignored.

After three successive sessions of errorless timed dictation trials, the next pretraining phase began with the additional letters assigned to that phase. The presession training was eliminated after 3 days of phase 3 and the subject's performance during the regular dictation exercise was timed. Rapid and accurate responding was again praised. The stopwatch was no longer used beyond session 20.

Responses during the letter naming exercise were never timed; the subject was just instructed to read quickly. Phases 1 and 2 lasted four sessions each, and phase 3 continued for 14 days.

Baseline 2. This phase was a reinstatement of baseline 1 conditions. For four sessions the dictation and naming exercises were conducted with no scheduled experimenter feedback.

Letter training phase 4. The basic conditions existing at the end of letter training phase 3 were reintroduced during this phase. There was a change, however, from the continuous delivery of praise for correct responses to a variable schedule of social reinforcement. Beginning with session 36, the child was praised, on the average, for every third correct response (range of 1 to 6) under both dictation and naming procedures. Technically, this is called a variable ratio three (VR 3) schedule of reinforcement. The VR 3 schedule of praise was introduced in order to maintain correct responding in the absence of experimenter feedback.

Postcheck. Four months following the termination of letter training a postcheck was conducted. The experimental procedures used during letter training phase 4 were employed.

RESULTS AND DISCUSSION

Following baseline 1, as shown in Figure 19-1, the child's (Subject 1) letter dictation and letter naming errors decreased in an orderly fashion across the first three letter training phases. The brief removal of the treatment conditions during baseline 2 resulted in an increase in both types of letter errors, which demonstrates that the training

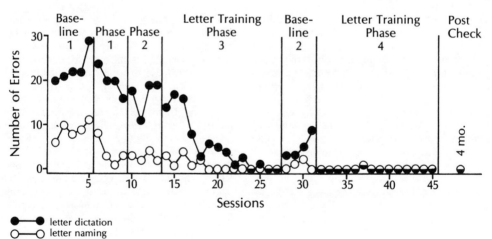

Figure 19-1. Subject 1: Number of letter dictation and letter naming errors (substitutions, omissions, and reversals) occurring in Experiment 1.

procedures were indeed responsible for the reduction in errors. When letter training was again employed during phase 4, dictation and naming errors were absent in 13 of 14 sessions. No errors occurred during the postcheck observation.

An analysis of the specific types of errors showed that most dictation errors were omissions, while both substitutions and reversals were evident during the letter naming activity. Some letters were consistently omitted during dictation and other letters were written upon first presentation, then omitted during the second exposure. Other errors included *b-d* and *p-q* reversals under both exercises, and substitutions were evident during the naming condition.

The results of this experiment demonstrate that a variety of written and oral letter errors can be effectively modified by behavioral intervention procedures. The presession letter training and social reinforcement for correct responses were probably the elements of treatment responsible for reducing the substitution and reversal errors. Although empirical evidence is lacking, it appears that the timed dictation exercise was an essential factor in reducing the omission errors. The timed procedure provided an opportunity to socially reinforce behaviors incompatible with dawdling and not remembering, which possibly are supported in the classroom by teacher attention.

EXPERIMENT 2

This study was designed to evaluate the effectiveness of the flash card and feedback procedures upon a child's digit reversals and to assess the generalization of this training to a regular classroom arithmetic activity.

METHOD

Subject and Target Behaviors

A second-grade boy, age 8 years, 1 month, participated in the study. The teacher referred the child for written number reversals that were observed during classroom arithmetic computations. For example, when writing either single digit or two-digit numbers that involved a *4* or *5*, the subject typically responded with the mirror images of these numbers. Two digit reversals (e.g., writing *31* for *13*) also occurred frequently. In an attempt to ameliorate numerical discriminations, the teacher pointed out the reversals to the child, modeled correct numbers, and gave specific instructions regarding the formation of these numbers on math papers. Also, the teacher tried to decrease the amount of attention directed toward the child's errors by scoring and attending to only correct answers, but reversals continued. It was decided that concentrated tutorial training would be scheduled along with concurrent monitoring of these sessions in the regular classroom.

Setting and Data Recording

Tutorial sessions about 10 to 15 minutes long were held two or three times per week at the subject's school. Data were the frequency of written number reversals which occurred during the following two exercises.

Tutorial number dictation. The subject was instructed to write all numbers from *12* through *19* in response to dictated cues from the experimenter. All numbers were presented twice in random order. The numbers *14*, *15*, *16*, and *17* were each presented a third time to yield a total of 20 numbers dictated per session. A different dictation list was used for 5 successive days, then the sequence of lists was repeated. Following each session, all written responses were scored by the experimenter for correct and reversed single digit and two-digit numbers.

Classroom worksheets. Ten sets of mimeographed worksheets were constructed, each with 20 addition number sentences on it (e.g., $8+6=$ —). The correct two-digit sums possible on each sheet were the same as those used during number dictation. The 20 problems were randomly selected (without replacement) from a pool of all possible permutation of these sums (116 problems). The subject worked the problems in the regular classroom with five other students the teacher felt could use the extra work on addition facts. The teacher organized the group and handed out the worksheets in the afternoon of each day in which tutorial training was conducted. At the end of the day the papers were turned over to the experimenter and scored for correct and reversed responses.

Reliability of observation. An independent judge scored the tutorial and classroom papers once during each experimental phase in the same manner as the experimenter using the appropriate dictation lists and answer sheets. Computations were derived as in Experiment 1. There was 100% agreement between observers on all occasions.

Procedure

Four experimental conditions were introduced according to an ABAB format during the tutorial number dictation exercise. Concurrently, the subject was exposed to the classroom worksheets to assess generalization of training effects.

Baseline. The child was exposed to the tutorial dictation exercise with no feedback from the experimenter following correct or incorrect responses. Similarly, the classroom worksheets were distributed and collected with no mention about specific items from the teacher or experimenter. This phase lasted 10 sessions under tutorial conditions and throughout the entire study during classroom worksheet activity.

Experimental condition 1. This condition consisted of two components: (a) presession flash card modeling of reversed target numbers and (b) differential experimenter feedback following student responses during the tutorial dictation exercise. During the presession activity, the experimenter randomly presented the names of the target numbers and the subject wrote the numbers on a practice sheet of paper. The experimenter raised all correct responses, while reversed single digit and two-digit numbers resulted in the experimenter showing the subject the correct number on a flash card and saying, "This is the number (*name*), write this number on your paper." All target numbers were presented twice. Prior to the dictation exercise, the child was encouraged to do his best and told that he would find out how many numbers he wrote correctly after the exercise. During dictation, praise statements (e.g., "My, you're doing nicely!") were delivered by the experimenter on a VR 3 schedule of reinforcement. No feedback occurred after reversed numbers. This phase lasted three sessions.

Reversal. This control condition differed from the return to baseline phase used in Experiment 1 (baseline 2). In this phase, the presession and dictation contingencies used during the experimental 1 condition were simply reversed. That is, for three sessions the subject was instructed and pretrained to write his numbers "backwards on purpose." This control procedure was used to provide further training on the features distinguishing correct from reversed numbers. Reversed responses during dictation were also praised according to the VR 3 schedule.

Experimental condition 2. This condition was a reinstatement of the experimental 1 training procedures and lasted 12 sessions.

Postchecks. Followup observations were conducted at 1 and 2 month intervals after the termination of experimental 2 training. The math exercise held in the regular classroom was used for these checks. Baseline conditions were still in effect.

RESULTS AND DISCUSSION
Tutorial Dictation

The upper half of Figure 19-2 depicts the child's (Subject 2) digit reversals as a function of the experimental phases during tutorial dictation. The flash card pretraining and differential experimenter feedback during the experimental 1 phase quickly reduced the two-digit errors produced under the dictation baseline condition. When the instructions and social reinforcement contingencies were reversed (reversal phase), errors increased to a level comparable to the frequency of baseline errors. A reinstatement of the original experimental procedures resulted in few two-digit reversals; for the 6 remaining days of this phase no two-digit errors occurred.

Overall, single digit reversals were infrequent during the study. The reversals apparent during the early baseline sessions diminished under repeated days of nonreinforced practice.

Classroom Worksheets

The lower portion of Figure 19-2 shows the frequency of reversals recorded in the classroom. The unconnected data plots signify those occasions when the teacher was unable to conduct the class exercise. Single digit reversals remained at a low level throughout the study. Two-digit reversals, however, were frequent under baseline conditions. As experimental 1 conditions lowered errors during tutorial training, two-digit errors in the classroom were also reduced. Thereafter, two-digit reversals remained infrequent while the reversal and experimental 2 conditions were implemented during tutorial dictation. There were no reversals during the two postcheck observations.

The results of this experiment suggest that isolated number discriminations established under tutorial conditions may generalize to a computational task involving those same numbers. Interestingly, as two-digit reversals increased during the dictation reversal phase, a corresponding in-

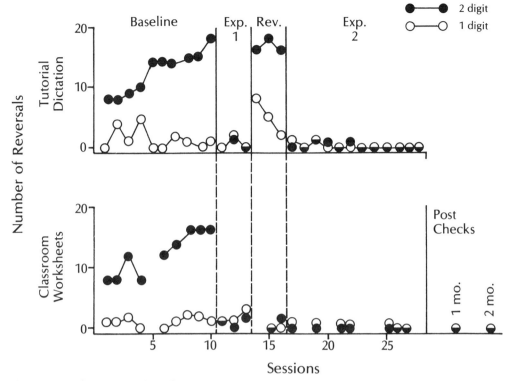

Figure 19-2. Subject 2: Number of single digit and two-digit reversals occurring in Experiment 2 under tutorial and classroom conditions.

crease in classroom reversals was not evident. The subject apparently discriminated the instructions and social reinforcement contingencies operating during the dictation reversal from the baseline conditions in effect in the classroom. Perhaps a longer dictation reversal period would have resulted in more classroom errors. Even though the reversal failed to increase errors, the dramatic decline in reversals at the onset of the experimental 1 phase suggests that the tutorial training was responsible for the improved classroom performance.

EXPERIMENT 3

The purpose of this study was to extend the use of flash card and social reinforcement procedures to a small group application.

METHOD
Subjects and Target Behaviors

The five children who participated in this experiment were selected from several regular third grade classes and assigned to a special remedial reading program. The mean age of the group was 8 years, 5 months, with a range of 8 years, 1 month, to 9 years, 5 months. The reading program was designed to assist those children who, according to standardized tests, showed at least average intellectual capabilities but were deficient in grade level reading skills. Reading programs such as this were conducted throughout the school district where this experiment took place.

The children had been exposed to the reading program for various lengths of time, but all continued to show reversal problems. Discriminations between *b-d* and *p-q* were particularly difficult for these children when given dictated cues.

Setting and Data Recording

Four or five sessions were held each week and were 20 to 30 minutes long. These times were the children's regularly scheduled remedial sessions. Instruction took place in a classroom designed for this program. The following dictation task was used to assess letter reversals during the study.

Letter dictation. All alphabet letters, except *i, l, o, t, v, w,* and *x,* were dictated twice to the children each session. The children were instructed to write only lower case letters on their paper. They wrote from the left hand to right hand margins on lined paper. The teacher dictated from one of five lists of random letters; after 5 successive days, the lists were reused. After each session, responses were scored by the experimenter and teacher for reversed and correct letter formations.

Reliability of observation. Papers of all children from one session of each condition were scored by an independent observer for reliability. The percentage of agreement was calculated as in previous experiments and there was 100% agreement in all cases.

Procedure

As in Experiment 2, there were four phases to this study plus two followup observations.

Baseline. Over a 5 day period, the children were presented the letter dictation exercise with no differential feedback from the teacher. The subjects remained in a standard column by row seating arrangement.

Experimental condition 1. This phase consisted of 3 consecutive days of letter discrimination training. The teacher prepared for each session by gathering the following materials: (a) letter flash cards (3×5 cards with individual letters printed in lower case), (b) letter choice cards (5×7 cards with the 19 dictated letters printed in lower case), (c) student writing boards, and (d) student notebooks and pencils. The target letters were *b, d, p,* and *q,* and these letters were selected from the individual flash cards. Training sessions began after the students were organized into a small half circle formation. Each child possessed a writing board, a notebook, and a pencil.

The training procedure involved three basic components: (a) the children matched letters dictated by the teacher to letters on a choice card; (b) the children wrote the letters in their notebooks without being able to look at the choice card; and (c) the children received teacher and peer praise and attention for all correct responses. An attempt was made to give each child an opportunity to match each target letter three times during a single session.

The teacher introduced training by demonstrating the procedures to be followed. A target letter was chosen and both correct and backward letters were identified on the choice card (e.g., both *b* and *d*). The teacher then pointed out why one letter was correct and why one was not by saying, for example, "The *b* has the circle on the right, and the *d* has a circle on the left." Next, another letter was selected and a single student was asked to find the matching and reversed letters on the choice card. The student was also asked to point out the distinguishing features of the letters. The teacher's choice card was then removed from view and all children were instructed to write the target letter in their notebooks. The students then held up their notebooks for checking by the teacher. Following a check on the student's written responses, another child was selected to match a dictated letter to the letter on the choice card, and so on.

Teacher praise and physical contact followed correct choice card matches by individual students, and written responses by all group members. The teacher said things like, "Good job (*student's name*)," "Now you're really trying," "That's using your head." Physical contact was made by shaking hands, touching hands, ruffling hair, or patting the child on the back. Other students were also involved in the social reinforcement process. All children joined in on congratulating the selected student by applauding and showing verbal approval.

If any children made a matching error, they were given a brief look at the appropriate flash card and asked to find the letter again. For example, the teacher would show the student the flash card and say, "This is the letter I want, find this letter on the choice card." The student was praised for a corrected match. Following a written error, the child was also shown the flash card and told to rewrite the letter. Social reinforcement followed a corrected written response.

The use of the teacher's choice card was gradually faded out as all children were able to consistently match both correct and backwards letters three successive times. The students were then told that they had been doing so well that the teacher wanted to see if they could write the letters without using the choice card. If reversals occurred, they were handled as outlined above. This phase of small group training continued for three successive errorless dictations of each target letter by all children.

A dictation test was given at the close of each small group training session. This test followed the same procedures that were used during baseline conditions. The children occupied their regular seating arrangement for dictation. After a child finished the test, no feedback regarding performance was given at that time. However, prior to the next day's training, each child that scored perfectly or showed inprovement was publicly praised. A child who did not perform in this manner was simply encouraged to do better on the current test.

Reversal. As in Experiment 2, this condition involved a reversal of experimental 1 instructions and social reinforcement contingencies. Thus, the students were now told to write two of the dictated target letters in reverse and were praised for doing so. (This reversal phase was to include all four target letters; however, this instruction was not effectively communicated to the teacher.) To demonstrate this activity, the teacher called each child to the chalkboard and said something similar to "If I dictate the letter *b*, what is the backward letter?" If the student wrote *d*, the teacher praised the child and said, "That's right. I want you to write only the backward letters on your paper." Both target letters were demonstrated in the same manner. The instructions were repeated if a child did not initially respond with the reversed letter. The regular seating arrangement was used during this condition which lasted 3 days.

Experimental condition 2. For the next 5 days, the training procedures used during the experimental 1 condition were again in effect.

Postchecks. Posttreatment observations were conducted at 1 and 2 month intervals. No small group training occurred; the children were only exposed to the previously outlined dictation procedures. Teacher feedback was withheld regarding specific responses by the students.

RESULTS AND DISCUSSION

Figure 19-3 illustrates the mean frequency of written reversals that occurred during the letter dictation tests. During the baseline sessions, the frequency of reversals varied across children, but each student made at least one error during three or more sessions. All letter reversals, however,

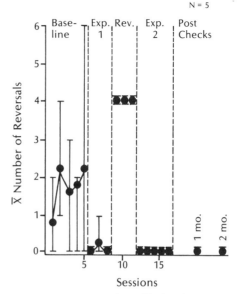

Figure 19-3. Mean number of *b–d* and *p–q* reversals occurring for the 5 subjects in Experiment 3. The vertical line through each data point indicates the range of reversal errors.

were quickly reduced during the first three small group training sessions (experimental 1). One child made an error on the second day of this phase. During the reversal condition, all children reversed the letter *b* and *d* on all four opportunities. When small group training was again instated (experimental 2), all students performed perfectly for 5 days. The errorless posttreatment observations suggest that the children's performance was enduring.

The results of this experiment extend the uses of flash card and social reinforcement procedures to eliminate the reversal errors shown by a small group of children. For educators working with similar populations, the present intervention techniques offer an effective means to teach letter discriminations, necessary prerequisites to beginning reading behaviors.

GENERAL DISCUSSION

The results of these experiments demonstrate the efficient application of behavioral procedures to remediate basic academic deficiencies associated with learning disabled children. The treatment technique used in Experiment 1 reduced a child's reversal, omission, and substitution errors that occurred under letter dictation and letter naming activities. For the child in Experiment 2, two-digit reversals were eliminated under tutorial training conditions, while a simultaneous decrease was observed during a math exercise in which no training occurred. During Experiment 3, letter reversals in a small group of children were eliminated via an application of the flash card modeling and social reinforcement procedures. In addition, followup observations showed that all treatment effects were maintained. These findings extend previous research that showed that behavioral assessment and remediation procedures successfully modified letter and number reversals (Hasazi & Hasazi, 1972; Smith & Lovitt, 1973; Stromer, 1975). Intervention procedures such as these appear to offer educators economical alternatives to indirect remediation strategies. The materials employed are readily available to most classrooms, and the tutorial duties could be conducted by a teacher's aide, volunteer parent, or capable student. Also, the use of praise and attention as reinforcers during training should facilitate the generalization of remediated skills to other learning materials and settings. However, the question of variables affecting generalization is one requiring further systematic research.

REFERENCES

Eisenberg, L. The epidemiology of reading retardation and a program for preventive intervention. In J. Money (Ed.), *The disabled reader*. Baltimore MD: Johns Hopkins Press, 1966.

Fisher, K. L. Effects of perceptual-motor training on the educable mentally retarded. *Exceptional Children*, 1971, *38*, 264–266.

Frostig, M., & Horne, D. *The developmental program in visual perception: Intermediate pictures and patterns. Teacher's guide*. Chicago: Follett, 1966.

Hasazi, J. E., & Hasazi, S. E. Effects of teacher attention on digit-reversal behavior in an elementary school child. *Journal of Applied Behavior Analysis*, 1972, *5*, 157–162.

Kelm, R. R. Visual-motor training, readiness, and intelligence of kindergarten children. *Journal of Learning Disabilities*, 1970, *3*, 256–259.

Kephart, N. C. *The slow learner in the classroom*. Columbus OH: Charles E. Merrill, 1960.

Mann, L. Perceptual training: Misdirections and redirections. *American Journal of Orthopsychiatry*, 1970, *40*, 30–38.

Smith, D. D., & Lovitt, T. C. The educational diagnosis and remediation of written *b* and *d* reversal problems: A case study. *Journal of Learning Disabilities*, 1973, *6*, 20–27.

Stromer, R. Modifying letter and number reversals in elementary school children. *Journal of Applied Behavior Analysis*, 1975, *8*, 211.

Waugh, K. W., & Bush, W. J. *Diagnosing learning disorders*. Columbus OH: Charles E. Merrill, 1971.

Wingert, R. C. Evaluation of a readiness training program. *The Reading Teacher*, 1969, *22*, 325–328.

20. The use of contingent skipping and drilling to improve oral reading and comprehension

THOMAS C. LOVITT   CHERYL L. HANSEN

Once students are ready to read contextual material, the first problem for the teacher of reading is placement. The teacher must place children in readers in order that they may, in time, become competent in decoding and comprehending written symbols. In order to increase the probability that pupils will, in fact, learn to read, they must be placed in readers that are just right for them, neither too easy nor too difficult. Pupils must be challenged to progress, but should not be frustrated by material that is too difficult.

Recently, we (Lovitt & Hansen, 1976) designed a procedure whereby children were placed in readers on the basis of their performance. Direct and daily measurement techniques were used, thus enabling us to place children in certain readers on the basis of their decoding and comprehending abilities.

After initial placement, the next major concern of teachers is advancement. Once children have been placed in readers and instruction has begun, how should they proceed through the readers?

As is true of placement, several strategies are used by teachers to advance pupils through readers and from one reader to another. Back in the olden days when the senior author (TCL) was a teacher, he used a method for advancing pupils from one story to the next that is still used by some teachers. He assigned all the pupils to various reading groups: jaguars, cougars, wolverines. The children in those groups took turns reading the same story; one child read a couple of paragraphs, the next child a few more, and so on until the story was completed. Then the class talked about the story. The next day a new story was assigned.

Since that time some reports have been published that describe methods for advancing pupils through stories and readers on the basis of pupil performance. Gormly and Nittoli (1971), for example, described a process whereby students were allowed to advance from one reading level to another if their comprehension scores for several stories were greater than 70%. Starlin (1970), in a doctoral dissertation, suggested that pupils should be advanced from one reading level to another when their correct oral reading rates were above 100 words per minute (wpm) and their incorrect rates were less than 2 wpm.

In this study we have combined the advancement criterion of those two reports. We allowed pupils to proceed from one section of a book to another on the basis of their comprehension scores *and* their oral reading rates. In fact, we allowed the pupils to skip several stories in their readers if, on the same day, their three scores—

From the *Journal of Learning Disabilities*, 1976, *9*, 481–487. Copyright 1976 by the Professional Press. Reprinted by special permission of Professional Press, Inc.

This research was supported in part by a National Institute of Education grant #OEG-0-70-3916(607), Project #572247.

oral correct rate, oral incorrect rate, and comprehension percentage—were better than criterion levels.

In this study we also incorporated a provision for pupils whose scores remained low. For those pupils, drill techniques were scheduled.

Whether the pupils skipped material or were drilled was contingent on their performance. Pupils were allowed to skip *only* when their reading abilities exceeded established levels, and were provided drill *only* when their reading abilities were inferior to the established levels.

SUBJECTS AND SETTING

The subjects for this research were seven boys, ages 8–12. They were categorized as learning disabled by their school district, and also, they were from one to three years, retarded in reading.

The setting for the research was the Curriculum Research Classroom, Experimental Education Unit, University of Washington. The purpose of this classroom is to conduct educational research with elementary-age children.

MATERIALS

The Lippincott Basal Reading series (McCracken & Walcutt 1970) was used during this project. Each reader in the series was divided into four sections (poetry and plays excluded). The stories in each section were then divided into 500-word segments. In stories where the last segment was more than 225 words, that part was considered a separate segment. If the last segment was less than 225 words, it was combined with the preceding 500-word segment.

The quarters were subdivided into 500-word segments in order to provide the same amount of reading material each day, and there were an equal number of comprehension questions daily.

The comprehension questions written for each 500-word segment were of four different types: recall, sequence, interpretation, and vocabulary. From the first- to third-grade readers, 10 recall, 10 sequence, and 10 interpretation questions were written. From the fourth- to sixth-grade readers, 5 recall, 5 sequence, 5 interpretation, and 5 vocabulary questions were written. Recall, sequence, and interpretation questions required short, written responses. A multiple-choice format was used for the vocabulary questions.

RELIABILITY

For oral reading, reliability checks were obtained an average of six times for each pupil. In order to conduct these checks, certain oral reading sessions were tape recorded. A second teacher then listened to the tapes and counted the correctly and incorrectly read words. Reliability was calculated by dividing the number of agreements between the two teachers by the number of disagreements plus agreements. This figure was then multiplied by 100. The average correct and incorrect rate reliability calculations were 98.8%.

Agreement for scoring answers to comprehension questions was determined by having a second teacher check a sample of 15 assignments for each pupil. The formula for calculating oral reading reliability was used. The average reliability for scoring comprehension answers was 99.6%.

PLACEMENT PROCEDURES

The instructional reading level for each pupil was determined by using a systematic informal reading inventory (Lovitt & Hansen, 1976). Each pupil orally read five 100-word segments from all Lippincott readers between levels D and K (grades one through six). They also responded to comprehension questions on all the readers.

After these data were collected, the mean oral correct and incorrect rates, and mean correct percentage scores for answering comprehension questions were calculated for each reader. Three scores, then, were calculated for all the pupils from the eight readers. These data were then used to place the pupils. Each pupil was placed in the highest reader in which his average oral correct rate was between 45 and 65 wpm, his oral incorrect rate was between 4 and 8 wpm, and his average correct comprehension percentage was between 50% and 75%. Using these criteria, one student was placed in Book D (1^2), one in Book E (2^1), three in Book F (2^2), and two in Book H (3^2).

INTERVENTIONS

In this study there were two interventions, skipping and drilling. Both were arranged contingent on pupil performance.

Skipping. After a 7-day baseline, average correct and incorrect oral reading rates and average percent correct comprehension scores were calculated for each pupil. Desired performance levels were then calculated for the intervention phase based on these scores. Desired performance levels were defined as 25% improvement. For example, if during the baseline, a pupil's average correct rate was 60 wpm, his average incorrect rate was 6 wpm, and his average correct comprehension percentage was 70, the desired scores for those corresponding behaviors throughout the intervention phase would be 75 wpm, 4.5 wpm, and 87.5%. This 25% improvement rule was used until the desired levels exceeded proficiency limits. Proficiency in oral reading was defined as 100 correctly read wpm or better, and 2.5 incorrectly read wpm or better. Our proficiency requirement for comprehension was 90% or better.

When the skipping provision was in effect the pupils were informed that they could skip all the remaining stories in the quarter of the book if, on the same day, all their scores equalled or exceeded the criterion scores. If a child's oral reading rates were better than 75 wpm correct and 4.5 wpm incorrect, and his comprehension score was better than 87.5%, he would be allowed to skip the remaining material in the section he was assigned to read.

Drilling. Three types of drill were used, one for each measured behavior: oral correct reading rate, oral incorrect reading rate, and comprehension percentage. For the correct rate drill, a pupil was required to read the last 100 words from the previous day's assignment. He repeated the passage until he could complete it at his criterion level.

When the incorrect rate drill was used, the teacher showed the pupil a list of the words he had misread during the reading session. These words were embedded in phrases from his reader. The pupil was required to rehearse the list of phrases until he could read all of them correctly to the teacher.

For the comprehension drill the pupil's answer sheet was returned to him with the incorrect responses checked. He was then required to rework his answers until they were all correct.

PROCEDURES

As described earlier, each reader was divided into four parts. Before a pupil read from each part he was given an opportunity to skim through all the stories in that group. He then told the teacher the order in which he preferred to read the stories. The reason for ordering the stories on the basis of pupil preference was because during parts of the study pupils could skip some stories if their performance surpassed a certain level. If some of their more preferred stories appeared at the end of a section, a pupil might want to read those stories and would, therefore, either hold back his efforts to avoid skipping, or would be disappointed if he did skip.

Throughout this study the pupils read 500 words orally each day. The only exceptions to this were those instances where the last segment of the story was less than 500 words. As was explained earlier, if this segment was less than 225 words, it was added to the previous 500-word segment; if more than 225, that amount constituted the assignment for the day.

The oral reading sessions were conducted in a small room off the main classroom. As the child read, if he mispronounced or was unable to pronounce a word, the teacher read it to him. During the oral reading sessions the teacher counted each correct and incorrect response. Incorrect responses consisted of substitutions, omissions, additions, and hesitations of longer than four seconds. Throughout the study the children were intermittently praised for fluent and accurate reading.

When the oral reading session was completed, the pupil was given a sheet of comprehension questions and asked to go to his desk to complete the assignment. A child could ask for help in reading the comprehension questions, but he could not refer to his reader to assist in answering the questions. The answers to the comprehension questions were checked by the teacher and the pupil was informed which ones he had answered incorrectly.

Data were kept pertaining to oral correct and incorrect rates and percentage of correctly answered comprehension questions. In oral reading, the data reported here were from the first two minutes, not from the time required to complete the total 500-word segment. The correct and incorrect rate data were obtained by dividing the number of correct responses by two, and the number of incorrect responses by two. In order to calculate the percentage for correctly answering comprehension questions, the number assigned was divided by the number correctly answered, and multiplied by 100. The pupils who answered questions from books one through three were assigned 30 questions each day, whereas the pupils who read from books four through six received 20 questions daily.

Baseline I. This condition ran for seven days. The circumstances described above prevailed. No additional feedback, instruction, or reinforcement techniques were scheduled. At the end of this condition the 25% improvement scores were calculated.

Skip and drill. Throughout this condition, which ran an average of 20 days, contingent skipping and drilling were arranged. As explained earlier, if, on the same day, a pupil's three scores were equal to or better than the desired scores, he could skip the remaining stories from that quarter of a book. Once established, the desired score levels for each student remained the same throughout the study.

If a pupil went seven days without skipping, drill procedures were instituted. He received drill, however, on only those aspects of reading that were below the desired scores. A pupil could receive drill on any one component, any two, or for all three. The various types of drill were scheduled shortly after the reading session. Drill procedures were in effect only until a pupil skipped a section. When a pupil skipped, another seven days had to elapse before drill was again scheduled.

Baseline II. Skipping and drilling were not arranged throughout this condition. The circumstances were identical to those in effect throughout Baseline I.

RESULTS

Baseline I. Throughout this condition, the average oral correct and incorrect rates were 50.7 and 3.1 wpm. The average comprehension score was 65.9%. The ranges of these rates were from 39.0 to 65.8 wpm, from 2.1 to 3.9 wpm, and from 55.2% to 78.3%. Had the skipping provision been in effect during this phase, there would have been an average of .02 skips per day (total skips divided by total days of pupils in the condition). Table I shows the average oral correct and incorrect rates and average correct comprehension percentages for the pupils for the three conditions of the study.

Skip and drill. During this condition the average and range of the correct and incorrect oral reading scores were 60.0 wpm (range from 47.7 to

Table 20-1. Fall quarter: Mean correct words per minute (c), incorrect words per minute (e) and percentage of comprehension (%).

Pupils		Base I	Skip & drill	Base II
MF	c/e	45.2/3.9	59.7/3.0	58.0/3.3
	%	63.4	74.9	79.7
TG	c/e	59.3/3.9	61.7/4.0	65.8/2.9
	%	55.2	63.4	74.5
DH	c/e	65.8/2.3	72.9/2.8	79.8/2.8
	%	64.8	79.2	71.0
DP	c/e	44.9/2.1	60.2/1.7	59.1/2.1
	%	71.4	84.3	86.4
MS	c/e	39.0/3.8	47.7/3.1	54.3/2.7
	%	78.3	84.0	89.7
TS	c/e	53.0/2.7	58.8/3.1	58.1/2.9
	%	59.5	74.0	76.0
BW	c/e	47.7/2.9	58.8/2.3	60.6/2.1
	%	68.8	84.9	84.0
x̄	c/e	50.7/3.1	60.0/2.9	62.2/2.7
	%	65.9	77.8	80.2

72.9 wpm) and 2.9 wpm (range from 1.7 to 4.0 wpm). When these data were compared to the baseline scores it was apparent that the correct rates for all pupils improved and the incorrect rates for four pupils improved. The mean correct rate improvement was 9.3 wpm (range from 2.4 to 15.3 wpm), and the mean incorrect rate improvement was .2 wpm (range from +.5 to −.9 wpm).

Meanwhile, the average comprehension score during this phase was 77.8% (range from 63.4 to 84.9%). The comprehension scores of all the pupils improved throughout this condition. The average improvement was 11.9% (range from 5.7 to 16.1%).

Throughout this condition 33 skips were made, an average of .24 per day. The students spent an average of 4.7 days per section before skipping (range from 2.2 to 12); 42% of the skips occurred on the first day of a section. On the average, when drill was instituted, 2.6 days elapsed before a pupil skipped.

Baseline II. When the skip and drill intervention was removed, the performance of the pupils generally maintained. In some instances performance actually improved.

Throughout this condition the average oral correct rate was 62.2 wpm with a range of 54.3 to 79.8 wpm. The average incorrect rate and range were 2.7 wpm, from 2.1 to 3.3 wpm. When these data were compared to the intervention phase, it was apparent that the correct rates

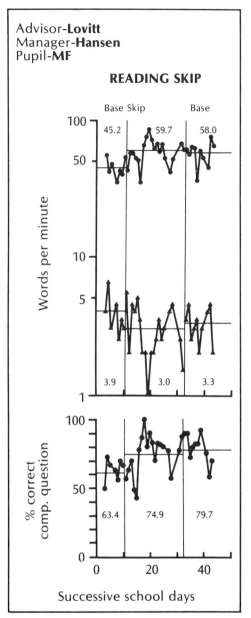

Advisor-**Lovitt**
Manager-**Hansen**
Pupil-**MF**

READING SKIP

Figure 20-1. The top graph shows the daily correct and incorrect oral reading rates for MF throughout the three phases of the study. The bottom graph shows his daily comprehension scores. The average rates and scores for the three conditions are included. The reason some data plots are not connected is that data were not obtained on some days (weekends, absences, field trips).

of four pupils improved and the incorrect rates of four improved.

The average comprehension percentage and range scores during this phase were 80.2%, from 71.0% to 89.7%. When these data were compared to those of the preceding phase, it was noted that five pupils improved. Had the skipping provision been in effect during this condition the number of skips per day would have been .16.

Figure 20-1 is included to show the daily oral reading and comprehension data from one pupil. All three aspects of this pupil's performance were influenced by the skipping and drilling interventions.

DISCUSSION

The data indicated that the intervention—skipping and drilling—was effective for all pupils in this study. Throughout this study, average correct and incorrect oral reading rates improved from 50.7 to 62.2 wpm and 3.1 to 2.7 wpm, respectively. The pupils also improved in their ability to comprehend; from 65.9% to 80.2%, despite the fact that they were continually reading more difficult material. From these data, however, we were unable to determine whether skipping or drilling, or the combination of the techniques, was responsible for the gains.

There is some possibility that the drill procedure alone could have been largely responsible for the improvements. Although our drill procedures were neither new nor different, they were related directly to specific reading problems and were contingently arranged. If, after seven days, for example, a pupil's correct rate was not fast enough, he received a correct rate drill. Similarly, if his oral incorrect rates were too high or his comprehension percentages were too low, he received drill for those features. It has been our experience that when simple instructional techniques are designed for specific problems and contingently arranged, improvement is immediate and significant.

Another possible explanation for the improvement of some pupils could be the threat of drill. For some children, drill could have been perceived as a punishing event; hence they sought to avoid it.

It is also possible that the improvement was due mostly to the skipping feature. The pupils in this study were, at the beginning of the year, reading from one to three years below grade level. All of them knew the level at which they were assigned and the level at which they should be reading (in spite of the coding systems used by various reading series). They also knew that most of their friends were reading from more advanced books than they were. It is quite possible, then, that being able to skip through books and approach or reach grade level was very reinforcing for these boys.

During the next two academic quarters we conducted studies designed to sort out some of the specific effects of skipping and drilling. In the winter quarter we formed three groups of subjects. Following a baseline phase, three pupils were assigned to a skip-and-drill condition, just like the one in the experiment just described. Meanwhile, two pupils, following a baseline, were placed in a drill-only condition; and two others were placed in a skip-only condition.

When the results were analyzed in regard to correct rate, it was revealed that the skip-and-drill and the skip-only groups gained more than the drill-only group. Both groups gained, on the average, 7.8 wpm. When incorrect rate improvement was studied, the skip-and-drill and skip-only groups fared the best. Average incorrect rates for both groups were lowered .1 wpm. When comprehension improvement was analyzed, the drill-only group showed the most improvement. The average gain for that group was 8.6%.

During the spring quarter, two pupils who had been in the skip-and-drill condition during the winter quarter continued in this condition. When their performances at the end of the spring quarter were compared to their efforts during the winter quarter, it was found that correct rates for both of them increased (2.9 and 3.9 wpm). The incorrect rate of one boy increased (.1 wpm), while for the other it decreased (.6 wpm). The comprehension scores for both increased (10.6% and 1.2%).

Although we ran these two additional studies, we were still unable to make definitive statements as to the relative merits of the two procedures since too few subjects were involved. However, the opportunity to skip, of itself, did appear to be reinforcing. In the major study we described, the drill procedures were never used for some pupils. In fact, 70% of all skips occurred without the necessity of drilling.

Throughout the year every pupil improved in every respect. The average correct rate gain was 32.9 wpm from beginning to end of the year. The average incorrect rate improvement was 3.3

wpm; and the average percentage comprehension score gain was 18%. In addition, all the pupils were reading at grade level at the end of the year. Throughout the year they gained an average of 1.9 grade levels (range from 1.0 to 2.5). Furthermore, the pupils attained grade level in an average of 15.7 weeks. Teachers of reading should be encouraged by the fact that, in spite of the short amount of time devoted to reading (average 25 minutes per child per day), all showed improvement. It should, however, be noted that this study was done with children whose reading comprehension was 65% to begin with and was raised to 80%. The technique has not yet been proven to be equally applicable for children with lower baselines for comprehension.

This procedure for teaching reading has several other features which should be considered by teachers. First, the idea of having pupils read about 500 words each day and answer several comprehension questions should be considered. By so doing, the teacher can measure progress in two important elements of reading.

A second matter for teachers to consider pertains to the interventions that were used. In this study, neither costly nor time-consuming teaching techniques nor reinforcement systems were used. The drill procedures were very simple; teachers have used the same techniques for years. The manner in which the drill procedures were used in this study was, however, somewhat special. Drill was not scheduled every day; it was arranged only if a pupil's performance fell below a certain level.

As to the reinforcement technique, only a skipping provision was arranged. The teacher did not resort to an elaborate motivational system such as a token economy that could have required additional costs or personnel.

A third, and perhaps the most important feature of this study for teachers to consider, was the manner in which pupils were advanced from one part of a book to another. In this study a pupil skipped from one quarter of a book to another only if his oral reading and comprehension scores were adequate. This same approach could be used for advancing pupils from one story to the next (if skipping is not desired), or from one reader to another. The significance of the approach is that advancement from one level to another is based on pupil performance, not on time, or that others in the group have passed, or other irrelevant factors. The method for advancement described here and the method used for placing pupils should be seriously considered by teachers who want to individualize reading instruction.

REFERENCES

Gormly, J., and Nittoli, M. J.: Rapid improvement of reading skills in juvenile delinquents. *J. Exper. Educ.*, 1971, *40,* 45–48.

Lovitt, T. C., and Hansen, C. L.: Round one—Placing the child in the right reader. *J. Learning Disabil.,* 1976, *6,* 347–353.

McCracken, G., and Walcutt, G. C.: Lippincott's Basic Reading. New York: Lippincott, 1970.

Starlin, C. M.: The use of daily, direct recording as an aid in teaching oral reading. Unpublished doctoral dissertation, Univ. of Ore., 1970.

21. The differential effects of reinforcement contingencies on arithmetic performance

DEBORAH DEUTSCH SMITH   THOMAS C. LOVITT

Reinforcement contingencies were introduced to classroom settings over ten years ago (Staats et al., 1962; Zimmerman & Zimmerman, 1962). Through the years these procedures have been refined for application with a variety of classroom activities. The use and frequent overuse of reinforcement contingencies has been well documented (Axelrod, 1971; Kazdin & Bootzin, 1972; Lipe & Jung, 1971; O'Leary & Drabman, 1971; Stainback et al., 1973). Although reinforcement contingencies have been applied in many different situations, little research has been conducted to verify the general use of such procedures for academic subjects— e.g., arithmetic, spelling, and reading. Occasionally one hears ardent claims that if teachers would use reinforcement contingencies, all educational problems will be solved, that undesirable behaviors will disappear and knowledge of academic subject matter will increase at record pace. Since some teachers have an affinity for applying contingencies, it is important to determine whether these procedures are appropriate in all teaching situations.

Research conducted in nonacademic areas indicates that reinforcement contingencies are not always effective. Ayllon and Azrin (1964), for example, found that when the initial performance level of mental patients in picking up appropriate eating utensils was close to zero, the application of reinforcement contingencies was not effective. When instructions were provided, the desired behavior began to occur immediately. Reinforcement contingencies were then used successfully to maintain the patients' ability.

In another study, Hopkins (1968) found reinforcement contingencies to be initially ineffective. His subject was an institutionalized boy who did not smile. When candy was offered to him initially, he maintained his solemnity and still did not smile. Instructions to smile then elicited a smile. Since the desired behavior was not in his repertoire at the beginning of the study, the reinforcement did not alter his behavior. Once he acquired the behavior, however, the boy's smiling increased when the candy reinforcement was repeated.

In both of these studies reinforcement contingencies were not initially effective because the desired behaviors were not in the repertoires of the subjects: The desired behaviors had to be acquired before reinforcement contingencies could be effective; then they served to increase and maintain satisfactory levels of performance.

In teaching academic subjects, classroom teachers work in three distinctly different situations: acquisition, proficiency, and maintenance. The acquisition situation occurs when the desired

From the *Journal of Learning Disabilities*, 1976, *9*, 21–29. Copyright 1976 by the Professional Press. Reprinted by special permission of Professional Press, Inc.

behavior is not in the repertoire of the child and the child does not know how to perform the desired task (i.e., he cannot correctly solve a particular type of arithmetic problem). In the proficiency situation, the child is able to accurately complete the task, but is unsure of the process and, therefore, is too slow at performing the task. In this case, a child's percentage scores indicate that he knows the subtraction facts, but his correct rate scores indicate that he does not know them well enough to solve the problems quickly. Once a child has acquired a new skill and has become proficient in his performance of that skill, the teacher must insure that the student maintains this level of proficiency.

The purpose of the research reported here was to determine whether reinforcement contingencies would be effective in two of these three academic situations—acquisition and proficiency. In the first of two experiments reinforcement contingencies were used for acquiring arithmetic skills. In the second experiment, reinforcement contingencies were applied to improve computational proficiency. A maintenance condition was then conducted to determine whether improved performance levels were retained.

GENERAL METHODOLOGY

Each of the many different types of arithmetic problems requires the ability to use a slightly different set of rules. Before a child can become proficient in arithmetic, he must know how to solve specific types of problems. In addition, for example, there are some general process rules—such as carrying over to the next column—which must be followed in order to solve all the variations of addition problems.

The child working arithmetic problems too slowly does not complete his work as fast as his classmates. As arithmetic assignments become more complex, this child often works even slower and completes fewer problems. Frequently, the reason for the difficulty is a lack of proficiency in using the basic facts that are the rudiments of larger problems.

In the first experiment, the children were presented with arithmetic problems which required process rules they did not know, such as borrowing or carrying, and they could not correctly solve these problems. They needed to acquire new arithmetic skills. In the second experiment, the children were presented with arithmetic problems which they were able to compute accurately, but they worked too slowly. In both experiments reinforcement contingencies were used as interventions.

SUBJECTS AND SETTING

Seven learning disabled boys, with an age range of 8–11 years, participated in this research. Three boys were involved in Experiment I; all particpated in Experiment II. All of the boys had been referred from one local school district to the Experimental Education Unit (EEU) at the University of Washington for one academic year because of general academic deficiencies. This research was conducted in the Research Classroom at the EEU; the primary purpose of this classroom is the investigation of various curricular materials and teaching techniques.

RELIABILITY

Reliability measures were obtained on timings, procedures, scoring, and graphing the data. Reliability scores were better than 99% on all measures.

MATERIAL CONSTRUCTION

Two types of arithmetic problems were selected for each child. Experiment I included problems not mastered by the child. Problems included were those for which the child had scored 0% for three consecutive school days.

Problems used in Experiment II were those which the child knew how to compute, but he was not proficient in arriving at the solutions. The criterion for selecting these problems was that the child's correct rate not exceed that of two-thirds of his peer group attending public school. Those rates were obtained by the authors before the research was conducted.

Once specific arithmetic problems were selected for each child, daily arithmetic pages were constructed The procedures for constructing the pages were constant regardless of the type of problem. If, for example, in Experiment I a child needed to learn to solve subtraction problems which required borrowing from a zero in the units colums, e.g.,

$$\begin{array}{r} 890 \\ -\,127 \end{array},$$

only problems of that type were used for his daily arithmetic sheets. Through the use of a table of random numbers, five arithmetic pages were constructed for each problem type. No problem was used more than once. The child received a different version of his arithmetic each day of the week.

In Experiment II, arithmetic fact problems were used. Since the number of fact problems available is smaller than that available for more complex arithmetic problems, the format for constructing these arithmetic pages varied slightly. For instance, if addition fact problems which have one digit in both addends and two digits in the sum were used, e.g.

$$\frac{9}{+9},$$

all problems of that type were identified. A table of random numbers was used to arrange the problems on the arithmetic sheets. Five different sheets were constructed for these problems. Since there are only 45 problems in this class, all problems were used more than once.

DESIGN

Every study in both experiments followed an *ABA* design. Criteria for change of condition, however, differed for the two experiments. In Experiment I, the baseline condition lasted three days; all the scores during that condition had to be 0%. The intervention condition lasted at least seven data days and was to be concluded when the last three scores for that condition were 100%. The intention was to follow with a maintenance condition. That condition was also to run at least seven data days and to be concluded when the last three scores were 100%.

During Experiment II the children's correct rates, rather than percent correct scores, were used as the basis for changing conditions. Each condition during these studies ran at least seven data days and was concluded when the last four scores were either decelerating or accelerating at a median slope not greater than X1.2.[1]

GENERAL PROCEDURES

In both experiments each child was given a different page of arithmetic each day of the week. The child wrote his name and the date at the top of the page. The experimenter gave the instruction: "Ready, start working," and at the end of two minutes for Experiment I and one minute for Experiment II the teacher said, "Pencils down." No other instructions were given. No feedback was provided the children regarding their performance during any phase of the research. The ex-

perimenter than collected the sheets and corrected them. She calculated percentage and correct and error rate scores, entered these on data sheets, and plotted the data. Partially completed and skipped problems were not counted as either correct or incorrect.

EXPERIMENT I

There were three phases to this experiment, each involving acquisition of new arithmetic skills.

PROCEDURES

The subjects were three boys. Kyle was assigned three-digit multiplication problems which did not require carrying, e.g.,

$$\frac{231}{\times 132}.$$

Brett computed subtraction problems which required borrowing from a zero in the units column, e.g.,

$$\frac{560}{-327}.$$

Stephan solved multiplication problems which required carrying, problems with one digit in the multiplier and two digits in the multiplicand, e.g.,

$$\frac{57}{\times 6}.$$

Baseline. No instructions, feedback, or reinforcement contingencies were in effect during this condition.

Contingent toy. On the first day of this condition, before a child was given his arithmetic pages, he was allowed to choose a toy model from a large selection. The experimenter wrote the boy's name and the cost of the model (10 points) on an index card which was affixed to the model and told him that he could purchase the toy model with points earned during arithmetic time.

The experimenter wrote "1:1" at the top of the arithmetic page, gave it to the boy, and explained the scoring: "For every problem you do correctly you will earn one point towards the model" (The experimenter had predicted that a child would do no more than five problems correctly each day and had established a ratio that would permit him to earn a model every two days.)

The children were allowed two minutes to work on the problems. The experimenter then collected the papers and corrected them. If any of the children had solved any of his problems correctly, the price on his chosen toy would have been reduced by the number of points he had earned; but none did.

Demonstration. Since none of the boys were able to master the problem types presented during the contingency phase, this demonstration condition was added to the experiment. After handing out the arithmetic pages, the experimenter went to the child's desk with a sample problem that she had previously written on an index card, and she demonstrated the appropriate process to follow as she worked the sample problem. She then left the child's desk, taking the sample problem with her. The child then worked on his arithmetic problems.

Maintenance. This fourth condition was a repetition of the baseline condition, with no instructions, feedback, or contingencies. It came after the added demonstration condition, following the complete failures in the contingent-toy condition.

RESULTS

Since none of the children improved his performance when the contingent-toy tactic was in effect, the demonstration condition was added. Figure 21-1 shows Stephan's data. Table 21-1 summarizes the results for the three subjects.

Baseline. All the boys scored 0% for the three days of this condition.

Contingent toy. This condition lasted seven days for each child. All of their percentage scores were zero.

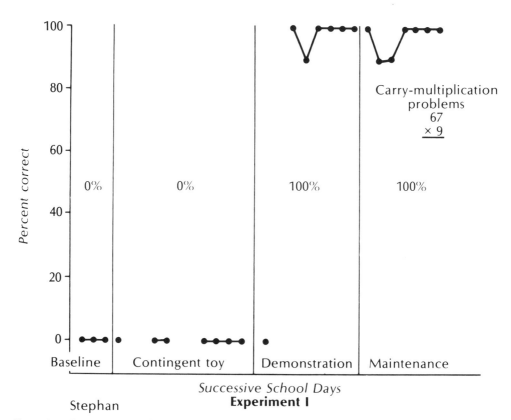

Figure 21-1. Percent correct for Stephan's problems assigned for Experiment 1. Only successive school days are connected by lines. Solid vertical lines indicate change of condition.

Table 21-1. Summary data for Experiment I reinforcement contingencies

Child's name	Problem type	Baseline		Condition Contingent toy		Demonstration		Maintenance	
		Median	Length	Median	Length	Median	Length	Median	Length
Brett	noo −xxx	0%	3	0%	7	100%	7	100%	7
Kyle	nn × xx	0%	3	0%	7	100%	7	100%	7
Stephen	cc × x	0%	3	0%	7	100%	7	100%	7

Demonstration. Median score for each boy was 100%.

Maintenance. During this condition baseline conditions were reinstituted. All the boys maintained their high level of performance and median scores were 100%.

DISCUSSION

During the baseline condition, the boys demonstrated they could not accurately compute the problems presented to them. When the contingent-toy condition was in effect, none of the boys improved his performance. Because the required performance was not within their repertoires, as indicated by their initial percentage scores of zero, the toys did not produce reinforcement. Reinforcement, by definition, increases the probability of a behavior occurring, but the behavior must have occurred before it can be reinforced.

Reinforcement contingencies, when used alone, will not positively alter behavior which must be acquired. Ayllon and Azrin (1964) and Hopkins (1968) arrived at similar conclusions when they unsuccessfully applied reinforcement contingencies to social behaviors which needed to be acquired.

CONCLUSION

The data from this experiment indicate that reinforcement contingencies are not appropriate to all teaching situations. When new skills need to be acquired, interventions other than reinforcement contingencies should be scheduled.

EXPERIMENT II

During this experiment, computational proficiency was the target, rather than accuracy. The children had already mastered certain computational skills, but needed to become proficient in performing these skills. Two types of reinforcement contingencies were used to increase the speed in solving arithmetic fact problems. The order of the interventions was the same for all the children. The first intervention was contingent free-time. During this condition, the children earned points which were redeemable for time to spend in preferred activities. The second intervention was contingent-toy models. Once again the children earned points for their computational arithmetic assignments, but now these points led to the purchase of toy models.

PROCEDURES

For this experiment six boys computed addition-carry facts and one boy subtraction facts. Addition-carry facts are those problems with single digits in both addends and two digits in the sum, e.g.,

$$\frac{8}{+8}.$$

Subtraction facts have single digits in the minuend, the subtrahend, and the remainder, e.g.,

$$\frac{5}{-2}.$$

The same procedures were used with all the children. After the baseline condition, the contingent free-time intervention was scheduled, followed by the contingent-toy intervention. The studies were concluded with a return-to-baseline phase.

Baseline. No instructions, feedback, or reinforcement contigencies were in effect.

Contingent free-time. During this condition, free time could be earned to spend as desired—

earned according to the number of correct problems computed each day.

A ratio (number of correct problems to amount of free time earned) was determined for each child before the condition was initiated by calculating the median correct rate score for the baseline condition. This score divided by five—the amount of time a child would earn if his daily correct rate score during this condition equaled his correct rate median for the prior condition—gave the number of problems the child had to solve correctly to earn one minute of free time. For example, if a child obtained a correct rate median of 10 problems during the baseline condition, 10 was divided by five. For every two problems the child computed correctly, he earned one minute of free time—i.e., if the child solved 14 problems accurately, he earned seven minutes of free time.

Each day before handing out the arithmetic pages, the experimenter wrote each child's ratio at the top of his page. Then, before the child did the arithmetic, the experimenter came to his desk and explained the ratio to him: "For every two problems you do correctly you will earn one minute of free time." No other instructions were given.

After a child worked on his assigned problems for one minute, he was told to stop and the experimenter came to his desk and collected his page. She corrected the problems, calculated the amount of free time he had earned, and told him how much time he was entitled to spend. The amount of time was also noted on a piece of paper posted at the front of the classroom. This was done to insure that the child spent only the amount of time he had earned. No praise was given the child for his performance.

Various activities were available for free time. Some children worked on shop projects, others put puzzles together, and so on, with many different activities chosen. They were permitted to spend their free time when they desired, so long as it was not saved for more than a two-day period.

Contingent toy. With this intervention, the children earned points which eventually led to the purchase of toy models. Before this condition began, the experimenter determined the ratio for points to number of correct problems by using a formula similar to that used in the contingent free-time condition. The toy models were priced for each child in this way: The median of the contingent free-time condition was divided by

the ratio multiplied by six. If in the previous condition a child obtained a correct rate median of 14 and the ratio used in that condition was 2:1, two was divided into 14. The answer, seven, was then multiplied by six. The cost of this boy's model was 42. The division step in this formula indicated the average number of points the child earned each day during the contingent free-time condition. If he retained his level of performance, the child earned his toy model in a reasonable length of time: six days. If he became faster in his computations, he earned his toy sooner.

On the first day of this condition, the child was allowed to select the toy model he wanted to purchase. Once he did, his name and the cost of the model were written on an index card and affixed to the model.

Each day, the child's ratio was written at the top of his arithmetic page. Before he started work, the experimenter came to his desk and explained the ratio to him; no other instructions or feedback were provided the child. After the child worked the problems on the page for one minute, the experimenter collected the page, scored it, and calculated the number of points the child had earned. She then went to the toy model and decreased the cost by the number of points the child had earned. Once a child earned enough points to purchase his model, it was given to him and he selected another model to work for.

Return to baseline. Baseline procedures were reinstituted. No instructions, feedback, or reinforcement contingencies were given.

RESULTS

For each condition in this experiment, medians, median slopes, and percent-of-change scores were calculated for each child's correct and error rates. Median slope scores were calculated to determine whether a child was becoming faster or slower in his computations within a condition. The percent-of-change score was calculated to show the amount of change in performance from one condition to the next. This indicated median-to-median changes. The following formula was used to obtain this score:

$$\frac{Md_2 - Md_1}{Md_1} \times 100 = \text{percentage-of-change score.}$$

For example, if the baseline median was 10 and the median correct rate score for the next condi-

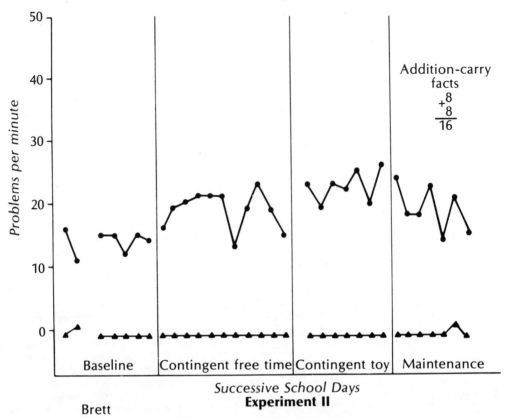

Figure 21-2. Correct and error rate data for Brett's problems during Experiment II. Dots indicate correct rate scores and triangles represent error rate scores.

tion was 15, the difference between these two scores was five. The baseline median was then divided into five. The percent-of-change score in this instance was 50%.

Table 21-2 shows the correct and error median rates, slopes, and percent-of-change scores for the seven children. Figure 21-2 presents the data for Brett.

Table 21-2. Summary data for Experiment II reinforcement contingencies

Subjects	Baseline				Percent of change		Contingent freetime			
	Median rate		Median slope				Median rate		Median slope	
	C	E	C	E	C	E	C	E	C	E
Brett	15.0	0	÷1.1	×1.0	+27	—	19.0	0	÷1.0	×1.0
John	21.0	0	×1.3	×1.0	0	—	21.0	0	×1.2	÷1.1
Kyle	33.0	0	÷1.2	×1.0	+ 9	—	36.0	0	×1.1	×1.0
Stephan	19.0	1.0	÷1.1	×1.0	+ 8	∞	20.5	0	÷1.1	×1.0
Rip	26.0	1.0	÷1.5	÷1.2	+19	∞	31.0	0	×1.0	×1.0
Rob	21.0	2.0	×1.1	÷2.7	+52	∞	33.0	0	×1.0	×1.0
Stewart	9.0	0	÷1.1	×1.0	+44	—	13.0	0	×1.0	×1.0

*means zero divided into zero
**means zero divided by or into a number

Baseline. The correct rate middle median for the seven children during this condition was 21.0 (range: 9.0–33.0). The error rate middle median was 0.0 (range: 2.0–0.0).

Contingent free-time. The correct rate middle median for the children was 21.0 (range: 13.0–36.0) and the error rate middle median for all was 0.0. The median level of improvement for all the children was +19% (range: 0–52%).

Contingent toy. The median improvement noted for the boy's correct rate medians was 19% (range: 0%–21%). The correct rate middle median was 26.0 (range: 16.0–39.0). The error rate middle median was 0.0 (range: 3.0–0.0).

Return to baseline. When the reinforcement contingencies were withdrawn, all of the children's correct rate medians decreased. The median child lost 9% of his correct rate (range: 6–25%). The correct rate middle median for the seven children was 23.0 (range: 12.0–36.0). The middle median error rate was 0.0 (range: 3.0–0.0).

DISCUSSION

When the children had the opportunity to earn free time for their arithmetic assignments, and the contingencies were aimed at increasing computational speed, most of the children's correct rate medians increased. One child's correct rate median score did not increase: it remained at the level of the baseline phase.

When the contingent-toy intervention was scheduled, all but one child showed an increase in correct rate medians. The median level of improvement was again 19%.

When baseline procedures were reinstituted, the correct rate madians for all the children decreased. All, however, concluded this experiment with a higher correct rate median than their initial levels. No appreciable rises in error rates were noted during this experiment. Although the children's correct rates improved, none obtained correct rates which indicated that they had become proficient in computing the problems presented to them.

Generally, both reinforcement contingencies were influential and stimulated increases in the children's correct rate scores. Each intervention brought the children's performances closer to the aim of 50 correct problems per minute. The interventions, however, did not produce identical results. Therefore, a comparison was made between the two reinforcement contingencies. The contingent free-time tactic fared slightly better than the contingent-toy intervention. Although the median percent-of-change scores for both intervention conditions were equal, a wider range of those scores was noted when the contingent free-time condition was in effect. The percent-of-change scores ranged from 0% to 52% while the contingent free-time intervention was scheduled; and 0% to 21% for the contingent-toy intervention. Several children made greater gains when the contingent free-time intervention was in effect.

There was one other advantage in using the free time tactic. Although the boy's error rates were not considerable, no child had an error rate median score above 0.0 during the contingent free-time condition. Several children had initial medians above 0.0, and some obtained higher error rate scores during the contingent-toy condition.

Percent of range		Contingent toy				Percent of change		No intervention			
		Median rate		Median slope				Median rate		Median slope	
	E	C	E	C	E	C	E	C	E	C	E
1	—	23.0	0	×1.2	×1.0	−21	—	18.0	0	÷1.4	×1.0
1	∞	25.5	1.5	÷1.1	×2.0	− 6	−33	23.0	1.0	÷1.1	÷1.1
7	—	39.0	0	÷1.1	×1.0	− 8	—	36.0	0	×1.1	×1.0
1	—	26.0	0	×1.2	×1.0	−12	—	23.0	0	×1.1	×1.2
6	∞	33.0	2.0	÷1.1	×1.0	− 9	0	30.0	2.0	×1.0	×5.1
0	∞	33.0	3.0	×1.0	÷1.5	−24	0	25.0	3.0	×1.3	÷1.4
9	—	16.0	0	÷1.1	×1.0	−25	—	12.0	0	÷1.2	×1.0

IMPLICATIONS

Two different educational situations were studied in this research—acquisition and proficiency. In the acquisition situation, the children did not know how to accurately solve various types of arithmetic problems. They did not know the appropriate computational rules required for solving the problems correctly. In the proficiency situation, the children knew how to solve the problems accurately, but at so slow a pace that this might have impeded future progress in computational arithmetic.

Reinforcement contingencies were applied in both academic situations. The results indicated that reinforcement contingencies could alter children's computational proficiency, but not acquisition. The major emphasis of this research was to demonstrate that some interventions are indigenous to certain educational situations and thus are effective only in specific circumstances.

The performance of the children who participated in both projects was remarkably similar. The children were classmates in a relatively small class, and we would like to encourage others to replicate our research to determine whether other children perform in a similar manner when given reinforcement for their arithmetic performance in both acquisition and proficiency situations. We also encourage others to conduct comparable research in different academic areas. It might be that such differential effects occur in reading, spelling, and handwriting.

For teachers to select the appropriate interventions for their pupils, they must first determine each child's educational levels. In computational arithmetic it is imperative that teachers identify the specific types of arithmetic problems that their pupils cannot compute accurately. It is also important for them to determine which problem types their pupils are not yet proficient in solving. After a diagnosis, teachers must then decide which intervention they will employ to remediate the computational deficits.

CONCLUSIONS

This research indicated that at least one type of intervention strategy is not appropriate in all types of educational situations. Reinforcement contingencies alone were not effective when children needed to acquire new computational skills. In that case, an instructional tactic brought the children to mastery level of performance.

When children's computational proficiency needed improvement, reinforcement contingencies influenced their computational speed. It is probable that other intervention strategies also have differential effects depending on the specific type of educational situation in which they are applied. It could be that there are varying levels of acquisition and proficiency which also influence the strength of the intervention strategies scheduled. Such information will only be discovered if educators clearly diagnose the educational situations before teaching tactics are implemented.

NOTES

1. A median slope was calculated through those data points. It was obtained by calculating a line which allowed for the least amount of variance by using the unsigned medians. The median slope indicates the trend of the data. Scores indicating that a child's rates were becoming faster are prefaced by an "X"; if a child's rates were becoming slower, the median slope score is prefaced by a " ÷ ".

REFERENCES

Axelrod, S.: Token reinforcement programs in special classes. Exceptional Child., 1971, 37, 371–379.

Ayllon, T., and Azrin, N. H.: Reinforcement and instructions with mental patients. J. Exp. Anal. Behav., 1964, 7, 327–331.

Hopkins, B. L.: Effects of candy and social reinforcement, instructions and reinforcement schedule leaning on the modification and maintenance of smiling. J. Appl. Behav. Anal., 1968, 1, 121–129.

Kazdin, A. E., and Bootzin, R. R.: The token economy: an evaluative review. J. Appl. Behav. Anal., 1972, 5, 343–372.

Lipe, D., and Jung, S. M.: Manipulating incentives to enhance school learning. Rev. Educ. Res., 1971, 41, 249–280.

O'Leary, K. D., and Drabman, R.: Token reinforcement programs in the classroom: a review. Psychol. Bull., 1971, 75, 379–398.

Staats, A. W., et al.: The conditioning of textual responses using "extrinsic" reinforcers. J. Exp. Anal. Behav., 1962, 5, 33–40.

Stainback, W. C., et al. Establishing a Token Economy in the Classroom. Columbus, O.: Charles E. Merrill, 1973.

Zimmerman, E. H., and Zimmerman, J.: The alteration of behavior in a special classroom situation. J. Exp. Anal. Behav., 1962, 5, 59–60.

22. A behavioral-educational alternative to drug control of hyperactive children

TEODORO AYLLON   DALE LAYMAN
HENRY J. KANDEL

Hyperactivity or hyperkinesis in the classroom is a clinical condition characterized by excessive movement, unpredictable behaviors, unawareness of consequences, inability to focus on and concentrate on a particular task, and poor academic performance (Stewart, Pitts, Craig, & Dieruf, 1966). It is estimated that about 200,000 children in the United States are currently receiving amphetamines to control their hyperactivity (Krippner, Silverman, Cavallo, & Healy, 1973).

Drugs such as methylphenidate (Ritalin) and chlorpromazine have been shown to control hyperactivity in the laboratory and applied settings. The evidence from the laboratory is based on recording devices actuated by the child's movements (Hollis & St. Omer, 1972; Sprague, Barnes, & Werry, 1970; Sykes, Douglas, Weiss, & Minde, 1971). In the classroom, children have been rated by their teachers along various dimensions to determine the effectiveness of stimulants on their behavior. Comly (1971) found that of 40 hyperactive children, whose behavior was rated twice weekly by teachers, those children receiving stimulants were rated as having better listening ability, less excitability, less forgetfulness, and better peer relationships. In a similar study, Denhoff, Davis, and Hawkins (1971) showed that teachers rated hyperactive children on

dextro-amphetamine (Dexedrine) as improved on measures of hyperactivity, short attention span, and impulsivity. In addition, global ratings by parents, teachers, and clinicians have shown that drugs such as methylphenidate (Ritalin) and dextro-amphetamine decreased children's hyperactivity in school and at home (Conners, 1971).

While there is still some conflicting evidence on drug effectiveness (Krippner et al., 1973), as well as a growing ethical concern for the morality and wisdom implied in administering medication to children (Fish, 1971; Hentoff, 1970; Koegh, 1971; Ladd, 1970), drugs are commonly used to control hyperactivity in the classroom.

Because the often-implied objective behind the use of drugs for the hyperactive child is that of enabling him to profit academically, it is surprising that few data directly support this belief. Most studies have measured the effect of medication on component skills of learning, e.g., attention, concentration, and discrimination. For example, Conners and Rothschild (1968), Epstein, Lasagna, Conners, Rodriguez (1968), and Knights and Hinton (1968) tested drug effects on general intelligence test performance. Sprague et al. (1970) studied children's responses of "same" or "different" to pairs of visual stimuli

Reprinted by permission from the *Journal of Applied Behavior Analysis*, 1975, *8*, 137–146. Copyright 1975 by the Society for the Experimental Analysis of Behavior, Inc.

The cooperative spirit of the parents and teachers of the children in this study is gratefully acknowledged. Special thanks go to Dr. E. Ensminger for his unflagging interest and encouragement.

presented on a screen. Conners, Eisenberg, and Sharpe (1964) studied the effects of methylphenidate (Ritalin) on paired-associate learning and Porteus Maze performance in children with hyperactive symptoms. Others (Conners, Eisenberg, & Barcai, 1967; Sprague & Toppe, 1966) concentrated their efforts on the effects of drugs on the attention of hyperactive children to various tasks. These laboratory studies investigated the effects of drugs on component skills related to learning, but they did not measure academic performance per se (e.g., math and reading) in the classroom.

Sulzbacher (1972) experimentally analyzed the effects of drugs on academic behaviors of hyperactive children in the classroom. Measures of correct solutions and error rates were taken in arithmetic, writing, and reading in three hyperactive children. In addition, measures were taken of the children's rates of talk-outs in class and their rates of out-of-seat behavior during class. The children were successively given a placebo, then 5 mg of dextro-amphetamine (Dexedrine), and finally 10 mg of dextro-amphetamine. The results showed that medication of 5 mg improved the children's academic responses; however, there was wide variance in academic performance when the children were administered 10 mg. The results for social behavior also varied. Of two children, one showed less hyperactive classroom behavior (talk-outs and out-of-seat behavior) at a dosage level different than the second child. However, the placebo had more effect on controlling the third child's behavior than did medication. The author's conclusion was that stimulant drugs "can effectively modify disruptive behaviors without adversely affecting academic performance in the classroom." Drug effects on academic performance, however, were highly variable.

Since Sulzbacher's major interest was in determining the role of drugs on hyperactivity and academic performance, he did not pursue behavioral alternatives to the control of hyperactivity. Yet, there is at present, a body of established findings indicating that such alternatives may be available. For example, O'Leary and Becker (1967) found that when children were rewarded for sitting, making eye contact with the teacher, and engaging in academically related activities, their misbehavior was virtually eliminated. Ayllon, Layman, and Burke (1972) showed that misbehavior may be also reduced, not by rewarding the child for good conduct, but by imposing academic structure in the classroom. This structure involved giving academic assignments with a short time limit for their completion. Ayllon and Roberts (1974) found that another behavioral technique to eliminate classroom misbehavior is to reward children for academic performance only. These findings suggest that disruptive behavior can be weakened by reinforcing incompatible academic performance. Using this method, the child performs well both academically and socially without treating the disruptive behavior directly.

The children in the above studies were disruptive, not hyperactive. Although the topography of the response is similar, hyperactivity differs from disruption in its magnitude, duration, and frequency. Illustrations of this difference are well documented, indicating that hyperactive children are in constant motion, fidget excessively, frequently enter and leave the classroom, move from one class activity to another and rarely complete their projects or stay with one particular game or activity. Their academic performance is typically poor (Campbell, Douglas, & Morgenstern, 1971; Freibergs & Douglas, 1969; Stewart, Pitts, Craig, & Dieruf, 1966; Sykes, Douglas, Weiss, & Minde, 1971).

Two questions arise: Can behavioral techniques used to decrease disruptive behavior be at least as effective as drugs in controlling an extreme form of classroom misbehavior such as hyperactivity? At the same time, can such techniques help the hyperactive child to grow educationally? The present study attempted to answer these questions.

METHOD

SUBJECTS AND SETTING

Three school children (Crystal, Paul, and Dudley), clinically diagnosed as chronically hyperactive, were all receiving drugs to control their hyperactivity.

Crystal was an 8-yr-old girl. She was 47 in. (118 cm) tall and weighed 76 lb (34.2 kg). She had an IQ of 118 as measured on the WISC. She was enrolled in a learning-disabilities class because of the hyperactive behavior she displayed before taking medication and because of her poor academic work. She had been on drugs since she was 5 yr old, when her doctor felt that her behavior was so unpredictable that he prescribed 5 mg of methylphenidate [four times a day] to calm her down.

Paul was a 9-yr-old boy. He was 53 in. (133 cm) tall and weighed 65 lb (29.2 kg). He had an

IQ of 94 as measured on the WISC. He had been enrolled in the learning-disabilities class for 2 yr before the study and had been taking 5 mg of methylphenidate [twice a day] for 1 yr to control his hyperactive behavior.

Dudley was a 10-yr-old boy. He was 55 in. (138 cm) tall and weighed 76 lb (34.2 kg). He had an IQ of 103 as measured on the WISC. He was enrolled in a learning-disabilities class for 2 yr before the study and on the advice of his doctor had been taking 5 mg of methylphenidate t.i.d. [three times a day] for 4 yr.

In addition to their drug treatment, Crystal and Dudley were under the care of a child psychiatrist and a pediatrician during the study.

The three children attended a private elementary school. They were enrolled in a self-contained learning disability class of ten children and one teacher. The children and the teacher remained together throughout the school day in the same room. Other personnel during the study consisted of two observer-recorders: one of the authors and an undergraduate student.

RESPONSE DEFINITION

Hyperactivity and academic performance across two academic periods, math and reading, were measured.

Math. Math was defined as addition of whole numbers under 10. The teacher wrote 10 problems on the board at the beginning of each class. The children were given 10 min to complete the problems. Problems were taken from Laidlaw Series Workbooks, Levels P and 1.

Reading. Reading was defined as comprehension and was measured by workbook responses to previously read stories in a basal reader. Each child had 20 min to complete a 10-question workbook page per day. The books were Merril-Linguistic Readers–3. In both math and reading, the written response served as a permanent product from which the percentage of correct answers could be determined.

The academic assignments in both math and reading increased slightly in difficulty as the child progressed through the work.

Hyperactivity. Since hyperactive behavior has overlapping topographical properties with other deviant behaviors, hyperactive behavior was defined using the same response definition as presented by Becker, Madsen, Arnold, and Thomas

for deviant behavior in the classroom (1967). To define and record deviant behavior, Becker and his colleagues used seven general categories of behavior incompatible with learning. These included gross motor behaviors, disruptive noise with objects, disturbing others, orienting responses, blurting out, talking, and other miscellaneous behaviors incompatible with learning. In the present experiment, the behaviors of the hyperactive children most often fell into the following four categories: gross motor behaviors, disruptive noise, disturbing others, and blurting out. The most frequently recorded category for these hyperactive children was gross motor behaviors, which included running around the room, rocking in chairs, and jumping on one or both feet. Disruptive noise with objects included the constant turning of book pages and the excessive flipping of notebook paper. Disturbing others and blurting out included the constant movement of arms, resulting in the destruction of objects and hitting others, screaming, and high-pitched and rapid speech. Categories that were not recorded with any consistency included orienting responses and talking, as in a conversation with another person. Thus, although the response definition for deviant behavior was used, the actual recording was heavily weighted on those behaviors described by Stewart et al. (1966) as being typical of hyperactive children.

Observational and recording procedure for hyperactivity. Initially, six children were identified by the school director as being hyperactive and receiving medication for it. These children were observed across two class periods: math and reading. The duration of each class period was 45 min. Each child was observed in successive order on a time-sample of 25 sec. At the end of each 25-sec interval, the behavior of the child under observation was coded as showing hyperactivity or its absence. At that time, the observer marked a single slash in the appropriate interval, on a recording sheet, if one or more hyperactive behaviors occurred. If no hyperactive behaviors were observed at that time, the appropriate interval was marked with an "O." The number of intervals of hyperactivity over the total number of intervals for each child gave the observer the percent of intervals in which each child was hyperactive. Each of the six children was observed a total of 17 times per 45-min class period. Using this recording procedure, it was possible to determine, during baseline, that the most chronically hyperactive children were Crystal, Paul, and Dudley. By dropping observations on the less-severely hyperactive children it was possible to increase the number of observations for the chronically hyperactive ones. Recording hyperactivity from one child to the next was now sampled about every 18 sec in the manner described above. Each child was now observed approximately 50 times each class period throughout the remaining phases of the experiment.

Observer agreement on academic performance and hyperactivity. The percentage of correct math and reading problems was checked by the teacher and one of the authors each day and the obtained agreement score was 100% on each occasion for each child.

Reliability checks for hyperactivity were taken by one of the authors and one of three undergraduate students in Special Education. The student was given the list of deviant behaviors described by Becker et al. (1967) one day before the reliability check to become familiar with the responses. The students were not told of the purpose of the study or of the changes in experimental conditions. Each observer during the reliability check used a watch with a sweep second hand. In addition, a prepared sheet showed the observers the sequence in which the children were to be sampled and the intervals at the end of which each observer was to look at the subject and record whether or not the behavior was occurring at that instant. Each observer sat on opposite sides of the room to ensure unbiased observations.

The percentage of agreement for hyperactive as well as nonhyperactive behavior was calculated by comparing each interval and dividing agreements in each by the total number of observations and multiplying by 100. Reliability checks were taken to include the baseline period under medication (Blocks 2, 3, 5, and 6; in Figures 1, 2, and 3), the period when medication was discontinued and no reinforcement was available (Blocks 7 and 9), and the final period when reinforcement was introduced in both math and reading (Block 11). Reliability scores for hyperactivity for each child were always more than 85%, with the scores ranging from a low of 87% to a high of 100%. The average reliability score was 97%.

Check-point system and back-up reinforcers. A token reinforcement system similar to that used by O'Leary and Becker (1967) in a classroom setting was used. Children were awarded checks

by the teacher on an index card. One check was recorded for each correct academic response. The checks could be exchanged for a large array of back-up reinforcers later in the day. The back-up reinforcers ranged in price from one check to 75 checks, and included such items and activities as candy, school supplies, free time, lunch in the teacher's room, and picnics in the park.

PROCEDURE

Each subject's daily level of hyperactivity and academic achievement, on and off medication, were directly observed and recorded before the behavioral program. In addition, using a multiple-baseline design, the relative effectiveness of the motivational system on (a) hyperactivity and (b) academic performance, in math and reading was evaluated. This type of design allowed each child to serve as his own control, thereby minimizing the idiosyncratic drug-behavior interactions that have the potential for confounding the interpretations and even the results when comparing one subject with another. This design is particularly useful in the study of the effects of discontinuing drugs on behavior, since as Sprague et al. (1970) and Sulzbacher (1972) have pointed out, the inherent problem in assessing effects of medication lies in the fact that each child reacts to the presence or absence of medication on an individual basis.

The design of the study included the following four phases:

Phase 1: *on medication.* Crystal, Paul, and Dudley were observed for 17 days to evaluate hyperactive behavior when they were taking drugs. Academic performance in math and reading was also measured.

With the full cooperation of the children's doctors and their parents, medication was discontinued on the eighteenth day, a Saturday. An additional two days, Sunday and Monday (a school holiday), allowed a three-day "wash-out" period for the effect of medication to disappear. It is known that these stimulant drugs are almost completely metabolized within one day. No measures of hyperactivity or academic performance were obtained during this weekend period.

Phase 2: *off medication.* Following the three-day "wash-out" period, a three-day baseline when the children were off medication was obtained. Time-sampling observations of hyperactivity were continued, as well as measures of academic performance. This phase served as the basis against which the effects of reinforcement on hyperactivity and academic performance could later be compared.

Phase 3: *no medication; reinforcement of math*. During this six-day period, the children remained off drugs while the teacher introduced a reinforcement system for math performance only. Observations of hyperactivity continued and academic performance was measured.

Phase 4: *no medication; reinforcement of math plus reading*. During this six-day phase, the children remained off drugs while reinforcement was added for reading and reinforcement of math was maintained. Observations of hyperactivity and measures of academic performance were continued.

RESULTS

When Ritalin was discontinued, the level of hyperactivity doubled or tripled its initial level. However, when reinforcement was systematically administered for academic performance, hyperactivity for all three children decreased to a level comparable to the initial period when Ritalin chemically controlled it.

Figure 22-1 shows that hyperactivity for Crystal during the drug phase in math averaged about 20%, while academic performance in math was zero. When Ritalin was discontinued, hyperactivity rose to an average of 87% and math performance remained low at an average of 8%. When math was reinforced, and Crystal continued to stay off drugs, hyperactivity dropped significantly from 87% to about 9%. Math performance increased to 65%. Hyperactivity in math was effectively controlled through reinforcement of math performance. However, the multiple-baseline design shows that concurrently Crystal's hyperactivity during reading class remained at 90% before reinforcement was introduced for correct reading responses.

At the same time measures were taken in the area of math, hyperactivity and academic performance were also measured in the area of reading. Crystal's hyperactivity during reading class averaged approximately 10% under medication. Academic performance in reading was zero under medication. When Crystal was taken off drugs, hyperactivity rose dramatically from 10% to an average of 91%. Academic performance remained low at approximately 10%. Only when reinforcement was administered for reading was hyperactivity in this area reduced from 91% to

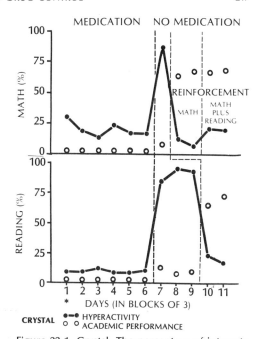

Figure 22-1. Crystal. The percentage of intervals in which hyperactivity took place and the percent of correct math and reading performance. The first and second segments respectively show the effects of medication, and its subsequent withdrawal, on hyperactivity and academic performance. A multiple-baseline analysis of the effects of reinforcement across math and reading and concurrent hyperactivity is shown starting on the third top segment. The last segment shows the effects of reinforcement on math plus reading and its concurrent effect on hyperactivity. (The asterisk indicates one data point averaged over two rather than three days.)

20%. Reading performance increased from 10% to an average of 69%.

Similar results were found for Paul and Dudley, as can be seen in Figures 22-2 and 22-3.

Figure 22-4 shows the pre and post measures of hyperactivity and academic performance for Dudley, Crystal, and Paul as a group. It can be seen that when the children were taking drugs, hyperactivity was well controlled and averaged about 24% during math and reading. When medication was discontinued and a reinforcement program was established to strengthen academic performance, the combined level of hyperactivity was about 20% during math and reading for the three children. This level (20%) of hyperactivity matched that obtained under medication (24%).

During the period when the children were taking drugs, their per cent correct in math and

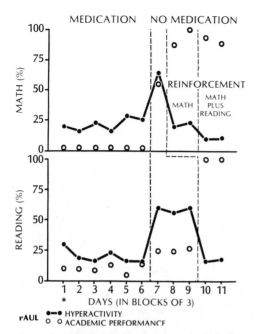

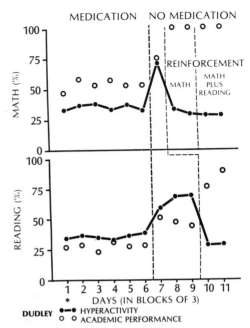

Figure 22-2. Paul. The percentage of intervals in which hyperactivity took place and the percent of correct math and reading performance. The first and second segments respectively show the effects of medication, and its subsequent withdrawal, on hyperactivity and academic performance. A multiple-baseline analysis of the effects of reinforcement across math and reading and concurrent hyperactivity is shown starting on the third top segment. The last segment shows the effects of reinforcement on math plus reading and its concurrent effect on hyperactivity. (The asterisk indicates one data point averaged over two rather than three days.)

Figure 22-3. Dudley. The percentage of intervals in which hyperactivity took place and the percent of correct math and reading performance. The first and second segments respectively show the effects of medication, and its subsequent withdrawal, on hyperactivity and academic performance. A multiple-baseline analysis of the effects of reinforcement across math and reading and concurrent hyperactivity is shown starting on the third top segment. The last segment shows the effects of reinforcement on math plus reading and its concurrent effect on hyperactivity. (The asterisk indicates one data point averaged over two rather than three days.)

reading combined, averaged 12%. When medication was discontinued and a reinforcement program was established, their average per cent correct in both academic subjects increased from 12% to 85%.

DISCUSSION

These findings show that reinforcement of academic performance suppresses hyperactivity, and they thus support and extend the findings of Ayllon and Roberts (1974). Further, the academic gains produced by the behavioral program contrast dramatically with the lack of academic progress shown by these children under medication (Note 1).

The multiple-baseline design demonstrates that

token reinforcement for academic achievement was responsible for the concurrent suppression of hyperactivity. Indeed, while this control was demonstrated during math periods, the children's concurrent hyperactivity during reading remained at a high level, so long as the reinforcement procedure for reading was withheld. Only when reinforcement was introduced for both math and reading performance did the hyperactivity for all three children drop to levels comparable to those controlled by the drug.

The control over hyperactivity by the enhancement of academic performance was quick, stable, and independent of the duration and dosage of the medication received by each child before the program. One child had been under medication for as long as 4 yr, another child for

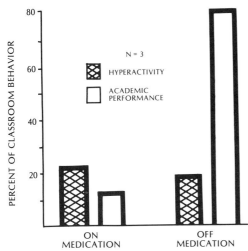

Figure 22-4. Average percent of hyperactivity and academic performance in math and reading for three children. The first two bars summarize findings from the 17-day baseline under drug therapy. The last two bars show results for the final six-day period without drug therapy but with a reinforcement program for both math and reading performance.

1 yr. Despite this extreme difference in history of medication, the behavioral effects were not differential to that history.

When medication was discontinued, hyperactivity increased immediately and to a high level in all three children. The effectiveness of medication in controlling hyperactivity, evaluated through direct observations of behavior, supports the data of earlier studies using recordings based on instrumentation (Hollis et al., 1972; Sprague et al., 1970; Sykes et al., 1971).

During the few days of no medication, hyperactivity became so severe that the teacher and parents freely commented on the gross difference in the children's behavior in school and at home. Their reports centered around such descriptions as "He's just like a whirlwind," "She is climbing the walls, it's awful," "Just can't do a thing with her," "He's not attending, doesn't listen to anything I tell him," and others. It was only with a great deal of support and counselling that the teacher and parents were able to tolerate this stressful period. It was this high level of hyperactivity shown by all three children that allowed the opportunity to test the effectiveness of a reinforcement program for academic performance in controlling hyperactivity.

Since both hyperactivity and academic perfor-

mance increased concurrently, as soon as medication was discontinued, it might be construed that these two dimensions are compatible. This may be an unwarranted conclusion, however, because the slight increments in academic performance concurrent with increments in hyperactivity may only reflect the type of recording method used in this study. For example, measures of the behavior of the children show that once they had finished their academic assignments, they became hyperactive. Thus, academic performance and hyperactivity could take place sequentially. When the time limit for academic performance had expired (e.g., after 10 or 20 min, depending on the subject matter) the child could engage in hyperactivity for the rest of the class period.

It usually took only one session for each child to learn that academic performance was associated with reinforcement while hyperactivity was not, suggesting that in the absence of medication these children react to reinforcement as normal children do. The classroom with reinforcement procedures now set the occasion for academic performance, rather than hyperactivity.

The present results suggest that the continued use of Ritalin and possibly other drugs to control hyperactivity may result in compliant but academically incompetent students. Surely, the goal of school is not to make children into docile robots either by behavioral techniques or by medication. Rather, the goal should be one of providing children with the social and academic tools required to become successful in their social interactions and competent in their academic performance. Judging from the reactions and comments of both parents and teacher, this goal was achieved during the reinforcement period of the study. The parents were particularly relieved that their children, who had been dependent on Ritalin for years, could now function normally in school without the drug. Similarly, the teacher was excited over the fact that she could now build the social and academic skills of the children because they were more attentive and responsive to her than when they were under medication.

On the basis of these findings, it would seem appropriate to recommend that hyperactive children under medication periodically be given the opportunity to be drug-free, to minimize drug dependence and to facilitate change through alternative behavioral techniques. While this study focused on behavioral alternatives to Ritalin for the control of hyperactivity, it is possible that another drug or a combination of medication and a behavioral program may also be helpful.

This study offers a behavioral and educationally justifiable alternative to the use of medication for hyperactive children. The control of hyperactivity by medication, while effective, may be too costly to the child, in that it may retard his academic and social growth, a human cost that schools and society can ill afford.

REFERENCE NOTE

1. For a systematic replication of this study see Layman, *unpublished*.

REFERENCES

Ayllon, T. and Kelly, K. Effects of reinforcement on standardized test performance. *Journal of Applied Behavior Analysis*, 1972, **5**, 447–484.

Ayllon, T., Layman, D., and Burke, S. Disruptive behavior and reinforcement of academic performance. *Psychological Record*, 1972, **22**, 315–323.

Ayllon, T. and Roberts, M. Eliminating discipline problems by strengthening academic performance. *Journal of Applied Behavior Analysis*, 1974, **7**, 71–76.

Becker, W., Madsen, C., Arnold, C., and Thomas, D. The contingent use of teacher attention and praise in reducing classroom behavior problems. *The Journal of Special Education*, 1967, **1**, 287–307.

Campbell, S., Douglas, U., and Morgenstern, G. Cognitive styles in hyperactive children and the effect of methylphenidate. *Journal of Child Psychology and Psychiatry*, 1971, **12**, 55–67.

Comly, H. Cerebral stimulants for children with learning disorders. *Journal of Learning Disabilities*, 1971, **4**, 484–490.

Conners, C., Eisenberg, L., and Barcai, A. Effect of dextro-amphetamine in children: studies on subjects with learning disabilities and school behavior problems. *Archives of General Psychiatry*, 1967, **17**, 478–485.

Conners, C., Eisenberg, L., and Sharpe, L. Effects of methylphenidate (Ritalin) on paired associate learning and Porteus performance in emotionally disturbed children. *Journal of Consulting Psychology*, 1964, **28**, 14–22.

Conners, C. and Rothschild, G. Drugs and learning in children. In G. Helmuch (Ed.), *Learning disorders*, Vol. 3. Seattle, Special Child Publications, 1968.

Conners, K. Recent drug studies with hyperkinetic children. *Journal of Learning Disabilities*, 1971, **4**, 476–483.

Denhoff, E., Davis, A., and Hawkins, A. Effects of dextro-amphetamine on hyperkinetic children: a controlled double blind study. *Journal of Learning Disabilities*, 1971, **4**, 491–499.

Epstein, L., Lasagna, L., Conners, K., and Rodriguez, A. Correlation of dextro-amphetamine excretion and drug response in hyperkinetic children. *Journal of Nervous and Mental Disease*, 1968, **146**, 136–146.

Fish, B. The "one child, one drug" myth of stimulants in hyperkinesis: importance of diagnostic categories in evaluating treatment. *Archives of General Psychiatry*, 1971, **25**, 193–203.

Freibergs, V. and Douglas, V. Concept learning in hyperactive and normal children. *Journal of Abnormal Psychology*, 1969, **74**, 388–395.

Hentoff, N. The drugged classroom. *Evergreen Review*, December, 1970, 6–11.

Hollis, J. and St. Omer, V. Direct measurement of psychopharmacologic response: effects of chlorpromazine on motor behavior of retarded children. *American Journal of Mental Deficiency*, 1972, **76**, 397–407.

Keogh, B. Hyperactivity and learning disorders: review and speculation. *Exceptional Children*, 1971, **38**, 101–109.

Knights, R. and Hinton, G. Minimal brain dysfunction: clinical and psychological test characteristics. *Academic Therapy*, 1968, **4**, 265–273.

Krippner, S., Silverman, R., Cavallo, M., and Healy, M. A study of hyperkinetic children receiving stimulant drugs. *Academic Therapy*, 1973, **8**, 261–269.

Ladd, E. Pills for classroom peace? *Saturday Review*, November, 1970, 66–83.

Layman, D. *A behavioral investigation: the effects of medication on disruptive classroom behavior and academic performance*. Unpublished doctoral dissertation, Georgia State University, 1974.

O'Leary, K. D. and Becker, W. C. Behavior modification of an adjustment class: a token reinforcement program. *Exceptional Children*, 1967, **33**, 637–642.

Sprague, R., Barnes, B., and Werry, J. Methylphenidate and thoridazine: learning, reaction time, activity, and classroom behavior in disturbed children. *American Journal of Orthophyschiatry*, 1970, **40**, 615–628.

Sprague, R. and Toppe, L. Relationship between activity level and delay of reinforcement. *Experimental Child Psychology*, 1966, **3**, 390–397.

Stewart, M., Pitts, F., Craig, A., and Dieruf, W. The hyperactive child syndrome. *American Journal of Orthopsychiatry*, 1966, **36**, 861–867.

Sulzbacher, S. Behavior analysis of drug effects in the classroom. In G. Semb (Ed.), *Behavior analysis and education*. University of Kansas, 1972.

Sykes, D., Douglas, V., Weiss, G., and Minde, K. Attention in hyperactive children and the effect of methylphenidate (Ritalin). *Journal of Child Psychology and Psychiatry*, 1971, **12**, 129–139.

23. The functional independence of response latency and accuracy: implications for the concept of conceptual tempo

MAURICE WILLIAMS   BENJAMIN B. LAHEY

Kagan developed the concept of conceptual tempo to add a new dimension to the understanding and assessment of human intelligence (Kagan, Rosmon, Day, Albert, & Phillips, 1964; Kagan, 1965a). In addition to simply quantifying intelligence in the form of IQ scores, Kagan proposed the assessment of a temporal aspect of "style" of cognitive functioning, conceptual tempo.

Specifically, response latency in choice tasks is believed to mirror a tendency to think over alternatives before choosing (reflective or to make decisions before thinking (impulsive tempo). The Matching Familiar Figures Test (MFF) developed by Kagan et al. (1964), the Kansas Reflection-Impulsivity Test for Preschoolers (KRISP) developed by Wright (1971), and other similar visual matching tests have been constructed to measure this putative trait. Research suggests that the tests have acceptable test-retest reliability, long-term temporal stability, and generality across tests (Kagan et al., 1964).

Studies contrasting children with different tempos have shown that impulsive children make more reading errors (Kagan, 1965b), have lower arithmetic achievement (Cathcart & Liedtke, 1969), make more errors on inductive reasoning tasks (Kagan, Pearson, & Welch, 1966a,b), sustain attention less well (Zelnicker, Jefferey, Ault, & Parsons, 1972), and learn discrimination tasks less rapidly than reflectives (Hemry, 1973; Massari & Schack, 1972). While this body of research apparently suggests that conceptual tempo is a valid and useful concept, its utility can be nevertheless questioned on several grounds.

First, the MFF, KRISP, and other tests classify children as impulsive or reflective on the basis of both latency and errors. Children with short latencies and high errors are termed impulsive, while the opposite group is labeled reflective. Because latency and errors are negatively correlated only to a moderate degree, $-.40$ to $-.65$ (Kagan, 1966), many children with short latencies and low errors, and long latencies and high errors, were excluded from the studies cited above. This suggests that error rates may be of as much importance (or more) as latency in determining the relationship between impulsivity-reflectivity and academic/intellectual performance. At a theoretical level, the moderate degree of negative correlation is a challenge to the construct of conceptual tempo that has never been answered. While it is easy to see that some slow-responding children might not be employing efficient cognitive strategies during their long latencies, how is it that children with very short latencies can score low in errors, when accurate

From the *Journal of Abnormal Child Psychology*, 1977, 5, 371–378. Copyright © 1977 Plenum Publishing Corporation. Reprinted by permission.

This article is based on a master's thesis prepared by the first author under the supervision of the second author.

responding requires reflective (long latency) decision processes in Kagan's model?

Second, a group of studies that have examined the modifiability of conceptual tempo suggest that response latency may not need to be taken into account in applied settings. A number of studies using instructions to respond slowly, modeling of long latencies, and reinforcement for long latencies found changes in latency but no corresponding changes in errors on matching tasks (Debus, 1970; Denney, 1972; Kagan et al, 1966a,b). These findings are reasonable since it is possible, and even probable, that low achievement subjects will extend their latencies without filling the time with productive cognitive activities. Studies in which treatments were aimed at errors, on the other hand, found decreases in errors that sometimes were accompanied by increases in latency (Errickson, Wyne, & Routh, 1973; Meichenbaum & Goodman, 1971; Ridberg, Parke & Hetherington, 1971; Egeland, 1974) and sometimes were not (Zelnicker et al., 1972).

Most of the training procedures that found increases in both accuracy and latency (Egeland, 1974; Michenbaum & Goodman, 1971; Ridberg et al., 1971) taught new, slow "reflective" cognitive strategies to their subjects, whereas the single study that found increases in accuracy without corresponding increases in latency (Zelnicker et al., 1972) trained their subjects using positive verbal reinforcement for correct responding on a task similar to the MFF. Errickson et al. (1973), however, found correlated increases in accuracy and latency using punishment (response cost) procedure for errors that did not involve the direct teaching of new cognitive strategies. It may be, however, that punishment produced increases in latency in this study independent of its effects on accuracy.

These data can be construed to support either of two alternate hypotheses:

1. With the exception of Zelnicker et al. (1972), the data suggest that (a) increases in latency without improvements in the actual reflective cognitive strategies employed will increase latency but not accuracy (the subjects will delay responding but may stare off in space while doing so); (b) directly teaching new reflective cognitive strategies will increase latency (because, as postulated by Kagan, reflective strategies are time-consuming) and decrease errors; and (c) indirectly encouraging more effective cognitive strategies through response consequences for errors will increase both accuracy

and latency for the reasons stated above. Considered in this manner, the data support the theoretical concept of conceptual tempo.

2. An alternate explanation is possible, however. Except for Errickson et al. (1973), the data could also mean that latency and accuracy are independent dimensions of responding, and that improvements in accuracy will be accompanied by increases in latency only when the training procedure *requires* it as an artifactual by-product. The results of Zelnicker et al. (1972) particularly suggest that accuracy can be improved without changing the latency of quick-responding children.

The clinical implications of these two explanations of previous data are very significant. The first explanation suggests that interventions designed to improve accuracy must also take latency into account, whereas the second explanation suggests that the focus could be on accuracy alone. This latter explanation would, then, argue against the necessity for the construct of conceptual tempo, which views latency and accuracy as necessarily related response measures.

In the present study, herefore, positive reinforcement was made contingent upon accurate responses in one group and long latencies in another to determine if these were independent dimensions. Most importantly, reinforcement for both accuracy and long latency was combined in one grop to determine if such a procedure was more effective than reinforcement for accuracy alone.

METHOD

Subjects

The twenty 4- and 5-year-old males and twenty 4- and 5-year-old females from a federally supported day care program serving low-income families who had the shortest latencies and highest number of errors on the KRISP from a group of 90 tested children were used as subjects. All of the children were black and all scored in the "impulsive" range of both latency and errors according to the KRISP norms for the age and sex of each subject.

Procedure

The subjects were randomly assigned to one of four experimental groups within two weeks of pretesting except that equal numbers of males and females were assigned to each group. Each child in each group was taken individually to a quiet room with one or two experimenters for a single treatment session. Immediately after treatment, the subjects were readministered the KRISP as a measure of generalization of change. A second observer was present on 17.5% of the KRISP trials and 22.5% of the baseline and the treatment trials for the purpose of assessing the reliability of latency scores.

The four experimental groups were as follows (the mean ages and KRISP scores of each group are presented in Table 23-1).

Table 23-1. Mean error and latency scores on the KRISP and ages of subjects in each experimental group

Groups	Pretest latency errors		Posttest latency errors		Mean ages
Control (C)	3.7[a]	8.6	6.4	2.9	5–10
Latency (L)	3.6	6.3	7.3	3.1	5–7
Accuracy (A)	3.7	7.1	4.9	2.8	5–7
Accuracy and latency (AL)	3.2	7.9	5.8	4.1	5–6

[a] Latency scores expressed in seconds.

Accuracy (A). During baseline, the subjects were shown a match-to-sample task composed of a sample and four horizontally arranged alternatives, one of which matched the sample. They were asked to find the alternative that matched the sample and point to it. The stimuli were composed of 1 to 3 lower-case letters (10 each) typed without spaces between them, similar to those used in Lahey & McNees (1975) and Lahey & Lefton (1976). Thirty different items were presented in baseline, with the consequences given to either correct or incorrect responses. During treatment, the 30-item block used in baseline was repeated three times as in baseline, except that after every correct response a token was given that could be exchanged later at the rate of 10 tokens per small toy. Contingent praise for getting the response right was also given. The contingency was explained to each subject prior to treatment ("Each time you point to the one that is exactly like the one over here you will win a token.")

Latency (L). The baseline phase of the L group was conducted in the same manner as the A group. Treatment differed, however, in that the tokens were made contingent on response latencies of six or more seconds (measured from the

presentation of the item to the response), regardless of accuracy. This figure was based on KRISP norms. The contingency was explained by telling the subjects, "Point to the one that is exactly like the one over here. Each time you take your time by waiting six seconds before you answer, you will win a token." Praise and correction was also given in these terms.

Accuracy and Latency (AL). In this group, all procedures were the same as in the A and L groups, except that tokens were given only when the response was accurate and had a latency of six or more seconds. The instructions described the contingency in these terms: "Each time you take your time by waiting six seconds before you answer and point to the one that is exactly like the one over here, you will win a token."

Control (C). The control group was conducted in the same manner during the first baseline block of 30 trials and on each of the three succeeding blocks of trials. No instructions or contingencies of any type were used.

RESULTS

Figure 23–1 shows the mean number of correct responses in each block of trials for each group and Figure 23–2 shows the mean response latencies for each group and block. A 2 (reinforcement or no reinforcement for accuracy) × 2 (reinforcement or no reinforcement for latency) × 4 (repeated trial blocks) ANOVA was conducted separately for accuracy and latency, and a 2 × 2 × 2 repeated measures ANOVA was con-

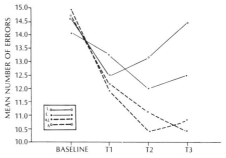

Figure 23-1. The mean number of correct responses in each block of 30 trials in the four experimental groups: reinforcement of accuracy (A), reinforcement of latency (L), reinforcement of both accuracy and latency (AL), and the control group (C).

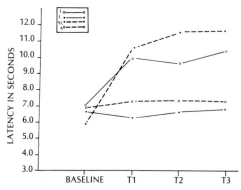

Figure 23-2. The mean response latency in each block of 30 trials in the four experimental groups: reinforcement of accuracy (A), reinforcement of latency (L), reinforcement of both accuracy and latency (AL), and the control group (C).

ducted for pretest-posttest KRISP administrations.

For the accuracy dependent variable, a significant trial blocks effect ($F = 10.02$, $df = 3/108$, $p < .01$) and a significant accuracy × trial blocks interaction was found ($F = 2.99$, $df = 3/108$, $p < .05$), with no other effects or interactions reaching significance. To further examine the accuracy × trial blocks interaction, a Newman-Keuls post hoc comparison was conducted. Because there was not a significant main effect or interaction for the independent variable of reinforcement of latency, the groups could not be separated across this dimension in the post hoc analyses. Therefore, the two groups in which reinforcement was given for accuracy (A and AL) were combined and compared to the two groups in which reinforcement was not given for accuracy (L and C). These analyses showed that the combined A and AL groups did not differ significantly from the combined L and C groups during baseline and the first trial block, but they did differ significantly on the second trial block ($p < .05$) and the third trial block ($p < .01$).

The analyses of the latency dependent variable yielded a significant latency effect ($F = 13.98$, $df = 1/108$, $p < .01$), a significant trial blocks effect ($F = 10.79$, $df = 3/108$, $p < .01$), and a significant latency × trial blocks interaction ($F = 8.65$, $df = 3/108$, $p < .01$). Due to the absence of a main effect or interaction for the independent variable of reinforcement of accuracy, post hoc Newman-Keuls tests were conducted on

the combined groups in which reinforcement was given for latency (L and AL) versus the combined groups in which reinforcement was not given for latency (A and C). These comparisons showed that the combined L and AL groups differed from the combined C and A groups on all trial blocks ($p < .01$) but not during baseline.

Analysis of the pre- and posttest KRISP accuracy scores yielded only a significant trial blocks effect ($F = 91.13$, $df = 1/36$, $p < .01$), and the analysis of KRISP latencies showed only a significant trial blocks effect ($F = 41.11$, $df = 1/36$, $p < .01$).

Interrater reliability for latency was assessed using a Pearson product-moment correlation coefficient yielding $r = .96$ for KRISP trials and $r = .95$ for baseline and treatment trials.

DISCUSSION

These results suggest that reinforcement of accuracy produces changes in accuracy but not in latency, and vice versa. Furthermore, reinforcement of both latency and accuracy (AL) was not different from the accuracy only group (A) in producing improvements in accuracy, even though AL showed concomitant increases in latency while A did not.

In this experiment at least, accuracy and latency were shown to be completely independent as far as improvements in accuracy were concerned. Although these data are only preliminary, they suggest that the concept of conceptual tempo may not be necessary in applied settings. Perhaps improvements in accuracy can be achieved without taking latency into account at all. These data also suggest that longer latencies could be produced in "impulsive" children if there were a practical reason for doing so, but as Skinner (1969) has suggested, low errors and short latencies are usually the desired end product in most educational and occupational situations.

These data do not necessarily mean, however, that visual search and other activities that subjects assumedly engage in between stimulus and response onset are not important. Egeland (1974), Ridberg et al. (1971), and Meichenbaum and Goodman (1971) produced decreases in errors by teaching more effective search strategies. The present data do indicate, however, that the functional dependence between latency and errors found by these investigators was an artifact of their perhaps artificially time-consuming search strategies. Search strategies and decision processes are important, but while they may occur in real time, their minimum durations are apparently within the limits of even "impulsive" children.

REFERENCES

Cathcart, W.. G., & Liedtke, W. Reflectiveness/impulsiveness and mathematics achievement. *The Arithmetic Teacher*, 1969 (Nov.), 563–567.

Debus, R. L. Effects of brief observation of model behavior on conceptual tempo of impulsive children. *Developmental Psychology*, 1970, *2*, 22–32.

Denney, D.. R. Modeling effects upon conceptual style and cognitive tempo. *Child Development*, 1974, *43*, 105–119.

Egeland, B. Training impulsive children in the use of more efficient scanning techniques. *Child Development*, 1974, *45*, 165–171.

Errickson, E. A., Wyne, M. D., & Routh, D. K. A response-cost procedure for reduction of impulsive behavior of academically handicapped children. *Journal of Abnormal Child Psychology*, 1973, *1*, 350–357.

Hemry, F. P. Effect of reinforcement conditions on a discrimination learning task for impulsive versus reflective children. *Child Development*, 1973, *44*, 657–660.

Kagan, J. Impulsive and reflective children: Significance of conceptual tempo. In J. D. Krumboltz (Ed.), *Learning and the educational process*. Chicago: Rand McNally, 1965. Pp. 133–161. (a)

Kagan, J. Reflection-impulsivity and reading ability in primary grade children. *Child Development*, 1965, *36*, 609–628. (b)

Kagan, J. Reflection-impulsivity: The generality and dynamics of conceptual tempo. *Journal of Abnormal Psychology*, 1966, *71*(1), 17–24.

Kagan, J., Rosmon, B. L., Day, D., Albert, and Phillips, W. Information processing in the child: Significance of analytic and reflective attitudes. *Psychological Monographs*, 1964, *78*(1, Whole No. 578).

Kagan, J., Pearson, L., & Welch, L. Conceptual impulsivity and inductive reasoning. *Child Development*, 1966, *37*, 583–594. (a)

Kagan, J., Pearson, L., & Welch, L. Modifiability of an impulsive tempo. *Journal of Educational Psychology*, 1966, *57*, 359–365. (b)

Lahey, B. B., & Lefton, L. A. Discrimination of letter combinations in good and poor readers. *Journal of Special Education*, 1976, *10*, 205–210.

Lahey, B. B., & McNees, M. P. Letter discrimination errors in kindergarten through third grade: Assessment and operant training. *Journal of Special Education*, 1975, *9*, 191–199.

Massari, D. J., & Schack, M. L. Discrimination learning by reflective and impulsive children as a function of reinforcement schedule. *Developmental Psychology*, 1972, *6*, 183.

Meichenbaum, D. H., & Goodman, J. Training impulsive children to talk to themselves: A means of developing self control. *Journal of Abnormal Psychology*, 1971, *77*, 115–126.

Messer, S. B. Reflection-impulsivity: Stability and school failure. *Journal of Educational Psychology*, 1970, *61*, 487–490.

Ridberg, E. H., Parke, R. D., & Hetherington, E. M. Modification of impulsive and reflective cognitive styles through observation of film-mediated models. *Developmental Psychology*, 1971, *5*, 369–377.

Skinner, B. F. *The technology of teaching*. New York: appleton-Century-Crofts, 1969.

Wright, J. C. *The Kansas Reflection-Impulsivity Scale for Preschoolers (KRISP)*. St. Louis: CEMREL, 1971.

Zelnicker, T., Jefferey, W. E., Ault, R., & Parsons, J. Analysis and modification of search strategies of impulsive and reflective children on the Matching Familiar Figures test. *Child Development*, 1972, *43*, 321–355.

IV
Behavior therapy
and pharmacological treatments

Three chapters elucidate the relationship between behavior therapy and the use of stimulant medications in Section IV. O'Leary and Pelham (Chap. 24), like the earlier chapter by Ayllon, Layman, and Kandel (Chap. 22), show that many hyperactive children can be taken off stimulant medications with no loss of improvement if their parents have been trained in the use of behavior management procedures. This study is important in dealing successfully with the important problem of weaning children from potentially harmful medications, but did not control for placebo or order effects (the behavior therapy might not have been as successful if it had not been preceded by drug therapy), and used the relatively weak dependent measure of parent rating scales. It does provide important confirmation within these limits, however, of the parent training program used by O'Leary, Pelham, Rosenbaum, and Price (Chap. 14).

The chapter by Wulbert and Dries (Chap. 25) illustrates the single-subject approach to the study of drug effects. In this methodology, multiple behaviors are continuously measured under a variety of different experimental conditions. In this study, the effects of both methylphenidate and behavior therapy were found to be specific to some behaviors and some situations, fortunately in ways that could be complementary to each other. This valuable methodology, therefore, revealed information that is generally hidden in large-group studies that obtain small amounts of information on a large number of individuals rather than obtaining a large amount of information on a small number of subjects. The fact that data were collected as part of an evaluation of a clinical case in an applied setting rather than as an experimental study is an excellent illustration of the value of single-subject designs in applied settings. An extensive discussion of these types of design can be found in Hersen and Barlow (1976).

In a sophisticated comparative study, Gittelman-Klein, Klein, Abikoff, Katz, Gloisten, and Kates (Chap. 26) found that behavior therapy plus placebo pills was not as effective in controlling high rates of inappropriate behavior measured in a variety of ways as either methylphenidate alone or methylphenidate plus behavior therapy. The combination of behavior therapy and stimulant medication was slightly superior to medication alone, but the differences were not statistically significant.

A more recent major study by Wolraich, Drummond, Salomon, O'Brien, and Sivage (1978) found stimulants and behavior therapy to be generally equal in controlling hyperactive behavior, but behavior therapy was clearly superior in improving classroom academic performance. These findings are particularly important since the study used the dosage level of methylphenidate (.3 mg/kg) suggested by Sleator and Sprague (1974) to be most effective in improving cognitive performance in laboratory studies.

Additional comparative studies are needed, of course, particularly ones using both of the behavior therapy techniques developed by Ayllon and the O'Learys, before the relative efficacy of these approaches can be fully assessed. For the foreseeable future, however, it is clear that both stimulant medications and behavior therapy will continue to see extensive use in applied settings.

REFERENCES

Hersen, M., & Barlow, D. H. *Single-case experimental designs: Strategies for studying behavior change*. New York: Pergamon Press, 1976.

Sleator, E. K. & Sprague, R. L. Dose effects of stimulants in hyperkinetic children. *Psychopharmacology Bulletin*, 1974, *10*, 29–31.

Wolraich, M., Drummond, T., Salomon, M. K., O'Brien, M. L., & Sivage, C. Effects of methylphenidate alone and in combination with behavior modification procedures on the behavior and academic performance of hyperactive children. *Journal of Abnormal Child Psychology*, 1978, *6*, 149–61.

24. Behavior therapy and withdrawal of stimulant medication with hyperactive children

SUSAN G. O'LEARY   WILLIAM E. PELHAM

Psychopharmacological intervention has been the most frequent treatment for hyperactive children for two decades. Recent estimates suggest that approximately 2 percent of all U.S. elementary-school children are receiving psychostimulant medication for hyperactivity (1). Dextroamphetamine (Dexedrine) and methylphenidate (Ritalin) are the most frequently administered psychostimulant medications. The efficacy of these drugs in changing teacher ratings of hyperactivity and improving sustained attention has been well established (2).

Despite the consistency of salutary effects of stimulants on hyperactive children in school settings, the exclusive reliance on drug treatment has been questioned repeatedly (3, 4, 5). The concern stems from several sources. First, such treatment appears to have no long-term effect on academic achievement (6, 7). Second, such treatment does not appear to be associated with long-term amelioration of social problems (7). Third, increases in heart rate and blood pressure have been observed (8), and decreases in the rate of height and weight gains have been found in some studies (4). Although the decrease in weight gain is probably reversible, the same may not be true of the decrease in height gains. Fourth, the child's attribution of his behavior change to the medication may have deleterious long-range effects. The child may learn that the only way to control his behavior is to take a pill (9). Fifth, because of the anorexic and insomnious effects of the stimulant medications, they are usually not administered in the late afternoon. Since the effects of the medication last only 3 to 5 hours, change in the children's behavior at home is often not observed (e.g., 10). Thus, the parents whose children are given medication without psychological consultation are often faced with serious problems at home. Because of these concerns, an increasing number of parents are seeking alternatives to medication, and many are particularly interested in successfully withdrawing their children from medication.

One possible alternative to medication, behavior therapy, has been effective in treating hyperactive children selected on the basis of measures used in previous psychopharmacological investigations (11, 12). These studies are limited by the brevity of their treatment (4 to 10 weeks) and their sole focus on school intervention. Further, the majority of the children in these studies had never received medication for hyperactivity. It might thus be argued that such subjects may not have been as severely disturbed as children who have received medication.

Two classroom studies involved direct com-

From *Pediatrics*. Copyright 1977, American Academy of Pediatrics. Reprinted by permission.

This research was supported in part by NIMH grant No. RO3MH27763. The opinions expressed herein, however, do not necessarily reflect the position or policy of NIMH. We are grateful to Carol Friedling for her help in testing and data collection and to Dr. Fred Mehlhop, pediatric consultant.

parisons of behavior therapy and stimulants with nonretarded children (13, 14). In the first study, a within subject analysis of three children in a special class showed that the effects of the two treatments were generally similar although the results are limited by the brevity of the behavioral intervention (12 days). The Gittleman-Klein et al. study involved 8-week treatments, and the psychostimulants were found to be superior to behavior therapy in changing school behavior. Mothers' ratings did not indicate differential improvement at home for the treated groups.

Attempts to withdraw children from medication are rare. In a single case study, Pelham (15) successfully withdrew stimulant medication while simultaneously implementing behavior therapy for a child who had been receiving drug therapy for 4 years. Withdrawal and treatment lasted for 9 months, and the results suggested that the child made substantially greater school improvement under the behavioral program than under the pharmacological intervention.

The present study was conducted to extend the evaluation of behavior therapy for hyperactive children being withdrawn from stimulant medication to include a focus on home as well as school problems.

METHOD
Subjects

Referrals were solicited through pediatricians, schools, and the news media for elementary-school children who were currently receiving stimulant medication for hyperactivity and whose parents were interested in an alternative to drug therapy. Children were not accepted for treatment if they were mentally retarded, psychotic, or showed evidence of organic brain damage. Of the ten families who contacted us, three did not complete the program. Two of these were dropped after the assessment phase since the children showed no significant behavior problems when their medication was discontinued. The third family withdrew during the course of the program because marital problems and lack of cooperation from the school obviated treatment implementation. The remaining seven children (Table 24-1) were functioning within the normal range of intelligence and displayed behaviors associated with the hyperkinetic syndrome, although S1 and S6 also exhibited behaviors characteristic of the unsocialized aggressive reaction of childhood.

Setting and staff

Treatment sessions were conducted at the State University of New York at Stony Brook and in the Children's schools. Three children were treated by the first author, a New York State certified clinical psychologist, and four by the second author, who was completing his internship in clinical psychology. A board-certified pediatrician served as medical consultant, and family physicians were advised of the children's participation and consulted regarding decisions to withdraw medication.

Dependent measures

Classroom observations. Trained observers recorded the frequency of off-task behavior when the children were engaged in independent seat work in their regular classes. Off-task behavior was defined as any behavior which disrupted the class and was not sanctioned by the teacher, e.g., aggression, playing with objects, being out of seat without permission, not attending to class work, and making noises or talking without permission. Observations were made on a 10-second observe/5-second record basis. During each half-hour observation session, observers alternately recorded the behavior of the experimental subject and a randomly selected same-sexed peer in 5-minute intervals, yielding 15 minutes of observation for each child per session. Reliability was assessed periodically by a second observer and was calculated by dividing the number of agreements by the number of agreements plus disagreements and multiplying by 100. The average reliability across the study was 67%.

Teacher rating scale. Using the abbreviated form of the Conners Teacher Rating Scale, TRS (16, 17), the classroom teachers rated the subjects' behavior during each assessment phase. Each of 10 items was rated on a scale from 0 (occurred not at all) to 3 (occurred very much). The mean ratings are reported in Table 24-2.

Parent rating scales. The mothers rated their children's behavior on the Werry-Weiss-Peters Activity Scale, WWP (18), during the first contact with the project and again during the post-treatment assessment phase. Each of the 22 items was rated on a scale from 0 (does not occur) to 2 (yes, occurs very much). The total scores (possi-

Table 24-1.

	Age (yrs/mos)	Grade	Class type	Type	Dosage	Duration	School	Home
S_1	8–8	3	Learning Disability (19 Students)	Ritalin	15 mg (AM) 15 mg (noon) 10 mg (night)	1½ yrs	destructive; immature; impulsive; short attention span	destructive; no friends; failure to complete work; inappropriate vocalizations
S_2	10–3	5	Regular	Ritalin	10 mg bID	4½ yrs	explosive outbursts; few friends; poor articulation	explosive outbursts; few friends; poor articulation
S_3	9–0	4	Regular (Open)	Cylert	37 mg qAM	½ yr	short attention span; failure to complete assignments	problems organizing himself, e.g., getting ready for school
S_4	8–1	3	Regular (Open)	Ritalin	10 mg (AM) 5 mg (noon)	1½ yrs	failure to complete work and to follow instructions	fighting; disobedience
S_5	8–6	3	Regular	Ritalin	10 mg (AM) 5 mg (noon)	½ yr	failure to complete work and to follow instructions	fighting; arguing
S_6	8–11	4	Regular	Cylert	75 mg qAM	¾ yr	noncompliance; tantrums; poor peer relations	noncompliance; tantrums; poor peer relations
S_7	7–3	2	Special Class (10 students)	Dexedrine	15 mg spansule qAM	1½ yrs	disobedient; failure to complete work	disobedient; arguing

ble range of 0–44) are reported in Table 24–2. Mothers similarly rated the children on the 35-item Aggressive-conduct disorder factor of the Conners Parent Rating Scale, PRS (19). Each item was rated on a scale from 1 (not at all) to 4 (very much). Mean item scores are presented in Table 24–2.

Procedure

Pretreatment assessment. During the initial contact with the parents, the treatment program was outlined; a detailed assessment of the family and the child's behavior at home was obtained; and the mother rated the child on the WWP and PRS. The initial contact with the teacher provided a detailed assessment of the child's behavior at school; the treatment program was outlined; and the teacher completed a practice TRS. The pretreatment assessment was then conducted. Children were evaluated in school for 1 week on-medication and for 1 week off-medication. Three classroom observations were made each week, and the teachers completed a TRS at the end of each week. Three children were randomly designated to be withdrawn from medication for week 1 and four for week 2. Teachers and observers were unaware of when medication was being given, although teachers were told that the children would be off-medication for 1 of the 2 weeks and that they could contact the therapist at any time if the child's behavior in class became intolerable. This occurred for one child (S1), and medication was reinstated after only 3 days.

Following pretreatment, a decision was made either to withdraw the child from all medication immediately or to withdraw medication gradually based on the degree of response to medication and the severity of the child's behavior off-medication. Four children (S3, S4, S5, and S7) received no further medication through the end of the school year. In two cases (S1, S2), the therapist, in conjunction with the teacher and family, elected to withdraw medication on a gradual basis. For S1 and S2, both AM and noon dosages were reduced, noon administration was eliminated, and finally AM administration was discontinued as the child's behavior in school improved. Complete withdrawal was accomplished for these Ss in 2.5 months.

Medication was initially withdrawn completely for S6, but his violent tantrums proved too disruptive for his school to tolerate. He was then placed on 10 mg Ritalin (5 mg bid); the medication was changed from Cylert as Ritalin is

more amenable to a program of gradual withdrawal. Complete withdrawal was not accomplished by the time therapist contact ended, but the parents continued withdrawal so that by posttreatment assessment the child was receiving a daily dosage which varied from 0 to 2.5 mg.

Treatment. During the 4 months following initial assessment the therapist conducted an average of 18 sessions (range 16–21) which were divided approximately equally between the family and the teacher. Initially, both the teacher and the family were seen on a weekly basis, but contacts were gradually reduced to once every 2 or 3 weeks.

Although individual variations in treatment procedures were developed for each child, all interventions included the following elements. Parents read and discussed with the therapist *Parents Are Teachers* (20), a manual designed to teach parents behavioral principles and methods for dealing with children's problems. Praise for appropriate behavior, ignoring minor disruptions, punishment (e.g., being sent to his room for brief periods), and if necessary, individual token programs were implemented in the home. Teachers were also taught to use these same procedures with respect to classroom behavior.

In all cases a daily report (11) was instituted at school. Each teacher in conjunction with the therapist developed a list of three to five problem behaviors on which to focus. Both academic and social behaviors were selected for the teacher to monitor and report to the parents. The behaviors and success criteria were changed periodically as the children progressed. For example, the daily report might initially be comprised of: (1) no tantrums, (2) began work immediately, (3) returned homework, and (4) completed two assignments. A later revision might include: (1) played nicely at recess, (2) completed all assignments, and (3) wrote neatly.

More specifically, S5 never completed any of his assigned work in school. Rather than requiring him to finish all of his work in order to receive a good daily report, the teacher set as an initial goal 50% of the math problems, a level slightly above his usual completion rate. In the following 5 or 6 weeks S5's criterion for math completion was gradually raised to 100%, a goal which he met regularly. Then a second similar criterion was established in another area, language, and the criterion was gradually increased for that subject. The same procedure was followed for each subject area until S5 was completing most of his assigned classwork on a regular basis. Care was taken to establish goals which the child was able to meet at least 75% of the time, so that communication between the school and the home was no longer one of failure but rather one of success. At the end of the day parents rewarded the child's successes with such consequences as praise, special after-school snacks, tokens incorporated into the home token program, or an extra half-hour of television. Daily reports were faded to weekly reports when possible, and family weekend activities were often used as rewards.

When necessary, therapeutic strategies other than daily reports and systematic teacher attention were employed in the schools. For example, S1 made minimal progress under the standard daily report procedure. He apparently was not able to delay gratification until the end of the day. Therefore, his teacher gave him immediate rewards in the form of coupons worth 5 minutes of extra TV time for completing each segment of his school work. S4 had a small reminder card taped on his desk each morning to prompt him to begin his daily routine quickly. A self-control procedure was instituted for S2. He recorded instances when he responded appropriately to teasing and occasions when he overreacted. This self-monitoring dramatically reduced the frequency of outbursts in the classroom. In two cases (S1 and S6) an exclusion procedure was used contingent upon severe tantrum behavior in the school. With this procedure, outbursts which included serious aggression and loud and continuous swearing and screaming resulted in the child's being sent home for the rest of the day and being restricted for that day from engaging in pleasurable activities.

In addition to individual variation in the children's school programs, adaptations of the basic therapy regimen were developed for some of the families. S4 was videotaped with his parents and brother while the family was engaged in a structured task. The therapist later viewed the tape with the parents and discussed how they controlled their children's behavior, e.g., the clear relationship between their behavior (nagging) and their children's behavior (continued misbehavior) was demonstrated. In other cases (S1 and S3) where token programs were being used in the home, parents were advised to include all their children in the program both to avoid sibling rivalry and to motivate the siblings to support the positive changes in the hyperactive child. Occasionally, therapy sessions were held

in small groups. Several parents commented that it was helpful to learn what procedures other parents with similar problems were finding effective.

At the end of the 4-month therapy period, the therapist stopped seeing the families and teachers. At this point parents and teachers were encouraged to continue any aspects of the program that they found helpful. The therapist had no contact with either the families or the teachers for the 4 weeks preceding posttreatment assessment.

Posttreatment assessment. When therapist contact had been terminated for 4 weeks, teachers and parents completed the appropriate rating scales and three classroom observations were conducted.

RESULTS
Classroom Observations [1]

Analyses of these data focused on three questions:

1. When the experimental children were not receiving medication, were they off-task more often than comparison children?

2. Was the off-task behavior of the treated children affected by medication?

3. Did the experimental subjects improve with behavioral treatment?

During pretreatment assessment and without medication, the hyperactive children were off-task significantly more than comparison children ($t = 5.46$, $df = 12$, $p < .001$). As can be seen in Table 24–2 and Figure 24–1, these two groups did not differ either when treated children were receiving medication or during posttreatment assessment. No significant changes were noted in the comparison children's behavior. Medication reduced off-task behavior ($t = 3.99$, $df = 6$, $p < .005$) for all children, and the average degree of improvement was 48%. An evaluation of the treated children's off-medication behavior pre- and posttreatment showed that their off-task behavior improved significantly ($t = 2.12$, $df = 6$, $p < .05$). The behavioral treatment effect was observed for five children, and the mean improvement for all seven children was 33%.

Teacher Ratings

Medication produced a significant effect on the TRS ($t = 2.19$, $df = 6$, $p < .05$). The effect was observed for six children, and all children im-

Table 24-2.

	% Off-task behavior						Abbreviated Connors teacher rating scale			Werry-Weiss-Peters activity scale (mother)		Aggressive-conduct factor (mother)	
	Pre-On		Pre-Off		Post-Off		Pre-On	Pre-Off	Post-Off	Pre-On	Post-Off	Pre-On	Post-Off
Subject	T	C	T	C	T	C							
1	28.7	25.3	73.3	13.3	18.3	38.9	1.1	2.1	.5	34.0	17.0	1.9	1.4
2	.0	3.9	11.6	41.5	13.9	8.3	1.4	3.0	2.1	18.0	15.0	2.2	1.9
3	48.9	32.2	65.0	28.3	35.0	37.2	.4	.6	.6	28.0	18.0	1.5	1.2
4	37.2	31.7	44.6	21.7	73.3	50.0	.5	.7	1.6	24.0	9.0	2.3	1.2
5	45.6	16.1	66.6	17.5	17.8	21.7	1.3	2.0	.9	17.0	10.0	2.0	1.6
6	35.0	32.2	50.0	25.5	33.9	42.8	2.5	2.0	.4	32.0	12.0	2.5	1.6
7	19.4	48.3	62.5	65.0	25.0	37.8	.0	.8	.4	25.0	7.0	1.7	1.5
Mean	30.7	27.1	53.4	30.4	31.0	33.8	1.0	1.6	.9	25.4	12.6	2.0	1.5

Data Pre- and Post-treatment Both On and Off Medication for Individual Subjects Including Classroom Observations of Treated (T) and Comparison (C) Children, Teacher Ratings, and Parent Ratings.

proved an average of 39%. Using the accepted cut-off of two standard deviations above the mean on the TRS (i.e., 1.5 or higher) to indicate hyperactivity (21), four of the seven children would have been so classified off-medication prior to treatment. Treatment resulted in significant improvement ($t = 1.97$, $df = 6$, $p < .05$) with five children showing reductions in problem behavior. The percentage of improvement for all children during treatment averaged 34%.

Parent Ratings

Significant treatment effects were found on the WWP ($t = 5.40$, $df = 6$, $p < .001$) and the Ag-

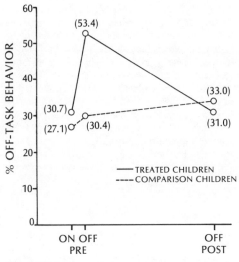

Figure 24-1.

gressive-conduct disorder factor of PRS ($t = 3.43$, $df = 6$, $p < .01$) with all children improving on both measures. The degree of improvement averaged 49% and 33%, respectively, on the two scales.

DISCUSSION

The present results suggest that behavior therapy is an effective and viable alternative intervention for some children who receive stimulant medication for hyperactivity. With respect to the group as a whole, the effectiveness of the treatment program was supported for changing behavior at school. On the observational measures, the children's posttreatment behavior in the classroom was virtually equivalent to the comparison children's behavior and to their own on-medication behavior prior to treatment. Similarly, the teachers' ratings after treatment were comparable to their ratings of the children while they were receiving medication, although the average rating at each of these times was one standard deviation above the mean for "normal" children (21).

The effectiveness of the school intervention for individual children varied, and the nature of that variation is instructive. The two children (S3 and S4) who showed the least improvement at school in terms of the TRS and the therapists' evaluations attended a school which was architecturally "open," i.e., several classes were conducted in a large space with no walls. These children were not acting-out, conduct problem children, and were not rated as particularly hyperactive on the Conners TRS. Rather, their problems were primarily attentional in nature.

They had difficulty completing tasks, organizing their work, and ignoring the many distractions in their environment. The therapists felt that these attentional problems went relatively unnoticed in the open environment.

The treatment appeared to be more effective for changing social behaviors in school than for improving attentional skills. With the exception of S2 who displayed infrequent but severe outbursts, the social behavior of all children improved dramatically. Although the results were generally not as striking for attentional skills, the two children (S1 and S5) who showed the most off-task behavior initially also showed the most improvement. Both of these boys were in highly structured rather than open school settings. Finally, a major variable which appeared to influence the changes occurring in the school setting was the degree of cooperation and commitment shown by the individual teachers and principals.

Psychostimulant medication, as it is currently administered, provides little aid to hyperactive children and their families after school hours and during the summer (10). The results of the present study clearly showed that behavior therapy resulted in significantly improved behavior at home as reflected in parents' ratings of their children's behavior on medication before behavioral treatment began and after the behavior therapy program. Ratings on the WWP Activity Scale decreased three standard deviations to within one standard deviation of the normal mean (18). Parents also rated their children as less aggressive on the Aggressive Conduct factor of the PRS. The parents reported changes in their sons' abilities to interact with other children, to control their impulses, and to cope effectively with everyday problems. In some cases (S1, S5, S6), the atmosphere at home changed radically from that of suspicion, expectation of problems, and hopelessness, to one characterized by shared responsibility, warmth, and an expectation for continued improvement. The factors influencing the effectiveness of the treatment for individual children at home are not clear, but improvement seemed to be related to a high degree of parental commitment to the therapy program.

The effects of the present withdrawal and treatment program are encouraging. However, it should be noted that behavior therapy is more expensive than drug treatment and should not be expected to benefit families who are not well motivated to attempt such an alternative to medication. Hopefully, future replications of withdrawal and behavior therapy programs will expand the sample size and include evaluations of academic behavior and long-term maintenance of treatment effects.

SUMMARY

Seven boys receiving stimulant medication for hyperactivity were withdrawn from that medication in conjunction with participation in a behavior therapy program. Withdrawal of medication was accomplished either immediately or on a gradual basis. Withdrawal decisions were determined primarily by the degree of severity of the child's behavior at school and the feasibility of dealing with that behavior in the academic environment. Although there was variability in the children's responses to both medication and behavior therapy, a realistic alternative to medication was substantiated. The children learned to function effectively in school without medication, and parents reported that their children behaved significantly better at home following behavior therapy than they had while on medication.

NOTES

1. All tests were one-tailed and analyses for correlated means were used for repeated measures on the same children.

REFERENCES

1. Krager, J. M., Safer, D. M.: Type and prevalence of medication used in the treatment of hyperactive children. *N Engl J Med* 291:1118, 1974.
2. Sroufe, L. A.: Drug treatment of children with behavior problems. In F. D. Horowitz (Ed.) *Review of child development research* (Vol. 4). Chicago: University of Chicago Press, 1975.
3. Sroufe, L. A., Stewart, M. A.: Treating problem children with stimulant drugs. *N Engl J Med* 289:407, 1973.
4. Safer, D. J., Allen, R. P.: *Hyperactive children: Diagnosis and management.* Baltimore: University Park Press, 1976.
5. Stewart, M. A., Olds, S. W.: *Raising a hyperactive child.* New York: Harper and Row, 1973.
6. Rie, H. E., Rie, E. D., Stewart, S., Ambuel, J. P.: The effects of methylphenidate on underachieving children. *J Consult Clin Psychol* 44:250, 1976.
7. Weiss, G., Kruger, E., Danielson, U., Elman, M.: effect of long-term treatment of hyperactive children with methylphenidate. *Can Med Assoc J* 112:159, 1975.
8. Rapaport, J. L., Quinn, P. O., Bradbard, G., Riddle, K. D., Brooks, E.: Imipramine and

methylphenidate treatments of hyperactive boys. *Arch Gen Psychiatry* 30:789, 1974.

9. Whalen, C. K., Henker, B.: Psychostimulants and children: A review. *Psychol Bull* 83:1113, 1976.

10. Sleator, E. K., von Neumann, A. W.: methylphenidate in the treatment of hyperactive children. *Clin Pediatr* 13:19, 1974.

11. O'Leary, K. D., Pelham, W. E., Rosenbaum, A., Price, G. H.: Behavioral treatment of hyperkinetic children: An experimental analysis of its usefulness. *Clin Pediatr* 15:274, 1976.

12. Rosenbaum, A., O'Leary, K. D., Jacob, R. G.: behavioral intervention with hyperactive children: Group consequences as a supplement to individual contingencies. *Behav Ther* 6:315, 1975.

13. Ayllon, T., Layman, D., Kandel, H. J.: A behavioral-educational alternative to drug control of hyperactive children. *J Appl Behav Anal* 8:137, 1975.

14. Gittleman-Klein, R., Klein, D. F., Abikoff, H., Katz, S., Gloisten, A. C., Kates, W.: Relative efficacy of methylphenidate and behavior modification in hyperkinetic children: An interim report. *J Abnorm Child Psychol* 4:361, 1976.

15. Pelham, W. E.: Behavioral treatment of hyperkinesis. *Am J Dis Child* 130:565, 1976.

16. Conners, C. K.: A teacher rating scale for use in drug studies with children. *Am J Psychiatry* 126:884, 1969.

17. Sprague, R. L., Sleator, E. K.: Effects of psychopharmacological agents on learning disabilities. *Pediat Clin North Amer* 20:719, 1973.

18. Routh, D. K., Schroeder, C. S., O'Tuama, L. A.: Development of activity level in children. *Dev Psychol* 10:163, 1974.

19. Conners, C. K.: Symptom patterns in hyperkinetic, neurotic, and normal children. *Child Dev* 41:667, 1970.

20. Becker, W. C.: *Parents are teachers: A child management program*. Champaign, Illinois: Research Press, 1971.

21. Werry, J. S., Sprague, R. L., Cohen, M. N.: Conners' Teacher Rating Scale for use in drug studies with children—an empirical study. *J Abnorm Child Psychol*, 3:217, 1975.

25. The relative efficacy of methylphenidate (Ritalin) and behavior-modification techniques in the treatment of a hyperactive child

MARGARET WULBERT   ROBERT DRIES

Two treatments for the hyperactive and disruptive child have become much used in recent years. Behavior-management techniques have been successfully taught to parents and teachers (e.g., O'Leary, Becker, Evans, & Saudargas, 1969; Wahler, Winkel, Peterson, & Morrision, 1965) and reinforcement regimes have been adapted to both home and school settings to control such behaviors as visual orientation (Quay, Werry, McQueen, & Sprague, 1966), out-of-seat and talking-out behavior (O'Leary & Becker, 1967), school attendance (O'Leary et al., 1969), aggression (Bernal, Duryel, Pruetl & Burns, 1968; Patterson, Jones, Whittier, & Wright, 1965; O'Leary & Drabman, 1971), self-control and self-reinforcement (Meichenbaum & Goodman, 1971; Palkes, Stewart & Kahana, 1968; Ridberg, Parke, & Hetherington, 1971), and actual school achievement (Hewett, Taylor, & Artuso, 1969). Simultaneously, the prescription of methylphenidate (Ritalin) and the amphetamines has also been on the rise (Grinspoon & Singer, 1973). Although the combined use of both behavior-modification techniques and stimulant drugs may be frequent in clinical practice, there is little or no research to support the assumption that use of stimulants facilitates or enhances learning beyond what might be expected from contingency management techniques alone (Conrad, Dworkin, Shai, & Tobiessen, 1971; Christensen & Sprague, 1973).

The effect of methylphenidate and the amphetamines on the behavior of the hyperactive child is now recognized as far from monolithic (Grinspoon & Singer, 1973; Sroufe, 1975). Global behavior ratings made by parents and teachers may show improvement with drug management, as compared to placebo (Sroufe, 1975). However, drug effects are dependent on several variables. The degree of structure in a given situation appears to be one such crucial variable. The medicated child, compared to the child on placebo, may be less active and more goal directed within the structure of the classroom (Cohen, Douglas, & Morgenstern, 1971; Sprague et al., 1970), but may be more active and less directed in the free-field situation of the playground (Millichap & Boldrey, 1967; Witter, 1971). Analogously, there is some evidence that parents are less able than teachers to discern drug effects from placebo effects within the relatively unrestrained home behavior of their child (Ellis, Witt, Reynolds, & Sprague, 1974). Hence, setting effects would seem to be significant.

Task effects are also apparent. Research reviews (Grinspoon & Singer, 1973; Sroufe, 1975)

Reprinted by permission from the *Journal of Applied Behavior Analysis*, 1977, *10*, 21–31. Copyright 1977 by the Society for the Experimental Analysis of Behavior, Inc.

The authors wish to thank Judith Jorgensen for her coordination of the double-blind prescription of medication, and Jayana Emery for his aid in the collection of data.

suggest that vigilance tasks, those requiring rote learning and/or fine motor control, are facilitated by medication. Problem-solving potential and abstract reasoning ability do not appear to be enhanced (Sroufe, 1975). Thus, evidence to date would indicate that the type of learning task involved needs to be specified in determining drug effect for these children. While the teacher's global rating of the child's classroom behavior may improve under medication as compared to placebo, the child's actual school achievement may be unaffected (Sroufe, 1975).

Another factor to be considered is that of the observation system employed in assessing the usefulness of the drug. Although literature reviews fairly consistently report positive findings for drug management when global ratings are used, there is less consistency when more specific behaviors are charted (Grinspoon & Singer, 1973; Sroufe, 1975). For instance, activity level as monitored by a stabilimeter, has actually increased with medication even when the child is rated as globally improved. (Millichap & Boldrey, 1967).

Yet another issue is that of whether enhanced attention-to-task in certain situations is a stimulant drug effect unique or "paradoxical" to hyperactive children. Since little or no research utilizing normal children as controls is available, it is not known whether methylphenidate and the amphetamines would have a similar effect on normal children (Sroufe, 1975).

The present study attempted to investigate several of the above variables. The relative efficacy of methylphenidate (Ritalin), placebo, and reinforcement contingencies was assessed with regard to several criterion tasks and specified behaviors. Further, drug *versus* placebo effects were monitored in two settings—a clinic setting, simulating a one-to-one school structure, and the relatively unstructured home setting. Hence, setting, task, and observation schema variables were taken into account in specifying drug *versus* reinforcement effects for a particular "hyperactive" child.

PROCEDURE
Subject

Arnold was 8-yr 11-months old, and had completed the third grade. He had been referred to a Community Mental Health Center for evaluation with regard to hyperactive behavior and poor school achievement. He was characterized by his

parents and by school personnel as exhibiting aggression with peers and sibling, noncompliance with requests and school routine, poor fine and gross motor coordination, little eye contact, mumbled, rapid speech; short attention span, and lack of age-appropriate play skills. The most salient feature of Arnold's problem, however, was his frequent engagement in repetitive, ritualistic behaviors, such as repeatedly smelling his hands or rolling imaginary minute objects between his fingers. Often, these hand rituals were accompanied by high-pitched, piercing noises or by "raspberries" blown on the back of his hands. Arnold had been diagnosed as "hyperactive" in the first grade and had been placed on Ritalin. Both parents and teachers concurred that Arnold was more "manageable" when medicated. However, the parents expressed concern that Arnold's repetitive behaviors might be exacerbated by Ritalin. Also, it was noted that Arnold was of significantly low height and weight for his chronological age, and Ritalin sometimes adversely affects growth patterns (Safer, Allen & Barr, 1972).

Despite medication and at least average intelligence (WISC IQ 109; Stanford-Binet IQ 115), Arnold produced almost no work within the classroom. Extensive psychological testing revealed extremely erratic performance, with great fluctuations on the same task administered on different days. One consistent finding was his difficulty in utilizing information presented visually, especially in tasks requiring visual sequential memory. Hence, in addition to the more classical signs of hyperactivity (poor peer relations, inability to follow instructions, poor school achievement, short attention span, high activity level), Arnold also evidenced motor deficits, an abnormal EEG, and idosyncratic, bizzare behaviors.

General procedure

Arnold was seen in the clinic for 90 min twice a week for eight weeks. During four of the eight weeks, he received medication; during the other four weeks, he received placebo in a double-blind design.

Arnold was seated at a small table in a 3- by 6-m room with a one-way mirror across one wall. The experimenters were a male and a female therapist who presented the tasks to Arnold during alternate sessions. The experimenter sat on the opposite side of the table and presented the tasks and poker chips as token reinforcers according to the prescribed schedule for a given session. Arnold was shown an array of possible prizes and told their cost in poker chips at the outset of each session. Prizes included such things as plastic models to assemble, a rubber bat, magnets, toy trucks, or planes.

TASKS

During each session, Arnold performed six sequential memory tasks. Recent recall tasks were chosen for two reasons. First, this represented an area of deficit for Arnold as designated by formalized testing. Second, according to previous research, methylphenidate should show its maximum effect on this sort of vigilance task, rather than on a task requiring abstract reasoning ability (Sroufe, 1975).

Three of the sequential memory tasks involved visual input and three involved auditory input. Auditory tasks had already been shown to be easier for Arnold than were visual tasks. Hence, drug and reinforcement effects could be assessed in relation to an area of comparative strength, as opposed to one of deficit.

Visual tasks

1. *Card sequence*. Arnold was shown a display of six playing cards of a single suit for 5 sec. The cards were then shuffled and handed to Arnold to arrange in the same sequence. Arnold was given five trials of different sequences at each session. A trial was scored as correct only if all six cirds were in the designated order.

2. *Memory for designs*. Arnold was shown a design drawn on a 7.5- by 12.5-cm card for 5 sec. The design was withdrawn, and Arnold was asked to produce the design with paper and pencil. Arnold was presented with five different designs at each session. Each reproduction was given a rating of 1, 2, or 3, depending on accuracy. The total number of points earned divided by a perfect score for each session.

3. *Imitation sequence*. The experimenter modelled a four-step, motor sequence and then asked Arnold to imitate the four actions. There were five such sequences at each session. The correct execution of each step was noted, and Arnold received a percent correct score for each session.

Auditory tasks

1. *Unrelated words*. Arnold was asked to repeat a sequence of six unrelated words just uttered by the experimenter. Five different sequences of six unrelated words were presented at each session. Each correctly repeated word was noted, and Arnold received a percent correct score for each session.

2. *Comprehension questions*. Arnold was read a short segment from a book or article appropriate to his grade level. He was then asked to answer seven questions related to the material just read to him. Each correct answer was noted, and Arnold received a percent correct score for each session.

3. *Auditory command sequence*. Arnold was given a verbal command involving four distinct steps. The correct execution of each step was noted. Five such four-step commands were given at each session, and Arnold received a percent correct score for each session.

Observation system

The accuracy of task performance was charted as the percent correct on each of the six tasks at each of the 16 clinic sessions. In addition, several other dimensions of Arnold's behavior were tracked within each clinic session. Ritualistic behavior, eye contact with the experimenter, and distractible behavior were charted. During each 1-min interval of a given session, each of the above behaviors was noted as either present or absent. Each session was composed of sixty to ninety 1-min intervals. The following definitions were used: (1) *ritualistic behavior:* any repetitive noise or repetitive gesture of the upper extremities. (2) *eye contact:* more than 5 sec of mutual eye contact with the experimenter during a given minute. (3) *Distractible behavior:* any surplus movement or a repetitive movement involving the lower extremities. During each session, Arnold received a percent score of 1-min intervals in which (1) ritualistic behavior, (2) eye contact with the experimenter, and (3) distractible behavior were observed to occur.

Observers and reliability

Three observers coded the above behaviors while observing through the one-way mirror. Two observers also functioned as the experimenters during alternating sessions. Observers were not informed of the medication regime.

During six of the sixteen clinic visits, two observers independently coded Arnold's behavior. The scoring of each 1-min interval was compared spearately for each of the beahvior categories. The percent agreement of the observers was obtained by dividing the number of intervals scored the same by both observers by the total number of 1-min intervals for that session. The mean percent agreement across the six reliability checks was: (1) eye contact 0.86, (2) ritualistic behavior 0.88, (3) distractible behavior 0.71. The mean percent agreement across all behavior categories over the six reliability checks was 0.82.

Home procedure

The mother administered a token economy for Arnold's appropriate behavior within the home throughout the eight weeks of the study. The mother and Arnold negotiated together what the prize would be and its cost in points. Typical prizes included a family outing to a drive-in movie, a box of colored pencils, a kite. Points were awarded by the mother for cooperative behavior with friends and sibling and for compliance with her requests. Arnold continued to accumulate points until a given prize had been won. Arnold was given 2 min of "timeout" in the bathroom following each observed aggressive act. Aggressive behavior was defined as a noxious motor action (i.e., hitting, poking, pushing, grabbing) directed toward another person.

The mother collected data on Arnold's behavior for three 5-min time segments each day. Five minutes of data were collected in the morning, 5 min in the afternoon, and 5 min in the evening. During each minute of the 5-min interval, the mother noted the occurrence of ritualistic, distractible, or aggressive behavior. If none of these occurred, the minute was scored as appropriate. No interobserver reliability information is available regarding the home-observation system. However, the mother did not know when Arnold received Ritalin and when placebo. An informal log or diary kept by the mother indicated that she was unable to guess correctly which weeks Arnold received placebo and which Ritalin.

Drug management

Before the study, Arnold had received 10 mg of Ritalin q.i.d. (four times per day). This had been established as his optimal dosage following several dosage trials under the direction of a private pediatrician. During the initial six weeks of the study, a staff psychiatrist prescirbed either 10 mg of Ritalin q.i.d. or placebo q.i.d. for Arnold. The mother was given an envelope contaning the medication for each week. Medication was dispensed in a double-blind design. Neither the experimenters, the mother nor Arnold were aware of when Arnold received Ritalin or when he received placebo. During each of the four two-week phases, however, it was understood that Arnold would be on Ritalin for one of the weeks and on placebo the other week. Thus, during each of the four phases of the study (Baseline, Treatment I, Treatment II, Reversals), Arnold was on Ritalin half the time and on placebo half the time. Medication changes occurred on Saturdays. Arnold was seen in the clinic on Tuesdays and Thursdays.

Reinforcement contingencies

The first two weeks, or four clinic visits, were a baseline condition. No poker chips were given to Arnold, and no prizes were available. Arnold performed the six sequential memory tasks at each session, and data were collected as to his task accuracy and his behavior.

Treatment Phase I occupied the next two-week period or second-four clinic visits. Poker chips, exchangeable for prizes at the end of the session, were introduced. These tokens were given for "hands down" and quiet behavior. All hand behavior was categorized into either ritualistic or "hands down, quiet behavior." "Hands down, quiet behavior" was incompatible with ritualistic behavior. Hands were required to be in a resting position or engaged in the handling of task materials without repetitive or bizarre gestures. Any verbalizations were required to be compatible with task requirements. A shaping process was employed. At first, Arnold received a chip for each 15 sec of "hands down" behavior not accompanied by bizarre noises. The experimenter placed a running stopwatch on the table. Each time Arnold raised his hands towards his face, engaged in ritualistic behavior, or made strange noises, the experimenter stopped the watch and turned away from Arnold for the duration of the ritualistic behavior. As soon as Arnold returned to the "hands down" position and was quiet, the experimenter again oriented toward Arnold, started the stopwatch, and resumed administration of the task. After 15 sec of "hands down" behavior, Arnold was handed a chip and told, "Good, you have your hands down and you are quiet". When Arnold had succeeded in earning chips for three consecutive 15-sec intervals, the time interval was lengthened to 30 sec. According to the same criteria, the interval was lengthened to 45 sec, 1 min, and eventually to 3-, 4-, and 5-min intervals on a random basis. During Treatment Phase I, no chips were dispensed for task accuracy. Chips were contingent only on lack of ritualistic behavior.

Treatment Phase II occupied the third two week period. During these four clinic visits, Arnold continued to receive poker chips contingent on the absence of ritualistic behavior, and also earned chips contingent on the accuracy of his task performance. Arnold earned a chip for each correct response as outlined in the section describing the tasks.

During weeks seven and eight, there were two reversals on the reinforcement contingencies. During Session 13, the tokens were given for task accuracy, but chips were not dispensed for "hands down" behavior. In Session 14, tokens were once again given for both task accuracy and "hands down", quiet behavior. In Session 15, the reversal was reinstituted, and poker chips were given contingent on task accuracy, but no chips were dispensed for "hands down" behavior. During the final session, chips were again given for both accuracy and "hands down" behavior. Two reversals were required in order to counter-balance for possible medication effects. During one of the reversals, Arnold received Ritalin. During the other reversal, Arnold received no medication.

The price of prizes was manipulated in such a way that Arnold was capable of "purchasing" a single prize at each session. Only once did he earn sufficient chips to buy two prizes at a single session. Hence, if chips were dispensed for both task accuracy and "hands down" behavior, the cost of a prize was increased for that session. Arnold was informed of the price at the beginning of each session.

The home program remained the same throughout the study. Points were earned for co-operation with peers and sibling and for compliance with requests. Timeout was administered for aggressive behavior. No points were given for lack of ritualistic or distractible behavior, although the mother collected data on these behaviors.

RESULTS

An analysis of variance, repeated measures design was employed to analyze the clinic data for drug and reinforcement effects with respect to: (a) task accuracy, (b) ritualistic behavior, (c) distractible behavior, (d) eye contact. Home data were analyzed separately to discern possible effects on ritualistic behavior, and aggressive behavior.

CLINIC DATA
Drug effects

The data on Ritalin *versus* placebo effects within the clinic are presented in Figure 1. There was no significant difference in Arnold's ability to perform either auditory or visual tasks whether on or off medication ($F \times 0.1$, $df = \frac{1}{2}$). He was better able to retain auditory than visual material whether on Ritalin or placebo.

Similarly, there was no main drug effect with respect to per cent time spent in: (a) ritualistic behavior ($F = 12.86$, $df = \frac{1}{2}$, (b), distractible behavior ($F = 1.00$, $df = \frac{1}{2}$), or (c) eye contact with the experimenters ($F = 0.3$, $df = \frac{1}{2}$). During Sessions 5 and 6, the first two sessions in which reinforcement was introduced, a shaping procedure was instituted, reinforcing 15, 30, and 45 sec of "hands down" behavior. Even though Arnold's behavior came under the control of this reinforcement system, the observation system did not immediately reflect the change. During baseline, Arnold had engaged in ritualistic behavior for 30 to 50 sec of every minute. During Sessions 5 and 6, Arnold might raise his hands towards his face only once or twice during the minute. However, according to the coding system, if any instance of ritualistic behavior occurred, the minute was scored as ritualistic. The data system was hence slow to reflect the actual changes in Arnold's behavior. Coincidentally, it happened that Sessions 5 and 6 were placebo sessions. The trend of the data in Table 1 to show less ritualistic behavior under Ritalin than placebo is probably due to this anomaly of the coding system, rather than to a trend of drug effect. In any case, there was no main drug effect nor any interaction effect between reinforcement and drug condition with respect to ritualistic behavior.

Reinforcement effects

The data on reinforcement effects are also evident in Figure 25-1 and Table 25-1. Arnold was

CLINIC DATA

RITUALISTIC BEHAVIOR ●━━━●
AGGRESSIVE BEHAVIOR ▪▪▪▪▪▪▪▪▪▪▪▪▪

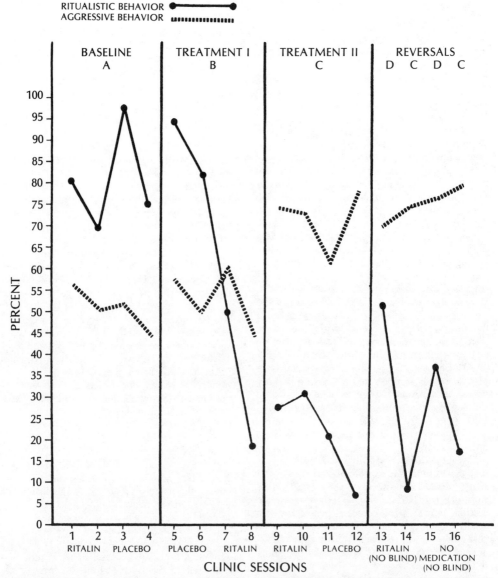

Figure 25-1. Clinic: Mean percent correct on tasks and mean percent 1-min intervals in which ritualistic behavior was observed to occur—(A) Baseline: no tokens for "hands down"; no tokens for accuracy. (B) Treatment I: tokens for "hands down"; no tokens for accuracy. (C) Treatment II: tokens for "hands down"; Token for accuracy. (D) Reversal: no tokens for "hands down"; tokens for accuracy.

significantly more accurate in performing the sequential memory tasks during sessions when he received poker chips for correct responses than during sessions when he did not receive chips for accuracy whether or not he was on medication $(F = 14.62,\ df = 2\%,\ p < 0.05)$. There is no significant interaction between reinforcement and drug effects $(F = 0.2,\ df = {}^2/_2)$.

Table 25-1. Reinforcement and drug effects in clinic

I. *Task Accuracy*—mean percent correct

	Ritalin	Placebo
A. Reinforcement for accuracy	0.73	0.77
No reinforcement for accuracy	0.51	0.50

	Auditory Tasks	Visual Tasks
B. Reinforcement for accuracy	0.77	0.70
No reinforcement for accuracy	0.65	0.49

II. *Ritualistic Behavior*—mean percent 1-min intervals

	Ritalin	Placebo
Reinforcement for "Hands Down, quiet behavior."	0.29	0.44
No reinforcement for "Hands Down, quiet behavior."	0.67	0.70

III. *Distractible Behavior*—mean percent 1-min intervals

	Ritalin	Placebo
Reinforcement for "Hands Down, quiet behavior."	0.21	0.32
No reinforcement for "Hands Down, quiet behavior."	0.36	0.40

IV. *Eye Contact*—mean percent 1-min intervals

	Ritalin	Placebo
Reinforcement for "Hands Down, quiet behavior."	0.44	0.37
No reinforcement for "Hands Down, quiet behavior."	0.09	0.16

There does appear to be a differential effect of reinforcement contingencies on auditory versus visual memory tasks (see Table 25-1). There is some gain in accuracy for both sorts of tasks when correctness is reinforced, but the majority of gain is seen in visual tasks. Hence, reinforcement effects are greatest in the area of initial deficit.

Significant reinforcement effects are also seen with respect to ritualistic behavior ($F = 76.00$, $df = {}^2/_2$, $p < 0.025$). Regardless of whether Arnold was on Ritalin or placebo, he showed less ritualistic behavior during sessions in which he received poker chips for "hands down, quiet behavior" than during baseline and reversal (no reinforcement) days. Again, there was no significant interaction between reinforcement and drug effects with respect to ritualistic behavior ($F = 26$, $df = {}^2/_2$).

There were also no significant reinforcement or interaction effects with respect to either distractible behavior or amount of eye contact with the experimenters. Reinforcement in the form of poker chips was never dispensed contingent on either of these behaviors. Distractible behavior and eye contact were monitored to gauge possible drug effects and to assess whether reinforcement effects might generalize to behaviors other

than those directly reinforced. This did not occur.

Figure 25-1 presents the clinic data for task accuracy and ritualistic behavior. Ritalin and placebo days are denoted, as well as changes in the reinforcement regime. This provides a graphic depiction of the maleability of Arnold's ritualistic behavior and accuracy of recall to reinforcing events. It also shows the relative imperviance of these behaviors to drug effects.

HOME DATA

Home data collected by the mother are presented in Figure 25-2. There was a significant drug effect with respect to ritualistic behavior. ($F = 36.15$, $df = {}^1/_6$, $p < 0.001$). Arnold engaged in significantly more ritualistic behavior during the weeks he received Ritalin than during the weeks he received placebo. There was no generalization to the home of the reinforcement contingencies applied at the clinic ($F = 2.55$, $df = {}^2/_{12}$). The amount of ritualistic behavior recorded at home was unrelated to any contingencies applied within the clinic. At home, no contingencies were applied to ritualistic behaviors.

There was also a significant drug effect with

HOME DATA

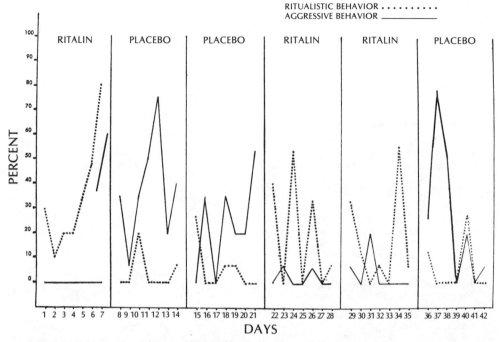

Figure 25-2. Home: mean percent of 1-min intervals in which ritualistic and aggressive behavior was observed to occur under Ritalin and Placebo conditions.

respect to aggressive behavior ($F = 50.63$, $df = {}^1/_6$, $p < 0.001$). Arnold was much less aggressive during weeks he received Ritalin than during weeks he received placebo. Aggressive behavior at home appeared unaffected by the reinforcement contingencies within the clinic ($F = 0.4$, $df = {}^2/_{12}$). Aggressive behavior was not in evidence in the clinic; Arnold was seen individually, and aggressive responses were typically directed at Arnold's sibling or peers. However, the effects of medication in possibly curtailing agression was a major concern of the parents. Aggressive behavior in the home was also monitored to assess possible generalization of clinic reinforcement procedures to behaviors never specifically reinforced.

Hence, while there were no significant drug effects within the clinic, a very different result was found within the home. Arnold showed an increase in ritualistic behavior but a decrease in aggressive behavior when on Ritalin as compared to placebo. None of the reinforcement programs in the clinic showed any generalization to the home.

DISCUSSION

Recent reviews on both drug management (Grinspoon & Singer, 1973; Sroufe, 1975) and behavior management (Berkowitz & Graziano, 1972) of children have stressed the notion that in future research, multiple problem behaviors need to be monitored in several settings to assess the breadth and generalizability of beneficial effects. In both fields, it now appears that behavioral changes may be more circumscribed than early studies seemed to indicate. Drug effects, for instance, for any particular child appear to be related to the degree of structure in a given situation and to the nature of the task posed to the child. The child on medication does not uniformly perform at a higher level in all settings and on all tasks than he does on placebo. Similarly, changes in behavior rendered by reinforcement contingencies do not appear to generalize to other settings or to other behaviors simply as a matter of course (Wahler, 1969; Wulbert, Barach, Perry, Straughan, Sulzbacher, Turner, & Wilts, 1974). Indeed, generalization must, itself, be programmed and reinforced. The present study attempted to delineate setting, task, and measurement variables in assessing the relative efficacy and possible interaction of drug effects and of contingency management in the treatment of a particular child.

For this child, no significant drug effects on any of the problem behaviors were discerned within the structure of the clinic setting, but definite drug effects were noted within the home. Arnold engaged in significantly less aggression but significantly more ritualistic behavior at home when receiving Ritalin rather than placebo. One might conjecture that initially, Ritalin did exacerbate Arnold's tic-like behavior, but that over time this ritualistic behavior became particularly strongly conditioned to stress or demand situations such as existed at school and in the clinic. Hence, ritualistic behavior eventually became relatively autonomous of drug effects in these stress situations, but remained a function of Ritalin within the relaxed structure of the home.

Reinforcement contingencies imposed within the clinic successfully diminished these repetitive behaviors within the clinic. However, since there were no contingencies for such tic-like behaviors imposed within the home, the ritualistic behavior remained a function of drug management in that setting. There was no automatic generalization, from the clinic to the home, of "hands-down," quiet behavior.

It is important to note that there were no interaction effects. Although clinical lore maintains that use of Ritalin and the amphetamines render hyperactive children more accessible to learning and reinforcement effects, there is little research to substantiate this notion. Arnold showed no tendency to respond more readily to a reinforcement regime when medicated than when on placebo. Hence, the present study does not support the common assumption that medication enhances learning effects.

Drug effects were purposely evaluated in the clinic setting with those aspects of Arnold's behavior where the *greatest* medication effect would be predicted control of excess activity level and accuracy of performance on vigilance-type tasks. Arnold had been maintained on Ritalin for 3 yr before the study because parents, teachers, and pediatrician were all convinced of its global beneficial effects. However, when specific behaviors were monitored, it was discovered that medication was actually associated with an increase in one of the problem behaviors (excess repetitive movement) in some settings.

Since the actual beneficial effect of Ritalin was restricted to a decrease in aggression at home, and since it was feared that Ritalin was adversely effecting Arnold's growth pattern, he was removed from medication as a result of this study.

The reinforcement regime was shown to be the potent variable in controlling Arnold's behavior within the clinic setting. It should be stressed, however, that reinforcement effects did not readily generalize to either other behaviors or to other settings. Increased eye contact with the experimenters and decreased excessive movement of the lower extremities were behaviors never specifically reinforced during the study. These behaviors did not change as a function of the reinforcement of increased task accuracy and decreased excessive movement of the upper extremities. In analogous manner, there was no evidence of the generalization of changes acquired in one setting to that of another setting. Although Arnold successfully decreased his ritualistic behavior in the clinic, a similar decrease did not simultaneously appear in the home where contingencies were unchanged. Thus, when Arnold was removed from medication, specific behavior-management programs had to be fashioned to the home and school. Arnold was placed in a special classroom that operates on a token economy. At home, a shaping procedure was instituted to control aggressive behavior.

It is hoped that the present study may serve in a pragmatic manner as a model for evaluating specific medication effects for the individual child. The idiosyncratic nature of drug effects for any particular child require monitoring several simultaneous dimensions. Global ratings of improved versus unimproved would appear inadequate in weighing the advantages and disadvantage for a particular child of maintenance on a drug whose long-term effects are unknown.

REFERENCES

Bernal, M. D., Duryel, J. S., Pruetl, H. L., and Burns, B. J. Behavior modification and the brat syndrome. *Journal of Consulting and Clinical Psychology,* 1968, **32**, 447–455.

Berkowitz, B. P. and Graziano, A. M. Training parents as behavior therapists: a review. *Behaviour Research and Therapy,* 1972, **10**, 297–317.

Christensen, D. E. and Sprague, R. L. Reduction of hyperactive behavior by conditioning procedures alone and combined with methylphenidate (Ritalin). *Behavior and Research and Therapy,* 1973, **11**, 331–334.

Cohen M. J., Douglas, V. I., and Morgenstern, G.

The effect of methylphenidate on attentive behavior and autonomic activity in hyperactive children. *Psychopharmacologia,* 1971, **22**, 282–294.

Conrad, W. G., Dworkin, E. S., Shai, A., and Tobiessen, J. E. Effects of amphetamine therapy and prescriptive tutoring on the behavior and achievement of lower class hyperactive children. *Journal of Learning Disabilities,* 1971, **4**, 45–53.

Ellis, M. J., Witt, P. A., Reynolds, R., and Sprague, R. L. Methylphenidate and the activity of hyperactivities in the informal setting. *Child Development,* 1974, **45**, 217–220.

Grinspoon, L. and Singer, S. B. Amphetamines in the treatment of hyperkinetic children. *Harvard Educational Review,* 1973, **43**, 515–555.

Hewett, F. M., Taylor, F. D., and Artuso, A. A. The Santa Monica project: evaluation of an engineered classroom design with emotionally disturbed children. *Exceptional Children,* 1969, **35**, 523–529.

Meichenbaum, D. H. and Goodman, J. Training impulsive children to talk to themselves: a means of developing self-control. *Journal of Abnormal Psychology,* 1971, **77**, 115–125.

Millichap, J. G. and Boldrey, E. E. Studies in hyperkinetic behavior II. Laboratory and clinical evaluations of drug treatments. *Neurology,* 1967, **17**, 467–472.

O'Leary, K. D. and Becker, W. C. Behavior modification of an adjustment class: a token economy reinforcement program. *Exceptional Children,* 1967, **33**, 637–642.

O'Leary, K. D., Becker, W. C., Evans, M. B., and Saudergas, R. A. A token reinforcement program in a public school: a replication and systematic analysis. *Journal of Applied Behavior Analysis,* 1969, **2**, 3–13.

Palkes, H., Stewart, M., and Kahana, B. Porteus maze performance of hyperactive boys after training in self-directed verbal commands. *Child Development,* 1968, **39**, 817–826.

Patterson, G. R., Jones R., Wright, J., and Wright, M. A behavior modification technique for the hyperactive child *Behaviour Research and Therapy,* 1965, **2**, 217–226.

Quay, H. D., Werry, J. S., McQueen, M., and Sprague, R. L. Remediation of the conduct problem child in the special class setting. *Exceptional Children,* 1966, **32**, 509–515.

Ridberg, E. H., Parke, R. D., and Hetherington, E. M. Modification of impulsive and reflective cognitive styles through observation of film mediated models. *Developmental Psychology,* 1971, **5**, 369–377.

Sprague, R. L., Barnes, K. R., and Werry, J. S. Methylphenidate and thioridazine: learning, reaction time, activity, and classroom behavior in disturbed children. *American Journal of Orthopsychiatry,* 1970, **40**, 615–628.

Sroufe, L. A. Drug treatment of children with behavior problems. In F. Horowitz, (Ed.), *Review of child development research,* 1975, **4**, 347–407.

Wahler, R. G. Setting generality: some specific and general effects of child behavior therapy. *Journal of Applied Behavioral Analysis,* 1969, **2**, 239–246.

Wahler, R. G., Winkel, G. H., Peterson, R. F., and Morrison, D. C. Mothers as behavior therapists for their own children. *Behaviour Research and Therapy,* 1965, **3**, 113–214.

Wulbert, M., Barach, R., Perry, M., Straughan, J., Sulzbacher, S, Turner, K., and Wiltz, N. The generalization of newly acquired behaviors by parents and child across three different settings: a study of an autistic child. *Journal of Abnormal Child Psychology,* 1974, **2**, 87.

26. Relative efficacy of methylphenidate and behavior modification in hyperkinetic children: an interim report

RACHEL GITTELMAN-KLEIN   DONALD F. KLEIN
HOWARD ABIKOFF   SIDNEY KATZ
AUDREY C. GLOISTEN   WENDY KATES

No rational, knowledgeable individual can dispute the efficacy of short-term stimulant treatment in the management of hyperkinetic children. Of all therapies in child psychiatry, it is the best documented. At the same time, legitimate concern has been expressed concerning the possibility of deleterious side effects which may result from long-term stimulant administration (Safer & Allen, 1975). Other nonmedical interventions, especially behavior modification techniques, have been suggested for the treatment of hyperactive children. The use of these techniques is not associated with physical side effects and, if equally effective, would offer a valuable alternative to medication in the treatment of hyperactive children. Werry and Sprague (1970) have recommended that pharmacotherapy of hyperactivity be undertaken only when behavior modification techniques are not realistically feasible. Others have turned the problem of how to treat hyperactive children into a moral issue (Grinspoon & Singer, 1973; Sroufe & Stewart, 1973). As usual, the intensity of the views held and the heat generated by the debate are inversely related to the amount of facts available on the point in question.

Little empirical evidence exists for the efficacy of behavior therapy in the treatment of hyperkinesis. The early studies of the effectiveness of behavior modification for hyperactive children took place in specially set up experimental classrooms (Doubros & Daniels, 1966; Patterson, 1965; Patterson, Jones, Whittier, & Wright, 1965; Pihl, 1967; Quay, Sprague, Werry, & McQueen, 1967). Unfortunatley, results obtained in such settings cannot be generalized to the ordinary school environment.

More recently, operant principles have been applied in regular classrooms. In an uncontrolled study of a 4-week behavior therapy program, Rosenbaum, O'Leary and Jacob (1975) found a significant improvement in teacher scale ratings of 10 hyperactive children. Since no control group was included, the specific therapeutic effect of the behavior modification techniques cannot be estimated. In a subsequent controlled study, O'Leary, Pelham, Rosenbaum, and Price (1976) treated children rated hyperactive by both parents and teachers for a 10-week period. After treatment the teacher ratings for the 9 children receiving behavior therapy were significantly better than those for the 8 untreated children. (The nature of the statistical analyses performed are not reported.) The above two studies of be-

From the *Journal of Abnormal Child Psychology*, 1976, *4*, 361–379. Copyright © 1976 Plenum Publishing Corporation. Reprinted by permission.

This study was supported in part by grant MH 18579, and by grant No. 3–621 from the Long Island Jewish-Hillside Medical Center. The authors wish to thank the behavior therapists, Drs. Jeffrey Felixbrod and Marion Pheterson, as well as Ms. Patricia Ramsey, who was responsible for data analysis.

havior therapy are unique in their use of scale measures which have been validated for both the identification of hyperactive children and the detection of drug effects. The authors indicate that the magnitude of treatment-induced improvement with behavior therapy, as measured by teachers' ratings, is equivalent to that reported in studies of stimulant effects in hyperactive children. By extension, the assumption is made that the two treatment approaches have the same degree of therapeutic efficacy. It is unfortunate that the descriptive data (mean values) after treatment are omitted.

Another approach, used by Ayllon, Layman, and Kandel (1975), argues for the usefulness of conditioning techniques in the treatment of hyperactive children. Three hyperactive girls were observed in the classroom under three nonrandom conditions—while receiving methylphenidate, while receiving no medication, and while off medication but receiving reinforcement for academic performance. Increases in correct mathematics performance as well as reduction in disruptive behavior were observed during reinforcement periods. The level of disruption during behavior modification was indistinguishable from that while the children were receiving methylphenidate.

A combination of behavior modification and medication has also been recommended as an alternative to medication alone in the treatment of hyperactive children. Arguments have been advanced that behavioral techniques and chemotherapy have discrete, independent actions; consequently, a combination of both modalities should be the treatment of choice (Eysenck, 1971; Sprague & Werry, 1971). Eysenck claims that stimulants enhance conditionability, and therefore, in behavior disorders which are indicative of early defective social conditioning, the combination of stimulants and conditioning should maximize the likelihood of behavioral amelioration.

Stimulants can be viewed as enhancing attentional processes and reducing restlessness, whereas social reinforcement may teach the child to internalize the value of appropriate behaviors. There is no direct evidence that stimulants facilitate operant conditioning in hyperactive children. Stimulants improve performance, but whether it is by removing maladaptive behavior, increasing attentiveness, or actually making the child more responsive to positive reinforcement is unclear (Gittelman-Klein & Klein, 1975).

Little empirical data exist regarding the advantages resulting from a combination of stimulants and behavior therapy. One study has reported the effects of methylphenidate in combination with conditioning in reducing inseat motor activity measured by a stabilimetric cushion in a laboratory setting (Sprague, Christensen, & Werry, 1974). Twelve hyperactive boys were assigned to either methylphenidate or placebo; seat movements were measured over 13 sessions: 2 sessions of baseline; 3 sessions of drug or placebo alone; 5 sessions of drug or placebo with conditioning, and 3 sessions following conditioning. Though methylphenidate was superior to placebo in reducing motor restlessness, the drug effects are difficult to interpret since the children in the placebo group were initially significantly more active than those in the drug group. The placebo group showed marked fluctuations in activity after initiation of placebo so that the only statistically significant change for the children receiving placebo was an increase in activity during the 3 placebo alone sessions compared to baseline. The conditioning contingencies significantly reduced motor activity only when compared to placebo period, not when compared to the baseline levels.

In the drug group, methylphenidate alone did not reduce motor activity. However, the combination of drug and conditioning significantly reduced motor activity. There was no significant difference between the drug alone condition and the combination of drug and conditioning. Thus, the results are unclear and only suggest that a combination of approaches may be optimal in the control of hyperkinesis.

Further data regarding the effects of combined behavioral treatments and methylphenidate have been presented by Christensen (1975) for a group of 13 hyperactive mental retardates in experimental classrooms. The children received 2 weeks of behavior therapy with methylphenidate (mean dose, 11.7 mg) and 2 weeks of behavior therapy with placebo in a crossover design. No difference was found between the two conditions on a variety of measures. The author concludes that "the additive use of stimulant medication produces few additional benefits" (p. 274). In view of the atypically low dosages used and the special nature of the clinical group, the study failed to test adequately the hypothesis of additive effects between the two treatment modalities in hyperactive children.

The studies reviewed demonstrate that, so far, there has been no adequate report of the relative merits of medication versus behavior therapy, or of combining these treatment tactics in hyperactive children. The study to be presented was designed to investigate the effects of behavior therapy, behavior therapy combined with methylphenidate, and methylphenidate alone in hyperkinetic children. The study is ongoing (a total of at least 75 subjects is projected).

PROCEDURE

SUBJECT SELECTION CRITERIA

The children had to meet the following criteria: They had to be between the ages of 6 and 12, attending elementary school, free of gross neurological disease and psychosis, and had to obtain either a Verbal or a Performance scale intelligence quotient of at least 85 on the Wechsler Intelligence Scale for Children. The parents had to be willing to participate in the study after it was explained to them.

A Conners Teacher Rating Scale was obtained for each child. The 39 scale items yield five factors: Factor I, Conduct Disorder; Factor II, Inattention; Factor III, Anxiety; Factor IV, Hyperactivity; Factor V, Sociability (Conners, 1969). To be accepted a child had to be rated hyperactive by the teacher, as defined by a minimum mean Hyperactivity factor score of 1.8 out of a possible 3. This cutoff score was based on results obtained in a study by Sprague et al. (1974), comparing normal and hyperactive children.

In addition, parents had to report that the child was hyperactive or had behavior problems at home. Thus, children who were *not* reported to be hyperactive or to have difficulties at home were not considered for the study, regardless of other clinical considerations.

The last requirement was the presence of observable behavior problems in the classroom recorded on a modified version of an observation code (unpublished) devised by O'Leary and coworkers. The index child and a classmate of the same sex, identified by the teacher as being average in comportment, were observed for 16-minute periods during structured lessons. The code consists of 14 categories; 9 were rated very infrequently and not included in the analyses. The 5 remaining categories are: 1. Interference: calling out, interruptions of others during work periods; 2. Off-Task: failure to attend to classroom assignments; 3. Gross Motor Movement: out-of-seat motor activity when it violates the class rules; 4. Minor Motor Movement: in-seat rump activity; and 5. Solicitation: seeking the teacher's attention.

The children were observed at least three times before treatment initiation, and weekly thereafter. The five behavioral categories were rated as present or absent for each 15-second interval of 16-minute observation periods. The scores represent the mean frequency of the behaviors over 16 minutes.

Except for the first 10 subjects, the observers were blind to the purposes of observation, and to the nature of the population studied. At all times, the observers were blind to the design of the study.

Criteria for the identification of hyperactive children were obtained from observations of normal children and children referred for hyperactivity. Mean cutoff observation scores which maximized the identification of hyperactive children and minimized false positives were selected; they were: Interference, 10; Off-Task, 3; Gross Motor, 3; Minor Motor, 21; Solicitation, 3. Elevated mean scores on at least two of the five behavioral categories were required. (The combination of Interference and Solicitation was not used since the two ratings are not always independent). The code and relevant procedures are detailed in another paper (Abikoff, Gittleman-Klein, & Klein, Note 1).

An overall index of disruptive classroom behavior was obtained by combining the categories of Interference, Off-Task, and Gross Motor Activity. The other two categories, Minor Motor Movement and Solicitation, were not included in the overall disruption estimate since in-seat movement has not been shown to be related to performance (Douglas, 1975). Solicitation is scored whether or not the child's demands on the teacher are appropriate. Therefore, it cannot be inferred that it regularly reflects disruptive, maladaptive behavior.

EXPERIMENTAL TREATMENTS

Children who met the study criteria were randomly assigned to one of three experimental treatments for an 8-week period: behavior therapy with methylphenidate; methylphenidate alone; or behavior therapy with placebo.

Behavior therapy. Behavior therapy was implemented in both the home and school. It followed operant conditioning principles. The specific behavioral approaches and techniques to be used in classrooms have been well described (O'Leary & O'Leary, 1972). Studies by O'Leary, Becker, Evans, and Saudargas (1969) and O'Leary and

Drabman (1971) indicate that an effective classroom management program can be introduced within a relatively short period of time, that a teacher with no previous experience can learn to implement a behavior modification program with regular professional consultation, and that tokens are the most effective form of reinforcement.

Similarly, the feasibility of using parents as agents of change has been demonstrated (O'Leary, O'Leary, & Becker, 1967; Salzinger, Feldman, & Portnoy, 1970; Wahler, Winkel, Peterson, & Morrison, 1965). Both mother and father had to participate in the program. Both were trained to assess and record the child's behavior. Reinforcements and punishments were identified for each child individually, and were revised as treatment progressed. Teachers dispensed points ("smile faces") to the children, who cashed them in at home for whatever backup reinforcement had been stipulated between therapist and parents.

The beginning of treatment was defined as the day on which reinforcement began to be dispensed, and did not include the 2- to 3-week prereinforcement period used for functional assessment at home and in school.

The behaviors most frequently reinforced in school were listening to teachers, not calling out, not interrupting, not leaving seat, doing the work, and not disturbing other children.

At home, the behaviors modified typically consisted of listening to parents, following stipulated rules, cooperating with duties, not fighting with siblings.

Medication. Pills (methylphenidate or placebo) were administered within 2 days of tangible reinforcement initiation. All children were prescribed 10 mg of medication per day for the first week, with gradual weekly increments. Teachers were called weekly and medication regulation was guided by the report of the parents and teachers. Dosage was increased only if problematic behavior was reported. All medication was administered twice daily, in the morning and at lunch. A maximum limit of 80 mg/day was set.

POSTTREATMENT EVALUATIONS

In the case of children receiving behavior therapy, all individuals involved in assessment were blind to the type of medication prescribed. Among children receiving methylphenidate alone, the observers were blind to the method of treatment, but other evaluators were aware of the fact that the child was not receiving behavior therapy.

After 8 weeks of treatment, another Teacher Rating Scale was obtained. In addition, teachers, mothers, and psychiatrists reported their overall impression of the child's status on an 8-point scale: 1. Completely Well, 2. Much Improved, 3. Improved, 4. Slightly Improved, 5. Unchanged, 6. Slightly Worse, 7. Worse, 8. Much Worse. The global ratings of the teachers and mothers reflect their own evaluaation of the child's progress. The psychiatrists, in contrast, made use of all information available. Therefore, these ratings represent a composite of several data sources: the school's evaluation, the parent's report of the child's behavior, and the psychiatrist's own observation and interview with the child. (Other scales dealing with such variables as symptoms, behavior at home and during psychometric testing were filled out by the mother, psychiatrist, and psychologist. Analysis of these measures has been postponed until completion of the study.)

DATA ANALYSIS

The data obtained from the Teacher Rating Scale and the observational code were analyzed to determine the effect of each treatment (within treatment effects), and to investigate whether treatments differed in relative efficacy (between-treatment differences). Within treatment effects were obtained by contrasting the pre- and posttreatment means of each treatment group with t tests for correlated means.

The between-treatment differences were tested by analyses of covariance, whereby the posttreatment scores were adjusted for the groups' initial, pretreatment values. If the covariance analyses yeilded significant F ratios, Tukey tests of Honestly Significant Differences (HSD tests) were computed to determine which group contrasts were significant. Since no clear prediction could be made concerning the relative merit of each treatment, the p values applied to the between treatment differences are two-tailed.

In addition, to determine the extent to which the treatments had normalized the children's behavior, the mean posttreatment scores obtained by the hype active children on the Teacher Rating Scale were compared, by means of t tests, to those obtained by Sprague et al. (1974) for 143 normal boys (treated vs. normal children). Posttreatment observation scores obtained by the hyperactive children were contrasted to those of their respective normal controls by means of t tests for correlated means.

For purposes of analysis, the global ratings of improvement were dichotomized. Ratings of Completely Well, Much Improved, and Improved make up the "Improved" category. Ratings of Slightly Improved, Unchanged, Slightly Worse, Worse, and Much Worse were combined to make up the "Unimproved" category. Chi square analyses were applied to the Global Improvement Ratings. If significant treatment differences were found across the three treatment groups, further chi square tests were done between groups.

RESULTS

A total of 36 children had entered the study at the point of this analysis. Two did not complete it. One child on methylphenidate was extremely sensitive to the drug, developing hypertension and tachycardia on as little as 5 mg/day. Another child was on methylphenidate for 2 weeks when his absent father returned home and refused to have the child on medication. The final sample consists of 34 children—32 boys and 2 girls, 32 white children and 2 black—with a mean age of 8 years 2 months. Thirteen children received behavior therapy with methylphenidate, 12 received methylphenidate alone, and 9 received behavior therapy with placebo. After 8 weeks of treatment, methylphenidate dosage ranged from 10 to 60 mg/day, with an average group daily dose of 35.6 mg.

TEACHER RATING SCALE

There was no significant difference among the treatment groups before treatment on any of the factors of the Teacher Rating Scale.

The pretreatment factor scores are presented for each treatment group and the total group in Table 26–1. As anticipated, the teachers' ratings of the hyperactive children were markedly more elevated than those obtained for normal boys($N = 143$), whose mean factor scores were: Factor I = .21; Factor II = .60; Factor III = .29; Factor IV = .56 (values for Factor V were not reported for the normal sample).

Within-treatment effects. The children in all three treatment groups were rated significantly less pathological after 8 weeks of treatment on the factors of Conduct Disorder, Anxiety, and Hyperactivity (p's from $< .05$ to $< .0001$). On the factors of Inattention and Sociability, the groups receiving behavior therapy with methylphenidate, and methylphenidate alone, were significantly improved. The group receiving behavior therapy with placebo did not show significant improvement on these two factors, though a trend was obtained ($p = .06$) for the behavior therapy alone group (see Table 26–2).

Between-treatment differences. Significant treatment differences were obtained on four of the five factors of the Teacher Rating Scale (Table 26–1). Both methylphenidate alone and the combination of methylphenidate with behavior therapy were significantly superior to behavior ther-

Table 26-1. Mean teacher rating scale factor scores

Groups	N	Factor I Conduct disorder Pre	Post[a]	Factor II Inattention Pre	Post[a]	Factor III Anxiety Pre	Post[a]	Factor IV Hyperactivity Pre	Post[a]	Factor V Sociability Pre	Post[a]
1. BT + M	13	1.29	.36	1.64	.64	1.02	.71	2.44	.56	−1.26	− .38
2. M	12	1.43	.38	1.94	.84	1.19	.63	2.70	.85	− .99	− .18
3. BT + P	9	1.38	1.00	1.74	1.45	1.10	.86	2.49	1.41	− .88	−1.03
Total	34	1.36		1.77		1.10		2.54		−1.07	
F ratios, 2,30 df[b]		.16	12.39	.91	10.50	.44	2.03	1.42	8.34	.96	9.23
$P <$		n.s.	.0002	n.s.	.0004	n.s.	n.s.	n.s.	.0013	n.s.	.0008
Tukey HSD[c], P			1vs2 n.s.		1vs2 n.s.				1vs2 n.s.		1vs2 n.s.
		—	1vs3<.01	—	1vs3<.01	—	—	—	1vs3<.01	—	1vs3<.01
			2vs3<.01		2vs3<.01				2vs3<.05		2vs3<.01

[a] Post scores adjusted for initial values.

[b] F ratios for pretreatment differences computed by analyses of variance. F ratios for posttreatment differences computed by analyses of covariance.

[c] Tukey Honestly Significant Differences. All p values are two-tailed. BT + M = Behavior therapy and methylphenidate; M = Methylphenidate; BT + P = Behavior therapy and placebo.

Table 26-2. T-test values for within-treatment group effects on teacher rating scale[a,b]

| | | | | Group[c] | | | | | |
| | $BT + M$ | | | M | | | $BT + P$ | | |
Factor	t	df	$p <$	t	df	$p <$	t	df	$p <$
I. Conduct disorder	7.71	12	.0001	5.69	11	.0002	2.88	8	.03
II. Inattention	7.16	12	.0001	7.97	11	.0001	2.19	8	n.s.
III. Anxiety	4.07	12	.002	2.79	11	.02	2.62	8	.04
IV. Hyperactivity	15.76	12	.0001	11.29	11	.0001	5.99	8	.0004
V. Sociability	4.22	12	.002	5.85	11	.0002	−0.34	8	n.s.

[a] See Table 26-1 for mean values.
[b] t tests for correlated means of pre- and posttreatment means within treatment groups, two-tailed tests.
[c] BT + M = Behavior therapy and methylphenidate; M = Methylphenidate; BT + P = Behavior therapy and placebo.

apy with placebo on the factors of Conduct Disorder (p's = .01), Inattention (p's = .01), Hyperactivity (p's = .01 and < .05) and Sociability (p's < .01). There was no significant difference between methylphenidate alone and methylphenidate combined with behavior therapy on any of the Teacher Rating Scale factors.

The only factor not yielding group differences on the Teacher Rating Scale was the Anxiety Factor.

Treated vs. normal children. After the 8-week treatment period, factor scores of children receiving behavior therapy with methylphenidate were indistinguishable from the scores of the normal children ($t = 1.27; -.16; -.27;$ 154 df, for factors of Conduct, Inattention, and Hyperactivity, respectively). However, they were significantly more elevated on the Anxiety factor ($t = 4.23,$ 154 $df, p < .01$).

Factor ratings of the children treated with methylphenidate alone were indistinguishable from ratings of the normals on Conduct Disorder and Hyperactivity ($t = 1.47,$ and 1.88, 153 df, respectively). On the Inattention and Anxiety Factors, however, the children treated with methylphenidate alone received significantly higher scores than the normals (153 df; $t = 2.64, p < .01; t = 3.44, p < .001$).

The postreatment scores of the group receiving behavior therapy with placebo were significantly more elevated than those of the normals on the factors of Conduct Disorder (150 df; $t = 5.66, p < .001$), Inattention ($t = 3.69, p < .001$), Anxiety ($t = 5.38, p < .001$), and Hyperactivity ($t = 3.65, p < .001$).

CLASSROOM OBSERVATIONS

Interobserver reliability was computed by a method previously reported by Blunden, Spring,

and Greenberg (1974). The number of interobserver agreements for the presence of a behavior within a 15-second interval (A) was divided by the sum of the agreements and disagreements (D) and multiplied by 100 to yield a percentage of agreement (A/A&D × 100). The percentage agreements obtained for Disruptive Behavior was 71%; for Minor Motor Activity, 74%; and for Solicitation, 66%.

The values obtained before treatment initiation were averaged. The hyperactive group was more elevated at baseline than their normal controls on all three observational measures (Disruptive Behavior, $t = 9.72,$ 33 $df, p < .0001$; Minor Motor Activity, $t = 4.01,$ 33 $df, p < .0001$; Solicitation, $t < 5.49,$ 33 $df, p < .0001$, two-tailed tests).

Within-treatment effects. The posttreatment scores of the classroom observations are the average of the scores obtained during the 7th and 8th week of treatment. The results of the t tests within groups for the classroom observations are presented in Table 26-3.

The level of Disruptive Behavior was significantly reduced in the two groups receiving medication (Behavior therapy with methylphenidate, and methylphenidate) (p's < .001). In contrast, this measure was not significantly affected by behavior therapy alone.

The amount of observed Minor Motor Activity was significantly reduced by all the treatments (p's < .01).

The degree to which the child sought the teacher's attention was not reduced by any treatment as reflected in the ratings obtained for Solicitation.

Between-treatment differences. The comparisons between treatments are presented in Table 26-4. After 8 weeks of treatment, the children receiving behavior therapy with methylphenidate and

Table 26-3. *T*-test values for within-treatment group effects on classroom observations[a,b]

	BT + M			*Groups*[c] *M*			*BT + P*		
Category	*t*	*df*	*p<*	*t*	*dt*	*p<*	*t*	*df*	*p<*
Disruptive behavior	4.50	12	.0008	5.38	11	.0003	1.41	8	n.s.
Minor motor activity	5.15	12	.0002	4.60	11	.0008	3.73	8	.006
Solicitation	0.36	12	n.s.	1.45	11	n.s.	0.81	8	n.s.

[a] See Table 26-4 for mean values.
[b] *t* tests for correlated means of pre- and posttreatment means within treatment groups, two-tailed tests.
[c] BT + M = Behavior therapy and methylphenidate; M = Methylphenidate; BT + P = Behavior therapy and placebo.

those receiving methylphenidate alone were observed to be significantly less disruptive than those treated with behavior therapy and placebo ($p < .01$ and $p < .05$, respectively). No statistically significant difference in disruptive behavior was found between the two groups treated with methylphenidate.

A significant difference in treatment efficacy was found in amount of inseat activity (Minor Motor Activity). The children treated with the combination of behavior therapy and methylphenidate were significantly less restless than those who received behavior therapy with placebo ($p < .01$). No difference in restless behavior was found between the group receiving methylphenidate alone and the two other treatment groups.

The amount of observed Solicitation was not differentially affected by treatment.

Treated vs. normal children. Results of the analysis comparing the post-treatment classroom observation scores of the hyperactive children and their normal comparisons are presented in Table 26-5. The children receiving the combined treatment of behavior therapy with methylphenidate were indistinguishable from their normal classmates. The group receiving methylphenidate alone continued to be significantly more disruptive ($p < .05$) and more fidgety ($p < .02$) than their comparisons. The children who received behavior therapy alone were significantly more disruptive than normal children in the same classroom ($p < .0001$).

Table 26-4. Classroom observations

			Pretreatment		*Posttreatment*[a]			
Measure	*Group*	*N*	*Means*	*Means +*	*F* 2,30df	*p*[b]	*HSD tests p*[b]	
Disruptive	1. BT + M	13	27.05	12.70			1vs2 n.s.	
behavior	2. M	12	34.62	15.36			1vs3<.01	
	3. BT + P	9	33.72	26.04	6.10	<.01	2vs3<.05	
	Total	34	31.48					
	4. Comparisons *Ss*	34	7.27	8.44				
Minor motor	1. BT + M	13	22.89	10.23			1vs2 n.s.	
movement	2. M	12	19.64	13.41			1vs3<.05	
	3. BT + P	9	18.53	16.90	4.22	<.05	2vs3 n.s.	
	Total	34	20.59					
	4. Comparisons *Ss*	34	15.38	11.57				
Solicitation	1. BT + M	13	2.84	2.91				
	2. M	12	4.99	2.86				
	3. BT + P	9	2.92	2.37				
	Total	34	3.62		0.12	n.s.	—	
	4. Comparisons *Ss*	34	.95	.94				

[a] Post scores adjusted for pretreatment values.
[b] Two-tailed tests.

Table 26-5. *T* values of posttreatment means of treated hyperactive children and normals on classroom observations[a]

Behavioral category	BT + M			Groups[b] M			BT + P		
	t	*df*	*p*	*t*	*df*	*p*	*t*	*df*	*p*
Disruptive behavior	.72	12	n.s.	2.45	11	.05	7.38	8	<.0001
Minor motor movement	.96	12	n.s.	.33	11	n.s.	1.68	8	n.s.
Solicitation	1.89	12	n.s.	2.75	11	.02	1.20	8	n.s.

[a] *t* tests for correlated means, two-tailed tests.
[b] BT + M = Behavior therapy and methylphenidate; M = methylphenidate; BT + P = behavior therapy and placebo.

GLOBAL IMPROVEMENT RATINGS

Teacher ratings. After 8 weeks of treatment, the teachers rated 100% of the children receiving combined behavioral and stimulant treatment as improved. Of the children receiving methylphenidate alone, 75% were evaluated as improved; 56% of the children treated with behavior therapy and placebo were similarly rated (Table 26-6). The combination of behavior therapy and methylphenidate was significantly superior to behavior therapy and placebo($\chi^2 = 4.39$, corrected, 1 *df*, $p < .05$). No difference in teachers' global improvement ratings was found between the other groups (i.e., methylphenidate vs. behavior therapy with placebo).

Table 26-6. Teachers' global improvement ratings[a]

Group	Improved	Unimproved	N
Behavior therapy and methylphenidate	13 (100)[b]	0 (0)	13
Methylphenidate	9 (75)	3 (25)	12
Behavior therapy and placebo	5 (56)	4 (44)	9 34

[a] $\chi^2 = 6.65$, 2 *df*, $p < .04$, two-tailed.
[b] Numbers in parentheses are percentages.

Mothers' ratings. The mothers' global ratings of improvement did not favor any single treatment group (Table 26-7). Rates of improvement varied between 67% and 85% across treatments indicating a relatively high level of perceived improvement by mothers for all the treatments ($\chi^2 = 0.97$, 2*df*, n.s).

Psychiatrists' ratings. The overall psychiatrists' improvement ratings are presented in Table 26-8. The psychiatrists' evaluations parallel those of

Table 26-7. Mothers' global improvement ratings[a]

Group	Improved	Unimproved	N
Behavior therapy and methylphenidate	11 (85)[b]	2 (15)	13
Methylphenidate	9 (75)	3 (25)	12
Behavior therapy and placebo	6 (67)	3 (33)	9 34

[a] $\chi^2 = .97$, 2 *df*, n.s.
[b] Numbers in parentheses are percentages.

Table 26-8. Psychiatrists' global improvement ratings[a]

Group	Improved	Unimproved	N
Behavior therapy and methylphenidate	13 (100)[b]	0 (0)	13
Methylphenidate	10 (83)	2 (17)	12
Behavior therapy and placebo	4 (44)	5 (56)	9 34

[a] $\chi^2 = 10.21$, 2 *df*, $p = .006$, two-tailed.
[b] Numbers in parentheses are percentages.

the teachers more closely than those of the mothers. Like the teachers, psychiatrists rated all children (100%) receiving the combination treatment as improved. Of the youngsters treated with methylphenidate, 83% were rated improved, whereas only 44% of those receiving behavior therapy and placebo were rated improved. A significant advantage was found for behavior therapy with methylphenidate over behavior therapy and placebo ($\chi^2 = 6.45$, corrected, 1 *df*, $p < .02$). No difference in global improvement was found between the groups on medication, nor between methylphenidate alone and behavior therapy ($\chi^2 = 1.97$, corrected, 1 *df*, n.s.).

DISCUSSION

A consistent pattern of treatment effects was obtained. All treatments produced significant clinical improvement, but the combination of methylphenidate and behavior therapy was regularly the best treatment; methylphenidate alone was next, and behavior therapy with placebo was the least effective. There was no exception to the above order. However, in no single instance was the combination of medical and behavioral treatment significantly superior to medication alone; the differences between the two were negligible. In contrast, behavior therapy with placebo was significantly less effective than methylphenidate on several measures obtained from teachers and objective observers in the classroom.

No untreated control group of hyperactive children was included in this study. Consequently, it is not possible to evaluate the degree of improvement induced by the experimental treatments against the effects of time alone. In a previous study done with hyperactive children in which a placebo group was included, little if any improvement was observed with placebo treatment (Gittelman-Klein, Klein, Katz, Saraf, & Pollack, 1976). Similarly, O'Leary et al. (1976) found no marked change among a nontreated control group of hyperactive children. Therefore, the improvement observed among the children receiving behavior therapy with placebo appears to be clinically meaningful, not merely equivalent to a time effect.

It may be inferred from these results that the behavior of hyperactive children can be ameliorated with behavioral management alone. Since the efficacy of methylphenidate also has been clearly established, a common fallacy in logic may follow whereby it is concluded that if two treatments "work," they are equivalent. This study highlights the pitfalls of generalizing about the merits of diverse therapies unless they have been studied simultaneously. Only investigations with random assignment and concurrent treatment groups allow for valid conclusions regarding the relative merits of interventions.

Through behavior therapy seems to be a useful clinical intervention when applied in the child's natural environment, it is significantly less effective than stimulant treatment. However, it cannot be assumed that the therapeutic advantage of the medication is absolute. The results are generalizable only to hyperactive children who are relatively severely disruptive since, in the present study, both mothers' and teachers' complaints

were a prerequisite for treatment and the scale criterion for admission was relatively high. The findings are limited also to children who receive comparable methylphenidate dosage. It cannot be assumed that the same pattern of treatment outcome applies to mild cases of hyperactivity, or to similar and other children treated with lower dosages.

Caution is also necessary in generalizing about the merits of behavior therapy. In this study, the behavioral treatment always involved both parents as well as the teachers, often the child, and was intensive. No limits were set on the amount of direct contact between the therapist and parents or teachers during the study period. A less dedicated effort might not yield the same magnitude of improvement.

Though statistically significant therapeutic changes are valuable, their clinical meaningfulness is dramatized if it can be demonstrated that, with treatment, the patients' behavior not only improves, but becomes indistinguishable from that of normals. Utilizing this criterion, the combined use of the two treatment modalities seems optimal. On all key measures, the children who received behavior therapy with methylphenidate were not significantly different after treatment from normals. The hyperactive children treated with methylphenidate alone continued to be rated as more inattentive by teachers ($p < .01$) and more disruptive by the observers ($p < .05$). The greatest contrasts between treated and normal children were found for the group receiving behavior therapy with placebo. Children in this group continued to be significantly different from normal children on crucial aspects of functioning; namely, teacher ratings of conduct disorder, inattention, and hyperactivity ($p < .001$), and classroom disruptive behavior ($p < .0001$). These findings further accentuate the lesser efficacy of behavioral treatment compared to methylphenidate.

It may be argued that behavior therapy was administered over an 8-week period only and that, given more time, results might have been quite different. True; however, behavior therapy is being compared to a treatment which produces marked amelioration in a very brief time span and the time factor itself can be considered a criterion of effectiveness. Further, as noted in a previous presentation (Gittelman-Klein, 1975, Note 2), children receiving behavior modification alone reached a plateau in behavioral improvement after 4 weeks of treatment.

Behavior therapy presents other disadvantages. Its cost is far greater than that of treatment with medication and its execution is often very difficult and fraught with practical problems. Implementing a behavior therapy program for a child in the public school system, at least in the greater New York area, is not a simple matter. Teacher responses to the pressures which the treatment induces vary (several children could not be accepted for treatment simply because their teacher refused to cooperate). Nevertheless, behavior modification led to significant improvement. Therefore, for children who cannot tolerate stimulants, or whose parents are resistant to its use, a behavioral approach offers a valuable, if not equivalent, therapeutic alternative. More importantly, should stimulants be proved to induce lasting major side effects, a realistic, albeit difficult and less effective, alternative is available for those vulnerable to the side effects.

Doubts regarding the quality of the behavior therapy used in this investigation may lead to reservations concerning the validity of the results obtained. Care was taken to hire individuals with a strong philosophical commitment to behavioral treatment, and individual management of the children was used in order to give each treatment the best chance. A more convincing argument, and more to the heart of the issue of quality of care delivered, is the magnitude of improvement obtained with behavior therapy. Children treated with behavior modification alone had a mean improvement of 1.48 on the Hyperactivity factor of the Teacher Rating Scale. This symptom reduction exceeds improvements of .82 and .93 scale points reported by others (O'Leary et al., 1976; Rosembaum et al., 1975) on the same measure, in 4- and 10-week studies done at a university nationally famous for research in behavior therapy. Arguments that the behavior therapy in this study was less than adequate seem unwarranted.

Some concerned laymen have claimed that stimulant medication inhibits children, transforming natural exuberance into robotlike complacency. Others have viewed behavior modification in the same light, that is, as a dehumanizing form of control aimed at inhibiting adjudged deviant behaviors to placate the demands of irrational authority (Schrag & Divoky, 1975). The classroom observational data present a direct challenge to this claim. The one variable insensitive to drug or behavior therapy was Solicitation, which reflects the child's spontaneous, self-monitored interaction with the teacher. The results do not support the notion that either stimulant medication or behavior therapy transforms

hyperactive children into abulic, overcomplaint, anergic youngsters.

The mothers reported somewhat more improvement with behavior therapy than the teachers and psychiatrists, and the advantage of drug treatment was least salient on the global ratings of mothers. This finding is felt to reflect a real clinical phenomenon. By the time the parents come for treatment, they typically feel helpless and demoralized regarding their ability to deal effectively with their child. The implementation of a behavioral treatment approach probably gives them a sense of mastery. In turn, their attitude toward the child may be more positive and accepting even if the child changes little. This shift in parental attitude is inferred from clinical observations; no empirical data were collected to measure it since it was not foreseen. These impressions suggest that measures of parental attitudes should be considered in the evaluation of various treatments of hyperactive children.

The treatment results presented are based on small samples and should not be construed as conclusive. Should the pattern obtained so far persist in the completed study, the data will support the conclusion that stimulant treatment is the intervention of choice for hyperactive children. If medication is not enough, behavior modification should be added. The reverse therapeutic strategy has been demanded by some (Grinspoon & Singer, 1973) who claim that behavioral techniques are the treatments of choice and medication is a last resort. Clearly, this view is not supported by the results of this study.

REFERENCE NOTES

1. Abikoff, H., Gittelman-Klein, R., & Klein, D. F. *Validation of a classroom observation code for hyperactive children.* Manuscript, submitted for publication, 1976.
2. Gittelman-Klein, R. *A preliminary report of the efficacy of methylphenidate and behavior therapy in hyperactive children.* Paper presented at the Annual Meeting of The American College of Neuropsychopharmacology, San Juan, Puerto Rico, December 1975.

REFERENCES

Ayllon, T., Layman, D., & Kandel, H. J. A behavioral-educational alternative to drug control of hyperactive children. *Journal of Applied Behavioral Analysis,* 1975, *8,* 137–146.
Blunden, D., Spring, C., & Greenberg, L. M. Validation of the classroom behavior inventory. *Journal of*

Consulting and Clinical Psychology, 1974, *42*, 84–88.

Christensen, D. E. Effects of combining methylphenidate and a classroom token system in modifying hyperactive behavior. *American Journal of Mental Deficiency*, 1975, *80*, 266–276.

Conners, C. K. A teacher rating scale for use in drug studies with children. *American Journal of Psychiatry*, 1969, *126*, 152–156.

Doubros, S. G., & Daniels, G. T. An experimental approach to the reduction of overactive behavior. *Behavior Research and Therapy*, 1966, *4*, 251–258.

Douglas, V. I. Are drugs enough? To treat or to train the hyperactive child. *International Journal of Mental Health*, 1975, *4*, 199–212.

Eysenck, N. T., & Rachman, S. T. The application of learning theory to child psychiatry. In T. C. Howells (Ed.), *Modern perspectives in child psychiatry*. New York: Brunner/Mazel, 1971. Pp. 104–169.

Gittelman-Klein, R., & Klein, D. F. Are behavioral and psychometric changes related in methylphenidate-treated children? *International Journal of Mental Health*, 1975, *4*, 182–198.

Gittelman-Klein, R., Klein, D. F., Katz, S., Saraf, K., & Pollack, E. Comparative effects of methylphenidate and thioridazine in hyperkinetic children. I. Clinical results. *Archives of General Psychiatry*, 1976 (in press).

Grinspoon, L., & Singer, S. B. Amphetamine in the treatment of hyperkinetic children. *Harvard Educational Review*, 1973, *43*, 515–554.

O'Leary, K. D., Becker, W. C., Evans, M. B., & Saudargas, R. Z. A token reinforcement program in a public school: A replication and systematic analysis. *Journal of Applied Behavioral Analysis*, 1969, *2*, 3–13.

O'Leary, K. D., & Drabman, R. Token reinforcement programs in the classroom. *Psychological Bulletin*, 1971, *75*, 379–398.

O'Leary, K. D., & O'Leary, S. G. *Classroom management in the successful use of behavior modification*. New York: Pergamon Press, 1972.

O'Leary, K. D., O'Leary, S., & Becker, W. C. Modification of a deviant sibling interaction pattern in the home. *Behavioral Research and Therapy*, 1967, *5*, 113–120.

O'Leary, K. D., Pelham, W. E., Rosenbaum, A., & Price, G. H. Behavioral treatment of kyperkinetic children: An experimental evaluation of its usefulness. *Clinical Pediatrics*, 1976, *15*, 274–279.

Patterson, G. R. An application of conditioning techniques to the control of hyperactive children. In L. Ullmann & L. Krasner, (Eds.), *Case studies in behavior modification*. New York: Holt, Rinehart & Winston, 1965. Pp. 370–375.

Patterson, G. R., Jones, R., Whittier, J., & Wright, M. A. A behavior modification technique for the hyperactive child. *Behavioral Research and Therapy*, 1965, *2*, 217–226.

Pihl, R. O. Conditioning procedures with hyperactive children. *Neurology*, 1967, *17*, 921–923.

Quay, H. L., Sprague, R. L., Werry, J. S., & McQueen, M. M. Conditioning visual orientation of conduct problems children in the classroom. *Journal of Experimental Child Psychology*. 1967, *5*, 512–217.

Rosenbaum, A., O'Leary, K. D., & Jacob, R. G. Behavioral intervention with hyperactive children: Group consequences as a supplement to individual contingencies. *Behavior Therapy*, 1975, *6*, 315–323.

Safer, D. J., & Allen, R. P. Side effects from long-term use of stimulants in children. *International Journal of Mental Health*, 1975, *4*, 105–118.

Salzinger, K., Feldman, R. S., & Portnoy, S. Training parents of brain-injured children in the use of operant conditioning procedures. *Behavior Therapy*, 1970, *1*, 4–32.

Schrag, P., & Divoky, D. *The myth of the hyperactive child and other means of child control*. New York: Pantheon, 1975.

Sprague, R. L., Christensen, D. E., & Werry, J. S. Experimental psychology and stimulant drugs. In C. K. Conners (Ed.), *Clinical use of stimulant drugs in children*. The Hague: Excerpta Medica, 1974. Pp. 141–163.

Sprague, R. L., & Werry, J. S. Methodology of psychopharmacological studies with the retarded. In N. R. Ellis (Ed.), *International review of research in mental retardation* (Vol. 5). New York: Academic Press, 1971. Pp. 147–219.

Sroufe, L. A., & Stewart, M. A. Treating problem children with stimulant drugs. *New England Journal of Medicine*, 1973, *289*, 407–413.

Wahler, R. G., Winkel, G. H., Peterson, R. F., & Morrison, D. C. Mothers as behavior therapists for their own children. *Behavioral Research and Therapy*, 1965, *3*, 113–124.

Werry, J. S., & Sprague, R. L. Hyperactivity. In C. G. Costello (Ed.), *Symptoms of psychopathology*. New York: Wiley, 1970. Pp. 387–417.

Index